How to Write Successful Fundraising Appeals

How to Write Successful Fundraising Appeals

Third Edition

Mal Warwick

with **Eric Overman**

JB JOSSEY-BASS™

A Wiley Brand

Cover design by JPuda
Cover image: © istockphoto

Published by Jossey-Bass
A Wiley Brand

One Montgomery Street, Suite 1200, San Francisco, CA 94104-4594—www.josseybass.com

Jossey-Bass books and products are available through most bookstores. To contact Jossey-Bass directly call our Customer Care Department within the U.S. at 800-956-7739, outside the U.S. at 317-572-3986, or fax 317-572-4002.

Wiley also publishes its books in a variety of electronic formats and by printon-demand. Some material included with standard print versions of this book may not be included in e-books or in print-on-demand. If the version of this book that you purchased references media such as CD or DVD that was not included in your purchase, you may download this material at http://booksupport.wiley.com. For more information about Wiley products, visit www.wiley.com.

Library of Congress Cataloging-in-Publication Data

Warwick, Mal.
    How to write successful fundraising appeals/Mal Warwick, Eric Overman. — Third edition.
        pages   cm. — (The Jossey-Bass nonprofit guidebook series)
Revised edition of the author's How to write successful fundraising letters, 2nd ed.
    Includes index.
    ISBN 978-1-118-54366-5 (paper); ISBN 978-1-118-57321-1 (ebk.);
    ISBN 978-1-118-57325-9 (ebk.); ISBN 978-1-118-61808-0 (ebk.)
        1. Direct-mail fund raising.   2. Nonprofit organizations—Finance.   I. Overman, Eric. II. Title.

HV41.2.W378 2013
658.15′224—dc23

2012048511

Printed in the United States of America

THIRD EDITION

PB Printing   10 9 8 7 6 5 4 3 2 1

The Jossey-Bass Nonprofit Guidebook Series

The Jossey-Bass Nonprofit Guidebook Series provides new to experienced nonprofit professionals and volunteers with the essential tools and practical knowledge they need to make a difference in the world. From hands-on workbooks to step-by-step guides on developing a critical skill or learning how to perform an important task or process, our accomplished expert authors provide readers with the information required to be effective in achieving goals, mission, and impact.

Other Titles in the Jossey-Bass Guidebook Series

Powered by Pro Bono, Taproot Foundation

Winning Grants Step by Step, 4th Edition, Tori O'Neal-McElrath

Content Marketing for Nonprofits, Kivi Leroux-Miller

The Nonprofit Marketing Guide: High-Impact, Low-Cost Ways to Build Support for Your Good Cause, Kivi Leroux Miller

The Executive Director's Guide to Thriving as a Nonprofit Leader, 2nd Edition, Mim Carlson, Margaret Donohoe

Strategic Communications for Nonprofits: A Step-by-Step Guide to Working with the Media, 2nd Edition, Kathy Bonk, Emily Tynes, Henry Griggs, Phil Sparks

The Budget-Building Book for Nonprofits: A Step-by-Step Guide for Managers and Boards, 2nd Edition, Murray Dropkin, Jim Halpin, Bill La Touche

Contents

Preface to the Third Edition ix

About the Author xiii

Introduction: Why You Should Read This Book 1

Part One   Motivating Your Audience

1   Why People Respond to Fundraising Appeals 9

2   How a Fundraising Appeal Is Like a Personal Visit 21

3   What Donors Really Think about Fundraising Letters 35

4   Characteristics of an Effective Fundraising Appeal 41

5   A Leisurely Tour through One Successful Appeal 47

Part Two   Your Plan of Action

6   What to Do Before You Write Any Fundraising Appeal 71

7   Eight Steps toward Successful Fundraising Appeals 85

8   The Cardinal Rules of Fundraising Letters 95

9   You're Writing for Results—Not for a Pulitzer Prize 115

Part Three   Customizing Your Appeal

10   Recruiting New Donors: Starting Intimate
     Conversations with Strangers 127

11   Recruiting New Supporters: Beginning the
     Cultivation Process Online 133

12   Welcoming New Donors: Treating People Like
     Part of the Family 141

13   Appealing for Special Gifts: Bringing Your
     Case Down to Earth 155

14   Asking for Year-End Contributions: Making the
     Most of the Holiday Spirit   167

15   Recruiting Monthly Sustainers: Offering Small Donors a
     Chance for Greater Impact   185

16   Soliciting High-Dollar Gifts: Framing the Case
     for Major Contributions   191

17   Going for Bigger Gifts: Persuading Donors to
     Make an Extra Commitment   203

18   Seeking Annual Gifts: Building Long-Term
     Loyalty, One Year at a Time   213

19   Thanking Your Donors: Friend-Raising before Fundraising   219

20   Promoting Legacy Gifts: Seeking the Ultimate Commitment   233

Part Four   Reinforcing Your Appeal

21   Rounding Out Your Appeal with Online Media and More   245

22   Writing Online Appeals   261

23   The New Keys to Success in Fundraising Today   297

Part Five   The Appeal Writer's Toolbox

A   Sample Multichannel Campaign Calendar   313

B   Twenty Great E-mail Subject Lines   317

C   Sixty Successful Outer-Envelope Teasers   319

D   Fifty-Four Strong Leads for Fundraising Appeals   329

E   Ninety Ways to Use the Word "You" in a
     Fundraising Appeal   331

F   Sixty-Three Ways to Handle Awkward
     Copywriting Transitions   335

G   Forty-One Powerful Ways to End a Fundraising Appeal   339

H   Fifty-Eight Ways to Start a P.S. in a Fundraising Appeal   341

I   Fifteen Ways How *Not* to Get Results   345

     Index   353

Preface to the Third Edition

Nearly twenty years ago I set out to develop the first edition of *How to Write Successful Fundraising Letters*. Measured against a geological timescale, two decades isn't a long time—but in fundraising terms the world has changed as surely and as dramatically as if the continents had drifted farther apart. Fundraisers today—those who were content to solicit funds by mail twenty years ago—face a *multichannel* environment, more complex, often baffling, and continuously changing.

The first edition of this book was exclusively about fundraising by direct mail. It represented my best effort to explain how and why the technique works—and how to make the most of it. Using abundant examples of successful and unsuccessful fundraising letters, I explained, step by step, what works and what doesn't in direct mail fundraising. I described all the different kinds of direct mail fundraising letters—if you're a beginner, don't be surprised that there are a lot of them!—and I explained why the differences matter and how to make them clear in your own writing.

For most nonprofits today, direct mail is still the workhorse in the development office, generating the largest number of new donors and raising by far the largest amount of net revenue for operations. But the number of ways that nonprofit organizations are raising money from the public has proliferated with the advent of e-mail, the World Wide Web, mobile computing, and social media, resulting in the multichannel environment that fundraisers confront today. That's why, from beginning to end, this book is dramatically different from its earlier editions. The changes include:

- *A new title, How to Write Successful Fundraising Appeals* (not just *Letters*), to reflect the changed reality that today's fundraisers confront

- *Three new chapters* ("Recruiting New Supporters: Beginning the Cultivation Process Online," "Rounding Out Your Appeal with Online Media and More," and "The New Keys to Success in Fundraising Today") and a fourth chapter thoroughly updated and expanded ("Writing Online Appeals")

- *New sample fundraising appeals* substituted for nearly all the examples found in the second edition

- *Revised text throughout*, with every single sentence weighed for its relevance to current conditions

- *Additions to the resources* at the end of the book

- *A website* dedicated to this book (www.josseybass.com/go/fundraising appeals), featuring numerous additional sample appeals (all in full color, of course).

If you want to cut to the chase and get a handle on the changes that time has wrought in the fundraising environment, I suggest you turn to the concluding chapter, "The New Keys to Success in Fundraising Today."

And if you're now using a previous edition of this book as a reference, you'd be well advised to consult this third edition instead. Yes, things have changed that much.

Three of my colleagues played pivotal roles in preparing this third edition. Eric Overman, vice president of digital strategy at Donordigital, reviewed the text for consistency with the current demands and opportunities of online communications, provided the substance of two of the new chapters, prepared two new resource sections for part 5, and supplied examples of online fundraising appeals from his work with clients. Eric spent a great deal of time on this project, and I'm very grateful to him. And my old friend Bill Rehm, vice president of Mal Warwick Associates, put in the hours too, suggesting substantial changes in the text, identifying out-of-date material to cut, and supplying the new direct mail examples featured in this edition. Finally, Amanda Melton, party planner/wordsmith/office manager/actor, secured most of the permissions for the illustrations used in this book, a truly thankless task for which I thank her anyway.

I couldn't possibly have produced this book without Eric's and Bill's help. They contributed a great deal to its freshness and new insights. Nonetheless, the final decisions about what to include or exclude were mine, so please blame me if you're unhappy.

I'm also indebted to my editors at Jossey-Bass, who were a pleasure to work with. They caught several potentially embarrassing slips on my part, and I'm grateful. Besides, they're the ones who actually publish the book!

If your job—or your personal predilection—keeps you engaged full-time in direct mail fundraising or in online fundraising and marketing, you may find what follows in this book a little disquieting. Get used to it. The days are long gone when we could hole up in our specialties and still meet ambitious fundraising targets. The world doesn't work that way anymore.

In any form of direct response fundraising, you'll find it essential nowadays to work closely with those who manage other aspects of direct response. Otherwise, you won't be able to maximize your fundraising returns. I hope this greatly revised book will help you on your way.

Berkeley, California   Mal Warwick
April 2013

About the Author

For more than thirty years, Mal Warwick has been widely known in the nonprofit sector as an author, consultant, and public speaker on marketing and fundraising for nonprofit organizations and in the private sector as an advocate for socially and environmentally responsible business policies and practices.

Mal is the founder and chairman of Mal Warwick | Donordigital (www .malwarwick.com), a full-service fundraising agency with offices in Berkeley, California, and Washington, DC. The firm specializes in integrated, multichannel fundraising and marketing, serving nonprofit organizations nationwide since 1979. It is a Founding B Corporation and is now employee owned.

Mal has written, coauthored, or edited a total of twenty books, including *Fundraising When Money Is Tight*, *Revolution in the Mailbox*, and several other standard fundraising texts. For twenty-five years, until February 2011, he also edited the free, monthly, electronic newsletter, *Mal Warwick's Newsletter: Successful Direct Mail, Telephone & Online Fundraising*™, which had more than ten thousand subscribers in sixty-nine countries. Over the course of his fundraising career, he has been widely in demand as a speaker and workshop leader throughout the world. Mal has taught fundraising on six continents to nonprofit executives from more than one hundred countries.

Among the hundreds of nonprofits Mal and his colleagues served over the years are many of the nation's largest and most distinguished charities as well as six Democratic presidential candidates and scores of small, local, and regional organizations. Collectively, Mal and his associates have been responsible for raising close to one billion dollars—largely in the form of small gifts from individuals.

Mal has played a leadership role in the fundraising and direct marketing fields both nationally and internationally. In 2009 and 2010, he cofounded and chaired the International Fundraising Congress Online, the world's first virtual fundraising conference, involving more than four hundred sites in forty-two countries, and he chaired its successor, Fundraising Online 2011. Previously, in 2007–2008, he served as chair of that event's sponsor, the international organization Resource Alliance (London, UK). The Resource

Alliance is the organizer of the annual International Fundraising Congress in The Netherlands and a leading force globally in developing the fundraising capacity of nongovernmental organizations, increasing their ability to build civil society. Having helped to establish one of its two predecessor organizations in the early 1980s, he was also an active member of the Direct Marketing Association Nonprofit Federation (Washington, DC). In addition, he served for ten years on the board of the Association of Direct Response Fundraising Counsel (Washington, DC), two of those years as board president.

In 2004, Mal received the Hank Rosso Outstanding Fundraising Executive Award from the Association of Fundraising Professionals, Golden Gate Chapter, and Northern California Grantmakers. In 2009, he was granted the Max L. Hart Nonprofit Leadership Award by the Direct Marketing Association Nonprofit Federation, in recognition of his lifetime contributions to direct marketing.

Mal chairs the board of GreatNonprofits (based in San Francisco), which is partnering with major institutions to bring the voices of donors, volunteers, and beneficiaries to the forefront in evaluating the impact of nonprofit organizations.

A serial entrepreneur and impact investor, Mal has been active in promoting social and environmental responsibility in the business community nationwide for more than two decades. He is the coauthor of *The Business Solution to Poverty: Designing Products and Services for Three Billion New Customers* (with Paul Polak), and of *Values-Driven Business: How to Change the World, Make Money, and Have Fun* (with Ben Cohen, cofounder of Ben & Jerry's). Along with Ben Cohen and others, Mal was a cofounder of Business for Social Responsibility in 1992, and he served on its board during its inaugural year. In 2001, after more than a decade as an active member of Social Venture Network, he began a six-year stretch (2001 to 2007) on its board, serving as chair for four of those years and as vice-chair for two.

Mal was a Peace Corps volunteer in Ecuador for more than three years in the 1960s. Since 1969, he has lived in Berkeley, California, where he is deeply involved in local community affairs. In 2006, he was awarded the Benjamin Ide Wheeler Medal by the Berkeley Community Fund as "Berkeley's most useful citizen," in recognition of his lifetime contributions to the community.

Mal is the grandfather of Dayna, Iain, Matthew, Gwen, Andrew, Kaleb, and Benjamin.

How to Write Successful Fundraising Appeals

Introduction:
Why You Should Read This Book

I immodestly recommend that you read this book for a number of reasons:

- If you write fundraising appeals for a hospital, a college or university, a museum, a health agency, a human service organization, a public interest advocacy group, or any other nonprofit that needs funds
- If you want to write appeals that raise more money for your organization
- If you serve in a leadership role in a nonprofit organization as executive director, development director, or marketing director
- If you are a member of a nonprofit's board of directors and you want to assess the effectiveness of your organization's fundraising appeals
- If you're involved in public relations, advertising, or marketing for a nonprofit organization or institution
- If you want to understand better how fundraising works
- If you want to understand how combining direct mail and online appeals can help you raise much more money
- If you want to learn how to write to get results
- If you want to be a more effective writer

If direct response fundraising is a science (a dubious proposition at best), its fuzziest, most inexact, least scientific aspect is writing the copy required for direct mail, e-mail, telephone, and other communications media now widely in use by nonprofit organizations and political campaigns. There are those in the field who claim fundraising packages can be written by formula, but I'm not one of them. Writing this stuff is tough work because what's effective for one organization may prove counterproductive for another. And what worked last year or last time may not work today.

Though there's no copywriting formula that's worth the pixels or paper it's printed on, there are principles and practices of grammar, syntax, word usage, and formatting that need to be respected. Call them rules, if you will. Your rules won't necessarily match my rules, but each of us has to be consistent—and that may mean obsessing over the minutest details. (To get a sense of what I mean by this, take a look at the edited copy reproduced in exhibit I.1. It shows the sort of thing I often do when I take on an editing job.)

EXHIBIT I.1
Editing Example, One Page of a Fundraising Letter

An attitude of energy conservation fits right into the vision of living more lightly on the earth and trying to do better with less.

you can

We can do it in the obvious areas: home, transportation, and appliances. We've put together a handy chart to show you how much energy could be saved by taking action in various areas. *I've enclosed a copy for you to* Please post and share with your friends.

But ... won't
You may think that changing a single light bulb won't make much of a difference. A single compact florescent light bulb uses 1/4 the energy and lasts 10 times as long as an incandescent bulb giving off the same amount of light!

to compact fluorescent
According to the Rocky Mountain Institute, if everyone in the U.S. switched to light bulbs, we could close 75 large power plants. That means we could close half our nuclear plants -- without touching anything but our lightbulbs! We could make an even bigger difference by using the most energy efficient electric appliances. *— shut down*

¶ As you can tell from the enclosed chart, we

Our society squanders immense amounts of energy on
Yet much of the energy used in the US is hidden from the consumer. Processed food; packaging; pesticides and fertilizers made from petroleum products; *and on* transport products across the nation and from around the world.

So other large
We must pressure businesses and institutions to become energy efficient, not only in their direct use of energy, but in the less obvious areas, too. It will take a lot of consumer *power to force such a big change in attitude!*

That's why Co-op America's 3E Program
Implementing our 3 Point Energy Efficient Economy Project will require more staff, time, and money.

to this historic new program
Once again we must ask for your help in this important project. Your contribution will help lay the foundation for an energy efficient and environmentally healthy economy. *] Note: don't underline here.*

We can and we must take control of the future of our environment by changing the way we spend our money.

We need to buy energy efficient and recyclable products, invest in technology that reduces our need for fossil fuels, and boycott companies that continue to produce energy wasting products. We also need to educate businesses on how they can improve the energy efficiency of their industries and demand that they do it. *← Speech again.*

Program for
Through your individual actions and your support of Co-op America's Energy Efficient Economy Project, you can play an integral part in shifting from a dirty, fossil fuel-based economy to a clean, efficient, renewable energy-based economy. *— shifting the US*

As a gesture of thanks for your
Please give as generously as you can. contribution of

The reality is that for most of us, writing of any sort is a royal pain in the neck. But there are ways to reduce the fuzziness and the pain and to raise the odds that your letters will bring in every nickel you need, and more. Talent helps, but experience counts for a lot too.

Over the years, I've read tens of thousands of fundraising appeals, written or edited thousands of those letters myself, and shared in the creative process as a manager or consultant in thousands of other mailings and online campaigns. All of this experience has given me a front-row seat in a never-ending "copy clinic"—a close-up view of what works and what doesn't (and sometimes even why). This book conveys what I've learned about writing fundraising appeals.

In other books I've written, I've explored many of the elements of fundraising. Most (though not all) of this work was about raising money by mail—from choosing mailing or e-mail lists to working with consultants, from measuring results to designing and producing packages, from strategizing to testing to scheduling. This book isn't about any of those things. It's about writing. My topic here is the effective use of written English in the pursuit of philanthropic gifts.

Over my varied career, I've written newspaper stories, magazine articles, book reviews, science fiction stories, and comic book scripts; ads for newspapers, magazines, radio, and television; sales letters, brochures, and pamphlets; technical manuals; e-mail promotions and copy for Web sites; speeches for others, including presidential candidates, and speeches for myself—not to mention all those fundraising appeals, plus more than a dozen other books about the craft of fundraising. I've written fiction and nonfiction, eulogies and humor, short pieces and long. I've written in three languages and translated from one to another.

Yet despite all this writing, I don't consider myself a particularly gifted writer. I'm no poet; my prose doesn't sing. I've written no unforgettable passage, contributed no timeless witticism to the language. But through long practice and difficult trial and error, I've learned to do one thing moderately well with my writing: get results. And there's just one result I want from this book: to help you write successful fundraising appeals.

This book is a guide to the techniques and approaches that have proved successful for me—a tool chest of ideas and examples that will help you sharpen your own writing. If you prefer, look on it as a comprehensive review to help you gain perspective on the challenges you face as a writer of fundraising appeals.

And there's one more result I hope to achieve with this book: I want you to enjoy reading it. I've found I do best what I enjoy the most—while those things I approach with deadly seriousness are least likely to turn out well.

I suspect you too will find that the more fun you have when you write your fundraising appeals, the more money you'll raise.

From Fundraising Letter to Fundraising Package

The title of this book refers to fundraising *appeals*. Note that this has grown out of the title of the first and second editions, *How to Write Successful Fundraising Letters*. What started largely as a direct mail phenomenon has grown into what is today a multichannel effort, employing a variety of techniques across mail, e-mail, web, phone, social media, and mobile communication channels.

However, what has *not* changed is that direct mail remains the workhorse in the fundraiser's toolbox. Despite the proliferation of media, direct mail continues to deliver the lion's share of the money, so it still deserves the most attention.

Direct mail is unique in many ways, but in no way more than this: a direct mail fundraising appeal consists of several components. You'll need an envelope for your fundraising letter. And almost all the time you'll need at least two other items as well: a reply device (variously called a response device, coupon, card, form, or something else) and an envelope to mail it back in. Without a reply device and an easy way to return it, most fundraising letters would generate precious few gifts.

However, in the new world of multichannel communications, those paper elements aren't enough. For a major fundraising campaign, you'll probably need e-mail copy, a telephone script, blurbs for Facebook and Twitter, and copy for your website as well. Things have gotten more complicated in the last decade. But the basics remain the same.

Why You Can Learn from the Examples—Even Though Your Organization Is Different

You'll find contemporary examples, new to this third edition, to illustrate the eleven types of fundraising appeal described in part 3. These examples are drawn from the work of my colleagues at Mal Warwick | Donordigital for our clients during recent years. There are additional examples on the website we've developed to accompany this book.

The causes and institutions appearing throughout this book cover a wide range of issues and activities—from fighting hunger and protecting animals to advancing the rights of women and cleaning up the environment. But what if your organization doesn't happen to fit into one of those categories? Or if it does fit, what if you're convinced it's really too different to benefit from the examples? In fact, you can learn a lot from fundraising appeals written by other nonprofit organizations. There are three reasons why I strongly believe this.

1. You can learn how the fundamental rules of writing apply (or don't apply) to the craft of writing fundraising appeals. These fundamentals have nothing to do with your cause or your constituency.

2. You can learn how the special techniques of fundraising and direct marketing can be put to work in fundraising appeals. These techniques change very little from one cause or constituency to another.

3. You can learn how to improve your fundraising copy if you distance yourself from the everyday needs and details of your organization's work. Often it's much easier to see the forest rather than the trees when you're looking into someone else's forest.

Take my word for that. I've been wandering around in other people's forests for a very long time. In a literal sense, I worked on the first edition of this book for more than three years, starting in 1989. In a larger sense, however, I started the project ten years earlier when I founded my direct mail fundraising firm, Mal Warwick Associates, or even in 1949, well over half a century ago, when I wrote my first "fundraising" letter home from summer camp. I've put a lot into this book. I hope you get a lot out of it.

To write successful fundraising appeals, it's essential that you understand the fundamentals of donor motivation and the dynamics of donor response. Those are the themes we'll cover in this first part of the book. You'll learn

- Why people respond to fundraising appeals when they're typically overwhelmed with them
- How a fundraising appeal is like a personal visit by a fundraising canvasser
- What donors really think about those fundraising letters cluttering their mailboxes
- The characteristics of an effective fundraising appeal, whether printed on paper or posted online

And finally, you'll take a leisurely tour through one successful appeal.

Chapter One:
Why People Respond to Fundraising Appeals

It's downright unnatural. Your fundraising appeal must persuade the recipient to take an action that much of humanity thinks peculiar: to give away money.

To accomplish this seemingly unlikely objective, your appeal needs to be built on the psychology of giving. Forget your organization's needs. Instead, focus on the needs, the desires, and the concerns of the people you're writing to. Your job is to motivate them.

Commercial direct marketers frequently say that there are five *great motivators* that explain response: fear, exclusivity, guilt, greed, and anger. But I believe the truth is much more complex: that there are at least two dozen and one reasons people might respond to your fundraising appeal. Any one of the twenty-five might suggest a theme or hook for your campaign, and it's likely that several of these reasons help to motivate each gift.

People Send Money Because You Ask Them to

Public opinion surveys and other research repeatedly confirm this most basic fact of donor motivation. "I was asked" is the most frequently cited reason for giving. And the research confirms that donors want to be asked. Focus group research also reveals that donors typically underestimate the number of appeals they receive from the organizations they support. These facts help explain why responsive donors are repeatedly asked for additional gifts in nearly every successful direct response fundraising program. When you write an appeal, keep these realities in mind. Don't allow your reticence about asking for money make you sound apologetic in your letter.

People Send Money Because They Have Money Available to Give Away

The overwhelming majority of individual gifts to nonprofit organizations and institutions are small contributions made from disposable (or discretionary) income. This is the money left over in the family checking account after the month's mortgage, taxes, insurance, credit cards, and grocery bills have been paid. Unless you're appealing for a major gift, a bequest, or a multiyear pledge, your target is this modest pool of available money.

For most families, dependent on a year-round stream of wage or salary income, the pool of disposable income is replenished every two weeks or every month. That's why most organizations appeal frequently and for small gifts. If your appeal is persuasive, your organization may join the ranks of that select group of nonprofits that receive gifts from a donor's household in a given month. If you're less than persuasive or if competing charities have stronger arguments—or if the family just doesn't have money to spare that month—you won't get a gift.

For example, if you write me a letter seeking a charitable gift, you may succeed in tapping into the $100 or $200 I'll probably have "left over" for charity during the month your letter arrives. If your appeal is persuasive, I might send you $25 or $50—$100 tops—because I decide to add you to the short list of nonprofits I'll support that month.

Now you may have the mistaken impression that as a businessman, a snappy dresser, and an all-around generous fellow, I have a lot of money. You may even be aware I've occasionally made much larger gifts to local charities. But you're unlikely to receive more than $50 because that's all I have available right now. Those few larger gifts I gave didn't come from my disposable income stream. They came from other sources (such as an investment windfall, a tax refund, or an inheritance) and required a lot of planning on my part.

People Send Money Because They're in the Habit of Sending Money

Charity is habit forming; giving by mail is a special variety of this benign affliction. When I became involved in direct mail fundraising in the late 1970s, I was told that only about one in four adult Americans was *mail responsive*—that is, susceptible to offers or appeals by mail. By the turn of the century, according to the Simmons Market Research Bureau, two out of every three adults were buying goods or services by mail or phone every year. Many purchases involved telemarketing—but there's no doubt Americans are now more mail responsive. Surveys also reflect the growing importance of direct mail appeals in the fundraising process. Research shows that fundraising letters are the top source of new gifts to charity in America.

But the charity habit isn't expressed solely through the mail. These days, with the proliferation of other fundraising channels, some people have gotten into the habit of giving online. Others prefer to respond to telephone calls (yes, telephone calls) or to television appeals. And once the hurdles are removed from giving via text messages on mobile devices, I'm sure people will get into that habit too.

People Send Money Because They Support Organizations Like Yours

Your donors aren't yours alone, no matter what you think. Because they have special interests, hobbies, and distinctive beliefs, they may support several similar organizations. A dog owner, for example, may contribute to half a dozen organizations that have some connection to dogs: a humane society, an animal rights group, an organization that trains Seeing Eye™ dogs, or even a wildlife protection group. A person who sees himself as an environmentalist might be found on the membership rolls of five or six ecology-related groups: one dedicated to land conservation, another to protecting the wilderness, a third to saving endangered species or the rain forest, and so on. There are patterns in people's lives. Your appeal is most likely to bear fruit when it fits squarely into one of those patterns.

People Send Money Because Their Gifts Will Make a Difference

Donors want to be convinced that their investment in your enterprise—their charitable gifts—will achieve some worthy aim. That's why many donors express concern about high fundraising and administrative costs. It's also why successful appeals for funds often quantify the impact of a gift: $35 to buy a school uniform, $40 for a stethoscope, $7 to feed a child for a day. Donors want to feel good about their gifts. Linking a donor's gift to something specific and tangible is always a plus.

Your donors are striving to be effective human beings. You help them by demonstrating just how effective they really are.

People Send Money Because Gifts Will Accomplish Something Right Now

Urgency is a necessary element in a fundraising letter, and even more so in an online appeal. Implicitly or explicitly, every successful appeal has a deadline: the end of the year, the opening of the school, the deadline for the matching grant, the limited pressrun on the book available as a premium. But the strong attraction in circumstances such as these becomes even clearer when no such urgent conditions apply. If the money I send you this week won't make a difference right away, shouldn't I send money to some other charity that has asked for my support and urgently needs it?

People Send Money Because You Recognize Them for Their Gifts

You appeal to donors' egos—or to their desire to heighten their public image—when you offer to recognize their gifts in an open and tangible way: a listing in your newsletter; a plaque, certificate, lapel pin, or house sign; a screen credit in a video production; a press release. If your fundraising program can provide appropriate and tasteful recognition, you're likely to boost response to your appeals by highlighting the opportunities for recognition in your letter or newsletter. Even if donors choose not to be listed in print or mentioned in public, they may be gratified to learn that you value their contributions enough to make the offer.

People Send Money Because You Give Them Something Tangible in Return

Premiums come in all sizes, shapes, and flavors: bumper strips, gold tie tacks, coffee-table books, membership cards, even (in one case I know) a pint of ice cream.

Sometimes, premiums (such as name stickers or bookmarks) are enclosed with the appeal; these so-called front-end premiums (or *freemiums*) boost response more often than not and are frequently cost effective, at least in the short run. In other cases, back-end premiums are promised in an appeal "as a token of our deep appreciation" when donors respond by sending gifts of at least a certain amount. Either way, premiums appeal to the innate acquisitiveness that persists in the human race.

People Send Money Because You Enable Them to "Do Something" about a Critical Problem, if Only to Protest or Take a Stand

Today we are bombarded by information about the world's problems through a wide variety of channels. Although we may isolate ourselves inside triple-locked homes, build walls around suburbs, and post guards at gateposts, we can't escape from knowing about misery, injustice, and wasted human potential. Often we feel powerless in the face of this grim reality. Charity offers us a way to respond—by helping to heal the sick or offer balm for troubled souls, imprint our values on a new generation, or feed the hungry. Your appeal will trigger a gift if it brings to life the feelings that move us to act, even knowing that action is never enough.

If you offer hope in a world drowning in troubles, your donors will seize it like the life jacket it really is.

People Send Money Because You Give Them a Chance to Associate with a Famous or Worthy Person

There are numerous ways that the identity, personality, or achievements of an individual might be highlighted in a fundraising appeal. For example, that person may be the celebrity signer, the organization's founder or executive director, the honorary chair of a fundraising drive, a patron saint, a political candidate, an honoree at a special event—or simply one of the organization's members or clients. If the signer's character or accomplishments evoke admiration or even simply a past personal connection, your donors may be moved to send gifts in response. The opportunity to associate with someone who is well known or highly esteemed may offer donors a way to affirm their noblest inclinations—or compensate for what they believe to be their shortcomings.

People Send Money Because You Allow Them to Get Back at the Corrupt or the Unjust

There are too few outlets for the anger and frustration we feel on witnessing injustice and corruption in society. Both our moral sense and the secular law hold most of us in check, preventing expressions of violence or vocal fury that might allow us to let off steam. For many, contributing to nonprofit causes or institutions is a socially acceptable way to strike back. Whether your organization is a public interest group committed to fighting corruption in government or a religious charity devoted to revealing divine justice, it may help donors channel their most sordid feelings into a demonstration of their best instincts.

People Send Money Because You Give Them the Opportunity to "Belong"—as a Member, Friend, or Supporter—and Thus You Help Them Fight Loneliness

Your most fundamental task as a fundraiser is to build relationships with your donors. That's why so many organizations use membership programs, giving clubs, and monthly gift societies. The process of solicitation itself can help build healthy relationships. Shut-ins, for example, or elderly people with distant family and few friends may eagerly anticipate the letters you send. Most of us are social animals, forever seeking companionship.

People Send Money Because You Enable Them to Offer Their Opinions

The act of sending a gift to some nonprofit organizations might itself constitute a way to speak out. Consider, for example, the American Civil Liberties Union or the Republican National Committee or the Human Rights Campaign; support for these groups makes an obvious statement about a donor's views. But almost any charity can offer donors an opportunity to state an opinion either by mail or online by including in an appeal an involvement device such as a membership survey, a petition, or a greeting card that might later be sent to a friend or family member. Although most donors may ignore the chance to offer suggestions, they may regard the invitation to do so as a strong sign of your respect and concern for them.

People Send Money Because You Provide Them with Access to Inside Information

Even if your organization or agency isn't an institution of higher education or a research foundation, you still possess knowledge many donors crave. Nonprofit organizations are often on the front lines of everyday, hands-on research, gathering important data day after day from clients, visitors, or program participants. Their staff members are likely to be specialists, and often experts, in their fields.

Every nonprofit possesses information that is not widely known to the public and that donors may perceive as valuable. A loyal supporter may be vitally interested in the health and well-being of your executive director (who was ill lately), the progress of a project you launched last year (after a spectacular start), or what your field staff learned last month (three months after the hurricane).

Disseminating inside information, which is intrinsically valuable and thus constitutes a gift from you, also helps build strong fundraising relationships by involving your donors in the intimate details of your organization.

People Send Money Because You Help Them Learn about a Complex and Interesting Problem or Issue

In most advanced industrial nations, citizens think it is largely government's responsibility to provide education, health care, and the arts. In contrast, the traditional American response has been to meet important needs such as these principally through private, voluntary action. Nonprofit organizations in the United States tackle issues or problems that society otherwise ignores or undervalues. Don't think just of the private schools and colleges, nonprofit hospitals, museums, and symphony orchestras. Think about Mothers Against Drunk Driving, Disabled American Veterans, Planned Parenthood, The Nature Conservancy, and the hundreds of thousands of other organizations like them that are far less well known. Often these organizations are on the front lines of research or public debate on the most challenging, the most controversial, the most engaging issues. If that's true of your organization, the emphasis you place in your appeal on your special knowledge may help motivate donors to give.

Your donors may even perceive the appeal itself as a benefit. As research frequently reveals, donors regard the letters they receive from charities as a source of special knowledge. I believe that helps explain why long letters containing hard facts and intriguing ideas often out-pull more emotional appeals.

People Send Money Because You Help Them Preserve Their Worldview by Validating Cherished Values and Beliefs

The very act of giving affirms a donor's dedication to a charity's worthy aims. Donors support your organization's work because you act on their behalf, pursuing your mission with time and effort they could never bring to bear themselves. In this passionate pursuit, you act out their values and beliefs—the deep-seated convictions that lead them to join in your mission. But you must constantly remind them of the connection.

If your organization's mission is congruent with widely shared values and beliefs—a commitment to piety, for example, or saving dolphins or promoting efficiency in government—you face an obvious marketing opportunity. But if your nonprofit is dedicated to an unpopular cause, such as prisoners' rights, you possess a similar (if unenviable) advantage: for that small number of donors willing to take a stand on an issue that others reject, the values and beliefs that make the act of giving a form of personal affirmation suggest to the fundraiser a language both may speak.

People Send Money Because You Allow Them to Gain Personal Connections with Other Individuals Who Are Passionately Involved in Some Meaningful Dimension of Life

A charity is an intentional community of sorts—a cooperative venture, an institutional expression of a shared creed or common hopes. Your job as a fundraiser is to strengthen the bonds that tie your community together. Your greatest asset may be the heroic members of your field staff, who daily risk their lives to right the world's wrongs, or simply a particular person within your community whom donors may regard as an inspiring example: a self-less, dedicated staff member; a passionately committed trustee; a model client or beloved beneficiary of your work. If you bring such people to life through your fundraising appeals, you enable your donors to live vicariously through them—and that can be a meaningful and rewarding experience for donors, as well as profitable for your organization.

People Send Money Because You Give Them the Chance to Release Emotional Tension Caused by a Life-threatening Situation, a Critical Emergency, or an Ethical Dilemma

The charitable impulse is often precipitated by special circumstances that cause pain, fear, or even embarrassment. Consider the enduring popularity of memorial gifts to commemorate the passing of friends or loved ones or the spontaneous outpouring of gifts to aid crime victims or the families of kidnapped children. People want to help relieve pain and suffering, if only because they share these feelings. And they want to respond to grave emergencies, if only because they fear death. Your appeal for funds may afford them an opportunity to ease their affliction.

People Send Money Because They Are Afraid

Fear motivates. The American public has been subjected to billions of fundraising letters expressly conceived to evoke fear. Fear of death. Fear of poor people or foreigners. Fear of Social Security benefit cuts. Fear of higher taxes. Fear of Democrats or Republicans, liberals or reactionaries. No Pollyannish view of human motivation can erase the evidence that vast sums of money have been raised by such appeals. Fear sells. Yet I believe with all my heart that it's often unseemly, at times ethically questionable—and ultimately counterproductive—to use this obvious stratagem.

Consider the would-be prophet who predicts Armageddon next year. Who will heed the prophet when next year has come and gone and the world is still in one piece? A fundraiser who builds the case for giving on the worst-case scenario may be building on quicksand.

People Send Money Because You Allow Them to Relieve Their Guilt about an Ethical, Political, or Personal Transgression, Whether Real or Imagined

Guilt undeniably plays a role in prompting some gifts. Think of the $1 or $2 cash contribution mailed in response to direct mail packages containing name stickers or greeting cards, the belated membership renewals that follow a long series of increasingly insistent demands, or the millions of small gifts sent every year in response to photographs of children with unsightly cleft palates. Our complex society allows few of us the luxury of acting out of purely ethical motives. Compromise is woven through the fabric of our daily lives. The fact is that none of us is likely to feel guilt-free at any time. Sometimes giving to charity, like throwing coins into the poor box in an earlier era, will help release the pressure.

Yet I believe guilt is highly overrated as a motivator. Rarely will donors who are moved primarily by guilt prove loyal over the years, and larger gifts from them are relatively rare. As a fundraising strategy, guilt may be just as counterproductive in the long run as fear.

People Send Money Because You Give Them Tax Benefits

No list of motivating factors for charitable giving is complete without at least passing reference to tax benefits. Without question, the charitable tax deduction has played a major role in stimulating many large gifts and legacy gifts, because the benefits to the donor are substantial. (This is particularly true of gifts of artwork or other forms of appreciated property to such institutions as museums, because the tax laws are specifically structured to encourage such gifts.) However, many small donors mistakenly believe they too gain a great advantage from the tax deductibility of their gifts. That's why it's always advisable when requesting a gift to inform the donor that it may be deductible: this information may not help, but it can't hurt.

Still, it's dangerous to construct an appeal exclusively on the basis of tax benefits, even an appeal to buy into a tax-reduction program such as a charitable remainder trust. Experts in planned giving advise that *donative intent*—the desire to help, to do good, to make a difference—is usually of far greater importance than any financial considerations. And there are lots of tax-reduction schemes available to well-to-do people from institutions with no charitable purpose whatsoever.

People Send Money Because They Feel It's Their Duty

Many of our religious traditions teach us that it's wrong to live life without observing our duty to others to relieve their pain, enlarge their opportunities, or brighten their lives. There is also a secular belief, widely shared in the United States, that as citizens in a democracy, we have an obligation to help make things better for our fellow citizens. Those who benefit from military training may acquire a heightened sense of duty.

Not every nonprofit organization can appeal explicitly to donors' sense of duty (though many charities can do so). But duty may nonetheless play a role in inspiring the gifts any nonprofit receives, for duty by its very nature is self-activating.

People Send Money Because They Believe It's a Blessing to Do so

The Christian belief that "it is more blessed to give than to receive" is deeply ingrained in Western civilization and far from limited to practicing Christians. In the Jewish concept of *mitzvah*, for example, or the Muslim *zakat* and *sadaqa*, many Americans find justification for believing that doing good is its own reward. Clearly—at least in our idealized vision of ourselves—we Americans celebrate the notion of charity. Our self-image as "nice people" derives in no small part from our generous response to charitable appeals.

People Send Money Because They Want to "Give Something Back"

The US economy has spawned millions of millionaires and more than a thousand billionaires, not to mention tens of millions of individuals who earn annual six-figure salaries. Huge amounts of cash slosh around in the melting pot that is American society. Although most of that money buys ever-larger homes and cars and increasingly contrived luxury goods, more each year is finding its way into the coffers of the nation's one and a half million nonprofit organizations. Why? Because many of those well-to-do people are motivated to share their good fortune with their communities or society at large. "Giving something back" is frequently cited by major donors as a principal reason for their gifts, and unquestionably it helps to account for the generosity of tens of millions of less-prosperous donors.

People Send Money Because You Offer Them a Choice of Specific Programs or Projects

Fundraisers have known for a long time that donors value choice. Like anyone else, they may be overwhelmed by a list of seventeen different options. But offered a chance to select one of, say, five projects your organization has under way, they might well respond more generously than if you solicit their support for just one of those programs, no matter how popular. As the *Chronicle of Philanthropy* reported in late summer 2012,

Boston's Jewish Federation "saw giving grow by 80 percent in 2011 and by 60 percent this year" by simply loosening its long-time insistence on unrestricted gifts.

Now that we've got a handle on two dozen and one of the reasons donors might respond to that fundraising appeal you're writing, let's take a look at the dynamics at work when they find your letter in their mailbox or inbox. That's the topic we'll take up in chapter 2, "How a Fundraising Appeal Is Like a Personal Visit."

Chapter Two:
How a Fundraising Appeal Is Like a Personal Visit

Most of us who mash words together to raise funds—or to sell products or services, for that matter—have a one-syllable answer to the question, "How do you know whether that will work?" *Test*.

A German professor of direct marketing named Siegfried Vögele has two answers. He's just as firmly committed as any of us to the rigors of head-to-head testing to determine which of two or more variations in copy, design, or content will secure the best response. But Vögele can also cite chapter and verse from a realm of research that uses such devices as eye-motion cameras and machines that measure subtle changes in skin chemistry. This research, conducted over many years, has given him profound and detailed knowledge of the ways human beings react when they hold direct mail materials in their hands.

Many of us guess about these things; we have insights or hunches. Siegfried Vögele often *knows*.

Vögele has been practicing and teaching his craft in Germany since the 1970s. He asserts that a direct mail letter works when it successfully involves readers in a silent dialogue with the signer. In 1980, he caused a sensation at the all-European direct marketing conference with his ideas, and he has taught his Dialogue Method throughout Europe ever since. Thousands of marketers have attended his seminars, and articles based on his eye-motion research have made their way to America. His *Handbook of Direct Mail*, published in German in 1984, has been translated into Italian, French, and English. In other words, the story's out.

This chapter sets out the essence of Vögele's Dialogue Method as it applies to writing direct mail letters—and I'll carry the translation one step further into the realm of multichannel fundraising.

What Happens in a Personal Fundraising Visit?

The doorbell rings. You trudge to the front door, switch on the porch light, and squint through the peephole.

Standing at your door is a young woman, nineteen or maybe twenty years old, scruffily dressed, a clipboard tightly gripped in one hand, and an eager smile pasted on her face. You may be thinking, "Is this another of those annoying canvassers? Do I have to write another check for twenty or twenty-five bucks to get her to leave? What group does she represent, and why are they bothering me? Am I really going to let this little pest inside my home?"

Nevertheless, you open the door, greet the young woman, and listen to her long enough to hear that she represents a charity called [fill-in-the-blank]. Not only that, but something she says tells you how what [fill-in-the-blank] is doing relates directly to things you care about. Besides, she's a beguiling young person who appears to have a bright future. You sigh, open the door a little wider, and (still reluctant) let her into the house.

Now, perched on the edge of your living room couch, the young canvasser launches into her pitch for [fill-in-the-blank]. You're not listening closely, but you get the gist of it. Every so often you nod, smile, or gesture. Encouraged, she plunges ahead, keeping her eyes on you all the while she speaks, emphasizing this or that or the other thing as you demonstrate more interest (or less) by the way you nod your head, fold or uncross your arms, or even occasionally ask a question or venture a comment. There are lots of questions on your mind, but you pose few of them, not wanting to drag out this unwanted conversation. And although you don't understand or agree with everything the fundraiser says, when you frown, shrug, or lift your eyebrows in a questioning way, she slips in a quick answer or makes a reassuring statement, then quickly rushes on to the next point. All this goes on for a few minutes until the fundraiser says something that really catches your attention.

Fully engaged for the moment, you make a casual reference to an experience related to what she has just said and—just to be polite—you ask her a pointed question. With a rush, she launches into a detailed answer. It's interesting for a few seconds, but then your eyes start glazing over. Noticing your disengagement, the young woman makes some comment about the lateness of the hour and immediately makes her pitch: "So, can I count on you for a gift of $50 tonight to help [fill-in-the-blank]?"

Fifty dollars is far too much, so you demur, settling for $25 instead. (Truth to tell, you're just as interested in getting her to leave you alone as you are in helping [fill-in-the-blank].) The canvasser gratefully volunteers to wait while you retrieve your checkbook. She accepts your gift with effusive thanks and departs, leaving behind a thin sheaf of papers with the latest developments at [fill-in-the-blank] and a promise that soon you'll be hearing from this group again so you'll know how your gift has been used.

Now, what has just happened here?

1. The canvasser got your attention by ringing your doorbell. You weren't expecting her, and as far as you're concerned, the evening would've been just as pleasant, if not more so, if she'd never shown up.

2. The moment you set eyes on her, barely conscious questions started welling up in your head in quick order: you wondered who she was and why she'd come and what she wanted you to do—and you answered most of those questions for yourself as quickly as they popped into your mind because the answers were obvious.

3. The young woman was representing an organization that's working on an issue you care a lot about. If she'd asked your help for some other cause or to address some other issue, you might just have smiled as politely as you were able and wished her better luck with the neighbors.

4. Her manner or her appearance—combined with something about your own mood and circumstances—induced you to let her into your home. You weren't planning to do so; it just happened. And you invited her in even though you knew perfectly well she was going to ask you for money.

5. Once inside, the young woman delivered her pitch, watching your body language all the while and answering every question you raised as responsively as she could, some more fully than others.

6. Something she said triggered a strong reaction in you—enough to provoke a comment of your own and a substantive question. Right away, the fundraiser gave you all the details you asked for and more.

7. As soon as she sensed your patience waning, she moved quickly to ask for a gift. She knew perfectly well you support the work of [fill-in-the-blank]. Her challenge was to make you admit it.

8. You declined to contribute the full amount she requested but did agree to give something. Since you had taken up so much of her time, it seemed the least you could do. Anyway, [fill-in-the-blank] does such valuable work!

9. The canvasser didn't just take your money and run. She thanked you for your support, reassured you it would make a big difference, and promised you would hear again soon from [fill-in-the-blank].

In short, you started the evening with absolutely no intention of giving a cent to [fill-in-the-blank]—or any other group for that matter, let alone a check for $25. You've done so anyway, and you feel pretty good about it!

Now let's consider a similar scene—one in which the appeal for funds comes by mail rather than in person. By comparing these two experiences, we'll gain important insight into Vögele's Dialogue Method.

How People Decide Whether to Open Fundraising Letters

You've just gotten home from a tough day at the office. You toss the mail into a heap on the coffee table, grab something to drink from the refrigerator, and collapse into the easy chair, flicking on the TV with the remote control with one hand and pulling the wastebasket close to your chair with the other. Now, one or two deep breaths later, barely paying attention in the flickering glow of the television screen, you retrieve a handful of mail and begin the daily ritual.

Plunk! Into the wastebasket goes the fourth duplicate copy of that clothing catalogue. Plunk! Again, in one smooth, unhesitating motion: another credit card offer. And again and again: that health charity that reminds you of things you want to forget, a packet of discount coupons from a store you wouldn't visit if your life depended on it, a promise of untold wealth from Publishers Clearing House, a picture of pathetic little children. Now you come to the gas and electric bill—and something else that may be worth a glance: an envelope from [fill-in-the-blank], the people who do all that good stuff about whatchamacallit. At least they spelled your name right (unlike the catalogue merchant and the senders of some of the other pieces of mail). You know whom it's from because the organization's name and address are right there in the upper-left-hand corner and, besides, there's a photo on the envelope that looks a lot like whatchamacallit. Anyway, it looks familiar.

Chances are that this is another fundraising appeal from [fill-in-the-blank]—but you never know for sure until you look inside. Maybe the group has something interesting to say, even if it is a solicitation.

Before you know it, you've turned over the envelope from [fill-in-the-blank], slit it open, and dumped the contents out onto your lap. Now there's no question what these people want from you: the self-addressed envelope with those telltale broad stripes and the reply card with a hefty checkmark and a big bold "YES!" above a string of dollar amounts leave no doubt whatsoever that this is a fundraising solicitation. But [fill-in-the-blank] is a fascinating group, and a photo and caption on the reply card give the impression this letter is definitely about whatchamacallit, so it's probably worth looking a little further.

Now let's take stock before we stumble deeper into the jungle of real-world fundraising. What's happening here, and how does it compare to the experience you've just had with that aggressive young canvasser?

1. You weren't expecting a fundraising letter from [fill-in-the-blank] any more than you were anticipating the young woman's visit to your home.

2. When you first glanced at [fill-in-the-blank]'s appeal, you weren't paying much attention at all—even less attention, no doubt, than you paid that canvasser. (After all, she was standing right there.) Vögele estimates we devote no more than 10 percent of our attention to reading unsolicited mail.

3. Despite your lack of attentiveness, you noticed one thing without fail: the group spelled your name correctly. That young woman didn't know your name, but she looked you in the eye, accomplishing much the same end.

4. Something else about the letter caught your attention, triggering curiosity or concern—enough to motivate you to open the envelope and pull out the contents. What did the trick? The [fill-in-the-blank] name? That photo of whatchamacallit? It's hard to know (but ultimately doesn't matter) exactly what made the difference, just as your decision to open your front door to that canvasser was impulsive and difficult to analyze.

5. As you opened the envelope and dribbled the contents onto your lap, a stream of questions started flitting nearly unnoticed through the depths of your consciousness, much like those that came to mind as the fundraiser delivered her pitch in your living room. These questions included the obvious ones ("What's this about? What do they want from me? What's it going to cost me?"), and many of them were answered at a glance as you observed the contents of [fill-in-the-name]'s appeal. These casual little traces of wonderment or confusion are what Siegfried Vögele calls *unspoken readers' questions*. As many as twenty such questions pop into the average reader's mind on picking up a direct mail solicitation.

But all this slips by with amazing speed. So far the whole incident—from your first glimpse of the [fill-in-the-blank] solicitation to your dumping the contents onto your lap—has taken a maximum of five to eight seconds.

To get a better sense of just how quickly five seconds flit by, follow the second hand on your watch, or count backward slowly by thousands. Those five long seconds spell the difference between the success or failure of a fundraising appeal. Tonight, for [fill-in-the-blank], they've been enough for a very good start.

Now, let's pick up the trail of our story again.

How a Fundraising Letter Is Like a Face-to-Face Dialogue

Taking a sip of your drink, then turning up the volume on the television set, you now fish out [fill-in-the-blank]'s letter from the jumble on your lap. Dangling it before you between thumb and forefinger, you glance at the front page. Briefly you take in a dramatic little photo in the upper-right-hand corner and note that the letter contains short paragraphs, subheads, and underlining. Then you quickly flip the letter over to the back page to see who's writing to you.

Your eyes temporarily fix on the signature and the typed name below it, then drop down to the postscript; it's only three lines long, so you read it through. Sure enough, [fill-in-the-blank] is hoping you'll send money to do something new about whatchamacallit. A whole new round of questions rushes to the surface—questions such as, "How are they going to pull that off again? Will my twenty-five bucks make a difference? Are they going to send me something if I mail them a gift?" So now you scan the subheads and underlined words in the letter at a rapid rate: first on the last page, then, very briefly, on the two interior pages, and finally on the first page again.

Now you begin reading the letter's opening sentence. It's the beginning of a story, and before you know it you're hooked. You read first one longish paragraph, then another—but that's enough. You're satisfied. [Fill-in-the-blank] is doing exactly what you'd hoped, and you're just as eager to be part of the act this year as you were before. Out of long-ingrained habit, you grab the reply card and scan it to be sure you didn't misunderstand what [fill-in-the-blank] expected of you. Satisfied there was no miscommunication, you add the reply card to [fill-in-the-blank]'s postage-paid return envelope and drop the little bundle on top of the gas and electric bill: both will go into the "bills to pay" file. You'll write both checks next Saturday—or at any rate, that's what you say to yourself.

Let's pause here to take stock again, reviewing what's taken place from the perspective of Siegfried Vögele.

1. You were still largely inattentive—after all, you had a drink in one hand and a TV set blaring—but something about the letter from [fill-in-the-blank] persuaded you to turn it over for a second look rather than toss it into the wastebasket along with the day's direct mail losers. Was it that photo on the first page? The way those short

paragraphs, subheads, and underlining suggested the letter would be quick and easy to read? No doubt both factors helped.

2. Pay close attention now: your eyes may have skipped through quite a number of words in scanning the first page of the letter, but you didn't actually read anything. The first words you read were the signature; the first element of text, the postscript. In other words, *the P.S. was the lead of this letter.* Siegfried Vögele says his eye-motion research reveals that the postscript is the first text read by more than 90 percent of all direct mail recipients.

3. But what was it you saw on the final page of the letter that motivated you, first to read the P.S. and then to scan the subheads and underlining? Was it the easy-to-read format and accessible language— or was there something genuinely involving in what you read? Was [fill-in-the-blank] making it worth your while to read on—by answering your unspoken questions with carefully crafted subheads, addressing your concerns through judicious underlining, spelling out the advantages you would receive by supporting their work? Vögele says yes: that only by answering your silent questions through such devices as these will a solicitation be involving enough to induce you to read on. If the letter doesn't answer those questions in the most obvious and accessible way, it's unlikely to be read at all.

4. Notice that the first time you read a complete block of copy was when you took in the P.S. The second time was after you read the opening sentence of the letter and learned it was interesting enough to engage you; then you read one or two complete paragraphs—and that was the point where you were finally hooked. In Vögele's way of looking at these things, there are two stages in a reader's involvement in a direct mail letter. As soon as you read one full block of text from beginning to end, you passed from the first stage to the second and final stage. At that precise moment, you began to participate in the *comprehensive second dialogue.* Here's how Vögele describes the process: "We answer unspoken readers' questions in a simple, easily understood way, first through a short 'dialogue' which makes the reader aware of the benefit to himself, then through a [second and] more detailed 'dialogue' built along the same lines as a real personal sales conversation."

5. But what was it that caused you to glide so smoothly from the *short dialogue* to the *comprehensive second dialogue*? Vögele would say many factors contributed—everything in the content, language, and format that made the letter easy to read, accessible, informative, and directly

responsive to your concerns. All are examples of the response boosters he calls *amplifiers*: little signs and gestures of positive reinforcement that help the reader spot encouraging answers to his unspoken questions.

In Vögele's lexicon, *filters* are the polar opposite of amplifiers. They're the negative forces that come into play in a direct mail package: the elements of formatting or the contents that make the package hard to read, uninteresting, off-putting.

Amplifiers provide you with little yeses to answer those unspoken questions. Filters produce noes.

The canvasser used her own arsenal of amplifiers by speaking intelligently (but not over your head), answering your questions (whether vocalized or not), watching and responding to your body language, and shutting up quickly when your patience flagged.

She skillfully moved you to answer yes to your own unvocalized questions—again and again and again. She avoided all the little traps (or filters)—the distractions, the boring lists of facts, the self-centered emphasis on [fill-on-the-blank]'s needs. Instinctively, she knew those missteps were a surefire way to lead you to answer your own unspoken questions with no—over and over again. Whoever wrote that letter for [fill-in-the-blank] did much the same thing, guiding you to answer yes far more often than you answered no.

As Vögele sees it, getting to that big YES!—a checkmark on the reply form, along with a check—is merely a matter of helping the reader answer yes a lot more frequently than he answers no.

But something else was going on here too, something much more basic: both fundraisers—the letter writer no less than the canvasser—took pains to *engage you in a dialogue*. They answered *your* questions (spoken or not). They both went out of their way to involve you in a conversation—silent and one-sided in the case of the letter but nonetheless involving.

Neither the young woman nor the writer of the letter was engaged in a monologue, preoccupied with [fill-in-the-blank]'s needs and problems. Both made the effort to *relate the organization's needs to you*—the listener or the reader—in a style, language, and presentation format that subtly moved you to adopt [fill-in-the-blank]'s needs as your own.

Answering Your Reader's Questions Before They're Even Asked

The trick to this craft, Siegfried Vögele tells us, is to anticipate the questions that will be on the reader's mind and answer those questions clearly and forcefully. He admonishes us to pay extra special attention to those questions that highlight the advantages the reader will enjoy (what we call *benefits*).

Your answers must find their way into photos or drawings (and accompanying captions) or into subheads or underlined phrases or words—because those are the items in your letter that the reader will notice before actually reading what you've written.

Much of the skill that a letter writer brings to the task, then, is to catalogue the questions readers are sure to ask and artfully weave the answers into the letter. Vögele says there are two types: *basic questions*—those that involuntarily leap to mind when someone picks up any fundraising letter—and *product questions*—those that relate specifically to your appeal and might not come to mind if your reader were instead examining an appeal from some other charity. Although Vögele's terminology is derived from the experience of commercial direct marketing, both categories of readers' unspoken questions have their equivalents in the realm of fundraising.

Here are some of the basic questions that donors or prospective donors might ask themselves when they pick up one of your fundraising letters:

- Where did this letter come from?
- What's inside the envelope?
- Who wrote this letter?
- Who signed this letter?
- Where did they get my address?
- What do they know about me?
- Why are they writing to me specifically?
- How much money do they want from me?
- Should I even bother to read this letter?
- Can they prove what they say?
- What happens after I respond?
- Do I have to sign anything?
- Do I have to put a stamp on it?
- What would my spouse think about this?
- What would my friends think?
- Can this wait?
- What would happen if I don't do anything?
- Can I throw this thing away?
- Have I received this before?
- Will they put my name on another mailing list?
- What's the catch?

Now consider some of the many product questions that might leap into your reader's mind at the first sight of your fundraising letter:

- Have I heard of this organization before?
- Have I given to these people before?
- Do they get any government funds?
- Do they really need my help?
- What difference will it make if I respond?
- Are they going to send me a newsletter?
- Will I get lots of other solicitations from these people?
- Will they expect me to give them money every year?
- How much of this gift will actually be used the way they say?
- How is this different from what other groups do?
- Are they going to send me a thank-you?
- Have they been doing this kind of work for very long?
- Is there a local branch of this organization?
- How do I know they're honest?
- Who runs this organization?
- Is there anybody famous who supports them?
- Is there a deadline?
- What do I have to do to fill out the reply card?
- Is there a better solution for this problem?

These questions are actually quite straightforward. Questions of both types are a natural human response to any unsolicited appeal, whether it comes by mail, by phone, through a website or an e-mail, through television, or in person. In a face-to-face visit, the fundraiser intentionally confronts the most promising of these questions and tries to provoke yet more questions, knowing that engaging a prospect in dialogue is the straightest path to a gift. In a written, scripted, or spoken fundraising appeal too, the skillful fundraiser seeks to anticipate the unspoken questions of readers, watchers, and listeners, knowing that the more directly prospective donors' true private concerns are met, the more involved these individuals will become in the silent dialogue.

The Four Waves of Rejection

If the writer doesn't properly anticipate and answer the reader's unspoken questions, instead of a preponderance of little yeses that add up to one big beautiful YES! the noes have it, Vögele says—and plunk! goes that letter. Rejection can come at any moment, he warns us. There are four possible stages in which the reader might give up on you—and, in one form or another, they are manifested in appeals delivered through any other communications channel as well.

Wave One

You've got up to twenty seconds to engage the reader—just long enough for her to open the envelope, examine the contents, and decide whether to spend any more time with your letter. And roughly the same holds true in e-mail and web communications as well as phone calls. Vögele refers to this as the *first run-through*. In this stage, you face your first and biggest hurdle; if your letter survives this test, the greatest danger is past. If, instead, the reader concludes, "I've never heard of these people before," or "I already sent them money this year," or simply "I'm not interested"—or any one of a thousand other possible excuses not to proceed—your appeal may well end up in the wastebasket or the computer trash bin, or be left dangling when the donor hangs up the phone. That's what happens to most. Even appeals to your most loyal and generous donors may suffer this ignoble fate: few people have the time or the inclination to read everything they receive in the mail, much less what they get by e-mail or access on the web.

Wave Two

If your appeal survives the first wave of possible rejection, your chances of securing a gift are greatly improved, but you don't have a lock on a gift. All that's happened, from Vögele's perspective, is that your reader has found satisfactory answers to the first round of silent questions. Now, reading more thoroughly, the reader looks for answers to a whole new round of questions. Previously, the reader has looked only at the pictures, read the subheads, and cruised through the underlined text. Now comes the true test: what you've written (or failed to include) in the blocks of text. What the reader encounters here must respond to her questions and spell out the benefits she will receive as a result of giving a gift. If the blocks of text in your letter or online don't speak to the reader, and if your text fails to provoke a preponderance of little yeses, chances are your appeal will make its way into the trash in this second throwaway wave.

Wave Three

Even if your letter survives the second wave of rejection, there's yet more potential trouble in store for you—for starters, the *filing-away*, or *archiving*, wave. If your letter succumbs to the near-universal human fondness for putting off until later what could just as easily be done right now, it won't find its way into the trash—at least not immediately. But, Vögele points out, time acts as a filter: the reader who was impressed enough with your appeal to put it away for later reference may no longer remember why she was so moved after a week or a month has gone by. The effect achieved is little better than a big fat NO! Rarely will archived appeals result in donations.

The hurdles are even greater with online and telephone solicitations. Once your message has been rejected, it's almost certain to be permanently forgotten.

Wave Four

Vögele distinguishes between the phenomenon of archiving (or filing away) and what he terms *putting to one side*. The difference lies in the reader's intentions: in putting aside your appeal, the reader has resolved to do something but can't quite decide what that will be. This may happen because you've presented her with a decision to make, a question to answer, a form to fill out, a comment or greeting to write—or because she simply doesn't have enough money in her checking account at the moment. Vögele estimates that 50 percent of the solicitations that are put to one side will ultimately get lost. He explains: "One day, they may well end up in the wastebasket too, even if the advantage offered in them was once recognized. In the meantime, a long period of time has elapsed. New pictures and information have taken precedence." However, we now have the ability to remind our donors via e-mail, phone, or both to pick your appeal back up and reconsider their decisions.

The Solution

Here's the key: the faster you get your reader to respond, the more likely she will. That puts an enormous burden on the first twenty seconds of your message's exposure to the reader's indifference. So let's conclude by going back to the beginning of this process: the first twenty seconds.

A Closer Look at the First Twenty Seconds in Your Letter's Public Life

Vögele divides the crucial first twenty seconds into three phases:

- *Phase one, before the envelope is opened—eight seconds on average.* During this time, recipients turn over the envelope, note how it's addressed, read the return address and any text, look for a way to open the envelope, and finally tear it open. With an e-mail, they'll consider who the message is from, how it's addressed, and most important, the subject line.

- *Phase two—approximately four seconds.* The reader picks up and examines the contents. Even before she has read a single word, the materials have an immediate impact on her. She unfolds or scrolls through them, forming a general impression of what they contain.

- *Phase three—another eight seconds.* In what Vögele refers to as the first run-through, the reader examines the pictures and headlines, finding short answers to her silent questions. If the writer has done a good job, the reader is now fully engaged in the short dialogue. This holds for both offline and online communications (but the process is a little more complex on the telephone).

Remember that the writer's objective is to involve the reader by persuading her to read some of the blocks of text in the letter—to become involved in the comprehensive second dialogue. "This means you need to get your reader's interest long before the twenty seconds are up," Vögele warns. The recipient will continue reading only if the benefits to her are obvious within the first few seconds. And that's why he insists a letter needs to "express the advantages to the reader by using pictures and headlines" and underlined words and phrases.

Now let's take a break from the quantifiable certainties of German research and venture into the realm of qualitative research—by taking a close look in chapter 3 at what donors really think about fundraising appeals.

Chapter Three:
What Donors Really Think about Fundraising Letters

Some years ago, as I was writing the first edition of this book, I took time out to observe a focus group in Los Angeles. For two hours I cringed behind a two-way mirror while ten people sat around a table, picking apart my direct mail fundraising letter for Camp Fire USA, then known as Camp Fire Boys and Girls. I was present because the leadership of Camp Fire had retained my firm to help launch a nationwide, direct mail fundraising program.

The letter those people were savaging was one I'd edited less than a week before. I'd thought the letter was pretty good to begin with, but I was convinced my brilliant editing had lifted it into the ranks of the fundraising hall of fame. Indeed, one of my senior associates went out of his way to congratulate me on my fine work, and for the first time ever, Camp Fire staff approved the text without changing a single word. They loved the letter. Nevertheless, Camp Fire had agreed that before mailing the letter, we would test our draft copy in focus groups and not rely exclusively on our own instincts. The Los Angeles group was the second of two organized exclusively for that purpose.

The group consisted of seven women and three men, diverse in age, ethnicity, religion, and income level as well as occupation: among them were a couple of retired people, a housewife, a teacher, a banker, and two business owners. Half had completed at least four years of college. Most had done volunteer work in the past three years.

Despite their differences, these ten people had one crucial element in common: in interviews over the telephone, they said they had previously contributed money by mail to human service organizations such as the Girl Scouts, Boys Town, Special Olympics, City of Hope, or Red Cross. In other words, they seemed to us like good prospects to support Camp Fire.

Now here's what happened.

How Ten People Reacted to My Pride and Joy

Under the skillful guidance of a professional moderator, the participants quickly warmed up to the subject at hand by discussing their views of direct mail fundraising and youth programs. They revealed what they knew—mostly what they didn't know—about Camp Fire. Prodded by the discussion leader, they cited examples of "good letters" from charities (ones that were "interesting" and contained "local examples so you can see the money at work"). Their biggest concern about fundraising letters was "authenticity." They were worried about getting sucked into scams "like you hear about on TV."

The group analyzed what was then Camp Fire's tagline—"The first fire we light is the fire within"—which most of them seemed to like. (A typical comment: "I'm not sure what it means, but I like it.") Then they critiqued one of our two candidates for the outer envelope design. That envelope featured the Camp Fire logo, name, address, and tagline along with smaller type reading "recycled paper," plus a much bolder and larger teaser: "Inside: Our free gift to you." Here's what the members of the focus group had to say about the envelope:

"'Recycled paper.' I like that."

"Pretty good as an envelope."

"Camp Fire caught my attention. The logo."

"I focused on 'Inside: Our free gift.'"

"There might be too much on it."

"It's very feminine. Like Camp Fire girls."

"You get the feeling there's something they're going to tell you about the spark" (a word nowhere to be found on the envelope).

"'Free gift'? I like that."

"They want something."

"I'd throw this away."

"Why are they offering a free gift?"

"I'd open it."

"So would I."

"I'd toss it."

"You think you have to send a gift and then they'll send something."

The reviews were mixed, but not too bad for starters. Then the moderator passed out copies of the one-and-a-half-page fundraising letter intended to be mailed in that envelope and asked the group to read it. This was the letter I'd edited, actually a version of a much longer letter my firm had drafted. My hunch was that a shorter letter would be better received in the market we expected to mail for Camp Fire, because appeals from many national charities already competing in that market were typically short.

Here's what the group had to say about the letter:

"I would throw it away."

"There's nothing in there that says anything about the free gift."

"There's not enough information in there."

"How are they going to teach kids to 'be somebody'?" (a promise made in the text of the letter).

"I don't know Camp Fire."

"I think it's very wordy."

"How do I know it's an authentic program?"

"It didn't sell me."

"There are a lot of programs out there that are trying to do the same thing."

"I'd rather contribute to an L.A.-based organization. I'd contribute if it said kids in L.A. would be helped."

"The letter just doesn't flow very well."

"I don't like this 'Dear Caring American' [the salutation]. Leave that out."

"Are these kids from poorer areas, or is this like the Boy Scouts?"

"Is 'kids' acceptable? Shouldn't you say 'children'? 'Teens'? 'Youth'?"

"This doesn't sound like Camp Fire. There's nothing camp-y here."

"They've been in business for over fifty years. Why don't they say that?"

"They need an 800-number. A hotline or somewhere you can call."

At various points along the way, the moderator turned the group's attention to specific elements in the letter copy:

- The letter's headline: "I'm gonna be dead by the time I'm 18."

  "It's not big enough."

  "It wouldn't mean anything unless I read the rest."

- The name we'd chosen for contributors of $12 or more: "Leadership Circle."

  "Too long a name."

  "Do I become a member?"

- The title we promised to early respondents: "Charter Member."

    "It sounds like the group [Camp Fire] is new."

    "I'm not important enough to be a Charter Member."

    "This letter's going to ten million people."

    "Just ask me for the money."

    "Does it mean they'll expect more money next year?"

To clinch matters, the moderator asked the group, "If you received this letter in the mail, would you consider making a contribution?" The unanimous response: "No."

Oh, ignominy! Oh, pain and suffering!

But am I glad that answer came from a focus group and not from an equally uncaring public—after Camp Fire spent a small fortune mailing 50,000 copies of the letter all over the country!

Why Did We Set Up That Exasperating Focus Group, Anyway?

Now listen to a few of the comments about the four-page version of the Camp Fire appeal our firm had drafted. That version led with a gripping story about an inner-city child whose life was turned around by Camp Fire:

    "I personally like this. I would give."

    "It gives you an actual person."

    "It's lovely."

    "The lead grabs you—real hard."

A similar sentiment had prevailed the evening before in a focus group assembled in Tulsa, Oklahoma. I'm told the Tulsa group had a somewhat different take on the first letter: they were much more familiar with Camp Fire, were much less critical of the copy, and showed none of the Los Angeles group's cynicism about charity. But emphasis and nuances aside, there's no question that both groups favored the longer letter instead of the shorter one, and by a huge margin.

Camp Fire didn't go to all the trouble and expense of organizing focus groups merely to choose between two versions of one appeal. Hearing unguarded comments from representative prospects helped us fine-tune our copy. We were able to answer major questions we hadn't anticipated and clear up ambiguities in the copy and artwork, any one of which might have had a profound impact on the results. In other words, we learned in advance what our readers' unspoken questions were likely to be and made changes in the copy to answer those questions. For example, each of the following comments was helpful in making final copy revisions:

"How come there are boys as well as girls?"

"What makes this organization different? What are they going to do?"

"Are there Camp Fire programs here in Los Angeles?" (There are.)

"What is AIDS counseling? As a parent, I would be very interested in knowing what approach they take."

"If it were Girl Scouts, we wouldn't be as critical. We see them here."

"Teaching kids how to survive. This is a key point."

"It doesn't tell exactly where the money goes—like, '30 percent to this.'"

"What's it going to do for my city?"

What Those Ten People Taught Me (All Over Again)

So lest you too stumble into the wilderness of indifference—armed only with a pitiful little one-and-a-half-page fundraising letter—please keep the following lessons in mind:

- *Donors need lots of information to be persuaded to send gifts by mail.* They may say they want to read only short letters, but what they really crave are answers to their questions. And questions produce doubt or disinterest, the parents of inaction. If it takes an extra page or two to answer every question you can anticipate, increase the budget and stifle your natural tendency to keep your message short and sweet. The results will vindicate you.

   In this respect, online appeals don't work the same way as direct mail letters. You'll need to pare down this long copy for a comparable appeal via e-mail or the web. (In part 4, I'll go into detail about how to modify your copy for e-mail and the web.)

- *Donors are skeptical.* It's best to head them off at the pass by volunteering information about the unique character, the impact, and the cost effectiveness of your work. And they want proof you're really doing the things you say you're doing. Abundant details— facts—will get that point across.

- *An appeal is too long only if it doesn't convey the information that donors want.* My one-and-a-half-page version was "wordy" because it lacked the particulars of the four-page letter. The longer version was not wordy even though it contained many more words.

- *Human interest sells—and probably doubly so in human service appeals.* A story, especially about children, is a great way to humanize a fundraising letter. That's what we did in the longer letter.

- *If there's a way to misunderstand your message, donors will find it.* They'll miss important points if you don't emphasize them. They'll be thrown off by awkward transitions, unfamiliar words, poor word choices, and attempts to gloss over details. Words matter.

- *Format and design affect understanding.* For the direct mail part of the appeal package, the only tools you've got are words, numbers, typography, pictures, paper, and ink. Use them all wisely; you have no other way to establish your credibility by mail. Online, format and design carry an even greater burden.

Most of the time, I remember all these lessons when I sit down to work on a fundraising package. Yet I still sometimes write copy that doesn't work well.

Raising money is an endlessly tricky business, and no amount of knowledge will equip a fundraiser to avoid occasional unpleasant surprises. But experience, insight, and market research like the focus group reported in this chapter can all help narrow the uncertainties and enlarge the odds of success.

Focus groups may not be cost effective for your organization, and they're certainly not needed for every fundraising campaign. But friends, family, and coworkers can informally evaluate your writing and the design of your package. That way, you too might find you're not achieving the effect you thought you were.

Now that we've examined what really happens to fundraising letters when donors receive them in the mail, let's examine the characteristics of an effective fundraising campaign—one that takes account of the insights we've gained through focus groups and other techniques that cast light on the whims and foibles of the human beings who read our appeals. Please join me in chapter 4, "Characteristics of an Effective Fundraising Campaign."

Chapter Four:
Characteristics of an Effective Fundraising Appeal

Most fundraisers apparently think fundraising appeals are all pretty much the same. Here's how their definition of a fundraising appeal seems to run: "A solicitation from a nonprofit organization, describing needs and requesting charitable gifts to fill them."

Right?

Wrong! Wrong on every count.

So banish that ill-conceived and misleading definition from your consciousness. Better yet, copy it down on a sheet of scratch paper, cross it out with bold strokes of your pen, slice it up with scissors, and deposit the whole mess in the nearest wastebasket.

Now you're ready to get started on the right foot! Read this next part carefully:

An effective fundraising appeal possesses three attributes.

Attributes of an Effective Fundraising Appeal

1. An effective fundraising appeal is a solicitation from one person to another.

2. An effective fundraising appeal describes an opportunity for the recipient to meet personal needs or achieve personal desires by supporting a worthy charitable aim.

3. An effective fundraising appeal invites the recipient to take specific and immediate action.

I'm sure you noticed that one all-important word is missing here: "money." Money—a request for a charitable gift—is an indispensable element in the overwhelming majority of fundraising appeals. Omit that request for funds, and your copy will fail the most basic test of effectiveness. What's worse, you'll almost certainly fail to raise much money.

But the action requested in a fundraising appeal doesn't always consist of sending money, at least not right away. The specific action requested might be to complete and return a survey; to use a set of stamps, name stickers, or greeting cards; or to authorize regular bank transfers. There are hundreds of possibilities. Especially nowadays with so many open channels of communication, our supporters can share personal stories, start fundraising campaigns on their own, contact members of Congress, or recruit new donors, in addition to responding with gifts. The appeal writer's first responsibility when writing for results is to determine what that action is. And understanding that duty leads to what I call a fundamental law:

The Fundamental Law of Writing Fundraising Appeals

When you set out to write a fundraising appeal, make sure you know precisely to whom you're writing and why—and be certain you make that point just as clear to them as it is to you.

That "point"—the equation that expresses the who, what, why, when, and how of your appeal—is what I've fallen into the bad habit of calling the *marketing concept*. I'll discuss this all-important notion in more detail in chapter 6, where I sum up the central message of this book. For starters, though, let's take a stab at a working definition:

- The marketing concept embodies your purpose in writing: to secure a gift of $500 or more, for example.

- The marketing concept identifies the person to whom you're writing: to extend the previous example, a donor who has previously given your organization at least one gift of $100 or more.

- The marketing concept incorporates the benefits the person you're writing to will receive as a result of responding—in this example, great satisfaction from knowing how much your organization can accomplish with $500 or more, plus special recognition for giving such a generous gift.

The fundamental law, then, is to work out the marketing concept before you write a single word—and then to be sure every word you write speaks to that concept.

Fundraising Campaigns: One Size Won't Fit All

Fundraising appeals are of many different types, serving a broad variety of ends and thus involving a great many different marketing concepts. To write an effective appeal, you must first determine the target audience and specific purpose you want to serve.

Determining the Target Audience

- Are you appealing to people who have never before supported your organization, asking them to join? That's an *acquisition* (or *prospect*) campaign that may be conducted either by mail or by e-mail. I cover that topic in chapters 10 and 11.

- Is your appeal to be sent to new members or donors, welcoming them to your organization? I call that a *welcome package* (when in the mail) or *welcome series* (when via e-mail); others may describe it as a welcome packet or kit or even a new-donor acknowledgment. Chapter 12 takes up this subject.

- Are you soliciting previous donors, appealing for additional gifts for some special purpose? That's a *special appeal*. You'll find examples in chapter 13.

- Are you addressing proven donors at the end of the year? That's a *year-end appeal*. The topic is covered in chapter 14.

- Are you asking your donors to enroll in a monthly giving program? That's a *sustainer*, *pledge*, or *regular giving program*, the subject of chapter 15.

- Are you writing to some of your most generous donors, seeking large gifts? I refer to an appeal of that sort as a *high-dollar letter*, the subject of chapter 16.

- Is the specific purpose of your letter to induce previous donors to increase their support? If so, you're writing an *upgrade appeal*. You'll learn about that topic in chapter 17.

- Are you approaching your new and regular supporters to ask them to renew this year's annual gift or membership dues? Then you're writing a *renewal*. That's the theme of chapter 18.

- Is your letter intended to acknowledge a donor's recent gift? That's a *thank-you letter*, the subject of chapter 19.

- Are you writing to encourage your donors to consider legacy (or planned) giving? That's a *legacy promotion*. It's the subject covered in chapter 20.

The second thing you need to start thinking about is the channel (or channels) through which you'll approach your donors or prospects. Will you use mail, e-mail, the web, social media, or mobile communications or some combination of these channels? Today's fundraising appeals often include multiple elements for which copy is needed, including the direct mail letter and package, e-mail communications, online landing pages and banner ads, and even social media and mobile content.

In the case studies in chapters 10 through 20, which contain examples of all eleven of these types of fundraising appeals, you'll learn how copy is modified to suit the various online channels that usually are part of multi-channel campaigns. That will prepare you for many writing challenges—but hardly all of them. No author can anticipate every need he may face. No book can supply you with models to follow in every contingency and copy for every possible channel.

But in spite of such great variety in fundraising appeals, the most productive ones I've read share six qualities.

Qualities of Successful Fundraising Appeals

1. *Clarity.* There's no doubt or ambiguity about the writer's intent or what the reader is asked to do. The message is delivered in unmistakably clear and simple terms that rule out guesswork. Early on, the reader gets the point of the appeal, and that point never wavers throughout the package.

2. *Cohesiveness.* Every element of the campaign works with every other to reinforce the message. If the message is complex—as, for example, in an appeal that combines a petition with a request for money—the close connection between the components is absolutely clear. The message isn't mixed. This means, for example, that an appeal for funds shouldn't be muddied by including a catalogue or a flyer that offers merchandise for sale, an invitation to a special event, or an update on a project discussed in an earlier appeal.

3. *Authenticity.* From beginning to end, the appeal is credible. The style and approach of the copy fit smoothly with what readers are likely to know about the signer, and the text includes enough revealing personal information to drive home that fit. Similarly, the nature of the appeal is consistent with what readers know about the organization and its work. In short, it's natural for this signer and this non-profit to be sending this particular appeal. Conversely, a Hollywood starlet, no matter how popular, might not be the most credible signer of an appeal from a research institute.

4. *Ease of response.* The appeal contains everything the reader might need to respond without a moment's delay after reviewing the appeal. At a minimum, the appeal will include a direct mail package that consists of a clearly marked response device and a preaddressed response envelope as well as a letter, and there's no doubt that the response form and envelope are included exclusively for the purpose of responding to the appeal. In all direct response, the fundraiser's job is to make it easy for the reader to respond. Experience shows that if it's not easy, the recipient is likely to set the appeal aside and never respond at all.

5. *Appropriateness.* The message is calculated to be of interest to the intended reader, and the appeal requests assistance of a sort that the reader might naturally be assumed to be able to provide. For example, I might write an extraordinarily interesting letter about the cuisine of Kyrgyzstan, but I would be unlikely to generate much response to my appeal unless I were writing to people with either a demonstrated interest in exotic cuisine or a fascination with Kyrgyzstan, or even less likely, both. In other words, it's always important to write to the audience. It's also important that what you write be suitable for the channel you're using. For example, copy that works in a direct mail package will probably need to be shortened for use in e-mail.

6. *Engaging copy.* There's something inherently intriguing about the appeal in the story it tells, the character of the request (or offer) it makes, or the language in which it's written. It's interesting and holds the reader's attention. Sometimes this can be accomplished with a clever outer envelope teaser or e-mail subject line (which is appropriately followed through inside the package or e-mail). Sometimes a fascinating personal story about a recipient of the agency's help connects with the reader on a deeply emotional level. Sometimes a writer's style is so fresh and compelling that the reader is inexorably drawn through the copy. Whatever it is, something catches the reader's attention—and holds it.

From a mechanical perspective, however, the only things common to all appeals are an *offer* (or *proposition*)—which incorporates the ask, if any, as well as the benefits to the donor—and the *case*—which is the argument that justifies the offer and spells out the benefits. If the appeal is framed as a letter, which is the central component in most successful fundraising campaigns, it's likely to include a salutation and signature that clarify the relationship between the letter signer and the person to whom the letter is addressed, a lead that starts off the letter, a close that ends it, a P.S., and a response device (or reply device) that the donor may use to return a gift. That's about it.

Many fundraisers relate these elements to a formula, insisting there's a standard structure or sequence a writer may follow in constructing an appeal. I disagree. To understand how to write successful fundraising copy, you must study appeals that have worked well, determine what made them successful—and then put them aside and focus on your own donors and your own organization. Your fundraising letters will be successful only if they reflect what's unique about your organization and uniquely attractive to your donors.

To bear down hard on this important point, let's turn now to chapter 5 and take a stroll through the pages of a single, well-written fundraising letter. By accompanying me on this paragraph-by-paragraph tour in the next chapter, you'll gain an overview of the approach I'll spell out later in more detail. In the process, you'll gain insight about how to frame the unique attractions of your own organization in ways that will be compelling to your donors.

Chapter Five:
A Leisurely Tour through One Successful Appeal

We'll meander slowly, paragraph by paragraph, through a four-page fundraising letter and its companion package components in an excellent example of the fundraiser's craft. Before we embark on our journey, however, I urge you to read the whole package in its entirety (exhibits 5.1 through 5.5). As you do, weigh it against the six qualities of successful appeals that I discussed in the previous chapter: clarity, cohesiveness, authenticity, ease of response, appropriateness, and engaging copy.

My colleague and friend Bill Rehm wrote this fundraising appeal for the San Francisco Conservatory of Music two decades ago. (The conservatory had retained our firm to assist it in building its membership base, part of a broader development strategy to lay the foundation for a significant capital campaign several years hence.) So, it's out of date, right? Yes and no. In its execution of fundamentals, this appeal is as strong as it was in 1992, and I'd be hard-pressed to come up with a newer example that's appreciably better. However, aspects of the appeal clearly reflect a time long past, and I've noted those instances in the text. To compare this appeal with one from the same organization twenty years later, go to this book's website (www.josseybass.com/go/fundraisingappeals), where I've posted a full-color version of a recent conservatory solicitation.

The San Francisco Conservatory of Music Appeal
The Outer Envelope

1. My eyes leap first to the signature in the upper-left-hand corner (called the *corner card*). Colin Murdoch, then and still president of the conservatory, signed the appeal inside, and printing his signature on the envelope (in blue ink, to contrast with the red of the logo and return

address) lends a personal touch that previous testing suggests may improve results—regardless of whether he's well known or not to a prospective donor.

2. With the same glance, I take in the extraordinary woodblock print in the corner card: the conservatory's logo.

3. The typefaces used in the conservatory's name and address are consistently repeated throughout the contents of the package, as they should be. A typeface can be an organization's signature as surely as the most distinctive logo design.

4. A postage meter has been used instead of a postal indicia (that is, a permit imprint). Testing sometimes shows that metered postage out-pulls an indicia (but both are usually far less successful, though not necessarily less cost effective, than first-class stamps).

EXHIBIT 5.1
Outer Envelope, San Francisco Conservatory of Music

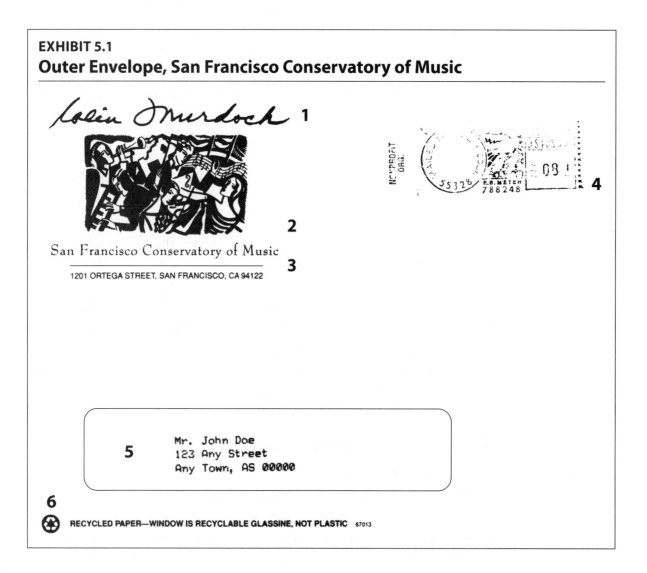

5. Now, you and I may have noticed all four of the features of this envelope I've already enumerated, but a recipient of this appeal is much more likely to have found her eyes leaping first to the mailing label. Why? Because, research shows, she'll notice her own name before anything else. So she sees a so-called Cheshire label, a strip of plain paper machine-affixed to a card inside that shows through a glassine (recyclable) window, revealing a computer-imprinted name and address plus a five-digit key code (upper right in the window) and a postal bar code. (Cheshire labels are virtually extinct today, when inkjet printers can address a reply device more cost effectively than a label, but window envelopes live on.) The bar code enabled the conservatory to mail this particular envelope at a savings of three cents off what was then the standard nonprofit bulk rate (8.1 cents versus 11.1 cents)—and don't you wish that postal rates were still that low?

6. The envelope advertises "recycled paper," though testing may show that using recycled paper doesn't improve results, even among donors who describe themselves as environmentalists. So what? As my grandmother would have said, "What can it hurt? And it might help!" Besides, it's the right thing to do.

The Letter
Page One

7. The size of the original page, 7 by 10 inches, is important. This so-called Monarch letter has a personal touch to it, because it's notably smaller than standard business size (8½ by 11 inches), much more like personal stationery. And there's that lovely logo again. It appears above the address—significantly, a street address, not a post office box—and a telephone number. Nowadays we would add a website address as well. Using the conservatory's actual address, telephone number, and web address may help inspire confidence in me as a prospective donor. If recent studies are correct, I would be likely to log onto the website before contributing to the conservatory. I might also be led to pay an unexpected visit or place a telephone call out of curiosity or suspiciousness—but that's much less likely.

8. The use of "Thursday afternoon" is a copywriter's conceit. Still, it may subliminally convey an illusion that the letter bears a specific date. There's no real date here because this appeal was mailed via bulk rate, making it probable that at least some of the letters would be delivered two weeks or longer after the mail date.

EXHIBIT 5.2
Solicitation Letter, San Francisco Conservatory of Music

7

San Francisco Conservatory of Music

1201 ORTEGA ST., SAN FRANCISCO, CA 94122
415/759-3463

8
Thursday afternoon

9
Dear Friend and Neighbor,

10   I'm writing to invite you -- and a select group of other music lovers in the Bay Area -- to take your seat, please.

11   Sit down, as our guest, at the Faculty Trio Concert this November 15th, and listen to some of the most beautiful chamber music that San Francisco has to offer.

12   It's our way of saying thank you -- for becoming a Friend of the San Francisco Conservatory of Music.

13   As the Conservatory begins its 76th season, we've set a goal of enlisting <u>333</u> <u>new</u> <u>Friends</u> <u>of</u> <u>the</u> <u>Conservatory</u>. We've chosen that number because there are exactly 333 seats in Hellman Hall -- the concert hall where we hold our New Member Concert each year.

14   I'd like to see all 333 seats filled with new members this year. And I'd like to see you in one of those seats.

15   In just a minute, I'll tell you about several other benefits you'll receive as a new member of the Conservatory. But first, let me tell you what your membership support means to the Bay Area.

16   Like the Bay Area itself, the San Francisco Conservatory of Music represents many things to many people. But above all else, the Conservatory is a community of musicians who experience the joy, the promise, and the pursuit of musical excellence. Every day, we celebrate the teaching, learning, composing, and performance of music.

17   That's been our proud mission for over 75 years

RECYCLED PAPER   67011 **18**

Page two **19**

20 -- ever since the Conservatory was first founded by pianists Ada Clement and Lillian Hodghead in 1917.

21   Today, the San Francisco Conservatory of Music is one of the most respected institutions of music education in the country, offering instruction to more than 1,500 students ranging from pre-school to post graduate levels.

22   Conservatory students, faculty and guest artists perform more than 300 concerts on campus each year.

23   And over the past seventy-five years, the Conservatory has trained some of our country's most brilliant musicians -- violinists Isaac Stern and Yehudi Menuhin, pianist Jeffrey Kahane, and guitarist David Tanenbaum, to name just a few.

24   The Conservatory's faculty of 78 professional musicians are drawn from some of the finest musical organizations in the country, including 32 musicians who are currently playing with either the San Francisco Symphony, the San Francisco Opera, or the San Francisco Ballet.

25   It goes without saying that all of us at the Conservatory share a love for music. But more than that, we possess the desire to help talented and motivated students realize their dreams.

26

With a student-faculty ratio of just six to one, teachers give special attention to every student.

Page three **27**

28   I see our role at the Conservatory as one of helping to nurture and develop the creativity, skill, and genius residing within each musician.

29   I also see it as the responsibility of the Conservatory to share the music we help create with the community.

30   Through the Conservatory's Community Service Program, our students give more than 400 performances each year. We bring music to hospitals, convalescent homes, day care centers, retirement homes -- reaching people who otherwise would never have the pleasure of hearing live classical music.

31

Conservatory students contribute to our community by performing more than 400 free concerts each year.

32   The San Francisco Conservatory of Music has a long, proud tradition of teaching and providing musical excellence to the Bay Area. And, I assure you, this will continue to be our overriding mission in the years ahead.

33   But the Conservatory is only as great as its supporters. Tuition and fees cover just 59% of our annual budget. The remainder must come from generous individuals in our community.

34   Currently, we have a very special group of Friends -- people like you -- who help support the Conservatory with a tax-deductible membership contribution each year.

35   That's why I hope you'll accept my invitation to become a Friend of the San Francisco Conservatory

Page four

36 of Music today -- and support one of San Francisco's oldest and most respected institutions.

37   When you become a Friend of the Conservatory, you'll receive <u>all</u> <u>these</u> <u>membership</u> <u>benefits</u>:

   38 o A subscription to <u>At the Conservatory</u>, the monthly newsletter and calendar of events.

   39 o Free tickets to the special Faculty Trio Concert for new members on November 15.

   40 o Free attendance at the "Friends Only" Tour and Concert in January, 1994.

   41 o Membership discounts for Conservatory concerts throughout the year and special discounts for Conservatory extension classes.

   42 o Advance ticket purchase for the <u>Sing-It-Yourself</u> <u>Messiah</u> concerts at Davies Symphony Hall this December.

43   Perhaps the greatest benefit you'll receive, though, is knowing you're helping to ensure that students will continue to get the best musical instruction available.

44   So please, right now while everything is in front of you, take a minute to write your tax-deductible check and send it to the San Francisco Conservatory of Music.

45   With many thanks.

                    46 Sincerely,

                    Colin Murdoch

                    Colin Murdoch
                    President

47 P.S. To reserve your free ticket to the Faculty Trio Concert at the Conservatory's Hellman Hall on November 15, we must receive your membership contribution by November 8. Please send your gift <u>today</u>. Thank you very much.

9. "Dear Friend and Neighbor" is a neat variation on the standard "Dear Friend." It's a signal that this appeal was mailed only locally. This is, in its way, a form of personalization, shortening the distance between the conservatory and me. However, since this letter is not addressed to me personally, it's obviously not personalized within the generally accepted meaning of that term. This is a bulk appeal, mailed in quantity, and there's no way around that.

10. In its five opening words, "I'm writing to invite you," this appeal simply and directly establishes the basis of a relationship between the signer and me. (Most people who receive this letter probably will flip to the bottom of page four to view the signature, to see who is sending the letter, and to read the P.S. But let's be orderly about this, and stick to our paragraph-by-paragraph story.) The opening sentence (the lead) identifies me in two important ways—as a music lover and a resident of the San Francisco Bay Area—and seizes my attention with an unfamiliar request: to take a seat.

11. The second paragraph quickly explains that unfamiliar request with specifics: what (a concert), when (on a particular day), and where (in San Francisco), in time-honored journalistic fashion. You'll note too that the conservatory is appealing to my love for chamber music. (How do they know that? They don't, of course. But they know how popular chamber music is among classical music fans.)

12. Now Colin Murdoch makes clear exactly why he's writing this letter to me. He wants me to become a "Friend" (and since I receive lots of letters like these, I've got a pretty good idea what he means).

13. Now come more facts—details that tell me this is a letter about something specific. Numbers and capitalized words capture my interest because they supply information that answers questions I may have about a topic that (as we've already established) is of general interest to me. The unusual number "333" is itself engaging, because it's unexpected. You'll also note that "333 new Friends of the Conservatory" is underlined—the only underlining on this page, so it really stands out. A different writer might have chosen different words to emphasize, but what's most important here is that underlining is used sparingly, to lessen the impression this is simply one more direct mail appeal.

14. That intriguing number is repeated. And so are the words "you" and "I," each for the third time so far. This is not an impersonal institutional appeal. It's a letter from Colin Murdoch to me.

15. There's "you" again: three more times. And "me" counts as a form of "I." Just as important, the concept of membership, broached in each of the two preceding paragraphs, is introduced in terms of its benefits, both

to me and to the area where I live (not San Francisco, you'll notice, but the entire, and much larger, Bay Area).

16. In this seven-line paragraph—the longest on all four pages of the appeal—the conservatory is described in emotional and conceptual terms, not as brick and mortar. Murdoch is connecting with me where I really live—on the plane of values: "joy," "promise," "excellence," "teaching," "learning," "music."

17. Note that only one line of this paragraph appears on this page: that's a device to draw my eye onto the second page.

18. There's that "recycled paper" again.

Page Two

19. This letter consists of two sheets of paper that form four pages. The notation "Page two" at the top helps orient me, minimizing the possibility I'll be confused (and thus less likely to send a gift).

20. Take note of specifics again. Facts and figures (used with reasonable restraint) heighten reader interest.

21. This reference to the conservatory's nationwide reputation helps establish credibility. The additional facts lend authority to the reference, making it more than a boast.

22. Here's a significant and surprising fact. Most concertgoers are aware that 300 performances per year is a very large number for any arts organization.

23. More facts here, and interesting ones at that. These names, familiar to classical music lovers, help reinforce my interest while enhancing the credibility of the appeal.

24. Facts again (numbers). By now, I'm really getting acquainted with the conservatory.

25. We're back to values and abstracts again: "love," "desire," "talented," "motivated," "dreams." This fellow Murdoch isn't sending me a press release. He's connecting with me about things that matter.

26. This intense and charming photograph and its handwritten caption convey important facts about the conservatory and its work. They also lend added human interest to the appeal.

Page Three

27. The words "Page three" reassure me that I'm on the right page. But I haven't been hit over the head with a "Next page, please" or the

equivalent on the bottom of page two. (No doubt some direct marketer has tested that obnoxiously condescending device and found it improves response. I tend to avoid using it. I doubt it makes much difference other than to serve as one more subtle but unwanted reminder that an appeal is really, after all, just an impersonal direct mail letter sent to large numbers of people.)

28. Again, Colin Murdoch reveals his personal feelings. He uses the lofty language that gets to the heart of the subject: the teaching of music.

29. Continuing in the first person, Murdoch now reveals the outward-looking dimension of the conservatory's mission: relating to the community—my community.

30. I see that by supporting the conservatory, I won't just be helping to bring out the genius in future world-class performers. I'll also help support my community's social safety net.

31. This photograph depicts an obviously diverse group of school-children, and the caption repeats the number "400." The effect is to drive home the point that the conservatory serves far more than its own students and faculty or affluent concertgoers like me. Those 400 concerts are free.

32. Now we're back to values again: "tradition" and "musical excellence." Even the word "mission" connotes passion and an orientation to values.

33. Citing the central financial fact about the conservatory brings me back into the picture once again. There's little doubt in my mind that I'm (supposedly) one of those "generous individuals."

34. Any doubt I may have is now quickly dispelled: Murdoch is talking about "people like" me. But the contribution he wants is more than simply that. It's "tax deductible," it buys me a "membership," and it's to be annual.

35. That, obviously, is what Murdoch means when he asks me to become a "Friend." But I'm going to have to go on to the next page to learn whether there's some qualification or exception to his request.

Page Four

36. There is no exception here—just another argument for supporting the conservatory: its long and respected institutional history.

37. Here, in the first underlined words since the phrase on page one, Murdoch introduces the subject of membership benefits. (Note that the

words are individually underlined. Some people prefer continuous lines, but I think the underlining of spaces distracts the eye from the message and focuses it on what's less important: the fact of the underlining itself. It also eliminates the spaces between words, which readers use to "swallow" words and phrases one bite at a time.)

38. As a "Friend," I'll receive a monthly newsletter and calendar. Murdoch cites the newsletter's name, emphasizing the unstated promise of events I may want to attend at the conservatory.

39. In fact, I'll receive free tickets to a specific concert—one that's coming up very soon.

40. More free tickets, and another event that's not too far off.

41. I'll get discounts—not only on admission to other concerts but for extension classes too. Here's a potentially important benefit that piques my curiosity. (I gave up trying the clarinet in fifth grade, but maybe I could learn it after all.)

42. Now—underlined again and deliberately placed last in the series, where it's most likely to be remembered—is a membership benefit that could well be the most attractive of all: the conservatory's wildly popular sing-along Messiah concerts at San Francisco's elegant Symphony Hall.

43. Despite all these tangible benefits of membership, Murdoch rushes to remind me I'll get something even more valuable: the satisfaction of knowing I've helped achieve something I value highly: the teaching of good music.

44. If I'm tempted to set this appeal aside and make my mind up later about whether to respond, Murdoch's suggestion that I do it now may have no effect on me, but at worst it's a throwaway line. And I'm reminded once again that my gift will be tax deductible, a fact that may be of special interest to me since the end of the year is fast approaching.

45. Ever hopeful, Murdoch thanks me.

46. He signs off "Sincerely," rather than with a more formal "Yours truly" or a flamboyant "See you at the Conservatory!" He is, after all, the president of a respected institution. His flowery signature has an artful flair; it's printed in dark blue ink, to set it off from the typed text and reinforce the illusion of personal (or, rather, business) correspondence.

47. As you'll remember, most readers read the P.S. first. This P.S. makes good use of that opportunity. It restates the date of the fast-approaching faculty concert and, for the first time, lays out a specific deadline for membership contributions. To be sure I'll beat that deadline,

I may really have to mail in my gift today, as I'm asked to do. (Although I rarely recommend including specific dates in letters written to recruit new members—or for that matter, in any other letters mailed at bulk rate—this case is an exception. The appeal was mailed within a narrow region and likely to be delivered well in advance of the concert date. And conservatory faculty and students perform so frequently that similar offers can be made almost any time of the year.)

Lift Letter

48. Yes, that intense-looking fellow in the upper-right-hand corner photo is the renowned cellist Yo-Yo Ma. Classical music lovers probably know that. It's likely to be the photograph that first caught your attention. That's what the eye-motion studies reveal. Then your eyes swept leftward to take in the musician's name, and finally down to the salutation and lead. This musical celebrity has signed what is called a *lift letter*—a brief, supplementary letter or note that strengthens the main appeal by emphasizing an important endorsement (as in this case) or providing significant information not found in the main letter.

49. While Colin Murdoch addressed me as a "Neighbor," Yo-Yo Ma finds common cause with me as a "Music Lover." It's a flattering reference. (He obviously never heard me play clarinet!)

50. From this first paragraph until the fifth and last, this testimonial lift letter from Yo-Yo Ma is a credibility-building exercise. It means a lot for one of the world's most illustrious concert performers to write about the conservatory's "high standards."

51. Similarly, it's useful—and impressive—for a celebrity in the world of music to name several of the conservatory's faculty members, who are far less likely to be known to the readers of this appeal. (I, for one, knew none of the three names cited.)

52. In a longer letter, Yo-Yo Ma might have revealed how frequently he visits the conservatory and how much time he spends there, thus establishing his authority as a judge of the conservatory's participation in the Bay Area community. In this context, I'm not impressed with the claim he makes in this paragraph.

53. He's back on more solid ground in this paragraph, speaking about musical tradition and the "next generation of musicians."

54. Most celebrities try to get off easy in lift letters like this one, omitting explicit endorsements such as the last paragraph. But without such a direct statement, a lift letter's value is limited. Now I know that Yo-Yo Ma

EXHIBIT 5.3
Lift Letter, San Francisco Conservatory of Music

48

YO·YO MA

49 Dear Friend and Music Lover,

50   Some of the finest cello teaching in the country today takes place at the San Francisco Conservatory of Music, where high standards are combined with an openness to new trends.

51   The San Francisco Conservatory of Music has a sense of tradition in the best sense of the word. Generations of great cello teachers from Margaret Rowell to Bonnie Hampton and Irene Sharp have nurtured some of the finest young cellists today.

52   The Conservatory is a working community -- it not only functions as an institution, but it participates as a vital member of the Bay Area community.

53   The high standards, tradition and a sense of community are the reasons why the San Francisco Conservatory of Music continues to be such a strong, creative force in producing the next generation of musicians.

54   I urge you to support this fine institution.

55   Sincerely,

Yo-Yo Ma

really wants me to lend a hand. (His appeal would have been even stronger if he had written, "I urge you to join me as a Friend of the San Francisco Conservatory," thus leaving not a shadow of a doubt about his own deep commitment.)

55. He signs off "Sincerely," his name alone sufficing to identify himself. His signature, like Colin Murdoch's, is printed in dark blue ink to set it apart from the typewritten text.

The Reply Device

56. "BRAVO!" What an appropriate variation on the more commonly used "Yes!" (The applause line is printed in dark red, as are the checkmark boxes and suggested gift amounts; the logo, name, address, and telephone number; and the headline below the line of dashes near the bottom. That bottom portion is tinted a gentle shade of red. All the text and every other element on this reply device is printed in black.)

57. In three terse sentences, the response device sums up the essence of the offer spelled out in Colin Murdoch's letter.

58. I'm offered three choices here. (Unfortunately, I have to read the text at the bottom of this reply device closely to be certain "Regular Membership" really entitles me to all the benefits I'll get as a "Friend" of the conservatory. It might have been better to label the $40 option "Friend of the Conservatory" and devise a new name for the $100 option, while spelling out special benefits for the higher level of support. But no appeal's perfect.)

59. Here I'm reminded of the deadline, November 8. It's also clear to me that the offer of free tickets to the Faculty Trio Concert is a serious one: this is an excellent and appropriate use of a premium in membership acquisition.

60. Here's the Cheshire label (noted in paragraph number five, describing the outer envelope).

61. That wonderful logo again!

62. I'm reminded, for the third time, that my gift will be tax deductible.

63. It's almost always wise to include instructions such as "Detach Here." Certainly I could figure out that the reply device is perforated along the line of dashes, but it's courteous to relieve me of the (admittedly very slight) burden of determining that for myself. Instructions of this sort also reinforce the action-oriented nature of direct mail appeals.

EXHIBIT 5.4
Reply Device, San Francisco Conservatory of Music

56 *BRAVO!*

57 I accept your invitation to become a Friend of the San Francisco Conservatory of Music. I want to help continue the long, proud tradition of musical excellence in San Francisco. Enclosed is my membership gift of:

58 ☐ **$40**   Regular Membership
☐ **$100**   Special Friend of the Conservatory
☐ $_____

59 ☐ Send me my FREE ticket(s) to the Faculty Trio Concert on November 15. Request must be received by November 8.   ☐ one ticket   ☐ two tickets

61

60 Mr. John Doe
123 Any Street
Any Town, AS 00000

San Francisco Conservatory of Music

62
Your contribution to the San Francisco Conservatory of Music is fully tax-deductible. Thank you very much.

1201 ORTEGA ST., SAN FRANCISCO, CA 94122
415/759-3463

63 ▲ DETACH HERE

- -

64 Your Membership Entitles You to Receive:

65 1. A subscription to *At the Conservatory*, the Conservatory's monthly newsletter and calendar of events.

2. A special New Member Fall Concert.

3. Membership discounts for Conservatory concerts throughout the year—and for Conservatory extension classes.

4. Advance ticket purchase for Sing-It-Yourself Messiah Concerts at Davies Symphony Hall.

5. Free attendance at the "Friends Only" Tour and Concert (January 1994).

66 *Please detach top portion, fold and return with your check in the enclosed postage-paid envelope. Keep bottom portion for your records.*

RECYCLED PAPER 67012B

64. Now any lingering doubt that I might not actually receive the wonderful benefits that Colin Murdoch's letter described is totally dispelled.

65. Those benefits are listed, described in the same words as in the letter.

66. The last thing I want to do when signing up for a membership in the conservatory is to fumble around with unfamiliar slips of paper of odd shapes and sizes, so I'm pleased to be told exactly what to do.

Reply Envelope

67. Once again I'm reminded that my gift to the conservatory entitles me to membership, with its attendant benefits. This handwritten tagline is printed in dark blue, like that of the signatures on both letters.

68. "Recycled paper" again!

69. This five-digit code helps production staff and envelope printers keep this envelope apart from those used with hundreds of other projects.

70. These vertical ruled lines are for the electronic scanning equipment used by the US Postal Service to route the mail.

71. The indicia and the horizontal ruled lines are for the naked eye: unmistakable signs that this envelope is, as the words to the left explain, "Business Reply Mail." At the time, it cost the conservatory approximately 40 cents per envelope returned. Currently, as of 2013, the charge for business reply mail is the amount of postage, plus 72¢. So, a postcard would be 99¢, a one ounce letter would be $1.18 and a one ounce flat would be $1.64. (Charges were a lot lower when this appeal was mailed!)

72. The envelope is addressed to the conservatory. In a more personal appeal—a membership renewal letter, for example—it might be appropriate to type Colin Murdoch's name above the institutional name.

EXHIBIT 5.5
Reply Envelope, San Francisco Conservatory of Music

New membership **67**
enclosed

70

NO POSTAGE
NECESSARY IF
MAILED IN THE
UNITED STATES

68 RECYCLED PAPER   67014 **69**   **71**

BUSINESS REPLY MAIL
FIRST CLASS MAIL PERMIT NO. 16779 SAN FRANCISCO, CA

POSTAGE WILL BE PAID BY ADDRESSEE

**72 SAN FRANCISCO
CONSERVATORY OF MUSIC**
1201 ORTEGA STREET
SAN FRANCISCO   CA   94122-4498

73

Its omission here is not a significant oversight: I would find it a little difficult to believe that the president of the San Francisco Conservatory of Music would be opening envelopes containing new memberships. Still, typing Murdoch's name on the reply envelope would reinforce the personality of this appeal; on balance, I would favor doing that.

73. This bar code enables the US Postal Service to sort returning envelopes with minimal human intervention: the vertical lines are computer language for the letters and numbers contained in the address.

What You Can—and Can't—Learn from This Example

This fundraising letter for the San Francisco Conservatory of Music is a singular appeal; it was written for a particular purpose on behalf of a particular organization at a particular time. As a result, there are several ways this letter may not work well as a model for your own fundraising efforts. The package was written to acquire members, whereas most fundraising appeals are written to proven donors. The appeal is benefit-driven, even to the point of offering prospective members admission to a specific performance, and most nonprofits have to reach far to come up with tangible donor benefits. There's a celebrity lift letter, a device that's appropriate for most nonprofits only in unusual circumstances.

Nevertheless, it's worthwhile for you to study this package so closely because it does its job so well. I chose this fundraising appeal because its varied contents illustrate how to meet so many different appeal-writing challenges and, more to the point, because it dramatizes how different a particular fundraising appeal can be from every other fundraising appeal. There's no question what the conservatory is offering. The marketing concept couldn't be clearer.

A Shorter Journey through a Letter That Doesn't Work Well

For a contrasting example, let's take a look at an appeal (exhibit 5.6) that's much closer to the dysfunctional definition of a fundraising letter that I referred to at the beginning of chapter 4.

A. Glance at the outer envelope. You can't miss the return address rubber-stamped in the upper-left-hand corner or the incomplete (and in many parts of the country undeliverable) address on the mailing label. The only thing this envelope has going for it is a first-class stamp. But you've probably guessed, just as I did, that the reason this was mailed first class was one of the following: (1) the quantity wasn't large enough to qualify the appeal for bulk mail, (2) the organization didn't have or couldn't get a nonprofit bulk mailing permit, or (3) the list was in such bad shape the organization couldn't bundle the mail properly to suit postal personnel.

B. Now take a look through the text on the first page of the letter. It has its positive points: short paragraphs, white space, underlined subheadings, language that's clear and relatively readable. But there are precious few personal pronouns anywhere in sight—except for "we" a few times—and the rest is argumentative and rhetorical. It's not really even clear this is an appeal for funds because I'm asked if I can "assist in other ways." But there's no way I can tell how my "financial contribution"—or any other sort of help I might give—is connected to anything else in this letter.

C. The second page continues in the same vein, compounding the problems of the first page: more statistics, more rhetoric, a laundry list of organizations (some of them little known), a dual signature—and no ask. It's hard to imagine a letter better calculated *not* to raise money.

D. Apparently the Federal Jobs Program outlined in the top two-thirds of this reply device is the principal program of the organization that sent this appeal, although I'm forced to guess that's really the case. Only at the bottom of the page do I find a way to respond to the letter (assuming I'd be so inclined). You'll note it's called an "Endorsement Form." However, there's no way for me to indicate my endorsement (for the Federal Jobs Program? the Campaign to Abolish Poverty?). There's also no suggested gift amount and no return address (in case the form becomes separated from the letter or the return envelope).

E. This rubber-stamped little reply envelope doesn't inspire confidence. Major gift fundraisers speak of an organization's readiness to receive big gifts. This organization doesn't appear ready to receive little gifts.

EXHIBIT 5.6
Outer Envelope (A), Campaign to Abolish Poverty

CAMPAIGN TO ABOLISH POVERTY
942 MARKET STREET #708
SAN FRANCISCO, CA 94102

Mal Warwick
2550 Ninth
Berkeley CA 94710

First Page of Letter (B), Campaign to Abolish Poverty

Campaign to Abolish Poverty

942 Market Street, #708, San Francisco, CA 94102 ● Ph: 415-397-4911 Fx: 415-434-3110

November 6, 1992

Dear Friend:

Electing Bill Clinton President certainly creates new opportunities in Washington, D.C. The pendulum is beginning to swing in the opposite direction.

But it remains to be seen how much difference Clinton will make, particularly for the poor and near-poor. If history is any guide, strong grassroots pressure will be necessary to push Clinton beyond his election-year program.

The Campaign to Abolish Poverty (CAP) aims to push the pendulum as hard as possible. Our current focus is to build support for the Federal Jobs Program -- a proposal to create two million new, permanent, public service jobs -- as a first step toward ending poverty in this country.

We urge you to help this effort by sending a financial contribution now, and letting us know if you can assist in other ways.

Clinton has committed himself to a number of good positions. But there is a downside to most of them.

Jobs

On the one hand, for example, it is encouraging that Clinton proposes federal funding for public works jobs. But he's only talking about one-shot infrastructure repair -- temporary jobs which largely would exclude women, minorities and low-income people who need them the most.

We need to persuade Clinton and Congress to support <u>sustained</u> federal funding for local human service jobs - jobs for which the poor and near-poor would qualify, with relevant on-the-job training.

Tax Reform

It is also positive that Clinton advocates increasing taxes on the wealthy. But his proposal would roll back only one-fifth of the tax breaks received by the top 2% of all households during the last fifteen years. If these families with annual incomes over $200,000 paid 34% of their income in federal taxes, as they did in 1977, $80 billion in addition to the $20 billion targeted by Clinton could be generated.

We need to persuade Clinton and Congress to restore 1977 tax rates for the wealthy. All other income groups are now paying higher federal taxes (including payroll taxes). The wealthy could pay what they paid in 1977 without undue hardship.

Second Page of Letter (C), Campaign to Abolish Poverty

Military Spending

Clinton's proposals for reductions in the military budget are inadequate. **We need to persuade Clinton and Congress to move in the direction of a 50% cut in military spending,** which could free almost $150 billion per year to help put Americans to work.

Federal Jobs Program

In consultation with a wide range of recognized experts and community organizations, CAP has developed a specific program -- the **Federal Jobs Program** -- that would appropriate $50 billion to create two million permanent public service jobs, paid for by higher taxes on the wealthy and reductions in the military budget (see enclosed).

A broad range of community-based organizations, community leaders, and elected officials have already endorsed this program, including American Friends Service Committee, Catholic Charities of San Francisco, California Legislative Council for Older Americans, Coleman Advocates for Children and Youth, San Francisco Lawyer's Committee for Urban Affairs, and Maryland United for Peace and Justice. Considering that we have been gathering endorsements only since early October, this support is very encouraging.

But in order to influence the next session of Congress, the Campaign to Abolish Poverty and its membership must broaden its base and press its case effectively in Washington. We have recently begun encouraging discussions with a number of national organizations with lobbyists in Washington to build support for our jobs program.

The desperation and misery experienced by growing millions of Americans compel us to make this effort and to continue until economic security for all is established as a human right.

So please give what you can financially, and if possible contribute time and energy as well. Please complete the form enclosed and return it with your tax-deductible donation as soon as possible.

With your help, we have a chance.

Sincerely,

Wade Hudson

Wade Hudson
Chair

Barbara Arms

Barbara Arms
Director

Reply Device (D), Campaign to Abolish Poverty

FEDERAL JOBS PROGRAM

<u>Purpose</u>: To appropriate $50 billion to create 2 million new public service jobs in both urban and rural areas, as the first step toward guaranteeing every adult the opportunity to work at a living wage. Each year, funding should increase by 20% until these jobs go begging due to lack of applicants.

<u>Types of Work</u>: These funds shall be used to hire workers in repair/maintenance/ rehabilitation of publicly-owned facilities, conservation/rehabilitation/ improvement of public lands, child care, health care, in-home caregiving, education (including tutorial services), peer counseling, housing and neighborhood improvement, recreation, arts programs, community centers, and other vital public services.

<u>Wages</u>: Wages shall range from $7-$12 per hour, plus benefits, and shall be indexed to inflation. The compensation for these positions shall not be less than the prevailing compensation for individuals employed in similar occupations.

<u>Allocation of Funds</u>: Two and one-half percent of all funds shall be allocated for Native American tribes and Alaska Native villages. Remaining funds shall be allocated by the Secretary of Labor to the states based upon the number of people living in poverty in each state.

<u>Administration</u>: The Secretary of Labor shall distribute the funds to the states for distribution to local governments. The cost of administration shall be no more than the standard for similar programs. Each recipient of funds shall be responsible for ensuring equal employment opportunities, equal pay for equal work, and the full participation of traditionally underrepresented groups, including women and racial and ethnic minorities.

<u>Displacement</u>: The following shall be prohibited: a) any displacing of current employees, including partial displacement such as a reduction in the hours of nonovertime work, wages, or employment benefits; b) impairing of existing contracts or collective bargaining; c) filling of openings created by related layoffs or terminations; or d) infringing on promotional opportunities of current employees.

<u>Oversight</u>: Prior to submitting its plan to the State, each eligible entity shall conduct an open public review and comment process, and during the year, shall conduct at least one public hearing to receive input into its evaluation process. Workers hired by these funds shall be encouraged to participate in this review process.

<u>Source of Funds</u>: The funds needed for this program shall come from increasing personal income taxes on the richest 2% of households and from reducing the military budget.

ENDORSEMENT FORM

___Please find enclosed a check for _____ (made payable to: Campaign to Abolish Poverty) to help with building support for the Federal Jobs Program. (Contributions are tax-deductible.)

___I would like to volunteer some time to help.

___Please send me more information about CAP and the Federal Jobs Program.

Name (print) _____

Organization (if any)_____

Address _____

City_____State_____Zip_____

Day Phone_____Eve Phone_____Fax_____

Reply Envelope (E), Campaign to Abolish Poverty

CAMPAIGN TO ABOLISH POVERTY
942 MARKET STREET #708
SAN FRANCISCO, CA 94102

Throughout the first journey we made, you must have recognized the emphasis I placed on the relationship between the conservatory and the donor. Relationship building is the essence of good fundraising; the biggest rewards come with time.

To gain perspective on the techniques that will allow you to use fundraising letters to maximum advantage in building strong, long-term relationships with your donors, please join me now in part 2, "Your Plan of Action."

It's nuts-and-bolts time. In this part, we'll approach the task of writing a fundraising appeal from a strictly practical, down-to-earth perspective. In successive chapters, we'll cover these topics:

- What to do before you sit down to write a fundraising appeal
- The eight steps I recommend you follow in crafting a fundraising package
- The eight concrete Cardinal Rules that determine whether your appeal will be a success (or a dud), along with two self-assessment forms that will help you evaluate the likely effectiveness of your fundraising letter and e-mail message in light of these rules
- The practical guidelines of style and syntax I urge you to follow when you're writing a fundraising appeal—or, for that matter, any other prose that's meant to persuade a reader to act

Chapter Six:
What to Do Before You Write Any Fundraising Appeal

How do you get started writing that fundraising solicitation that's due at the printer's next month?

You *think*.

Effective writing begins with clear, uncluttered thinking. Before you write a single word of your next fundraising appeal, you must understand precisely to whom you're writing, why you're writing, and what you're writing. That's what the following twenty questions are about. Asking yourself these questions won't guarantee you'll write a better appeal (much less a more successful one), but it will help you think clearly about the task at hand and focus your writing on the specific points you most need to make.

Answering these questions will enable you to construct a powerful *marketing concept*, the idea that's at the core of any piece of writing conceived to produce results. The marketing concept is a tapestry woven of need, opportunity, and circumstance. It's the pure essence of the message you're conveying. Or think of it as an executive summary of your letter.

The marketing concept is at the heart of the dialogue that Siegfried Vögele describes (see chapter 2). Incorporated into it are the answers to many of your readers' unspoken questions.

Never forget this: the words you write will obtain the objectives you desire only to the extent that those words convey a marketing concept powerful enough to motivate your donors. You must appeal to them clearly and unambiguously, which requires that you begin with an absolutely clear understanding of why you're writing an appeal in the first place. That's where the twenty questions start.

The Twenty Important Questions You Need to Ask Before You Begin Writing

First, Think about Why You're Writing This Particular Appeal

1. What is the purpose of your appeal? To acquire new donors or members? Solicit larger gifts or major gifts? Urge your donors to consider planned giving? Reactivate lapsed members or donors? Or meet any of a multitude of other specific fundraising needs?

Now, Think about the People You're Writing To

2. What do the people you're writing to have in common with one another? For example, do they share a powerful experience: an earthquake, a religious conversion, new citizenship, a rare disease, a crushing personal loss? Are they patriotic or dedicated to a particular cause? Are they all likely to be concerned about global climate change?

3. What fact, or facts, may be true about almost all of these people—facts to distinguish them from the rest of the world's population? Are they all over the age of sixty? Do they all live in a single community? Were they all once patients in your hospital? Are they all women? Baby Boomers? Donors? Nondonors? Members?

4. What do you know about the feelings of the people you're writing to? Are they likely to be angry (or elated) about a recent turn of events in the world or in your local community? Have recent economic setbacks made life more difficult for them, or changes in tax laws made them more comfortable? Are they likely to be skeptical about charity? Concerned about declining moral values? Fearful of old age?

5. What's the relationship of these people to your organization? What do they know about you, your organization, or the issue or problem you're addressing? What don't they know? What do they want to know? Have they been contributing regular gifts for several years and demonstrated interest, even commitment, to your nonprofit? Is the typical reader of the letter you're about to write a longtime subscriber to your newsletter or a new donor who lacks basic information about your work? Is there likely to be a personal relationship between the readers and your executive director or a member of your board?

6. Consider the typical recipient of your letter. What experiences, feelings, and thoughts is that person likely to have that would help her understand the issue or problem you're addressing? Is it likely that this

typical reader will feel very deeply, based on her own personal experience, about some issue or problem that underpins your agency's work? For example, if you serve the homeless, is she likely to come into contact with homeless people on a daily basis—or almost never? Put yourself in her position, and think how she might think and feel about the challenges your organization faces every day.

7. What leads you to believe that the typical person you're writing to will respond favorably? Does she have a long history of supporting your agency or, at least, other organizations like yours? Has she expressed interest in knowing how she might help? Is there some personal connection, such as a child who was a patient, a parent who benefited from your services, or an old school tie? Is this a time of crisis, and have earlier appeals to the same or similar groups amply demonstrated that people like those you're writing to now are likely to respond?

Now, Think about What You'll Ask People to Do

8. What is it exactly that you want recipients to do? Renew their memberships? Send larger annual gifts than they did last year? Join an exclusive giving club? Commit to making monthly gifts via electronic funds transfer? Support a special new project? Respond to an emergency with an additional $10 or $15?

9. What is the minimum amount of money (if any) that you hope to receive from each recipient? Few other questions are more important. The amount of your ask, particularly the minimum amount, will often predetermine the amount you receive. A prospective donor may be incredulous at a request for $1,000, while a long-loyal supporter thinks the same sum too small. (That's one reason why the same appeal usually can't be sent to both prospective and proven donors.) To be successful, your appeal must ask for a specific amount, and that must be the right amount. Now, both in direct mail and in the digital arena, you can even use dynamic *ask strings* on your donation forms, strings that change based on each donor's giving history or other factors.

10. Is there anything else you want recipients to do right now? Will your appeal ask for a cash contribution and nothing more? Or will you request a three-year pledge, a monthly commitment, a signature on a credit card authorization form—or something entirely different? For example, will your appeal include an involvement device, such as a postcard or e-mail to the governor, a membership survey, or an offer to supply information about wills and bequests?

Now, Think about the Circumstances in Which You're Writing This Appeal

11. What problem, need, issue, or opportunity prompts your agency to send this appeal? Be specific; don't state the need as simply that "funds are tight" or "we need money." Think about the particular set of circumstances that makes it necessary for your agency to raise funds right now. Is there a profoundly exciting new opportunity that your organization wants to meet by launching a new program? Has there been an unanticipated demand for your services—or a shortfall in funding from corporate and foundation donors? Is a trustee or a friendly foundation offering a challenge grant (or willing to do so)?

Think about the Person Who Will Sign the Appeal

12. What is the signer's name? It's dangerous to draft an appeal not knowing who will sign it. A fundraising appeal—a letter from one person to another—is most powerful when it reflects the personal views and feelings of both people—the sender and the receiver. The appeal will be most effective when you can bring it to life with a relevant anecdote or two, or a typical statement that will ring true—something that might cause a knowledgeable reader to nod and say, "Yes, that's old Fred in a nutshell, all right!"

13. What is the connection between the signer and the problem, need, issue, or opportunity that prompts the appeal? If the signer is your president or executive director, the connection may be obvious—and rife with possibilities to bring that opportunity to life. If the signer is instead someone who has no day-to-day connection with the events or circumstances that prompt your appeal, think about what might move that signer to write an emotional appeal at this particular time. Is there something in her past: her education, her childhood, her experience as a soldier at war, her business achievements?

14. What is the connection between the signer and those who will receive the appeal? Do they share the experiences of a generation? For example, are most of them over the age of fifty-five—or under forty? As loyal members of a single organization, have they shared a particular event or intense experience: the death of a president, a Super Bowl victory, the landing on the moon, the fall of the Berlin Wall, or 9/11? Or are they all well-to-do, or members of a particular community or political party? Have they received similar honors, attended the same school, watched the same shows on television? In today's sophisticated fundraising

campaigns, you'll often need to develop conditional content to reach different segments of your audience with variations on your message.

15. What are the signer's feelings and thoughts about the problem, need, issue, or opportunity that underlies the appeal? If you don't know the answer to this question, ask it. Sometimes the signer—even an in-house, staff, or board signer—can suggest a powerful line of argument or an evocative story that will bring your appeal to life. Emotional copy is usually more effective than intellectual copy, but a powerful fundraising letter is built on ideas and facts as well as feelings. Look for both to flesh out your appeal.

Consider What Benefits People Will Get If They Respond to Your Appeal

16. List all the *tangible* benefits, if any. Are you offering a newsletter, for example, or discounts on products or services, or the promise of invitations to events with celebrity supporters? Or have you enclosed a premium such as a bookmark, name stickers, photographs, or a calendar?

17. List the *intangible* benefits of sending a gift in response to your appeal. Will donors help you change the course of human history, or save the life of a tiny child? Will they be ensuring that their values and beliefs will be passed along to generations of descendants or raising the quality of life in their community? Will donors gain salvation, learn about a headline-grabbing issue, prevent the abuse of pets?

Now, Why Do the Readers of Your Appeal Need to Respond Right Now?

18. Is there an especially urgent need or opportunity that justifies this appeal? Is Thanksgiving approaching, and with it increased demand for the hot meals your agency serves to the poor? Is a regional war about to break out, shutting down communications with your field office? Is the congressional debate that will affect your issue drawing to a close? Will the board of directors be forced to shut your program down soon if funding goals aren't met?

19. Is there a deadline by which you must receive responses? For instance, have you arranged—or can you arrange—a challenge grant with an imminent deadline? Is the end of the calendar year approaching, and with it the opportunity for donors to save on this year's taxes? Is Easter special to your organization, representing a traditional time for your supporters to demonstrate their compassion for the less fortunate? And when

you appeal by e-mail, are you prepared to send out your message the day before or the very day of a deadline? Does your matching offer expire at midnight tonight?

20. What will happen if you don't receive responses before that deadline? Will you lose the challenge grant? Will poor people go hungry? Will children be turned away from the door to your agency? Will small animals die, or the supply of autographed books run out, or people with AIDS suffer needless pain?

If you crave a shorthand way to remember these twenty questions, think of the journalist's old saw about including the who, what, when, where, and why in a story's lead (and add a how for good measure). You can even diagram these thoughts as follows:

Who?	Who will sign the letter?
	Who will receive the letter?
What?	What is it you want the reader to do?
	What will the reader receive in return?
When?	When do you want the reader to respond?
Where?	Where will the proposed action take place?
Why?	Why should the reader take this step?
How?	How will the proposed action make a difference?

How to Write a Marketing Concept

Once you've answered those twenty questions (or cheated by using the table I just gave you), sum up all this information in one paragraph. Be as specific and precise as possible, and write the paragraph in the first-person singular (just as you'll have to do when you write the appeal itself). Address it to that one typical individual who will be receiving your letter. This paragraph will be the marketing concept for your appeal. Once you've written it, the rest of your job will be easy.

Keep in mind that the marketing concept is not the appeal itself or even its opening paragraph; it's simply a way to get started. Others might call it the *copy platform*. It's the foundation on which you'll construct your appeal. It's what you'll write about: facts, information, feelings, circumstances—that is, specifics. The marketing concept is the skeleton on which you hang them all together. In writing your appeal, you'll put flesh on these bones.

To help you get the hang of it, here are two examples of typical marketing concepts:

Because you've been so generous to the Center in the past, you've heard from me from time to time about exciting new developments here. I've told you before how far we stretch your contributions to serve the underserved in the Community. Now, a renewal gift from you of as little as $25 will go twice as far as before! Your $25 will help house the homeless children of the Community by enabling the Center to buy $50 or more worth of lumber and tools—because your gift will be matched, dollar for dollar, by an anonymous donor through the Center's new Matching Gift Program. That way, you'll get double the satisfaction from your act of generosity—and bring new hope to twice as many of your neighbors in the Community.

You may not know me, but I'm sure you're familiar with the Museum, which has been the centerpiece of my life during the past twenty years of my tenure as its Director. I'm writing to you, a fellow resident of the City, because I want you to be among the first to know about the Museum's unique new Charter Membership program. As a person who appreciates the finer things in life, you'll cherish for many years to come each magnificent issue of our new bimonthly magazine on the visual arts. You'll receive the magazine absolutely free of charge as a Charter Member of the Museum. And you'll have the satisfaction of knowing that your Charter Membership contribution of $45, $75, $150, or more will help us to showcase the exciting work of emerging new artists in our region.

If cramming so much information into one paragraph strikes you as daunting (or silly), it may be useful to consider the construction of a marketing concept as a multistage process. Begin by answering the twenty questions I posed earlier. Then read all the available material that might help you flesh out the concept with those telltale facts that often work like magic in a fundraising appeal: reports from program officers, foundation proposals, postings on the organization's website, and so forth. If necessary, ask questions of senior staff members, program officers, clients or beneficiaries, gift processing staff members, or donors. Then think some more before you (finally) draft the marketing concept. Once you're pleased with the result, shop it around the office. Ask your colleagues to poke holes in your argument and identify shaky claims or missing facts. Revise accordingly.

Often, but not always, the reply device in a successful direct mail fundraising package restates the marketing concept. That's why many experienced direct mail copywriters (including me) tackle the reply device first when they set out to write a package. Keep in mind that the reply device has four functions: to affirm the donor's decision to take the action you're requesting, to restate the marketing concept, to detail the donor's benefits, and to guide gift processing.

To get a stronger grip on the central role of the marketing concept in the reply device, study the examples in exhibits 6.1 through 6.4. You'll soon get the gist of the marketing concept behind each of the fundraising appeals from which these response forms were selected. It stares you right in the face. That's what your marketing concept needs to do every time you write an appeal!

EXHIBIT 6.1
New Donor Enrollment Form, Doctors Without Borders

YOU CAN HELP SAVE A LIFE

Yes, I want to help Doctors Without Borders USA bring medical humanitarian relief around the world. I am making a tax-deductible gift of:

☐ **$35**　　☐ **$75**　　☐ **$100**　　☐ **$200**　　☐ **$500**　　or ☐ $ _____

We desperately need your financial support. Please help us.

MEDECINS SANS FRONTIERES
DOCTORS WITHOUT BORDERS

F306256291 ADQ070301A1V

Mr. Mal Warwick
~~2763 Ashby Pl Apt E~~
~~Berkeley, CA 94705-2393~~

DOCTORS WITHOUT BORDERS
MEDECINS SANS FRONTIERES
PO BOX 5023
HAGERSTOWN MD 21741-5023

A1

Please make your check payable to Doctors Without Borders USA. TO CHARGE YOUR GIFT, PLEASE SEE OTHER SIDE.
Please tear at perforation and return this reply slip with your gift. Thank you for your support.

Printed on Recycled Paper
Q73A-1

✂ *Detach here*

© Kris Torgeson

"*Many people tell us that this is the first time that they have seen a qualified doctor and received treatment. People have told me that they don't know what might happen to them if we weren't here and there were no international witnesses to what they are going through.*"

– Matthias Hrubey, MD for Doctors Without Borders,
Kass, South Darfur, Sudan

Your contribution to Doctors Without Borders allows our volunteers to save lives around the world.

$35 – Supplies a basic suture kit to repair minor wounds.

$75 – Provides 1,500 patients with clean water for a week.

$100 – Provides infection-fighting antibiotics to treat nearly 40 wounded people.

$200 – Supplies 40 malnourished children with special high-protein food for a day.

Thank you for your generosity.

MEDECINS SANS FRONTIERES
DOCTORS WITHOUT BORDERS

www.doctorswithoutborders.org

Always remember that your reader has only twenty seconds to get the message and even less with e-mail. (Think back to Siegfried Vögele's eye-motion research.) If your message—the central reason that your readers should respond—isn't clear at a glance, there's little chance your letter will be read at all, much less generate contributions.

Join me now in chapter 7 on a step-by-step journey through the route I usually take when setting out to write a fundraising appeal.

Fill in the following to charge to your credit card:

American Express, MasterCard, Visa, and Discover accepted.

Authorized signature   _Date_

Account number   _Expiration date_

Name as it appears on your credit card

Doctors Without Borders Meets. or Surpasses All Standards

Doctors Without Borders has consistently met all standards of watchdog agencies and has recently been awarded an "A" rating from the American Institute of Philanthropy. The watchdog agencies' reports are available to the general public.

Please read our *Commitment to Our Supporters* at http://www.doctorswithoutborders.org/donate/donorcommitment.cfm.

For more information, please call Donor Services at 212-763-5779.

Doctors Without Borders, PO Box 5023, Hagerstown, MD 21741-5023

In 2005, donations to Doctors Without Borders USA, Inc. were spent as follows:

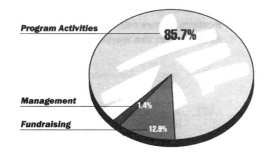

Program Activities — 85.7%
Management — 1.4%
Fundraising — 12.8%

Doctors Without Borders strives to direct at least 85% of our spending to program activities, which include emergency and medical programs, program support, and public education.

We have surpassed this standard every year from 1995 to 2005. We are committed to this goal.

NOTICE TO CONTRIBUTORS

EXHIBIT 6.2

New Donor Enrollment Form, Ocean Conservancy

New Member Reply Form

☐ **YES!** I want to help protect dolphins, whales, sea turtles and other endangered marine wildlife. My tax-deductible gift (made payable to The Ocean Conservancy) is for:

Your gift of this level or higher will really help!

☐ $50   ☐ $25   ☐ $15*   ☐ $10   ☐ Other $_____

* For your gift of $15 or more, you'll receive full membership benefits *plus* our exclusive Ocean Conservancy sea turtle plush!

☐ Please put my gift to work entirely for the oceans— don't send me the sea turtle.

07DPBCKAAX 27102297101

Mr William P Rehm
XXXXXXXXXXXXX
XXXXXXXXXXXXXX
lllllllllllllllllll

The Ocean Conservancy
Advocates for Wild, Healthy Oceans

Please return this form with your check, or complete the reverse to give by credit card. Thank you!

62305

The Ocean Conservancy • 2029 K Street, NW • Washington, DC 20006 • www.oceanconservancy.org   7-PB2A

Charge my credit card: ☐ MasterCard ☐ VISA ☐ American Express ☐ Discover

Card Number: ☐☐☐ ☐☐☐☐ ☐☐☐☐ ☐☐☐☐   Exp. Date: _____

Print name (as shown on card): _____

Signature: _____

A copy or summary of the current Financial Statement or Annual Report and Registration filed by The Ocean Conservancy may be obtained by contacting: The Ocean Conservancy, 2029 K. St. NW, Washington, DC 20006, (202) 429-5609. In order to reduce our fundraising expenses and to find new members who can help us in our critical work, The Ocean Conservancy may occasionally share the names of our members with other carefully screened organizations. If you would prefer us not to share your name, please contact us. Arizona: 1-800-458-5842. Maryland: For the cost of copies and postage, Office of the Secretary of State, State House, Annapolis, MD 21401 or call 1-800-825-4510. Michigan: Registration number is MICS 9972. New Jersey: INFORMATION FILED WITH THE ATTORNEY GENERAL CONCERNING THIS CHARITABLE SOLICITATION MAY BE OBTAINED FROM THE ATTORNEY GENERAL OF THE STATE OF NEW JERSEY BY CALLING 973-504-6215. REGISTRATION WITH THE ATTORNEY GENERAL DOES NOT IMPLY ENDORSEMENT. New York: A COPY OF THE LATEST ANNUAL REPORT MAY BE OBTAINED FROM THE ORGANIZATION OR FROM THE OFFICE OF THE ATTORNEY GENERAL, DEPT. OF LAW, CHARITIES BUREAU, 120 BROADWAY, NEW YORK, NY 10271. North Carolina: Financial information about this organization and a copy of its license are available from the State Solicitation Licensing branch at 1-888-830-4989. The license is not an endorsement by the state. Pennsylvania: The official registration and financial information of The Ocean Conservancy may be obtained from the Pennsylvania Dept. of State by calling toll-free within the state, 1-800-732-0999. Registration does not imply endorsement. Virginia: State Division of Consumer Affairs, Dept. of Agricultural and Consumer Services, PO Box 1163, Richmond, VA 23218, 1-800-552-9963. Washington: Charities Division, Office of the Secretary of State, State of Washington, Olympia, WA 98504-0422, 1-800-332-4483. West Virginia: Residents may obtain a summary of the registration and financial documents from: Secretary of State, State Capitol, Charleston, WV 25305. Registration does not imply endorsement. Florida: A COPY OF THE OFFICIAL REGISTRATION AND FINANCIAL INFORMATION MAY BE OBTAINED FROM THE DIVISION OF CONSUMER SERVICES BY CALLING TOLL-FREE, 1-800-435-7352 WITHIN THE STATE. REGISTRATION DOES NOT IMPLY ENDORSEMENT, APPROVAL, OR RECOMMENDATION BY THE STATE. FLORIDA REGISTRATION #SC-00944. Mississippi: The official registration and financial information of The Ocean Conservancy may be obtained from the Mississippi Secretary of State's office by calling 1-888-236-6167. Registration by the Secretary of State does not imply endorsement by the Secretary of State. Registration with any of these states does not imply endorsement.

EXHIBIT 6.3
New Donor Enrollment Form, Interfaith Alliance

07 0418457

I Want to Help Preserve Our Constitution!

☐ Yes, I am disturbed by the manipulation of religion for political gain. The Religious Right must be stopped from using the alleged "war on Christianity" as a tactic to advance their divisive agenda. To help protect religious freedom, promote inclusive policies, and advocate for civility in politics, I am joining THE INTERFAITH ALLIANCE with my gift of:

Mr. Stephen Hitchcock
XXXXXXXXXXXXXXXXX
XXXXXXXXXXXXXXXXX
Ilobolollooillooilooboloboloboloillooiloboli

P107031T

THE
INTERFAITH
ALLIANCE

1331 H Street, NW
11th Floor
Washington, DC 20005
Toll-Free: (800) 510-0969
Fax: (202) 639-6375
www.interfaithalliance.org

☐ $25   ☐ $50   ☐ $100   ☐ $250   ☐ Other $_____

Please make your check payable to **The Interfaith Alliance.**
To make your contribution by credit card, please complete
information on reverse side.

By signing up for timely e-mail updates, you can stay informed about the activities of The Interfaith Alliance and issues that impact you. **My e-mail address is:**

_____@_____._____
(We will never sell or share your e-mail address.)

Mr. Hitchcock, it's so important that you and I tell President Bush and Members of the 110th Congress to stop funding religion with government dollars. We must remind our leaders that we, as people of faith, good will and conscience, believe the separation of church and state is good for both religion and government. Please include the petition below along with your gift and return this entire form to The Interfaith Alliance. We will deliver your message to the President, *thank you!*

PETITION TO THE PRESIDENT

FROM: Mr. Stephen Hitchcock
        Albany, CA

As a person of faith, good will and conscience, I am offended by the Religious Right's attempts to curtail religious freedom under the guise of a "war on Christianity."

I am opposed to all attempts to funnel my tax dollars into houses of worship and religious organizations, and to any other efforts that undermine the appropriate relationship between government and houses of worship as dictated by the First Amendment.

President Bush, I believe with all my heart that my values call for understanding, healing, and inclusion — not intolerance, divisiveness, and bigotry.

I respectfully urge you to preserve freedom of — and from — religion for ALL Americans, as mandated in the Constitution.

Sincerely,

_____   _____
SIGNATURE   CITY, STATE

☐ I prefer to charge my contribution of $ _____ to my:

☐ **VISA**   ☐ **MasterCard**   ☐ ▨   ☐ **DISCOVER NOVUS**

Card Number _____   Expiration Date _____/_____

Authorized Signature _____

E-mail _____ @ _____ . _____

Religious or Spiritual Affiliation (optional) _____

Your gift could go twice as far if your company has a matching gift program. Please ask your personnel office for the appropriate forms and guidelines.

The Interfaith Alliance is making a difference in America by promoting the positive role of religion in public life and challenging religious political extremism. TIA is located at 1331 H St., NW, 11th Floor, Washington, DC 20005 and can be reached at (202) 639-6370. Contributions to TIA are not tax-deductible for federal income tax purposes. TIA is a 501(c)(4) non-profit organization. You may obtain a copy of the charity's financial report by writing to the charity's name and address. NY – New York residents may obtain a copy of TIA's annual report by writing to the Office of the Attorney General, Department of Law, Charities Bureau, 120 Broadway, New York, NY 10271; PA – The official registration and financial information of The Interfaith Alliance may be obtained from the Pennsylvania Department of State by calling toll-free, within Pennsylvania, 1-800-732-0999. Registration does not imply endorsement. WV – Residents may obtain a summary of the registration and financial documents from the Secretary of State, State Capitol, Charleston, WV 25305; WA – A notice of solicitation required by law is on file with the Washington Secretary of State. You may obtain financial disclosure information by contacting the Secretary of State at 1-800-332-GIVE; MD – Copies of documents and information submitted by TIA under the Maryland Charitable Solicitations Act are available for the cost of copies and postage from the Secretary of State, State House, Annapolis, MD 21401, 410-974-5534; VA – A financial statement for the most recent fiscal year is available upon request from the Division of Consumer Affairs, Department of Agricultural and Consumer Services, P.O. Box 1163, Richmond, VA 23209, 804-786-1343; Registration by the Secretary of State does not imply endorsement; NC – Financial information about TIA and a copy of its license are available from the State Solicitation Licensing Section at 888-830-4989. The license is not an endorsement by the state; FL – Registration # CH9499. A COPY OF THE OFFICIAL REGISTRATION AND FINANCIAL INFORMATION MAY BE OBTAINED FROM THE DIVISION OF CONSUMER SERVICES BY CALLING TOLL-FREE, WITHIN THE STATE, 1-800-435-7352 or 1-800-FLA-Yuda POR ASTENCIA EN ESPANOL; NJ – INFORMATION FILED WITH THE ATTORNEY GENERAL CONCERNING THIS CHARITABLE SOLICITATION MAY BE OBTAINED FROM THE ATTORNEY GENERAL OF THE STATE OF NEW JERSEY BY CALLING 973-504-6215. KS: TIA's registration number is: 339-588-6 and Epsilon's registration number is ID# 0000027. The annual financial report for the preceding fiscal year is on file with the Secretary of States, 1st Floor, Memorial Hall, 120 SW 10th Ave., Topeka, KS 66612. Registration with any of these government agencies does not imply endorsement.

Made in the USA

EXHIBIT 6.4
New Donor Enrollment Form, AmeriCares

Please Help AmeriCares Save More Lives Around the World

Mr. Hitchcock, here are some examples of how your gift can save lives:

- ❑ $25 can provide 125 patients with tests for tuberculosis and malaria
- ❑ $50 can provide 1,000 children with treatments for cholera
- ❑ $100 can provide 1,500 infants and children with oral-rehydration treatments
- ❑ $250 can provide 5,000 children with anti-parasitic treatments
- ❑ $500 can provide 400 patients with rapid malaria tests
- ❑ Other $_____

802228278   Q071101196
Mr. Stephen Hitchcock
XXXXXXXXXXXXX
XXXXXXXXXXXXX

AmeriCares
★★★★★★★
HUMANITARIAN LIFELINE TO THE WORLD
88 Hamilton Avenue
Stamford, CT 06902
www.americares.org

To receive updates and information via e-mail, please provide your e-mail address:
_____ @ _____

Contributions to AmeriCares are tax-deductible to the extent permitted by law. Please make check payable to AmeriCares.

Contribute to AmeriCares with Confidence

For nearly 25 years, the success of AmeriCares has been characterized by timely response, meaningful impact and intense passion. For every $100 donated to AmeriCares, more than $3,000 in aid is delivered due to partnerships and in-kind contributions.

Four Star Charity

★★★★
CHARITY NAVIGATOR

For the past five years, AmeriCares has been awarded the highest four-star rating from Charity Navigator, the nation's premier independent charity evaluator.

"The fact that we cannot solve all the world's problems does not absolve us of the responsibility of solving the ones we can."
– Bob Macauley
AmeriCares Founder & Chairman

AMC-Q0711-PBRply

Chapter Seven:
Eight Steps toward Successful Fundraising Appeals

Not long ago, a man who has been raising money by mail for more than thirty years bragged to me that he rarely spends more than an hour or two writing a fundraising letter—and he has been responsible for some big winners. Some of the most successful appeals he has ever written, he claimed, took no more than forty-five or sixty minutes of work.

You may choose to believe his claim or not. (I, for one, am skeptical.) But you won't hear me making similar assertions. I've been known to spend hours—even, occasionally, days—wrestling with a marketing concept before I set a single word down on paper.

In other words, I sometimes spend just as long thinking about what I'm going to write as another writer might require to do the job from start to finish. It's usually time well spent as far as I'm concerned. Once I know what I'm going to write, the rest goes much more smoothly (at least most of the time).

Developing the marketing concept is just the first of eight steps I take when writing a fundraising appeal, but it may occupy half or three-quarters of all the time I spend on a project.

The eight-step sequence I follow may not work for you. In fact, you may believe you're better off working like my former colleague Stephen Hitchcock, who swears he writes in order to think (rather than the other way around). I suspect the truth is that Steve simply thinks a lot faster than most of the rest of us. You may too. Nevertheless, I hope you'll try it my way at least once. You might even like it!

So let's run through the eight steps, one by one. Assume that you've been assigned the task of writing a simple, straightforward special appeal to the active donors of a charity called Hope Is Alive! Here is the way I recommend you go about the project.

Step 1: Develop the Marketing Concept

Write a complete marketing concept, so you'll understand the offer you'll be making in the letter. Writing this concept down will force you to decide how much money to ask for, who will sign your appeal, and whether you'll include a donor involvement device (such as a survey), a premium, or a deadline—all the things you're writing about. In this case, let's say you've determined that the marketing concept runs as follows:

> *As Executive Director of Hope Is Alive! I've written you many times in the past about the terrible challenges faced by the homeless in our city. Now I'm writing to you, as one of our most loyal and generous supporters, to tell you about a challenge that's a wonderful opportunity: two members of our Board of Trustees have volunteered to match your gift on a dollar-for-dollar basis if we receive it before January 15—up to a total of $10,000. The money raised in this Challenge of Hope will be used to outfit our new shelter, so that thirty more homeless families can find a warm and secure place to sleep in the difficult weeks still to go before winter ends.*

Now you're *almost* ready to start writing the appeal itself.

Step 2: Determine the Contents of Package

Exactly what are you going to write? A long letter or a short one? A window envelope with text (a *teaser*) on the outside or a businesslike, *closed-face* (no window) envelope with no printing except the name Hope Is Alive! and the return address? An e-mail using only text, or one that includes photos or video? In other words, it's time to determine how your marketing concept will be implemented as a fundraising campaign. What will the appeal consist of? In preparing this particular appeal, you might decide the following components are adequate to the task:

Basic Elements of the Appeal

- A Number 10 closed-face outer envelope printed in black on the front only, with the addressee's name and address laser-printed on the front, and mailed first class with a postage stamp
- A two- or three-page letter, 8½ by 11 inches, printed in two colors, on one side only of two (or if necessary, three) sheets, with page one laser personalized and subsequent pages printed to match but not personalized

- A reply device, approximately 3¼ by 8½ inches (to fit unfolded in a Number 10 envelope), printed on one side only, in two colors, on card stock, with name, address, and the ask amounts laser personalized

- A Number 9 business reply envelope printed in one color on one side only

Other Elements of the Appeal

- A two-part e-mail series (especially if your appeal is calculated to cultivate current supporters), one sent before the letter, the other one afterward

- A *hero image* at the top of your website, consisting of a photo and text designed to provoke interest in your appeal among site visitors

I suggest you write all this information down on a sheet of paper. Label it something like "Contents of Package." And take the time necessary to describe in some detail the paper stock and other specifications for each of the items you've decided to include in the package.

These should never be casual choices. Here, you've settled on a closed-face outer envelope with no teaser because you reason that committed donors will be inclined to open an appeal from Hope Is Alive! without an extravagant promise on the envelope. You've picked a two- or three-page letter with no brochure or other graphic enclosures because the story of the matching gift challenge is easily told and the January 15 deadline fosters a sense of urgency that might be undermined by a photo brochure that takes time, trouble, and expense to design and print. You have e-mails scheduled to hit the right segments of your audience as the deadline approaches.

Note how much closer you're getting now to knowing exactly what you're going to write. If you were writing a package to acquire new members rather than solicit support from proven donors, you might feel the need for a longer letter, a bigger reply device (perhaps to accommodate a full listing of membership benefits), plus a brochure or other insert, and maybe a premium such as name stickers as well as one or more additional e-mail messages. You might also find that laser personalization and e-mail are both impractical in such a member acquisition package (because they're unlikely to be cost effective). Before you actually write the direct mail copy, you need to know such things for two reasons: (1) the person in charge of getting the letter printed and mailed will need to secure printing and lettershop bids, and (2) you need to know the space limitations you'll be facing when you write.

Even what might seem like inconsequential details can make a big difference in the way you go about writing an appeal. Take, for example, the way the choice of printing technology affects the choice of minimum suggested gift levels in the letter. The choice of personalization on the reply device (both in the mail and online versions) and the first page of the letter allows you to ask for gifts commensurate with each individual's giving history, because those amounts appear in the same computer file as the names and addresses. However, if you don't laser-personalize the letter's subsequent pages, you can't repeat the specific ask amounts printed on page one. If the final page of the letter is to be reproduced on an offset printing press rather than a laser printer, any ask amounts printed there will be identical in all the letters—something of a disadvantage, since it's customary and advisable to repeat the ask close to the end of an appeal.

Several of the same considerations need to be made for the online components of your appeal. What is the audience segment of your current file that you want to solicit? What artwork or images will you include so your audience will associate your e-mail and web appeals with the letter you're mailing? Will your data setup allow you to segment and match the ask to each donor's giving history, or will work-arounds need to be devised? In addition to direct mail and e-mail messages, do you need social media and mobile components too?

But now let's say your choices have been made. You know what you're writing, and you're ready to start.

Step 3: Draft the Reply Device

Drafting the reply device may take no more than a minute or two, since you've already written a complete marketing concept. And as you write the device, whether your reply device is in the letter package or on an online donation page, you may find yourself fleshing out the marketing concept. For instance, if there are to be several different ask levels or segments in your appeal for Hope Is Alive! now's the time to think through the implications. A gift of $500 might require a dramatically different justification from one of $25. Waiting until later to figure that out might oblige you to do a lot of rewriting.

But this appeal, I've said, is simple and straightforward. So let's assume different versions of the letter aren't needed for different donor segments. The language on the reply device, then, will read somewhat as follows:

Yes, I'll help meet the Challenge of Hope! so that thirty more homeless families can find a safe, warm place to sleep in the difficult weeks remaining before winter ends. To beat the January 15 deadline—so my gift is matched dollar-for-dollar by the Trustees—I'm sending my special tax-deductible contribution in the amount of:

☐ *$[Last + 50%]*   ☐ *$[Last + 25%]*   ☐ *$*————————

Step 4: Write the Outer-Envelope and E-mail Subject Lines

Here's the point where I'm likely to get hung up all over again, even after developing a gem of a marketing concept. If a letter I'm writing requires an outer-envelope teaser—one of those brassy, cute, provocative little half-statements and promises—I might find myself dithering for hours before I can get past this crucial fourth step in the process. And the same can be said for an e-mail subject line, the online equivalent of an outer envelope teaser. I can write two thousand words in the time it takes me to devise a really good teaser. Sometimes, if I decide (or, more often, a client decides) that a teaser is essential, I'm forced to settle for one that's less than ideal. And it's usually essential to come up with a subject line for an e-mail as well, ideally one that makes a big difference in whether the e-mail is opened or not. Fortunately, e-mail subject lines can be tested in advance, so it's best to come up with several and then determine which one induces more readers to open your e-mail.

A teaser can entice the reader to open the envelope, which nothing else may be able to bring off. And certainly, a subject line does this for e-mail. A teaser that's doing its job will challenge, question, or intrigue the reader, drawing her more deeply into the silent dialogue that may later give birth to a gift.

Like everything else in a fundraising package, the teaser must be appropriate to the appeal type. For example, it's hard to imagine how any of the following teasers or subject lines could be used for a donor acquisition package: "It's time to renew!" "Special Bulletin for Members Only," or "Your newsletter is enclosed." All of these are teasers as surely as the most outrageous come-on for a "free gift" or a petition to the president of the United States. So are such seemingly offhand statements as "First Class Mail" or "Official Documents."

Often the best teaser in direct mail is no teaser at all. Fundraising letters are almost always crafted to mimic personal letters, so teasers may well cheapen or undermine the effect the writer hopes to achieve. In fact, my agency's extensive testing suggests that response isn't necessarily higher when you use a teaser, even when it seems eminently appropriate to do so. I believe that only *really good* teasers have the intended effect. Teasers that fall short of the mark probably have no effect whatsoever—or worse, they may persuade the reader *not* to open the envelope. After all, for most people, teasers are a dead giveaway for what all too many reflexively look on as junk mail. And remember, you may very well need a different teaser for the outer envelope than the one that works for a subject line, so now is the time to start thinking through both.

The outer envelope in exhibit 7.1, an oversized (9 by 12 inches), closed-face carrier, was part of a high-dollar fundraising package. The envelope bears first-class stamps, and the only words in sight are those in the address and the corner card, where the return address appears. There is no teaser in the generally accepted sense of that term. But for that appeal, at that time, the absence of a teaser was the best possible come-on. Words calculated to call greater attention to the contents or otherwise hype the appeal would likely have depressed response rather than boosted it. That's why I regard the teaser in exhibit 7.1 as the best ever, bar none.

Let's assume that you've decided the appeal you're crafting for Hope Is Alive! will be mailed in a closed-face, personalized outer envelope with no teaser. You're ready to move along to the fifth step.

EXHIBIT 7.1
Exemplary Outer Envelope, Mills-Peninsula Hospital Foundation

Arthur H. Bredenbeck

Mills-Peninsula
Hospital Foundation

100 South San Mateo Drive, San Mateo, CA 94401

Mr. John Doe
123 Any Street
Any Town, AS 00000

Step 5: Write the Lead

If the opening paragraph of a letter, whether it's sent via direct mail or e-mail, doesn't engage the reader's attention, he's unlikely to read further. Research shows the lead of the letter has higher readership than any other element but the outer-envelope copy and the P.S. The lead paragraph—a simple sentence, more often than not—is one of the most important elements in a fundraising letter, which may help explain why the lead is another one of those points where I've been known to clutch.

You won't clutch, however. You know exactly how you're going to lead off your letter for Hope Is Alive! You'll begin with a brief, inspiring story about a six-year-old client of the agency who personifies everything that's best about its work—something like this:

> *Jennifer just <u>knew</u> things were going to get better. Molly told her so.*
>
> *Jennifer was only six years old, and she'd spent most of those years on the streets. Drifting from town to town with a dad who could never find work that lasted. No school. No friends, really. No pretty clothes like the other girls she saw sometimes.*
>
> *But one day Jennifer and her dad showed up at our Front Street shelter. Molly D'Alessandro was on duty and greeted the new arrivals. You might say it was love at first sight.*

Telling a story is just one of several common approaches to writing a lead. You might also respond to or elaborate on the outer-envelope teaser or e-mail subject line, ask a provocative question, challenge the reader, make the offer, or simply establish the reader's relationship with the signer. Some of the most powerful letter leads combine several of these elements. This is also the time to start remembering that the copy for the direct mail and copy for the e-mail will likely vary, while needing to tell the same story. I'll tell you more about how to modify the copy for e-mail later in this chapter and in depth in chapter 22.

While you're engaged in writing this lead, you might find it convenient to write the close of the letter as well. Just as the lead ought to be directly connected to the subject line of an e-mail or outer-envelope teaser, if any, the close should relate to the lead. If you began by asking a question, answer it now. If you started by challenging the reader, refer to the challenge again, and note how the offer you've made will enable the reader to respond in a meaningful way. Complete the circle; round out your letter with a satisfying close. In this case, you'll want to be sure that Jennifer and her dad and Molly D'Alessandro all figure in the way you wind up the letter.

Step 6: Write the P.S.

We've learned from Siegfried Vögele that the postscript is the real lead more than 90 percent of the time because that's where readers usually turn first. So, this step deserves your full attention in both direct mail copy and in e-mail, where it often is the final drive to action.

After a lot of thought, you've decided to use the P.S. to emphasize the deadline for receipt of matching gifts in the trustees' challenge grant campaign. The postscript would go something like this:

> *P.S. Your gift will be matched dollar-for-dollar—but only if we receive your check by January 15. In this difficult winter, please help us outfit the new shelter and take thirty more homeless families off the streets!*

This P.S. conveys three of the strongest elements of the appeal—the deadline, the dollar-for-dollar match, and the thirty families who will benefit—at just the place in the letter that's bound to have the highest readership of all.

Don't conclude on the basis of this example that you should use the postscript to restate and reinforce the ask. The overwhelming majority of fundraising letters make that mistake. Simply pleading with the reader to "act now" or "send your gift today" is a waste of this valuable real estate. That's boring. Use the P.S. instead to disclose some benefit or intriguing fact or to comment on an enclosure in the package that's not discussed in the body copy. Make the P.S. irresistibly interesting. After all, its function is to involve the reader and motivate him to turn to the lead of the letter.

Now you're ready to move along to the body of the letter itself.

Step 7: Consider Subheads and Underlining

Do you remember Vögele's observations about the behavior of real-world direct mail recipients—how they skip about the text, glancing at a phrase here and a highlighted word or two there? If so, you'll want to decide at the outset what points to highlight visually in the body of the letter. This is another area of variance between off-line direct mail copy and e-mail copy, where underlining also indicates a *link* that can be clicked, and where the text is often shorter and needs fewer subheads (or none). See chapter 11 for more on this, but remember, the points to highlight will stay the same.

Now here's a subtle but significant lesson: the items to underline or to feature in subheads aren't necessarily the ones you think will break up the text at the most convenient intervals or help convey your tone of voice. Rather, subheads and underlining must *appeal directly to the reader*. Ideally, such emphasis is used to spotlight donor benefits, tangible or intangible—the payoff to those who respond to the appeal with contributions.

Let's assume you've decided that subheads are inappropriate for the appeal you're writing for Hope Is Alive! Perhaps they're out of character for the signer, the executive director, who tends to be a bit stuffy, or perhaps you think subheads detract from the upscale image the agency wants to convey. There's still an easy way for you to accent the benefits offered in your appeal, answer readers' unspoken questions, and make your letter easier to read: use underlining. Do it sparingly, on only a few key words and phrases. Limit yourself to no more than three or four per page, and emphasize donor benefits. If possible, choose them before you write the body of the letter. One way you can determine which points warrant underlining (or subheads) is to outline the letter before you write it. If you construct your outline paying particular attention to the benefits you're offering, the appropriate words and phrases may jump off the page.

As you may be aware, this advice of mine on underlining flies in the face of common practice in the direct mail fundraising field. Pick up almost any fundraising letter at random, and what are you likely to find? Sentence after sentence, paragraph after paragraph, line after line—underlined. Overuse of underlining defeats its purpose, which after all is emphasis. Emphasize everything, and you emphasize nothing.

In this case, you'd be likely to decide that among the points requiring underlining are these two important ones:

> *If you respond by January 15, <u>your gift will be matched dollar-for-dollar.</u>*

> *With your generous support, Hope Is Alive! will be able to open the new shelter on time—and <u>thirty homeless families will be off the streets</u> for the rest of the winter.*

Instead of emphasizing Hope Is Alive!'s $10,000 budget to outfit the new shelter, you've wisely chosen to stress the thirty homeless families who will have a warm and secure place to sleep. Obviously, your readers will care much more about Jennifer and her dad and the other families than about an agency's budget!

Step 8: Write the Text (at Last!)

This is the easy part. You've already written the reply device; you've developed the lead, the close, and the P.S.; you've drafted the principal underlined points. What else is there to do? A game of fill-in-the-blanks.

Take care, though; it's all too easy to stumble off course in the stretch. And remember, you may have to vary your copy based on whether you're writing a letter, an e-mail, or copy for the web. Tell the story you started about Jennifer and Molly, but don't turn it into a novelette. Make sure the story shows the benefits the reader will receive if she accepts your offer: that Jennifer now has hope for a better life, and so will dozens of other good people trapped in terrible circumstances. Stick to the points you selected for emphasis by underlining. You picked those points because they answer the unspoken questions you know your reader will have—and because they emphasize the benefits that you hope will motivate the reader to send a gift without delay. If you stay on this course, Hope Is Alive! will raise its $10,000, and those thirty families will be off the streets. You, the author, will be a hero. And so will everyone who responded to your appeal.

In the next chapter let's recap the essentials by reviewing what I call the *Cardinal Rules of Fundraising Letters*.

Chapter Eight:
The Cardinal Rules of Fundraising Letters

In many ways, the techniques required to write an appeal for funds share a lot with any other sort of writing that's intended to persuade or otherwise produce results. But there are guidelines that apply specifically to writing fundraising letters. I call these axioms the *Cardinal Rules of Fundraising Letters*.

The Cardinal Rules

To illustrate the eight rules spelled out below, I'll refer to the direct mail package in exhibits 8.1 through 8.6. It's an appeal mailed by St. Joseph's Indian School, in Chamberlain, South Dakota; this package was one of several efforts to secure an additional gift from one of my newsletter's correspondents in the year after he sent the school an unsolicited $15 check as part of an annual exercise to learn how nonprofits responded to small gifts. The appeal isn't without flaws, but it does illustrate the eight rules.

Rule 1: Use "I" and "You" (But Mostly "You")

"You" should be the word you use most frequently in your fundraising letters. Your appeal is a letter from one individual to another individual, not a press release, a position paper, or a brochure.

Studies on readability supply the fundamental reason the words "you" and "I" are important: they provide human interest. Stories, anecdotes, and common names (and capitalized words in general) have some of the same effect, but the most powerful way to engage the reader is by appealing directly to her: use the word "you."

And online this point is paramount. Online, a donor is more likely to feel that she is changing the world, and not just helping your organization change the world. Electronic communication brings the immediacy and directness of an appeal to the fore.

EXHIBIT 8.1
Appeal Letter, St. Joseph's School

St. Joseph's Indian School
Chamberlain, South Dakota 57326

October 30, 1992

Dear Friend,

You are a dream catcher.

The Lakota (Sioux) believe that good dreams and nightmares float in the air, and that a special willow frame strung with sinew can screen out nightmares and let only good dreams pass through.

They call the ornament a dream catcher and put one in every tipi and on the cradle board of every baby.

The other evening I was walking through the William House, one of our childrens' homes. I peeked in on some of the younger kids who were already asleep. I watched the children sleeping and dreaming peacefully.

Sweet dreams are something new for so many of the children. They've come from such troubled homes — and nightmares are far more common on the reservations. I thought about the Lakota (Sioux) dream catcher and my thoughts turned to you.

You protect our children from nightmares. You save them from poverty, illiteracy, and despair — a nightmare fate that befalls so many Native Americans on the reservations.

You bring them good dreams — of a bright future as well-educated, young adults with a purpose and strong values. And you help make those dreams come true. You are a dream catcher!

Because you are a guardian of good dreams for the children of St. Joseph's, we want you to have a special gift. I've enclosed a Thanksgiving Card that features the Lakota dream catcher.

I hope you'll keep this card to bring good dreams to yourself and your family, or pass it on to bring good dreams to a faraway loved one at Thanksgiving.

Because so many of our friends are interested in Lakota traditions, we have ordered a small number of Lakota dream catchers in antique brass.

If you can send a special gift today of $25 or more, I'd love to send you one of these unique ornaments as a special gift from the children of St. Joseph's.

These highly detailed dream catchers make wonderful gifts for children and new parents, and make unique Christmas Tree decorations.

In any event, please send a gift today of whatever you can afford to bring dreams of hope to the children of St. Joseph's. Without people like you, their lives would be a nightmare.

Thanks!

Yours in Christ,

Bro. David Nagel
Director

P.S. Thanksgiving is a special, happy time around here. It's one of the few times when America remembers all the gifts Native Americans gave to this country — and how little they received in return. Please remember the children of St. Joseph's when you offer thanks over your Thanksgiving dinner. We'll be praying for you.

EXHIBIT 8.2
Appeal Reply Device, St. Joseph's School

Dreams of Hope for the Children

2150050. 079

Mr. Karps:
Send a gift today of $25 or more, we'll send you a beautiful antique brass Dream Catcher ornament as a special gift from the children of St. Joseph's.

YES!

I want to be a dream catcher to help bring dreams of hope to the children of St. Joseph's.

2150050. 079

Enclosed is my gift of:

(   ) $25   (   ) $15   (   ) $48   (   ) $_____

(   ) I have enclosed a gift of $25 or more, please send an antique brass Lakota dream catcher ornament.

Please make your tax-deductible gift payable to St. Joseph's and mail it with this slip. Use the other side for your prayer requests and intentions. Please be sure the return address on the reverse side shows through the window of the enclosed envelope.

St. Joseph's Indian School Chamberlain, South Dakota 57326

PRAY FOR ME

Dear Brother David, I am in need. Please pray for the following intentions.

☐ For the health of my loved ones   ☐ For my peace of mind

☐ For the strength of my marriage   ☐ For my children

☐ Other _____   ☐ For my health

_____

_____

☐ Please send information about your Charitable Gift Annuity.

Please be sure this address shows through the window of the enclosed envelope:

ST. JOSEPH'S INDIAN SCHOOL
CHAMBERLAIN SD 57326

EXHIBIT 8.3

Dreamcatcher Premium, St. Joseph's School

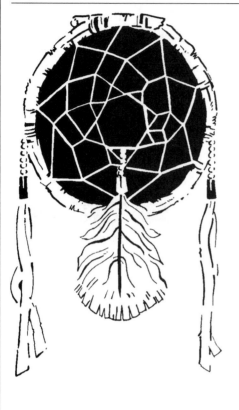

THE LEGEND OF THE DREAMCATCHER

The native Americans of the great plains believe that the air is filled with both good and bad dreams.

Historically, the dream catchers were hung in the tipi or lodge, and also on a baby's cradle board.

Legend has it that the good dreams pass through the center hole to the sleeping person. The bad dreams are trapped in the web, where they perish in the light of dawn.

EXHIBIT 8.4

Dreamcatcher Thanksgiving Card, St. Joseph's School

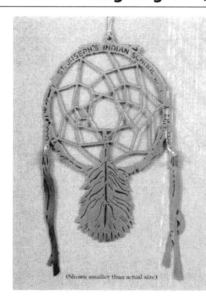

Dreamcatcher

This Dreamcatcher is produced in solid brass. The beautiful details of the brass hanging are brought out by the antique finish. For a special gift I will send you this beautiful Dreamcatcher for you to display in your home.

Bro. Dave

(Shown smaller than actual size)

EXHIBIT 8.5
Appeal Outer Envelope and Reply Envelope, St. Joseph's School

A Lakota Gift for You!

NONPROFIT
ZIP + 4

CHAMBERLAIN
SD

U.S.POSTAGE
0.08 8
PB METER
681085

573

PLEASE
PLACE
STAMP
HERE

EXHIBIT 8.6

Charitable Gift Annuity Brochure, St. Joseph's School

<u>make a note!</u>

It's Time For
A Little
End Of The Year
Pre-Planning

You may discover that a timely charitable contribution this time of the year could increase your personal joy of helping the Lakota boys and girls at St. Joseph's and play an important role in reducing your income taxes.

With a little PRE-PLANNING NOW, you may pleasantly learn that you have more charitable gift possibilities than you realize!

One of the ways, as you know, to save on your taxes and do some good at the same time is with a gift to charity. Those who have adequate deductions to itemize, may include their gifts as charitable deductions.

Perhaps you have found in the past that you did not have enough deductions to benefit by itemizing. However, a Larger-Than-Usual gift this year, might enable you to hoist your deductions and allow you to itemize as you benefit from a tax savings.

As we advance toward the final months of 1992, it is wise to begin making plans for gifts that could help you before the year ends.

THIS IS AN IDEAL TIME OF THE YEAR TO CONSIDER A ST. JOSEPH'S CHARITABLE GIFT ANNUITY.

If you have been "thinking about" an annuity but kept putting it off — NOW, BEFORE THE YEAR'S END — is a good time to find out how our Gift Annuity works.

Keep in mind, it is a Gift as well as an Investment! With a St. Joseph's Gift Annuity you are giving to some of the neediest children in our country as well as guaranteeing yourself a lifetime income. PLUS, you are allowed definite tax advantages the year the gift is made. About 45 to 50 percent of your initial gift is considered a charitable deduction by the IRS, and as we pay you, part of your annuity is not taxed.

Our Gift Annuity program is very simple: you give a specified amount ($1,000 or more) to the school and we in turn pay you a FIXED rate of return for as long as you live. The older you are the higher the return. You may be interested in the Single Life contract only — or perhaps the Joint Life plan may be best (even if rates are a bit lower) if you are married.

If you are between the ages of 50 to 65, you might like to investigate our Deferred Gift Annuity plan. With this type of annuity, you contribute your gift right away and claim the Charitable Deduction portion the year it is given. However, your income payments do not begin until a later-specified time, perhaps the year you retire. In the meantime, your gift

is safe and accruing interest. This is a very useful plan for individuals or married couples who could use the Charitable Deduction during their working years but will not need the income until they retire.

You may wish to consider exchanging appreciated stocks or bonds for a St. Joseph's Charitable Gift Annuity. This can be a wise way to make a gift, which may eliminate some of your capital gains tax, and earn a charitable deduction the year the gift is made.

Now as the year is rapidly ending it is an excellent time to find out more about a St. Joseph's

Charitable Gift Annuity. Fill out the attached coupon and return it to us. We would be delighted to send you a personalized proposal before the year ends.

REMEMBER

1) Donations made to St. Joseph's on or before December 31 are deductible this year if you itemize.

2) A gift that is larger-than-usual might enable you to itemize for your 1992 taxes.

3) Consider a gift of appreciated stocks and avoid capital gains tax or receive a considerable savings if exchanged for a Charitable Gift Annuity.

4) This is a beautiful time of the year to give a memorial gift in honor of a loved one while making a charitable gift to us.

5) The IRS allows a charitable deduction for gifts of property such as antiques, artwork, jewelry, and any type of collection if we can actually use it for the school. The deduction would be for the fair market value of the object given.

6) The joy and satisfaction of making a major type gift to the Lakota boys and girls at St. Joseph's Indian School.

It is always wise to consult your tax advisor before any final contribution is made that may affect your tax outcome.

Special Gifts
St. Joseph's Indian School
P.O. Box 100
Chamberlain, SD 57325-0100

Dear Brother David,

Please use the following information to calculate my Gift Annuity benefits. I understand that I am under no obligation and this personalized proposal is FREE.

☐ Immediate Gift Annuity   ☐ Deferred Gift Annuity (payments to begin year _____)

Amount of Gift Being Considered: $_____ (Minimum Annuity Amount $1,000.)

Frequency of Payment Desired: ☐ Annual   ☐ 2 Times/Year   ☐ 4 Times/Year   ☐ Monthly
($5,000 Min.)   ($10,000 Min.)

Name (Mr., Mrs., Miss) _____

Address _____

City _____ State _____ Zip _____

Telephone _____

☐ We are interested in a Two (Joint) Annuity plan.

Name of Second Annuitant: _____

Birth Date: Month _____ Day _____ Year _____

Name of Second Annuitant: _____

Birth Date: Month _____ Day _____ Year _____

Relationship of Second Annuitant: _____

Please Note: For proposed annuitant(s) less than 50 years of age, we write only Deferred Payment Annuities—payments typically to start at age 65.
(All information is confidential.)

In the St. Joseph's Indian School fundraising letter (exhibit 8.1), notice how Brother David Nagel uses these powerful personal pronouns to establish intimacy:

> You are a dream catcher.
>
> I peeked in on some of the younger kids who were already asleep. You protect our children from nightmares. You save them from poverty, illiteracy, and despair . . .
>
> I hope you'll keep this card to bring good dreams to yourself and your family . . .

Note that the singular "Dear Friend" is used here—and the same singular salutation appears even if the letter is addressed to a married couple. (Only one person at a time reads a letter.) Abolish the plural "you" from your vocabulary (as in "Dear Friends," for example). Try to avoid the royal "we" too; it smacks of condescension and will detract from the personal character of your appeal.

Use of the singular will require that you stick to a single letter signer. You'll cause yourself two problems by using more than one signer. First, you won't be able to enliven your letter with the personal details and emotional asides that might come naturally in a letter from one person to another. And second, with multiple signers you'll sacrifice suspension of disbelief: your reader's willingness to accept that your letter is actually a personal, one-to-one appeal.

Think about it: how am I, as the receiver of this letter, to believe that two or three busy people who don't live together or work in the same office have collaborated in writing a fundraising letter to me? Which one of them typed the letter? (Or was it really someone else?) Did they both actually sign it? These are not questions you want your readers to be asking!

When to Break Rule 1   You may write a letter in the first-person plural if—and only if—there's a special reason to do so—for example, if the letter is to be signed by a married couple or your organization's two venerable cofounders or a famous Republican and a famous Democrat. Even in such exceptional cases, however, I advise you to craft the letter *as though it were written by only one* of the two signers, in much the same manner as one of those annual family letters that arrive by the bushel every December. Something like this: "When Bob and I agreed to co-chair this fundraising drive, it was absolutely clear to both of us that we'd have to turn first to the agency's most loyal and generous donors—people just like you."

Rule 2: Appeal on the Basis of Benefits, Not Needs

Donors give money because they get something in return (if only good feelings). To tap their generosity, describe what they'll receive in return for their money—such benefits as lives saved, or human dignity gained, or larger causes served. And don't be shy about emphasizing tangible benefits. Donors may tell you they give money for nobler reasons, but premiums often make a difference. (Most donors read your letters in the privacy of their own homes. They don't have to admit their own mixed motives to anyone—not even themselves.)

Look at how Brother David bases his request for funds to the St. Joseph's Indian School on the benefits to the donor, both tangible and intangible:

> *If you can send a special gift today of $25 or more, I'd love to send you one of these unique ornaments as a special gift from the children of St. Joseph's.*
>
> *These highly detailed dream catchers make wonderful gifts for children and new parents, and make unique Christmas Tree decorations.*
>
> *In any event, please send a gift today of whatever you can afford to bring dreams of hope to the children of St. Joseph's. Without people like you, their lives would be a nightmare.*

When to Break Rule 2 If you're sending a genuine emergency appeal, you'd be foolish not to write about your organization's needs—and graphically so. But if it isn't a real emergency (and you'll really be in trouble if you habitually cry wolf), then write about benefits, not needs. In the long run, you'll raise a lot more money that way. An annual "emergency" could put you out of business!

Rule 3: Ask for Money, Not for "Support"

Almost always the purpose of a fundraising appeal is to ask for financial help. Be sure you do so clearly, explicitly, and repeatedly. The ask shouldn't be an afterthought, tacked onto the end of a letter; it's your reason for writing. Repeat the ask several times in the body of the letter as well as on the reply device. A successful fundraising appeal might include as many as half a dozen asks. It may even be appropriate to lead your letter with the ask.

Note in the St. Joseph's appeal that the ask appears twice in the letter and twice again on the reply device (exhibit 8.2). Notice, too, how clear and explicit the requests for funds are: ". . . send a special gift today of $25 or more," ". . . please send a gift today of whatever you can afford," "Send a gift today of $25 or more," and "Enclosed is my gift of . . ."

When to Break Rule 3 Many direct mail packages are structured not as appeals for funds but as invitations to join a membership organization. Others feature surveys or other donor involvement devices. In these cases, deemphasize the financial commitment, and highlight membership benefits—or stress the impact of completing the survey or mailing the postcard you've enclosed.

Rule 4: Write a Package, Not a Letter

In direct mail, your fundraising letter is the single most important element in the package, but it's only one of several items that must fit smoothly together and work as a whole. In a multichannel campaign, the direct mail package is only one of as many as three or four elements making use of different channels.

At a minimum, your direct mail package will probably include an outer (or carrier) envelope, a reply envelope, and a reply device in addition to the letter. When you sit down to write, think about how each of these components will help persuade donors to send money now. Make sure the same themes, symbols, colors, and typefaces are used on all elements, so the package is as memorable and accessible as possible. And be certain every element in the package relates directly to the big idea or marketing concept that gives the appeal its unity. (I spoke about marketing concepts in chapter 6.)

Notice that the St. Joseph's Indian School package contains seven components:

- Outer (carrier) envelope (exhibit 8.5)

- Two-page letter (exhibit 8.1)

- Reply device (exhibit 8.2)

- Photograph in full color of the dream catcher premium (exhibit 8.3)

- Dream catcher Thanksgiving card (exhibit 8.4)

- Charitable gift annuity brochure (exhibit 8.6)

- Reply envelope (exhibit 8.5)

Examine these components carefully, and you'll see several earmarks of a successful effort to package the contents of this appeal in a unified way:

- *Theme.* The dream catcher theme, the big idea in this appeal, is emphasized on every component of the package except for the brochure on gift annuities and the nearly text-free reply envelope.

- *Subtext (or underlying theme).* The subtext of gift giving is explicit almost everywhere and implicit everywhere else. There's no mistaking that this is an appeal for funds, but it's couched as an exchange of gifts.

- *Color.* Although you can't see them in this book's black-and-white reproduction, the colors used on the outer envelope, the letter, and the reply device are identical: black text with bright orange accenting and imagery. The brochure is printed in red and black.

When to Break Rule 4 Sometimes it pays to spend a little extra money on a package insert that doesn't directly relate to the marketing concept.

For example, a premium offer might be presented on a *buckslip*—an insert designed to highlight the premium—and that offer might not appear anywhere else in the package (with the possible exception of the reply device). Often, in fact, a buckslip works best when it doesn't use the same color and design as other package elements, so that it stands out more clearly.

Rule 5: Write in Simple, Straightforward English

Use compact, powerful words and short, punchy sentences. Favor words that convey emotions over those that communicate thoughts. Avoid foreign phrases and big words. Minimize the use of adjectives and adverbs. Don't use abbreviations or acronyms; spell out names, even if their repetition looks a little silly to you. Repeat (and underline) key words and phrases.

Brother David's simple, unadorned language, free of pretense, in his letter (exhibit 8.1) helps convey the strength of his appeal: "good dreams and nightmares," "the younger kids," "You bring them good dreams," and "to bring dreams of hope to the children."

When to Break Rule 5 A letter that could have been written by a twelve-year-old might not look right bearing the signature of a college president or a US senator, so follow this rule judiciously. But don't make the mistake of confusing big words, complex sentences, and complicated thoughts with intelligent communication: the most literate fundraising letter needs to be clear and straightforward. The very best writing is easy to understand.

Rule 6: Format Your Letter for Easy Reading

The eye needs rest, so be conscious of the white space you're leaving around your copy:

- Indent every paragraph.
- Avoid paragraphs more than seven lines long, but vary the length of your paragraphs.
- Use bullets.
- In long letters, try subheads that are centered and underlined. Underline sparingly but consistently throughout your letter—enough to call attention to key words and phrases, especially those that highlight the benefits to the reader, but not so much as to distract the eye from your message.

Take another look at the St. Joseph's appeal in exhibit 8.1. Notice that not a single paragraph in the body of the letter is longer than five lines (and there's only one that long). Only the P.S. exceeds that limit, with seven lines. Every paragraph is indented the standard five spaces, although the letter is printed on Monarch-sized paper. There are neither underlined phrases nor bulleted points in Brother David's appeal, but they aren't needed here; the letter is short enough and sufficiently appealing. It's easy to read.

When to Break Rule 6 Don't mechanically follow this rule. Some special formats, such as telegrams or handwritten notes, have formatting rules of their own. Don't ignore them. Remember that you want the reader to believe—or at least to *act* as though she believes—that you've sent her a telegram, a handwritten note, or a personal letter (or whatever else the communication might be).

Rule 7: Give Your Readers a Reason to Send Money NOW

Creating a sense of urgency is one of your biggest copywriting challenges. Try to find a genuine reason that gifts are needed right away: for example, a deadline for a matching grant or an approaching election date. Or tie your fund request to a budgetary deadline so you can argue why "gifts are needed within the next 15 days." There is always a reason to send a gift now. And the argument for the urgency of your appeal may bear repeating.

Keep in mind, though, that urgency isn't a simple matter of time alone. Circumstances such as children dying of hunger, troops massing for an invasion, or the imminence of an environmental catastrophe may require urgency despite the absence of deadlines.

There are several ways Brother David builds a sense of urgency in his appeal for the children of St. Joseph's Indian School:

- The emphasis on Thanksgiving in an appeal dated October 30 provides a natural and easily understood deadline.

- The brochure headlining "It's Time for a Little End of the Year Pre-Planning" (exhibit 8.6) sets a fallback date, December 31, thus laying down a second line of urgency.

- Brother David's comment that "we have ordered a small number of Lakota dream catchers" implies that the supply could run out quickly, leaving the donor *without* "wonderful gifts for children and new parents."

- The topic of "poverty, illiteracy, and despair," set out in the letter, is freighted with urgency all its own.

When to Break Rule 7 In direct mail, be *very* careful about fixed deadlines if you're mailing by bulk rate, which might delay delivery by two weeks or more. (Instead of giving a date, use a phrase like "within the next two weeks.") Don't overuse particular arguments for urgency, lest your credibility suffer. And try not to depend on deadlines based on actual dates in large-scale mailings to acquire new donors: the value of those letters will almost always be greater if you can continue to use the same letter over and over again.

When communicating online, however, you can fine-tune your message by the hour, if necessary, and reach out right up until the final hour before a deadline, if you wish.

Rule 8: Write as Long a Letter as You Need to Make the Case for Your Offer

Not everyone will read every word you write, but some recipients will do so, no matter how long your letter. Others will scan your copy for the information that interests them the most. To be certain you push their hot buttons, use every strong argument you can devise for your readers to send you money now. And to spell out every argument may mean writing a very long letter; it may also mean repeating what you've written to the same donors many times in the past. But don't worry about boring your readers by restating your case: research repeatedly reveals that even many of the most active donors remember very little about the organizations they support.

Brother David's appeal for St. Joseph's is only two pages long. If all the information contained in the two inserts devoted specifically to the dream catcher offer were to be included in the letter rather than printed as separate items, the appeal would run to three pages. (It's much better the way it is.) Still, this letter doesn't convey enough information about St. Joseph's to answer the questions that might occur to a prospective donor who has never before heard of the school. (For starters: "How many kids attend the school? Where is Chamberlain? Does all the money come from donors like me, or does the government pay too?") This appeal was mailed to a previous donor, who presumably has already had those questions answered.

I've already hinted that the e-mail version of your appeal will need to be shorter. While St. Joseph's letter is only two pages, Brother David would probably have to cut that copy by half in its e-mail counterpart. Some online testing has shown that with a highly motivational story, a long e-mail can out-perform a short one. However, even a long fundraising e-mail is usually shorter than many corresponding direct mail appeals. Normally, you'll need to be briefer and more direct in the online version of your copy.

When to Break Rule 8   Not every organization and not every appeal calls for a long letter. A well-known organization with a readily identifiable purpose—the American Red Cross, for example, or a prominent children's hospital—might be able to make its case with only a sentence or two. Similarly, in writing to your proven donors, you can sometimes state the argument for a straightforward membership renewal or special appeal in just a few words. "It's time to renew your membership" is a good example.

Three More Things to Keep in Mind

If you follow the eight rules I've just described, you won't go far wrong when you write your next fundraising appeal. But I suggest you also keep in mind the psychology of the position you've placed yourself in as the signer of your letter. You might want to consider the following as three additional rules of writing fundraising letters:

1. You (the signer) are an individual human being, with hopes, fears, convictions, and experiences. Look at how Brother David takes up that challenge, writing about "sweet dreams," "nightmares," "despair," "loved ones," and "wonderful gifts." This is no masterpiece of self-revelation, but it gives a sense of a man who is engaged in his work and feels strongly about the children at the school.

2. You are writing to one person, the addressee, who has hopes, fears, convictions, and experiences too. Notice how Brother David appeals directly to the donor's feelings: "You bring them good feelings"; "to bring good dreams to yourself and your family"; "Without people like you, their lives would be a nightmare."

3. Regardless of its mission, your organization addresses human needs on many levels, intangible as well as concrete, emotional as well as practical. Those are the things people care about. Remember that Brother David doesn't write about budgets, fiscal years, and funding shortfalls. He writes about *the kids*—their dreams, their nightmares.

Rating Your Writing

Some people think that writing fundraising appeals is pure art. Others insist the work is simply a matter of building on well-known formulas. Judging from the hundreds (sometimes thousands) of fundraising appeals I've seen over the years, they're both wrong. There's precious little art in evidence. And if formulas really work in writing fundraising appeals, they're not well known because their influence doesn't show either.

Without a formula for success, most level-headed folks would be likely to think that there is no systematic way to assess the effectiveness of a fundraising letter. But as a lifelong contrarian, I maintain that there are two ways to do so:

- *The standard way*. Just mail the letter, and you'll see how well it works. However, if you've been doing a little too much of that and with too little to show for it, you might try using the following method to review your work before the market renders its own, possibly costly, opinion.

- *My way*. With my Cardinal Rules as a point of departure, I've developed a simple self-assessment form for a direct mail fundraising letter, reproduced as exhibit 8.7. (Note that in the course of converting the Cardinal Rules into a method of evaluation, I've lent more weight to some factors and less to others.) If this is a formulaic approach, so be it. It works for me.

Let's move on now to chapter 9, where we'll examine some of the more general considerations that come into play when you're writing for results.

EXHIBIT 8.7

How to Assess a Direct Mail Fundraising Package

First, rate package on each criterion by circling your rating: 5 = best, 0 = worst.

#	Criterion	Rating	Weight	Total
1	Speaks *to* the reader, *from* the signer. Uses the singular personal pronouns "you" and "I."	0 1 2 3 4 5	× 2 =	
2	Talks about benefits, not needs.	0 1 2 3 4 5	× 3 =	
3	Has an unmistakably clear *offer*. Benefits to donor are compelling. Asks for a specific amount of money or other explicit act.	0 1 2 3 4 5	× 5 =	
4	Establishes urgency—that is, makes the case to take action *now*.	0 1 2 3 4 5	× 2 =	
5	Is unified into a whole package, with components reinforcing each other.	0 1 2 3 4 5	× 2 =	
6	Has a powerful writing style: short words, emotion, short sentences, short paragraphs; no ten-dollar words, foreign expressions, abbreviations, acronyms.	0 1 2 3 4 5	× 2 =	
7	Is formatted and designed for easy reading. Uses white space, indents, bullets, underlining, a P.S.	0 1 2 3 4 5	× 1 =	
8	Letter is as long (or as short) as necessary to make the case. Must address all the unspoken questions a reader's likely to have.	0 1 2 3 4 5	× 1 =	
9	Outer envelope commands attention, provokes curiosity.	0 1 2 3 4 5	× 3 =	
10	Response device makes it easy to take action.	0 1 2 3 4 5	× 2 =	
11	Effectively uses color, graphics, white space to emphasize essentials: benefits, deadline, call to action.	0 1 2 3 4 5	× 1 =	
	TOTAL *(Total the 11 ratings. Remember: 0 × 5 = 0!)*			

Second, evaluate your score. With as many as 5 points available for each of the eleven criteria, and weighting factors that total 24, a perfect score is 120 points. You may translate a numerical score into a letter grade as follows.

Rating	Letter grade	Meaning
110–120	A+	No more need be said.
100–109	A	Give that writer a pat on the back!
80–99	B	Shows lots of promise.
60–79	C	Needs some improvement.
30–59	D	Requires a lot of work. Maybe better to start from scratch!
0–29	F	Uh oh!

Source: Copyright © 1996, 2003, 2013 by Mal Warwick.

Chapter Nine:
You're Writing for Results—Not for a Pulitzer Prize

My brother has never forgiven me. Art was eighteen and about to enter his first year of college. He has since become a respected psychiatrist and has taught at universities that rival any I've ever attended. But back then—to my mind, at least—he was just my snot-nosed younger brother. And Art was absolutely, positively guaranteed to stumble over freshman English—or so everyone else in our family was convinced.

Since I was three years older than my brother and a veteran of hundreds of essays, letters, stories, reviews, and critiques, not to mention a few political speeches, our mother pressed me into service during that summer of 1962. As a former English teacher, she was suffering from acute embarrassment in addition to her maternal fear for Art's future.

"Make yourself useful for a change," she told me. "Help your brother. Teach him how to write."

This assignment pleased neither Art nor me, but orders were orders. (Our parents were still paying the bills, after all.) With mutual ill will, we took up our new roles: I as a teacher, he approximating the role of the obedient younger brother.

Things went from bad to worse after I gave Art his first assignment: a 500-word essay entitled "How to Tie Your Shoelaces."

Art wrote and then rewrote that essay at least a dozen times, each successive draft a mosaic of my notations in red, blue, and black pencil. The essay was finished only after painful daily sessions stretching over several weeks. Along the way, there were countless changes in word order and sentence structure. We discarded adjectives and adverbs, shifted prepositions, changed verbs, and thumbed through Roget's Thesaurus for sparkling new nouns. But when the job was complete and we were ready to proceed with the second assignment, it was obvious that what Art had learned about writing had little to do with any of the changes we'd made in his labored drafts. The essence of what he had learned (and I had "taught") was this:

Lessons Learned

1. To write clearly and effectively, the writer must *think* before setting pen to paper (or, more likely now, fingers to the keyboard). Clearly written communication is nothing more—and nothing less—than a reflection of disciplined, logical thinking.

2. When writing to achieve results, the writer must *make things easy for the reader.* Unless held at gunpoint or facing the loss of a job, the reader has no obligation to the writer and nothing to fear. The reader is free to abandon what she or he is reading and turn to something more personally rewarding—like badminton or Beethoven, for example.

3. The right word is not necessarily the most colorful or even the most precise. The right word is the strongest, the most expressive word—the word that communicates the writer's meaning most effectively.

4. A skillful writer can make any subject interesting, amusing, or at least palatable.

Perhaps I'm kidding myself. Art may never have learned those four things at all. Or his freshman English teachers may have forced some discipline into his writing where I'd utterly failed. But I cherish the thought that my brother's subsequent academic success had at least a little to do with my drill sergeant's brand of summertime writing instruction.

As in so many of the other times in my life when I thought I was helping someone else, I was really helping myself a lot more. That summer, acting in the belief that a good teacher needs to be thoroughly familiar with his text, I reread Strunk and White.

If you're not familiar with this legendary little volume, I suggest you pick up a copy and devour it. If you already know the book, reread it before you start your next writing job. Its title is *The Elements of Style*, its coauthors William Strunk Jr. and E. B. White. It's readily available in inexpensive paperback editions throughout North America, and—perhaps best of all—*The Elements of Style* is truly a little book. My 1950s-vintage paperback version is all of seventy-one pages long.

Some writers claim they can get along quite well without Strunk and White or any other grounding in the basics of writing. I'm told there are hugely successful advertising and public relations copywriters who learned everything they know on the job. I'm skeptical of this assertion, which I ascribe largely to the self-promotion that's so common among people who traffic in myths. But for the sake of argument, let's accept the claim that copywriters can learn their craft even if they're ignorant of the fundamentals of English style. That doesn't mean it's a good idea to violate all the rules. In fact, I believe the copywriter's life will be easier—and probably more successful—if it starts with training in the basics. That brings us to Rudolf Flesch.

Rudolf Flesch's Rules of Effective Writing

Generations of Americans have turned to Rudolf Flesch for advice on effective writing and speaking, and no wonder. Flesch's books, written decades ago, contain insights as fresh today as when they were newly written. I especially recommend *How to Write, Speak and Think More Effectively* (an inexpensive and widely available paperback published by NAL/Signet). Flesch's "Rules of Effective Writing" are well worth reading in full, but here's the gist of them:

- Write about people, things, and facts.
- Write as you speak.
- Use contractions.
- Use the first person.
- Quote what was said or written.
- Put yourself in the reader's place.
- Don't be too brief.
- Plan a beginning, middle, and end.
- Go from the rule to the exception and from the familiar to the new.
- Use short forms of names.
- Use pronouns rather than repeating nouns.
- Use verbs rather than nouns.
- Use the active voice.
- Use small, round figures.
- Be specific. Use illustrations, cases, and examples.
- Start a new sentence for each new idea.
- Keep sentences and paragraphs short.
- Use direct questions.
- Underline for emphasis.
- Make your writing interesting to look at.

These aren't arbitrary rules of taste or style. They're the result of Flesch's studies of readers' reactions to written material.

Rudolf Flesch is the all-time master of the study of *readability*, which means the likelihood that what you've written will actually be understood (and possibly remembered) by your readers. Flesch held sway in an era when numerical measurements inspired more faith than they do in today's skeptical society, but his charts, graphs, and scores are still useful. In fact, they're incorporated into the readability statistics offered by Microsoft Word.

Flesch found, for example, that two key indicators of the readability of writing were the number of syllables per 100 words and the average length of a sentence (expressed in number of words).

I won't go into the precise way Flesch defined these two measurements. You can read it yourself in his book (and I hope you will). But look at how Flesch interprets these measurements (exhibit 9.1).

In Flesch's lexicon, "very easy" writing is to be found in comic books. "Standard" writing is the earmark of such magazines as *Time*, and "very difficult" writing is found in scientific and professional journals.

This chapter averages eleven words per sentence, according to Microsoft Word—pretty easy reading, Flesch would say. Judge for yourself whether you find my writing readable.

But short words and short sentences alone won't make your writing easy to read. Flesch insists (and I agree) that a factor of equal importance is the human interest in what you write. Human interest is a function of the proportion of personal words (such as personal pronouns and proper names), the frequency with which quotations are used, and the extent to which you engage the reader by challenging, questioning, or directly addressing her.

Flesch's suggestions about how to increase readability are equally useful. Here are some of them:

- Focus on your reader.

- Focus on your purpose.

- Break up sentences and paragraphs.

EXHIBIT 9.1
Rudolf Flesch's Measurement of Readability

Description of style	Syllables per 100 words	Average sentence length (number of words)
Very easy	123	8
Easy	131	11
Fairly easy	139	14
Standard	147	17
Fairly difficult	155	21
Difficult	167	25
Very difficult	192	29

- Find simpler words.

- Help your reader read (emphasize, anticipate, repeat, summarize).

- Learn to cut unnecessary words.

- Rearrange for emphasis.

- Write to be read aloud.

- Don't write down to your reader.

To write for results, you'll need to do more than polish your writing style. Writing for results is different from writing meant merely to describe or report to the reader. Let's take a look at the differences now.

How Writing for Results Is Different from Writing to Describe or Report

There are at least nine differences between writing for results and writing merely to describe or report, all of which might prove to be crucial elements in your fundraising appeals.

1. *Colloquialisms*. Writing for results requires you to use everyday language and patterns of speech because you need to communicate readily, without delay or complication and without forcing the reader to work for understanding. There are exceptions to this rule, but like much else that can be said about writing for results, the exceptions revolve around the audience, not the writer.

In many fundraising appeals (depending, of course, on the signer and the cause), I might use such phrases as "No way!" or "Guess again" to underline the informality of the solicitation. Such examples of colloquial speech and even slang are more than just acceptable; they're sometimes essential. Like a chatty personal letter, a masterpiece of copywriting will read much more like a conversation at the supermarket than an article in the *Harvard Business Review*.

2. *Clichés*. Most people think, speak, and write in clichés. That, I believe, is not a good thing, but it's important for the copywriter to take it into account. Clichés, after all, are only one step removed from garden-variety colloquialisms; precisely because of their familiarity, they offer an easy way to communicate thoughts rapidly. For the same reason, many readers also find clichés boring, so a tired and overused turn of speech shouldn't be your first line of defense against the difficulty of explaining a complex set of circumstances or making a subtle argument. But sometimes when writing for results, an old chestnut can help you fill the understanding gap.

Consider, for example, that old cliché the "pot of gold at the end of the rainbow." I wouldn't be caught dead using this phrase in everyday speech, even in a defenseless moment. But I can think of no other phrase that more readily communicates the concept of fabulous wealth and could better provide an appropriate image for a sweepstakes featuring large cash prizes. (Naturally, it's been used—time and time again.)

3. *Figures of speech.* You'll probably remember from high school English that similes and metaphors are among the earmarks of fine literature. A simile is one of those hard-working figures of speech that crawls up the hillside "like a train trailing a hundred cars." In contrast, a metaphor forces the reader to do much of the work, taking it on faith that an abstraction in a figure of speech might be a train, a Bengal tiger, or a pot of gold.

I have a simple rule about the use of similes and metaphors in writing for results: *don't use them.* Metaphors require thought; even similes can slow the reader down, or worse. These figures of speech help communicate complex thoughts and feelings, but only by indirection; any complexities in your message need to be spelled out more directly, or you may lose your readers.

4. *Humor and irony.* Creative advertising copywriters notwithstanding, humor is rarely advisable in writing for results. (How many times have you laughed at a commercial on TV and then utterly forgot what it was about, no matter how many times you saw it?) And entirely avoid irony, that wry, sophisticated form of humor. It's not just that some people have no discernible sense of humor or even that what's humorous to one person might seem tragic to another. The fundamental problem, I believe, is that the written word is an imperfect medium to convey good humor.

In speaking to an audience, you might get a laugh for even a poorly told joke by communicating the humor through tone of voice, gestures, facial expressions, and even the use of props, aided by the natural tendency of most people to feel sympathy for you when you're standing right there. You have none of those advantages when writing to that same audience. I suggest you keep the jokes to yourself, or tack them up on your refrigerator or the office bulletin board.

5. *Sentence structure.* I'll call her Miss Forsythe because, truth to tell, I can't remember her name. More than half a century ago, she taught me in ninth-grade English that every sentence must contain a subject and a predicate. Among a great many other rules, all of them delivered in

commanding tones and in language that inhibited questions, Miss Forsythe also insisted that a sentence must never begin with "and" or "but" and must never end with a preposition.

In some forms of writing, those rules are as true today as they were in the 1950s. But not in writing for results. To convey meaning simply and clearly—to respect the informal practices of natural, spoken language and place emphasis where it's needed—Miss Forsythe's rules sometimes need to be ignored. The result may be writing that fails all the tests of conventional sentence structure, punctuation, and grammar—but yields the results you want.

Try these rules instead of Miss Forsythe's:

- A sentence expresses a single thought. Sometimes a thought can be expressed in just one word. One. And one's enough.
- Don't worry about ending sentences with prepositions. Sometimes a preposition is the very best word to end a sentence with.
- And it's OK to start a sentence with a conjunction. (But don't overdo it. Two sentences in a row that start with "but" are likely to confuse the reader.)
- If at first you're not convinced by these three rules, reread them carefully. You might change your mind.

6. *Punctuation*. We'll look at three specific forms of punctuation here.

Semicolons. I despise semicolons. My thoughts tend to break up into little pieces that don't quite justify sentences of their own, but I still refuse to follow the grammarian's rulebook and set one apart from another with a semicolon. Much better, I think, just to pretend I've written a sentence. Miss Forsythe would disapprove with her customary hauteur. But no matter: I get no complaints from my latter-day readers. And when I'm seeking results with my writing—when I want my readers to take action—I am especially zealous to root out all the semicolons.

Why? Because sentences are easier to read without semicolons. The eyes glaze over at the sight of long sentences. Periods provide rest and comfort. The capital letters that begin new sentences heighten interest. Besides, Miss Forsythe isn't here to kick me around anymore.

Dashes. In writing for results, it's often wise to use a dash—what typesetters call an *em dash* (about twice the width of a hyphen—technically, the width of a capital M). I use a lot of dashes when writing fundraising letters—and I don't feel guilty in the least, no matter what Miss Forsythe might say. Dashes lend emphasis to your thoughts by setting them apart and increasing the white space that surrounds them. (The German professor you met in chapter 2 insists that dashes arrest the reader's eye and make writing less readable, but I choose to ignore his advice on this highly personal matter of style.)

Ellipses. Miss Forsythe would cringe . . . but I don't care. Ellipsis points (. . .) have much the same effect as a dash, particularly when they're set off by blank spaces before and after the points. Both help convey meaning by splitting complex or urgent thoughts into their component pieces.

7. *Contractions.* Lawyers, top business executives, and even some journalists advocate the sparing use of contractions. Don't pay any attention to them if you want your readers to take action. Listen instead to Rudolph Flesch. And to me.

Purists would rather you spell out every word, erring on the side of precision, so there can be absolutely no confusion in the minds of your readers. I'd rather you use fewer words, favoring informality and natural speech patterns, so your readers won't feel that you're talking down to them.

Contractions such as "I'm," "you've," "don't," and "can't" are usually preferable in copywriting to the longer expressions they're derived from: "I am," "you have," "do not," and "cannot." The shorter form is more easily taken in by the ear, and the eye quickly comprehends the meaning of contractions. Also, negatives catch the reader's attention, sometimes conveying precisely the wrong impression. The word "not" may lodge in the reader's eye like a cinder, causing him to misread the following sentence—or the point of the whole letter.

8. *Repetition.* Grammarians are often repelled by writing intended to persuade because it's likely to be riddled with repetition. The repetition is not accidental. Just as a journalist leads an article with the most important piece of news, the copywriter is likely to emphasize the points of greatest potential interest to the reader by repeating them—the ask in a fundraising letter, for example.

The English language possesses almost unmatched variety, so a writer can describe any benefit or make any offer in a hundred or a thousand different ways. The demands of writing a letter intended to sell products or secure contributions may force the writer to use precisely the same words over and over again.

9. *Underlining and italics.* Miss Forsythe told us never to italicize words unless they're book titles or come from a foreign language. In the days when handwriting and using a typewriter were the writer's only options, she meant we shouldn't underline words. Today some editors follow the same rule: I sometimes find my articles or columns appearing shorn of

all their carefully chosen italicized emphasis. I keep submitting articles peppered with italics anyway, in hopes my editors will wake up and see what's obvious to me: *italics enhance the reader's understanding*—when used sparingly. Emphasizing important facts or thoughts makes it easier for the reader to grasp the writer's meaning and easier to review and remember key points. However, in most fundraising letters, I generally prefer underlining instead of italics.

When Does the Fun Start?

Some writers can produce readable copy in a first, fluid draft. It seems as though the words just keep streaming out of their fingertips, all neatly arranged in precisely the right order. (Grrr! I hate those people!) Within the ranks of the top freelance writers, stories abound about the geniuses who can sit down at the keyboard (a typewriter, often enough) at 9:00 in the morning and type without interruption for three hours. I actually knew one of these guys. Years earlier, when he was working his way through college by writing pulp fiction, he would knock off for an hour's lunch, return for four more hours of unruffled word processing in the afternoon—and end the day with five thousand salable words, or even ten thousand. But people like him write hundreds of books or thousands of stories or articles, or both. (He did.) They've had a lot more practice than you're likely to get. And I don't mind admitting they've got a lot more innate talent for writing than I have.

So most of us have to revise and rewrite and revise again. Don't make the mistake of believing you've got it right the first time. Chances are, you don't. Whatever it is you're writing, set it aside for a day or two or a week after you've completed your first rough draft. Then take a fresh look at it. And don't forget to read your letter aloud. If you can't find something on every page that cries out for revision, you're either a far better writer than I am or you're kidding yourself.

Now it's time to consider your appeal in the context of a full-fledged, multichannel fundraising campaign. As you'll see, reinforcing a simple direct mail appeal by adding e-mail and web messaging will help you raise more money.

There's nothing magical about multichannel marketing. As you're probably all too well aware, when you see a TV commercial for a strong national brand, you're likely to come across a very similar use of imagery and text in magazine ads, on billboards, and possibly in other media as well. Why? Because messages delivered to the same person through various channels are much more likely to be noticed, remembered, and acted upon. An integrated fundraising campaign simply makes use of this fundamental marketing lesson.

With this understanding in mind, let's now cast our eyes about the nonprofit sector and identify the various ways that direct response communications might be put to use in the interest of raising more money. I invite you to accompany me now on a long walk through part 3, "Customizing Your Appeal."

In the following eleven chapters, I'll take you on a walking tour through the thickets of fundraising, visiting, one at a time, each of the most common types of fundraising appeals. We'll examine their unique characteristics and the distinctive demands they impose on a writer. In the course of part 3, we'll study appeals designed to

- Recruit new members or donors
- Start the cultivation process
- Welcome new donors
- Appeal for a special (additional) gift
- Request a year-end contribution
- Recruit monthly sustainers
- Solicit larger, high-dollar gifts
- Persuade donors to send bigger gifts
- Seek annual gifts
- Thank donors
- Seek legacy gifts

You'll find additional examples of these appeals on the website dedicated to this book at www.josseybass.com/go/fundraising appeals.

Part Three: Customizing Your Appeal

Chapter Ten:
Recruiting New Donors

Starting Intimate Conversations with Strangers

The term *direct mail* is most commonly associated with the letters that non-profits mail, often in extremely large quantities, to enlist new members or donors from among a broad population of prospects. In reality, the other types of fundraising letters covered in the following chapters are in many ways (such as the substantial net revenue they generate) far more important to the financial health of nonprofit organizations than the *acquisition* (or *prospect*) packages that bring in new donors. Still, it's the acquisition letters that make the rest of the process possible by supplying a steady stream of new, first-time donors.

Online, the acquisition process is different. I'll cover that in the next chapter.

The reply device in exhibit 10.1 is typical of those used to accompany acquisition letters mailed to prospective donors. (The full package may be found, in color, at www.josseybass.com/go/fundraisingappeals.)

How do you know this form comes from an acquisition (or prospect) package? Because the temporary 2012 membership card, the generic nature of the appeal (encompassing the full range of Earthjustice's mission), the tote bag (a typical introductory membership premium), and the broad array of suggested gifts (the gift string) suggest that Earthjustice knows very little about Bill Rehm and is writing to recruit him as a new member. This form is typical of acquisition packages in several other ways as well:

- On the back of the reply device, you'll find a long list of legally required notices from state charitable regulation agencies—in what may be the smallest typeface known to humankind. These notices are rarely found on appeals to existing or former donors. They're almost always a dead giveaway for acquisition appeals.

- Just below the state registration notices, you'll find a checkbox followed by the sentence, "Please do not share my name with other

EXHIBIT 10.1
Acquisition Package Reply Device, Earthjustice

PETITION TO CONGRESS
PROTECT OUR ENDANGERED WILDLIFE
BEFORE IT'S TOO LATE!

Dear Speaker of the House John Boehner,

America's majestic wildlife is threatened with extinction due to irresponsible industrial development and corporate greed. We must prioritize the well-being of wildlife ahead of profits. Please uphold your charge to protect our nation's wildlife by answering science and oil spill response questions before approving offshore oil drilling in the Alaskan Arctic or longline fishing in the Gulf of Mexico. If we lose our polar bears, sea turtles, and other iconic species, then we will have lost a big part of what makes our country great. Please do all you can to protect these animals and to protect our country's natural heritage.

Sincerely,

224318303   PQ1208MGOLAWBXSD2
_____
Bill Rehm
Berkeley, California

PETITION TO CONGRESS
PROTECT OUR ENDANGERED WILDLIFE
BEFORE IT'S TOO LATE!

Dear Senate Majority Leader Harry Reid,

America's majestic wildlife is threatened with extinction due to irresponsible industrial development and corporate greed. We must prioritize the well-being of wildlife ahead of profits. Please uphold your charge to protect our nation's wildlife by answering science and oil spill response questions before approving offshore oil drilling in the Alaskan Arctic or longline fishing in the Gulf of Mexico. If we lose our polar bears, sea turtles, and other iconic species, then we will have lost a big part of what makes our country great. Please do all you can to protect these animals and to protect our country's natural heritage.

Sincerely,

224318303   PQ1208MGOLAWBXSD2
_____
Bill Rehm
Berkeley, California

I prefer to charge my contribution to my: ☐ Visa   ☐ MasterCard   ☐ American Express   ☐ Discover

Card # _____   Signature _____

Exp. Date _____   Amount $_____

Earthjustice is a nonprofit law firm dedicated to protecting the environment, located at 50 California Street, Suite 500, San Francisco, CA 94111, and may be reached at (415) 217-2000. Earthjustice has retained Mal Warwick Associates to assist in this direct mail fundraising. You may obtain a copy of Earthjustice's financial report by writing to Earthjustice. Residents of the following states may obtain information as follows:

Arizona: Financial information filed with the Secretary of State, State Capitol, 1700 West Washington, 7th Floor, Phoenix AZ 85007-2808, is available for public inspection or by calling toll-free, (800) 458-5842. California: The official registration and financial information regarding Earthjustice can be obtained from the Attorney General's Web site at http://caag.state.ca.us/charities/. Colorado: Earthjustice's registration number (**20023003777**); Colorado residents may obtain copies of registration and financial documents from the Secretary of State by calling (303) 894-2680 or at www.sos.state.co.us. FLORIDA: A COPY OF THE OFFICIAL REGISTRATION AND FINANCIAL INFORMATION MAY BE OBTAINED FROM THE DIVISION OF CONSUMER SERVICES BY CALLING TOLL-FREE [(800) 435-7352] WITHIN THE STATE. REGISTRATION DOES NOT IMPLY ENDORSEMENT, APPROVAL, OR RECOMMENDATION BY THE STATE. Georgia: A full and fair description of Earthjustice's programs and our financial statement summary are available upon request at the office and phone number indicated above. Illinois: Contracts and reports regarding Earthjustice are on file with the Illinois Attorney General. Kansas: Earthjustice's Kansas registration number is (**213-160-5**), and Mal Warwick's Kansas registration is #0000118. The annual financial report for the preceding fiscal year is on file with the Secretary of State, 1st Floor, Memorial Hall, 120 SW 10th Ave., Topeka KS 66612. Maryland: Copies of documents and information submitted by Earthjustice under the Maryland Charitable Solicitations Act are available for the cost of copies and postage from the Secretary of State, State House, Annapolis MD 21401, (410) 974-5534 [(800) 825-4510 within Maryland]. Michigan: Earthjustice's Michigan registration number is MICS 9715. Mississippi: The official registration and financial information of Earthjustice may be obtained from the Mississippi Secretary of State's office by calling (888) 236-6167. New Jersey: **INFORMATION FILED WITH THE ATTORNEY GENERAL CONCERNING THIS CHARITABLE SOLICITATION AND THE PERCENTAGE OF CONTRIBUTIONS RECEIVED BY THE CHARITY DURING THE LAST REPORTING PERIOD THAT WERE DEDICATED TO THE CHARITABLE PURPOSE MAY BE OBTAINED FROM THE ATTORNEY GENERAL OF THE STATE OF NEW JERSEY BY CALLING (973) 504-6215 AND ARE AVAILABLE AT** www.state.nj.us/lps/ca/. New York: New York residents may obtain a copy of Earthjustice's annual report by writing to the Office of the Attorney General, Department of Law, Charities Bureau, 120 Broadway, New York, NY 10271. **North Carolina: Financial information about this organization and a copy of its license are available from the State Solicitation Licensing Branch at (888) 830-4989 (toll-free in North Carolina) or (919) 807-2214. The license is not an endorsement by the State.** Pennsylvania: The official registration and financial information of Earthjustice may be obtained from the Pennsylvania Department of State by calling toll-free, within Pennsylvania, (800) 732-0999. Vermont: **How Contributions Are Allocated Between Charity and Fundraiser:** For information on how much of your contribution goes to Earthjustice and how much to Mal Warwick Associates, contact the Vermont Consumer Assistance Program, Morrill Hall, UVM, Burlington VT 05405, tel. (800) 649-2424, or the Vermont Attorney General's Internet website, www.state.vt.us/. Virginia: A financial statement for the most recent fiscal year is available upon request from the Division of Consumer Affairs, Department of Agriculture and Consumer Services, P.O. Box 526, Richmond, VA 23218; (804) 786-1343. Washington: A notice of solicitation required by law is on file with the Washington Secretary of State. You may obtain additional financial disclosure information by contacting the Secretary of State at (800) 332-GIVE. West Virginia: West Virginia residents may obtain a summary of the registration and financial documents from the Secretary of State, State Capitol, Charleston, WV 25305. Los Angeles, CA: INFORMATION CARD NO. M0056: Issues Pursuant to Los Angeles Municipal Code, Chapter IV, Article 4, Philanthropy. **Activity:** Direct Mail, Telemarketing and Web Site Appeal through December 31, 2011. **Solicitation Dates:** January 1, 2012 through December 31, 2012. **Purpose:** Net proceeds to provide legal services to environmental and conservation organizations in environmental matters of a broad public nature. **Previous Activity:** 2010-2011 activity collected a total of $4,988,444, of which $2,871,874 (57%) was applied to expenses and $2,116,570 was donated to charity.

REGISTRATION WITH A STATE AGENCY DOES NOT CONSTITUTE OR IMPLY ENDORSEMENT, APPROVAL OR RECOMMENDATION BY THAT STATE.

☐ Please do not share my name with other organizations.

PRINTED ON RECYCLED PAPER WITH SOY-BASED INKS.

organizations." Some nonprofits, obviously including Earthjustice, prefer to place this standard notice in the most inconspicuous place possible—to minimize response, of course. Others might make it more prominent. But few organizations make this offer anywhere but on the letter that makes the first contact with a donor—an acquisition package such as this one.

- The two "Petitions to Congress"—*involvement* or *action* devices—aren't unique to acquisition packages, but they are more commonly found there, since such devices are known to boost response.

- The amount $25 is circled on the gift string and appears under the handwritten phrase "This would really help us!" All this is part of Earthjustice's effort to elicit a higher than average gift from Bill. In an appeal mailed to him as an existing donor, Bill's donor history would be the basis for the ask. The gift string would be less spread out. (I typically advise suggesting no more than two or three gift options to existing donors.)

How Donor Acquisition Letters Differ from Other Fundraising Appeals

Even if you're new to fundraising, you've probably seen letters like these a thousand times. They're by far the most familiar sort of direct mail, and they represent what the public thinks of when the subject comes up.

Successful appeals written to recruit new donors or new members come in all sizes, shapes, and flavors. They may be fat or thin, colorful or drab, up-to-the-minute or timeless. They're frequently mailed using third-class bulk postage—either precanceled nonprofit bulk stamps or postage-metered nonprofit bulk *indicia* (stamp-like printed copy in a rectangle)—or occasionally even with first-class postage. But there are five characteristics that the majority of donor acquisition letters share:

1. Donor acquisition letters are often long and occasionally arrive in packages that contain lots of additional material too: brochures or folders, flyers, lift letters, buckslips, and premiums. Many charities fare better without using any of this stuff. Some well-known groups can get away with short letters too. Chances are, though, that a letter you write to prospective donors will need to be at least a little longer than the letters you usually write to previous donors. Otherwise, prospects may not have enough information about your organization to decide whether they'll make a gift.

2. They typically appeal to prospects to support a nonprofit's larger agenda: its goals and the full range of its programs (though one project or aspect of the work may get the lion's share of the attention in the letter). If prospective donors send gifts in response to such a letter, they're more likely to respond favorably when asked later for additional support.

3. References to "you" (the reader) are normally vague and general. Although your organization may know a great deal about the people on one of its donor lists, it probably knows next to nothing about those on its other lists. With these other people, there isn't much to hang a relationship on. Chances are the demands of economy will require that you mail the same letter, unchanged, to all your prospect lists.

4. Typically, acquisition letters are undated and make few references to time or the calendar. That's because you'll probably want to use this appeal over and over. Not just because of the need to economize but also because it normally takes repeated trial and error to fashion a really successful acquisition letter, with modifications tested and retested over time.

5. The minimum suggested gift amount tends to be low. Most charities seek to maximize the number of new donors: asking for less at the outset may serve that purpose.

So much for *direct mail* acquisition. How about *online* acquisition? Join me now in chapter 11, where we'll explore the very different nature of trolling for new donors online.

Chapter Eleven:
Recruiting New Supporters

Beginning the Cultivation Process Online

Two decades ago, when the novel idea of raising money online first became more than a fantasy with the advent of the World Wide Web, those of us who began thinking seriously about the prospect were fixated on the notion that we would simply operate online exactly as we had in direct mail: sending out donor or member acquisition appeals—but via e-mail rather than terrestrial mail.

Well, unfortunately, that simply didn't work.

Throughout the 1990s, as early adopters in online fundraising gained experience, we gradually came to understand that e-mail messages just didn't do an effective job of introducing prospective donors to new organizations *and*, at the same time, persuading them to send money. Not that it never happened—just that it didn't happen often enough to make the technique viable. Eventually, we all learned that acquisition online requires much more patience than it does with direct mail. Online, the key to success is *cultivation*.

As you'll see in the example below, online acquisition typically begins not with an invitation to give a gift or become a member but with an opportunity for the prospect to become involved in your mission by taking action of some sort. It is only later, once those who take action have had the chance to learn more about your organization, that they may show interest in supporting you financially.

The Children's Health Fund (CHF) is dedicated to making sure that kids throughout the United States have a fair chance at securing basic health care services when they're needed. Far too many American children don't have that chance—*one in five kids in America today live in poverty*. As part of celebrating its twenty-fifth anniversary, CHF wanted to increase the number of voices joining it in this cause.

CHF created an online campaign—"Healthy Kids = Healthy America"—to allow individuals to stand up for kids by joining forces with CHF. In CHF's wide-ranging campaign, this pledge generated e-mail addresses from multiple sources, as thousands across the country helped to provide a voice for kids who don't have one, and to get them the health care they deserve. CHF then cultivated pledge takers with an e-mail welcome series highlighting CHF's impact on the lives of thousands of kids—and, more important, the impact the pledge takers can have directly as supporters of CHF.

Like the acquisition campaigns conducted by many other nonprofits, the Healthy Kids campaign involved more than just online communications. For example, cofounder Paul Simon highlighted the organization's impact over the past twenty-five years at a concert in Radio City Music Hall . . . along with a few of his friends—and what a great musical event it was! Building excitement around the event also helped bring new supporters into the CHF fold, supporters who agreed right up front that they "choose to care." CHF billed this exciting event as a thank-you for standing up for children— and offered people a chance to win tickets to the concert.

The principal goal of the Healthy Kids campaign was to recruit new advocates for the one in five American children who lack access to health care.

Driving Pledge Activity

CHF used three initial methods to recruit supporters for the Healthy Kids campaign:

- A Facebook campaign (exhibit 11.1)
- A Change.org petition campaign (exhibit 11.2)
- A coregistration, opt-in campaign (exhibit 11.3)

Each of these elements required a slightly different approach, with different copy in turn, but all three required the message to be distilled to its very essence. This is common in online media: sometimes you're limited to just one sentence to drive the action you want.

With the Change.org petition in exhibit 11.2, you can see the main call to action and the fundamental facts about the Healthy Kids campaign in the headline and the single, seventy-one-word paragraph that space allowed.

The Children's Health Fund also launched a *coregistration* campaign to bring new supporters to the cause. With a coregistration campaign, online users are offered a chance to learn about CHF while they are completing an unrelated online registration of some sort. They might be making a purchase, requesting information, or signing up for a newsletter, actions not necessarily even related to children but requiring a registration process. As users complete the registration process, they are offered a chance to learn about helping children in need. In other words, they're not only registering

EXHIBIT 11.1
Facebook Page, Children's Health Fund "Healthy Kids" Campaign

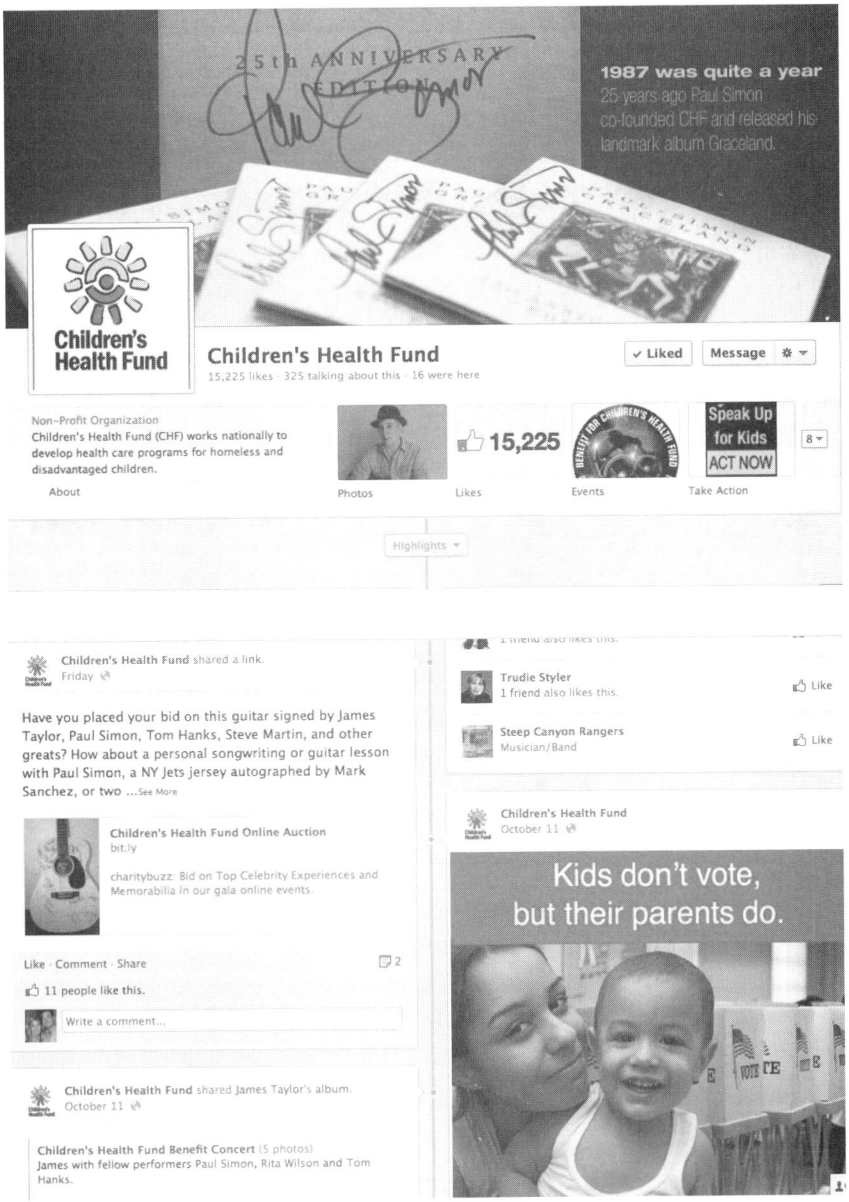

for whatever product or information they were originally seeking, but they also coregistered to receive information from CHF by clicking the button. In exhibit 11.3, you'll note that CHF needed to drive action exclusively through a two-sentence explanation that was relevant to both its mission and the campaign.

CHF carried out the third component of the campaign through Facebook. The organization placed paid ads across the social network (exhibit 11.4), driving new potential supporters to its Facebook page (exhibit 11.1),

EXHIBIT 11.2
Change.org Petition, Children's Health Fund "Healthy Kids" Campaign

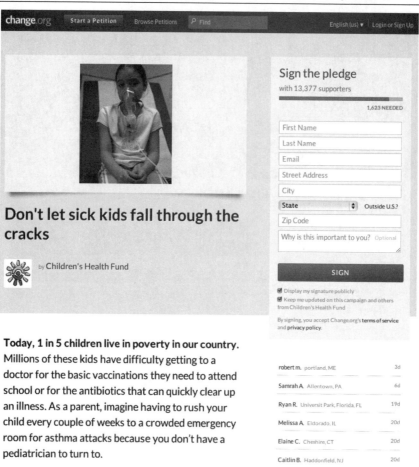

Today, 1 in 5 children live in poverty in our country. Millions of these kids have difficulty getting to a doctor for the basic vaccinations they need to attend school or for the antibiotics that can quickly clear up an illness. As a parent, imagine having to rush your child every couple of weeks to a crowded emergency room for asthma attacks because you don't have a pediatrician to turn to.

EXHIBIT 11.3
Coregistration Campaign, Children's Health Fund "Healthy Kids" Campaign

○ Yes ○ No | **The health & well-being of our kids is critical.**
Give children a healthy future by standing up to help them today. Privacy Policy

Submit

Please only click once.

Offer preview 120 by 90:

EXHIBIT 11.4
Facebook Ads to Generate "Likes" for Children's Health Fund

Children's Health Fund

1 in 5 children live in poverty, many without access to a doctor. Help us help them

You like this.

Children's Health Fund

Every child deserves a chance at a healthy future. Like us if you agree.

You like this.

EXHIBIT 11.5
Landing Page, Children's Health Fund "Healthy Kids" Campaign

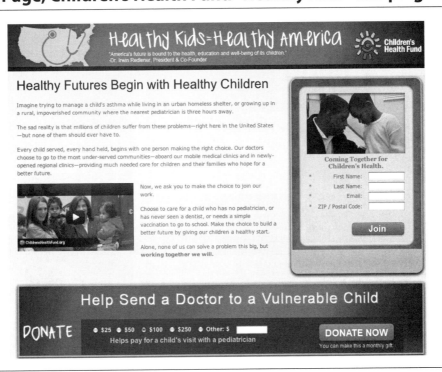

EXHIBIT 11.6

Welcome Series E-mail #1, Children's Health Fund "Healthy Kids" Campaign

Welcome

Dear Donor,

Imagine having a child with a painful ear infection with no antibiotics to treat it. Or watching your child gasp for breath from untreated asthma as you rush to the emergency room.

For millions of children here in America, this is how they live — held back from school and childhood experiences because they can't get proper health care. And sadly, sometimes their parents have to choose between putting food on the table or paying for a doctor.

As a pediatrician, I believe every child in every neighborhood deserves a doctor. Children's Health Fund is committed to breaking down the barriers to health care for children, but we can't do it without you.

We work tirelessly to bring doctors and medicines to America's most vulnerable children and their families. Across the country, our fleet of 50 mobile clinics — each a complete "doctor's office on wheels" — have helped reach so many children who otherwise would not have had the care that they needed, when they needed it most.

Again, thank you for showing your support, and urging our presidential candidates to remember that our nation's future depends on the health of our children.

We have some exciting opportunities for you to help these children, and we invite you to experience the inspiring stories of our kids and doctors.

We're grateful to have you,

Irwin Redlener, MD
President & Co-Founder

25 Years of Care

Co-Founded by Paul Simon and Dr. Irwin Redlener in 1987, Children's Health Fund has been bringing quality care to America's most disadvantaged children for over 25 years.

Learn More

Dr. Elliott Attisha and patient

Click to update your information or to unsubscribe.
This e-mail was sent by Children's Health Fund, 215 West 125th Street, Suite 301, New York, NY 10027

and from there drove them to take the pledge on its website. (In the future, CHF will likely build the pledge directly on its Facebook page, so as not to require any outside link.)

Using the Web and E-mail

First from its Facebook campaign, and shortly thereafter through a variety of other efforts, including e-mails to its current e-mail address file, website promotions, and contest giveaways, CHF drove traffic to its online pledge page (exhibit 11.5). CHF then initiated an e-mail welcome series as each new supporter's pledge came online. The first e-mail in the series is illustrated in exhibit 11.6.

Notice the following in exhibit 11.6:

- E-mail tells the CHF story

- Personal message from the organization's cofounder

- Prominent "Learn More" button

- Single image supports content and mission

- Received within one week of taking pledge

- Invites you to read inspiring stories online

- Clear "Welcome" message right at top

Additional welcome series e-mails asked supporters to watch and forward a video, share content on social media, read a story about the impact of their support, and make a donation (or a sustaining gift, if this welcome series was instead going out to new donors).

So that's how acquisition is done online. Notice that the Children's Health Fund campaign did *not* include a wave of e-mail acquisition appeals sent to rented or borrowed lists. Such lists are available, but only very rarely is it advisable to spend time and money approaching them. Almost invariably, response rates are simply too low (a tiny fraction of one percent, sometimes measured in hundredths).

Assume, then, that we've managed to enlist new donors via direct mail or, over time, through online media. What's next? Isn't it time to welcome them into the family? I'll cover that topic in the next chapter, "Welcoming New Donors."

Chapter Twelve:
Welcoming New Donors

Treating People Like Part of the Family

Fundraisers are finally coming to understand that direct response cannot be treated simply as a way to haul in gifts. The communications we send our donors or members are just as important for the contributions they make to the relationship-building process that lays the groundwork for more and larger gifts over a long period of time. That relationship-building process involves both online and direct mail messaging:

- An e-mail welcome series launches immediately upon receipt of a donor's or member's first contribution, ideally within hours but no more than a day or two after the gift is received. In the course of the three to five e-mail messages in a welcome series, you'll reinforce the donor's good intentions—combat *buyer's remorse*, to borrow a phrase from commercial marketing—and enumerate some of the best ways for new donors to become engaged in your organization. In exhibits 12.1 to 12.3 you can see the messages that make up a typical e-mail welcome series.

- A direct mail welcome package for new donors or new members rounds out the welcome process. These packages, mailed soon after the receipt of a donor's or member's first gift, are intended to open a dialogue between the individual and the organization. They lay out, simply and clearly, succinctly, and within a single direct mail package, all the benefits of supporting the organization and all the ways that a supporter may become directly involved. The response device in exhibit 12.6 comes from such a welcome package for new members.

EXHIBIT 12.1
Welcome Series E-mail #1, Share Our Strength

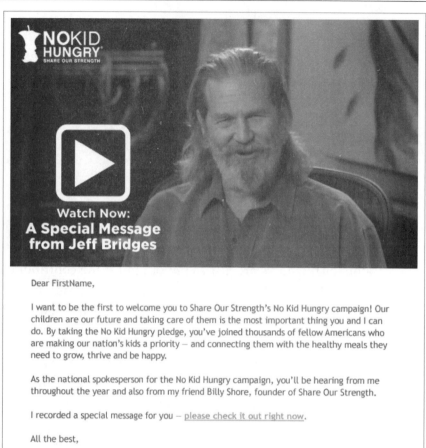

Dear FirstName,

I want to be the first to welcome you to Share Our Strength's No Kid Hungry campaign! Our children are our future and taking care of them is the most important thing you and I can do. By taking the No Kid Hungry pledge, you've joined thousands of fellow Americans who are making our nation's kids a priority — and connecting them with the healthy meals they need to grow, thrive and be happy.

As the national spokesperson for the No Kid Hungry campaign, you'll be hearing from me throughout the year and also from my friend Billy Shore, founder of Share Our Strength.

I recorded a special message for you — please check it out right now.

All the best,

Jeff Bridges
National Spokesperson, No Kid Hungry

NO **KID** HUNGRY

Find us on
Facebook

©**Share Our Strength**, 1730 M Street NW, Washington, DC 20036
Web site: www.strength.org
Email: contactus@strength.org
To unsubscribe: unsubscribe

Source: Share Our Strength's No Kid Hungry Campaign.

First, then, let's see what a full e-mail welcome series looks like. Read the copy in exhibits 12.1 through 12.3. The purpose of these messages couldn't be more obvious, could it?

EXHIBIT 12.2
Welcome Series E-mail #2, Share Our Strength

Having problems seeing this message? View in your browser
Share this message with a friend

NO KID HUNGRY
SHARE OUR STRENGTH

TAKE ACTION!
Speak Up for Children

Dear Reader,

Congress is at work on the 2012 Farm Bill.

You may be thinking, so what? Well, the Farm Bill includes funding for critical federal nutrition programs like SNAP (Supplemental Nutrition Assistance Program), formerly known as food stamps, that help feed hungry kids. And that's why I'm writing to you today.

Drastic cuts to SNAP are on the table for the Farm Bill and nearly half of all SNAP participants are children. If Congress cuts funding for this poverty relieving program, it will affect millions of children and families, leaving them even more vulnerable to hunger.

Will you speak up for children right now, asking your members of Congress to protect SNAP from devastating cuts? Please contact your members of Congress now and urge them to protect SNAP and the kids who rely on this program.

Federal nutrition programs like SNAP are vital to helping struggling families put food on the table. The proposed funding cuts would mean more hungry kids in America. I can't stand for that and I hope neither will you.

Please take a minute to contact your members of Congress using our simple online tool and urge them to stand up for our nation's kids by protecting federal nutrition programs. They need to hear from you, loud and clear.

Thank you for taking action on this very important issue.

Sincerely,

Billy Shore
Founder and CEO

The Farm Bill includes funding for critical federal nutrition programs that help feed hungry kids.

Urge Congress to kids by supporting SNAP and other federal nutrition programs covered by the Farm Bill.

Contact Congress

NOKIDHUNGRY

©**Share Our Strength**, 1730 M Street NW, Washington, DC 20036
Web site: www.strength.org
Email: contactus@strength.org
To unsubscribe: unsubscribe

Source: Share Our Strength's No Kid Hungry Campaign.

In addition to an e-mail welcome series, wise fundraisers may also send a direct mail welcome package. The distinguishing characteristics of such packages are typically the following:

- The welcome message is hard to miss on the outer envelope, which often reads simply "Welcome!"

- The salutation in the letter reads "Dear New _____ Member." Nothing subtle there!

EXHIBIT 12.3
Welcome Series E-mail #3, Share Our Strength

Having problems seeing this message? View in your browser
Share this message with a friend

$20 CAN CONNECT A CHILD TO 200 MEALS

Dear Firstname/Friend,

Increasingly, the face of hunger in this country is the face of a child. With the help of No Kid Hungry pledge takers like you, we're changing that and reaching more children than ever before.

Right now, we are rolling out breakfast challenges, preparing summer meal sites, recruiting schools and governors and mayors, and working to connect kids across the country to healthy meals. But we need your help.

You've already pledged to fight childhood hunger and taken action to strengthen the campaign. Will you take the next step and make your first gift to support the No Kid Hungry campaign?

2012 MEMBERSHIP CARD

[FirstName LastName] [XXXXXXXXX]

Will you help us reach more hungry children than ever before?

Become a Member

When you make your first gift to support the No Kid Hungry campaign, you will join thousands of other supporters dedicated to the cause. Here are just a few things we've accomplished together in the last year:

- Launched an aggressive campaign to reach children during the vulnerable summer months when free school meals are not available. In fact, in six of our No Kid Hungry campaign states we increased the number of meals served by nearly 1 million compared to the year before!

- Dramatically increased the number of children receiving a healthy breakfast by providing grants and supporting school breakfast challenges. As a result, 128 schools in six No Kid Hungry Campaign states started alternative breakfast programs and ensured that thousands of children at risk of hunger started the day ready to learn.

- Provided nearly $7 million in grants to more than 400 community organizations nationwide working to ensure that kids receive nutritious meals on a regular basis.

- Taught nearly 18,000 families how to get more food for their money and cook healthy meals through Cooking Matters.

While we have many successes to celebrate, we have much more work to do to bring an end to childhood hunger. That's why we need your help today.

Missing meals on a regular basis bears long-lasting and harmful effects on a child. It can stunt their physical growth, compromise their immune system, and distract them from school work and other activities.

Imagine the difference you can make in a child's life when you join Share Our Strength and help connect children facing hunger to healthy meals where they live, learn and play! Please give $20, $35 or whatever you can afford today — remember every $1 equals 10 meals for a hungry kid.

From all of us at Share Our Strength, thank you for taking the No Kid Hungry pledge, taking action to speak out for children, and bringing hope to those who need it most..

Sincerely,

Billy Shore
Billy Shore
Founder and CEO

Donate Now

NOKIDHUNGRY

Source: Share Our Strength's No Kid Hungry Campaign.

- The reply device includes a detachable membership card, labeled "your new _____ membership card."

- Both in the letter and on the reply device, a welcome package offers new members the opportunity to enlist in the organization's action alert and its monthly sustainer program. Testing has repeatedly shown that the optimal time to recruit new monthly pledges is shortly after a new member's or donor's first gift is received.

Case Study: Global Fund for Women

On the website dedicated to this book, you'll find two excellent examples of welcome packages, both developed for nonprofit membership organizations that offer members substantial benefits. But what sort of welcome package might a *donor-based* organization provide to newcomers? Without a hefty list of benefits, is there any way to craft a welcome package that will strengthen the relationship with donors?

The answer—you guessed it—is yes. Exhibits 12.4, 12.5, and 12.6 display the welcome package employed by the Global Fund for Women. As you can see, this simple package incorporates most of the elements routinely found in a welcome package—with just a few sheets of paper and without the need to dwell on extensive donor benefits. Witness:

- The letter is personalized and acknowledges the new donor's gift by amount and date.

EXHIBIT 12.4
New Donor Welcome Letter, Global Fund for Women

This is your tax receipt.

No goods or services were provided to the donor in consideration of this gift. The entire amount of this contribution to the Global Fund for Women is tax-deductible.

Global Fund for Women

1375 Sutter Street, Suite 400
San Francisco, CA 94109
415-202-7640
www.globalfundforwomen.org

Ms. Jane Doe
GFW07YB/Ongoing/Pkg. 1: Low$ Welcome
123 Main Street
Anytown, AS 111111

Dear Ms. Doe,

Warm greetings from the Global Fund for Women! Thank you for your contribution of $35.00 on 05/15/07. I am excited to welcome you to our international network of women and men committed to gender equality, social justice, and peace.

I've enclosed a booklet for you that illustrates how your contribution supports women and girls around the world. Thank you again for embarking on a partnership with women on every continent who are standing up—often against the steepest odds—to bring a better future for women, girls, and their communities.

With sincere appreciation and best wishes,

Kavita N. Ramdas
President and CEO

P.S.   We'd like to know more about what issues are important to you. If you can, please take a few moments to fill out the information below. Thank you!

7-YA2W

EXHIBIT 12.5
New Donor Welcome Reply Device, Global Fund for Women

Please take a moment to review and complete the following options. Please detach the survey from your tax receipt above and return your response in the enclosed postage-paid envelope. ▲ ▲ ▲

1. THANK YOU for your recent contribution of $35.00. It is heartwarming to know you share our vision for a better world. Please consider becoming a supporter for ongoing change by making a monthly investment of in the power of women.

☐ YES. I authorize the Global Fund for Women to deduct the following amount each month from my checking account/credit card as indicated below. **I understand I can change the amount or cancel at any time.**

[ ]   [ ] $_____

123456
WELS

Signature: _____

☐ Please deduct the amount indicated above from my checking account each month. I've enclosed a void check.

OR

☐ Please charge the amount indicated above to my credit card each month:
    ☐ Visa   ☐ MasterCard   ☐ American Express

Card # _____ Exp. Date: _____

2. DONOR SURVEY

Please complete this Donor Survey so that we can learn what issues are important to you and verify that our contact information for you is correct.

a) Name: Ms. Jane Doe/GFW07YB/Ongoing/Pkg. 1: Low$ Welcome
b) Address: 123 Main Street
              Anytown, AS 111111

c) Email: _____
d) Home phone #:   (___)_____

e) How do you prefer to be addressed?
    ☐ Ms.   ☐ Mrs.   ☐ Miss   ☐ Mr.   ☐ Dr.   ☐ _____

f) Date of birth: MONTH _____ DAY _____ YEAR _____

Please see over ▶

- The reply device, which is printed on the same sheet as the letter and separated by a perforation, consists of a thank-you, a suggestion that the donor may enlist in the Global Fund's monthly giving program, and a detailed donor survey, which concludes with an ask for an additional contribution.

g) Do you have children? ☐ YES   ☐ NO

h) Below is a list of issues facing women across the globe today. Please check those that are of greatest importance to you.

☐ Violence against women
☐ Access to economic opportunities
☐ Access to health care and sexual and reproductive rights
☐ Girls' access to education
☐ Trafficking and forced prostitution
☐ Political participation and legal rights
☐ Peace building and conflict resolution
☐ Traditional religious and cultural practices
☐ Other _____

i) What regions of the world are of particular interest to you?
☐ Africa   ☐ Middle East and North Africa
☐ Asia   ☐ Eastern Europe
☐ The Caribbean   ☐ Oceania
☐ Latin America   ☐ Other _____

j) If you read and speak a foreign language, please indicate which language(s): _____

3. COMMUNICATION PREFERENCES

The Global Fund for Women takes pride in respecting the wishes of our donors. Please take a moment to check only those boxes that are relevant to you.

a) All current donors receive our print newsletter.

I prefer not to receive this newsletter. ☐

b) Donors with email addresses receive our bi-monthly e-bulletin with current updates.

I prefer not to receive this e-bulletin. ☐

c) You can help us recruit new donors and expand our network by allowing us to exchange your name with other nonprofits we think may be of interest to you.

I do not wish to help in this way. Please do not share my name. ☐

4. PLEASE SEND ME the following:

☐ How to spread my gift over the year (pre-arranged monthly giving)
☐ How to give a gift of stock
☐ How to leave a legacy by making a bequest
☐ How to volunteer my time
☐ How to host a House Party
☐ Annual Report
☐ Recent Global Fund for Women newsletter

5. ADDITIONAL CONTRIBUTION

I'd like to make an additional contribution to help women's groups protect and promote the rights of women and girls and build stronger communities around the world. Here is my gift of:

WEL

☐ **$25**   ☐ **$50**   ☐ **$75**   ☐ **$_____**

☐ I've enclosed a check payable to *Global Fund for Women*.

☐ I prefer to use my credit card.
   Please charge my: ☐ VISA ☐ MasterCard ☐ Amex

Card Number _____

Exp. Date _____ Signature _____

☐ I'd like to make this gift in honor/memory (please circle one) of:

_____

Please send a card acknowledging this gift to:

Name _____

Address _____

City, State, Zip _____

Please return to: **Global Fund for Women**   1375 Sutter Street, Suite 400   San Francisco, CA 94109

- The brochure ("Welcome to the Global Fund for Women") sets the tone for the relationship between the organization and the new donor, reviews the case for giving, and lists several ways that donors may become involved in the work of the fund.

EXHIBIT 12.6
New Donor Welcome Brochure, Global Fund for Women

Warm greetings!

Thank you for choosing to support the courageous efforts of women all over the world working to create communities free from poverty, violence and discrimination.

We are immensely grateful for your support and welcome you to our international network of women and men committed to equality, social justice and peace.

At the Global Fund for Women we believe philanthropy is an opportunity for each of us to participate in social change and to support the issues we believe in.

Unlike most nonprofits, we do not categorize our donors by gift amount. We see all of our supporters as equal partners in our work.

If you have any questions, please contact us. You'll find specific contact information on the back page. Thank you for your contribution, and welcome to our network!

Kavita N Ramdas

Kavita N. Ramdas
President and CEO

The Global Fund for Women is the largest grantmaking foundation in the world that focuses exclusively on women's rights globally.

We believe that women themselves know best how to determine their needs and propose solutions for lasting change. Our flexible grantmaking approach is designed to empower women at the local level.

Unlike most international funders, the Global Fund for Women accepts requests for funding in any format—handwritten, emailed or typed. We also accept requests in any language. This makes us truly accessible to even the most remote or underresourced groups.

All around the world, women and girls are taking the initiative to solve problems in their own communities. These inspiring, courageous leaders are not afraid to encounter opposition, and often risk their lives in pursuit of equality.

Only 7.3% of US philanthropic dollars directly benefit women internationally.

—Foundation Center

We Invest Your Money Wisely

The way in which we do our work is as important as what we do. This philosophy is reflected in our respectful and responsive style of grantmaking and fundraising.

We award grants to women's organizations directly. We depend on the expertise and guidance of a global network of advisors from diverse backgrounds to inform our grantmaking decisions. Grantees provide specific feedback reports on what they have achieved with our grants.

Since 1987, the Global Fund for Women has given away more than $56 million to seed, strengthen and link 3,300 women's groups in over 160 countries.

"At this time, we at SWAA are humbled by the generosity and solidarity of all our partners. You are the ones who have made possible SWAA's efforts to ease the suffering of the people infected and affected by AIDS."

—Society for Women and AIDS in Africa, Sudan

> **"Women face violence, health care inequities, and educational barriers. And yet there's hope ... I know I'm affecting women's lives in a direct way."**
>
> **—Jennifer Weber**
> **Global Fund for Women donor**

The Global Fund for Women provides grants ranging from $500 to $20,000 to women's rights organizations around the world. We fund groups that focus on advancing the rights of women and girls by addressing critical issues, including:

+ Economic independence
+ Women's health and reproductive rights
+ Access to education for women and girls
+ Violence against women
+ Harmful traditional practices
+ The rights of women with disabilities
+ Women's political participation
+ Women in peace-building efforts
+ Access to media, communications, technology and the Internet

This work is only possible with the help of individuals like you. Thank you!

PHOTOGRAPHS BY:
PETER ADAMS; TERRY LORANT;
MARK TUSCHMAN;
STINA KATCHADOURIAN;
REBECCA JANES.

Get Involved!

Your gift of money, resources or time is an opportunity to make a difference in the world. Here's how you can support the work of the Global Fund for Women:

House Party

Organize a House Party and invite your friends and family to learn about the Global Fund for Women. Contact us for your free House Party kit.

Monthly Gift

Provide a consistent contribution each month through our monthly giving program, the *Corazón Network*. Your pre-authorized monthly contribution will ensure we can continue to provide funds where and when needed.

Celebration Gift

Celebrate Mother's Day, the lives of loved ones, birthdays, holidays and other events with a dedicated donation to the Global Fund for Women.

Leave a Legacy

Leave a legacy that represents the things you believe in. Once you have taken care of your loved ones in your will, please consider including a bequest to the Global Fund for Women.

We Invite You to Contact Us
(415) 202-7640

www.globalfundforwomen.org

Global Fund for Women

1375 Sutter Street, Suite 400
San Francisco, CA 94109

 RECYCLED & RECYCLABLE / SOY INK   7-YA5W

Welcome to the Global Fund for Women

How New Donor Welcome Packages Are Different from Other Fundraising Appeals

In nonprofits' continuing search for heightened donor loyalty and higher renewal rates, welcome packages for new donors have become increasingly common. These packets of information mailed to newly recruited members or donors may be fat or thin, elaborate or simple. Typically, however, they share five attributes:

1. They strive to be warm, emphasizing the organization's appreciation rather than its needs and offering additional information. Short copy is common. The welcome letter's purpose is usually to inform the new donor about the organization's programs and its donor benefits and services.

2. Any copy that refers to the new member personally is likely to be vague and general; usually the charity knows too little to personalize the letter in any meaningful way. One important exception is the amount of the initial gift, which may be inserted in the cover letter if it's personalized, or noted on a gift receipt.

3. Some charities use the opportunity to request a second gift or even to suggest that a new donor join a giving club, such as a monthly sustainer program. But it's more common—and I think, more advisable—not to seek a gift with this package. For example, if you've decided that the best time to invite members to join a monthly pledge program is immediately after they join, I suggest you *first* mail them a welcome package and *then*, perhaps a week or ten days later, send the pledge invitation.

4. To introduce new donors to the organization's work, a recent issue of its magazine or newsletter is often enclosed. Sometimes brochures about organization programs and services are included. Welcome packages are often heavy and expensive. They're an investment in future fundraising efforts.

5. Welcome packages frequently offer new donors multiple opportunities to respond—through surveys, requests for additional information, *member-get-a-member* programs, donor options, or other involvement devices.

Six Reasons You Should Send an E-mail Welcome Series and Direct Mail Welcome Packages

Let's take a look first at the many roles that an e-mail welcome series and a direct mail welcome package are created to play. Then we can review several possible elements you might consider including in your own welcome efforts.

It seems to me there are six reasons to go to all this trouble:

1. All donors expect to be thanked for their support. A simple receipt, whether online or in the mail, is probably not enough to make them think you're being nice. And treating members well increases the chances they'll renew their annual support. This is especially important if (like most other charities these days) your nonprofit has a very low first-year renewal rate.

2. Donors are most receptive to your message immediately after making their first gifts. This is the best time to approach them about such fundraising options as monthly sustainer programs or *friend-get-a-friend* efforts. (However, it's not necessarily the best time to ask for a second gift.) If you can move a new member to take action right after joining—almost any action, in fact—you'll be well on your way to building a strong, mutually beneficial, long-term relationship. But timing is important here; receptivity fades fast, and donors can all too easily forget having contributed to a charity that's new to them.

3. Donors' first impression of your organization is likely to affect their views of all subsequent communications. A cheap thank-you, such as a postcard or an impersonal letter, may impress a few donors with its frugality, but far more donors are likely to be flattered by a carefully prepared, well thought out introductory package that underscores how very important their financial support is. I'm convinced most donors secretly think you're wasting money when you send fancy packages to other people but not when you spend money on them.

4. Donors are too often skeptical about how their contributions are put to use. They sometimes need to be persuaded that their gifts accomplish more than raising additional money. By describing your work in detail and offering opportunities for members to contribute more than money, a series of welcome efforts can drive home the message that your organization is lean, hard working, and cost effective. This is true even when an individual member has no interest at all in contributing volunteer time or attending events. The offer and the opportunities communicate an important message.

5. New donors probably won't understand your organization and its programs unless yours is a local group that provides a single, direct, easily grasped service. Any nonprofit that's engaged in multiple projects—especially if it's a large, decentralized, complex nonprofit— will need a well-organized series of welcome messages so donors will understand its work and the role they can play in it. Once donors do understand your organization well, they're much more likely to respond favorably when you ask for additional support.

6. Not all donors are created equal. Some may be delighted to send small monthly contributions. Others may want to contribute only once per year. Still others might be interested in joining a high-dollar giving club. The welcome package is an excellent opportunity to test their preferences on these and other fundraising questions by giving them a questionnaire or at least by clearly offering several different fundraising options and an easy way to request more information about them.

If your organization mails new donors more than a simple tax receipt or thank-you note, you may already be addressing some of the six opportunities I've just listed. But there may be a number of other ways you can accomplish a whole lot more. You might consider adding some enclosures to your thank-you letter or a full-fledged new donor welcome package. Possible enclosures include the following:

- A small brochure or folder that catalogues membership services and benefits

- An involvement device that includes a brief new member survey

- An explanation of how the organization works, either in a brochure or flyer or in the cover letter copy

- A membership card, with an abbreviated listing of membership benefits on the reverse

- A brochure about your monthly sustainer program

- A brochure about your bequest and planned giving programs, if any

- A flyer that includes an order form for merchandise you sell, featuring a discount offer for new members

Now that we've gotten donors in the door and welcomed them properly, we'll turn to the next step: soliciting additional donations. That's the subject of chapter 13, "Appealing for Special Gifts."

Chapter Thirteen:
Appealing for Special Gifts

Bringing Your Case Down to Earth

A special appeal urges donors or members to focus on one of the organization's individual programs, a specific issue, a season of the year, or a particular need or opportunity. Normally, the letter makes clear that funds contributed in response to a special appeal are undesignated—in other words, that they provide general operating support—even though the letter may heavily emphasize a single issue or project.

For example, take Be The Match®. For more than twenty years, the National Marrow Donor Program®, which operates Be The Match, has been helping patients receive life-saving transplants. The Be The Match Foundation® is dedicated to raising the funds needed to help all patients get the transplant they need. What could be more natural for Be The Match than to solicit its donors with a matching gift appeal?

Exhibits 13.1 through 13.5 show the full contents of Be The Match's 2012 direct mail special appeal. In many ways, it's representative of the thousands of special appeals mailed every year by nonprofit organizations to their previous donors.

- The teaser on the outer envelope and headline on the response device ("Special Matching Offer" and "$100,000 Challenge Fund Campaign") both suggest that this is an appeal mailed exclusively to Be The Match donors, and the language in the "Yes" statement just below the headline as well as the phrase "2012 Challenge Fund" on the envelope make that clear, since a particular foundation has pledged to match up to $100,000 by a certain date. It's extremely unlikely that Be The Match would send this appeal to anyone but those who had previously contributed to its work. It just wouldn't be cost effective to do so.

EXHIBIT 13.1

Special Appeal Response Device, Be The Match

$100,000 CHALLENGE FUND CAMPAIGN

YES, I want to double the impact of my gift to Be The Match®—and help patients in need of a life-saving transplant! I understand the Jeff Gordon Children's Foundation will match my contribution dollar-for-dollar if sent before August 31, 2012. Enclosed is my gift:

☐ $100   ☐ $150   ☐ $200

☐ My check is enclosed.
☐ Please charge my credit card. *(See reverse.)*

12ACSDA   000000

Mr. Bill Rehm
#########
###############

BE ✦ **THE MATCH®**
3001 Broadway Street NE | Suite 601
Minneapolis, MN 55413-1753
BeTheMatch.org   2515
                                  12-AC2

▽ Please choose the gift form with the amount you want matched. Be The Match is a 501(c)(3) organization and your contribution is fully tax-deductible. Thank you!

BE ✦ **THE MATCH®**   *This check is non-negotiable, but represents funds from the special matching grant that will match your gift.*
3001 Broadway Street NE | Suite 601
Minneapolis, MN 55413-1753

Check #: 23160
Date: July 20, 2012

Challenge Fund Calculation	
Your check for:	$100
	x2
Total value of your gift:	$200

Pay to the Order of   Be The Match Foundation® $100.00

One Hundred and 00/100   Dollars

Mr. Bill Rehm
#########
###############

Christine Fleming
Authorized Signature

BE ✦ **THE MATCH®**
3001 Broadway Street NE | Suite 601
Minneapolis, MN 55413-1753
BeTheMatch.org

MEMO   With your check for $100, this grant will increase your gift to $200.

BE ✦ **THE MATCH®**   *This check is non-negotiable, but represents funds from the special matching grant that will match your gift.*
3001 Broadway Street NE | Suite 601
Minneapolis, MN 55413-1753

Check #: 23161
Date: July 20, 2012

Challenge Fund Calculation	
Your check for:	$150
	x2
Total value of your gift:	$300

Pay to the Order of   Be The Match Foundation® $150.00

One Hundred and Fifty and 00/100   Dollars

Mr. Bill Rehm
#########
###############

Christine Fleming
Authorized Signature

BE ✦ **THE MATCH®**
3001 Broadway Street NE | Suite 601
Minneapolis, MN 55413-1753
BeTheMatch.org

MEMO   With your check for $150, this grant will increase your gift to $300.

BE ✦ **THE MATCH®**   *This check is non-negotiable, but represents funds from the special matching grant that will match your gift.*
3001 Broadway Street NE | Suite 601
Minneapolis, MN 55413-1753

Check #: 23162
Date: July 20, 2012

Challenge Fund Calculation	
Your check for:	$200
	x2
Total value of your gift:	$400

Pay to the Order of   Be The Match Foundation® $200.00

Two Hundred and 00/100   Dollars

Mr. Bill Rehm
#########
###############

Christine Fleming
Authorized Signature

BE ✦ **THE MATCH®**
3001 Broadway Street NE | Suite 601
Minneapolis, MN 55413-1753
BeTheMatch.org

MEMO   With your check for $200, this grant will increase your gift to $400.

Gift Designation Options

- ❏ Where most needed
- ❏ Supporting Patient Assistance Programs
- ❏ Supporting Research Programs
- ❏ Adding Potential donors to the Be The Match Registry®

BE ❋ THE MATCH®

Be The Match Foundation® raises funds to help patients who need a bone marrow or umbilical cord blood transplant find a donor and receive treatment.

I want to give using my credit card

❏ MasterCard   ❏ VISA   ❏ AMERICAN EXPRESS Cards   ❏ DISCOVER NOVUS

Card Number _____

Expiration Date _____ $ _____ Gift Amount

Cardholder Signature (Required) _____

My E-mail Address _____

Please contact me by e-mail with information and opportunities to help.

Instructions: Please make your check payable to Be The Match Foundation®. To make a gift with your credit card, please fill out the form to the left. Mail your gift with one or more of the Matching Grant checks in the enclosed envelope. Your gift to Be the Match Foundation is fully tax-deductible. Thank you very much.

Gift Designation Options

- ❏ Where most needed
- ❏ Supporting Patient Assistance Programs
- ❏ Supporting Research Programs
- ❏ Adding Potential donors to the Be The Match Registry®

BE ❋ THE MATCH®

Be The Match Foundation® raises funds to help patients who need a bone marrow or umbilical cord blood transplant find a donor and receive treatment.

I want to give using my credit card

❏ MasterCard   ❏ VISA   ❏ AMERICAN EXPRESS Cards   ❏ DISCOVER NOVUS

Card Number _____

Expiration Date _____ $ _____ Gift Amount

Cardholder Signature (Required) _____

My E-mail Address _____

Please contact me by e-mail with information and opportunities to help.

Instructions: Please make your check payable to Be The Match Foundation®. To make a gift with your credit card, please fill out the form to the left. Mail your gift with one or more of the Matching Grant checks in the enclosed envelope. Your gift to Be the Match Foundation is fully tax-deductible. Thank you very much.

Gift Designation Options

- ❏ Where most needed
- ❏ Supporting Patient Assistance Programs
- ❏ Supporting Research Programs
- ❏ Adding Potential donors to the Be The Match Registry®

BE ❋ THE MATCH®

Be The Match Foundation® raises funds to help patients who need a bone marrow or umbilical cord blood transplant find a donor and receive treatment.

I want to give using my credit card

❏ MasterCard   ❏ VISA   ❏ AMERICAN EXPRESS Cards   ❏ DISCOVER NOVUS

Card Number _____

Expiration Date _____ $ _____ Gift Amount

Cardholder Signature (Required) _____

My E-mail Address _____

Please contact me by e-mail with information and opportunities to help.

Instructions: Please make your check payable to Be The Match Foundation®. To make a gift with your credit card, please fill out the form to the left. Mail your gift with one or more of the Matching Grant checks in the enclosed envelope. Your gift to Be the Match Foundation is fully tax-deductible. Thank you very much.

Gift Designation Options

- ❏ Where most needed
- ❏ Supporting Patient Assistance Programs
- ❏ Supporting Research Programs
- ❏ Adding Potential donors to the Be The Match Registry®

BE ❋ THE MATCH®

Be The Match Foundation® raises funds to help patients who need a bone marrow or umbilical cord blood transplant find a donor and receive treatment.

I want to give using my credit card

❏ MasterCard   ❏ VISA   ❏ AMERICAN EXPRESS Cards   ❏ DISCOVER NOVUS

Card Number _____

Expiration Date _____ $ _____ Gift Amount

Cardholder Signature (Required) _____

My E-mail Address _____

Please contact me by e-mail with information and opportunities to help.

Instructions: Please make your check payable to Be The Match Foundation®. To make a gift with your credit card, please fill out the form to the left. Mail your gift with one or more of the Matching Grant checks in the enclosed envelope. Your gift to Be the Match Foundation is fully tax-deductible. Thank you very much.

EXHIBIT 13.2
Special Appeal Letter, Be The Match

2515

3001 Broadway Street NE | Suite 601
Minneapolis, MN 55413-1753
BeTheMatch.org

July 20, 2012

Dear Mr. Rehm,

I'm writing to you today with some wonderful news—for you and also for Be The Match®. We just received confirmation that one of our longtime friends and philanthropic partners has stepped forward with a $100,000 Matching Gift Challenge!

If you are able to make a gift between now and August 31st, your contribution will be matched—dollar-for-dollar—by the Jeff Gordon Children's Foundation. For the next 42 days, you can double the impact of your support for Be The Match.

Be The Match has received this special Matching Gift Challenge opportunity whereby the first $100,000 contributed by supporters like you will be matched. If we receive $100,000 by August 31st, it will actually mean that $200,000 will be available for Be The Match to grow our Be The Match Registry® of potential new marrow donors and bring hope and healing to more patients and their families.

This Matching Gift Challenge from the Jeff Gordon Children's Foundation comes at a particularly good time. As you may know, since our founding in 1987 more than 50,000 patients have received transplants. But each year, more than 10,000 patients with life-threatening diseases such as leukemia and lymphoma need a marrow transplant from an unrelated donor—and so many of our patients are children.

But we must raise $100,000 from Be The Match contributors like you to fully qualify for the matching gift funding.

> **That's why I'm turning to you for help. Your gift of $100 was particularly helpful, so I hope you'll consider making another gift of that amount again today. Your $100 gift will actually be worth $200 if we receive it before August 31st.**

Jeff Gordon—through his own philanthropy and the generosity of the Jeff Gordon Children's Foundation—has been an extraordinary partner in helping Be The Match to match children who need marrow transplants from unrelated donors—and helping kids like six-year old Parker in the enclosed photo.

Mr. Rehm, please know that I am extremely grateful for your last gift to Be The Match in 2011, and that your participation in our Matching Gift Challenge Campaign will also make a big difference in our ability to provide patients with the resources and services they need to improve the quality of life after a transplant.

(over, please)

♻ RECYCLED & RECYCLABLE / SOY INK 12-AC1

Your support makes all our work possible.

Every year, there are more than 10,000 patients in the United States who need a life-saving marrow transplant from an unrelated donor. Be The Match helped 5,200 of those patients receive a transplant last year—approximately one half.

Our goal, in the year ahead, is to improve those odds.

With your support, we want to increase the number of patients for whom we help find a match—including the number of children—to at least 10,000 patients each year. Additionally, we want to educate more doctors about transplant advances in matching and caring for their patients post transplant, and provide more funding for researchers in the science of transplants.

In short, our mission is to lead the way for patients and their families through the entire transplant journey, from diagnosis through survivorship—and with your continuing gifts to Be The Match, you are helping to advance these endeavors.

I ask you to send the most generous gift you possibly can before our $100,000 Matching Gift Offer deadline expires on August 31st, knowing that your support will be matched dollar-for-dollar and will have twice the impact on our ability to help children across the county receive the transplants they need.

Your generosity and compassion are critical to our success—and will help propel us forward in the year ahead.

With many thanks,

Christine Fleming

Christine Fleming
President

P.S.   Your contribution will offer hope and healing to children—and their families—who need marrow transplants to stay alive. And remember, the amount and impact of your gift will be doubled if we receive it within the next 42 days. Please help us reach our $100,000 goal by participating in our Matching Gift Challenge before August 31st! Please don't delay.

EXHIBIT 13.3
Special Appeal Lift Note, Be The Match

Your gift—matched by the Jeff Gordon Children's Foundation—will help children like Parker receive marrow transplants they need!

Each year 10,000 patients with leukemia, lymphoma and other life-threatening diseases need a marrow transplant—<u>but</u> <u>only</u> <u>half</u> <u>receive</u> <u>one</u>. The Jeff Gordon Children's Foundation wants to improve those odds, *and* the number of children who receive life-saving transplants.

This summer, the first $100,000 in contributions from Be The Match® donors like you will be matched—dollar for dollar—by an extraordinary matching gift from the Jeff Gordon Children's Foundation. Your gift, if received by August 31ˢᵗ, will have twice the impact, and will help Be The Match bring hope and healing to more patients and their families.

Please send your gift—of any amount—to Be The Match today!

"Parker is amazing. His courage in the face of cancer is heroic, and his determination to help other children win their fight inspires me to do more."

—Jeff Gordon

BE ❖ **THE MATCH®**

3001 Broadway Street NE, Suite 601 | Minneapolis, MN 55413-1753 | BeTheMatch.org | 1-800-Marrow-2   12-ACS

EXHIBIT 13.4
Special Appeal Outer Envelope, Be The Match

BE ❖ **THE MATCH®**

3001 Broadway Street NE | Suite 601
Minneapolis, MN 55413-1753

INSIDE: Special Matching Offer *Your gift to Be The Match is worth twice as much!*

2012 ❖❖
CHALLENGE FUND ❖❖

♻ RECYCLED & RECYCLABLE / SOY INK   12-ACS

 94610$1014 C011   Ihlodoladhmulllhmulllhmulhlolololulmll

---

- The first underlined phrase in the letter uses the language "supporters like you," confirming that Bill Rehm has already donated at least once to Be The Match. Besides, the personalized salutation, while not unique to donor appeals, is uncommon in new-donor acquisition letters.

EXHIBIT 13.5
Special Appeal Reply Envelope, Be The Match

3001 Broadway Street NE, Suite 601
Minneapolis, MN 55413-1753

PLEASE RUSH:
My Challenge Fund Gift Enclosed

BE THE MATCH®
GIFT PROCESSING CENTER
3001 BROADWAY STREET NE SUITE 601
MINNEAPOLIS MN 55413-2659

♻ RECYCLED & RECYCLABLE / SOY INK 12-AC6

This was produced by the Be The Match Foundation, which will receive 100% of the contributions. Our principal office is at 3001 Broadway Street NE, Suite 601, Minneapolis, MN 55413-2659. Phone: 1-800-MARROW-2. Contributions to Be The Match Foundation are tax deductible for federal income tax purposes. We are committed to extending and improving the lives of patients by creating and delivering innovations in cellular transplant therapies. Requests for copies of recent financial statements or other information may be directed to the address and telephone number listed above. Residents of the following states can also request copies of our annual report to the state, registration, financial information, license in that state and/or summaries of these (items of file vary by state) by writing or calling as indicated: FL: Reg. # CH624. A COPY OF THE OFFICIAL REGISTRATION AND FINANCIAL INFORMATION MAY BE OBTAINED FROM THE DIVISION OF CONSUMER SERVICES BY CALLING 1-800-435-7352 (toll free within FL); MD: Documents and information submitted under the Maryland Solicitations Act are also available, for the cost of postage and copies from the Secretary of State, State House, Annapolis, MD 21401; MS: The official registration and financial information of Be The Match Foundation may be obtained from the Mississippi Secretary of State's office by calling 1-888-236-6167; NJ: INFORMATION FILED WITH THE ATTORNEY GENERAL CONCERNING THIS CHARITABLE SOLICITATION AND THE PERCENTAGE OF CONTRIBUTIONS RECEIVED BY THE CHARITY DURING THE LAST REPORTING PERIOD THAT WERE DEDICATED TO THE CHARIABLE PURPOSE MAY BE OBTAINED FROM THE ATTORNEY GENERAL OF THE STATE OF NEW JERSEY BY CALLING (973) 504-6215 AND IS AVAILABLE ON THE INTERNET AT www.state.nj.us./lps/ca/charfrm.htm; NY: Office of the Attorney General, Department of Law, Charities Bureau, 120 Broadway, New York, NY 10271; PA: The official registration and financial information of Be The Match Foundation may be obtained from the Pennsylvania Department of State by calling toll-free, within Pennsylvania, 1-800-732-0999. VA: State Division of Consumer Affairs, Department of Agricultural and Consumer Services, PO Box 1163, Richmond, VA 23218; WA: Charities Division, Office of the Secretary of State, State of Washington, Olympia, WA 98504-0422, 1-800-332-4483; WV: Residents may obtain a summary from the Secretary of State, State Capital, Charleston, WV 25305; NC: Financial information about this organization and a copy of its license are available from the State Solicitation Licensing Section at 1-888-830-4989. REGISTRATION OR LICENSE IN ANY OF THE ABOVE STATES DOES NOT IMPLY ENDORSEMENT, APPROVAL OR RECOMMENDATION BY THE STATE OR ANY OFFICE THEREOF.

- The gift string, or *ask* string, on the response device is limited to three tightly clustered ask amounts. Clearly, Be The Match knows something about this fellow Bill Rehm, because he previously donated $100 (as a single gift, in all likelihood). In special appeals such as this, the lowest ask amount is usually based on a donor's highest previous contribution, and the asks that follow represent upgrades from that level.

- The check-like involvement devices below the reply device bring into tight focus the specific amounts noted in the gift string. Although it's not unknown for nonprofits to use devices such as this in new-donor acquisition appeals, the amounts specified are much higher than would be the case in most prospect mailings.

- On the reverse of the reply device and involvement devices, the left-hand column offers Bill Rehm an opportunity to choose how his gift may be used. Donor choice is relatively uncommon in acquisitions but is frequently used in special appeals, where it makes more of a difference.

This matching gift appeal was an integrated campaign that also included the materials in exhibits 13.6 through 13.8.

EXHIBIT 13.6
Online Appeal E-mail #1, Be The Match

Having trouble viewing this e-mail? View online

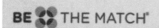 BE THE MATCH®

First $100,000 raised by August 31 will be *doubled*

Dear Eric,

Jeff Gordon, an extraordinary partner both through his own philanthropy and the generosity of the Jeff Gordon Children's Foundation, has presented an exciting opportunity right when we need it the most. The Jeff Gordon Children's Foundation has offered to match the first $100,000 we raise!

This means that from now until August 31 every dollar you donate will be doubled — up to $100,000.

This extraordinary generosity comes at the perfect time. Dollars are much harder to raise in the summer, but patients' needs for help in finding marrow donor matches and transplant assistance is only growing.

That's why taking full advantage of this opportunity is vital. From adding new, lifesaving matches to the registry, straight through to patient recovery assistance — every dollar will go twice as far in helping marrow transplant patients like six-year-old Parker (pictured at right) get their second chance at life.

You can help us secure every dollar possible for patients by sending your gift now.

Thank you for standing strong with us for the thousands of patients every year needing a bone marrow transplant. Your compassion is their best chance of finding a lifesaving match.

Sincerely,

Christine Fleming

Christine Fleming, President
Be The Match Foundation

P.S. Don't forget to send your gift by August 31 to be matched by the Jeff Gordon Children's Foundation.

(l to r) Jeff Gordon and Parker

"Parker is amazing. His courage in the face of cancer is heroic, and his determination to help other children win their fight inspires me to do more." - Jeff Gordon

Through the *Jeff Gordon Children's Foundation*, the first $100,000 donated will be matched.

MAKE A GIFT

MAKE A GIFT

BeTheMatch.org | update your contact information | privacy statement | unsubscribe
© 2012 National Marrow Donor Program

If you unsubscribe, your e-mail address will be removed from general Be The Match® and Be The Match Foundation® e-communications. If you're a member of the registry and receive the registry member monthly e-newsletter, you will continue to receive it. We must keep our registry member e-mail list separate to protect your confidentiality. Every e-newsletter includes a link at the bottom you can use to unsubscribe from the e-newsletter if you wish.

Be The Match® is operated by the National Marrow Donor Program®
3001 Broadway St. N.E., Suite 100, Minneapolis, MN 55413-1753 | (800) MARROW-2

EXHIBIT 13.7
Online Appeal E-mail #2, Be The Match

Having trouble viewing this e-mail? View online

DONATE NOW TO HAVE YOUR GIFT DOUBLED!

Dear Eric,

The August 31 deadline for the Jeff Gordon Children's Foundation Matching Challenge is fast approaching, and we're so close to reaching our $100,000 goal!

We need your help to cross the finish line! Please make a gift by August 31 to capture every dollar possible to help blood cancer & blood disease patients and their families.

Your gift, combined with Jeff Gordon's matching dollars, means more lifesaving potential donors on the registry, greater assistance to recovering patients, and more second chances at life.

Every dollar you donate before the deadline will be doubled. Make your gift now and take full advantage of this opportunity.

Thank you for your dedication,

Christine Fleming

Christine Fleming

P.S. Don't forget to make your gift today, to be matched by the Jeff Gordon Children's Foundation.

Last chance to have your gift matched by Jeff Gordon Children's Foundation!

DOUBLE YOUR GIFT

EXHIBIT 13.8
Landing Page Hero Image for Online Appeal, Be The Match

How Special Appeals Are Different from Other Fundraising Appeals

Most special appeals share the following six characteristics:

1. They contain specific time references because special appeals are usually mailed only once, through a narrow window on the calendar. To emphasize their urgency and underline how different they are from other solicitations from the same charity, most special appeals refer to passing conditions or one-time opportunities or circumstances—as in the case illustrated here—or a particular holiday or season.

2. The ask amount is (normally) variable. Usually, a special appeal is segmented; that is, different versions of the appeal are sent to distinct groups of donors. For example, those who've never contributed more than $50 at any one time might be asked for $75, and previous donors of between $200 and $499 would be urged to send a minimum of $500.

3. In most cases, there are specific program references. These are, after all, special appeals. More often than not, the funds requested are to support one particular project or program.

4. Special appeal letters are frequently short—just one or two pages. Many low-budget organizations, as well as some that are well heeled, include few inserts. The assumption is that proven donors are well acquainted with the charity's work and need few reminders about its value. This assumption is questionable, but it's common nonetheless. Also, inserts such as brochures or flyers may make a mailing seem less personal, blunting its effect. (There are many exceptional circumstances that justify such inserts, however. The dream catcher package from St. Joseph's Indian School, shown in chapter 8, is a good example. But even the letter in that package is a short one.)

5. A special appeal is far more likely than a donor acquisition mailing to be personalized. It's also more likely to use *live postage* (stamps) and high-quality paper. The extra expense is often considerable, and it's magnified by the lower volume that's also typical of mailings to proven donors. But the resulting higher cost per unit tends to be justified by the response, which is customarily about five to seven times as great as that from a donor acquisition mailing.

6. The copy is likely to be warm and personal. It's built on individual donor histories. A charity knows a few things about its proven donors, such as when they started giving, the sizes of their largest gifts, and the number of gifts they've sent. In a well-run fundraising program, those things are reflected in the frequent special appeals mailed in search of additional support.

Those six characteristics apply to special appeals in general. However, there are also several types of special appeals, and they are distinctive in their own ways. The first of these, year-end appeals, is the topic in the next chapter.

Chapter Fourteen:
Asking for Year-End Contributions

Making the Most of the Holiday Spirit

For the overwhelming majority of Americans, the final weeks of the calendar year are a time for giving. It's no accident that a hugely disproportional share of the funds that nonprofit organizations raise each year is realized in the several weeks before New Year's. Nor is it coincidental that virtually every nonprofit organization that has its fundraising act together mails a year-end appeal to its donors or members.

There are many types and formats of year-end appeals. The examples in this chapter illustrate two of those types that my colleagues and I have found especially productive: a year-end survey (Union of Concerned Scientists), and a holiday card (Center for Victims of Torture).

The business end of most year-end appeals resembles the reply device in the Center for Victims of Torture (CVT) appeal (exhibit 14.1) and the top segment of the 8-by-14-inch sheet from the Union of Concerned Scientists (UCS) (exhibit 14.2).

At least two elements show that both these letters are obviously year-end appeals to donors:

- They say so. You can't mistake the words "my special year-end gift" on the CVT response device or "my tax-deductible year-end contribution" in the UCS copy. No subtlety here (and none called for).

- CVT's ask amounts are high enough to suggest that the people to whom this appeal was mailed have a history of support for the organization. Few nondonors would seriously consider gifts so generous. Although the ask amounts in the UCS package are low, they all fall within a narrow range, probably indicating that John Doe sent one

EXHIBIT 14.1

Year-End Appeal Response Device, Center for Victims of Torture

MY 2011 YEAR-END SUPPORT

<u>Yes</u>, I want to support torture victims around the world. Enclosed is my special year-end gift to help survivors reclaim their lives.

❏ $100   ❏ $200   ❏ $_____

☐ My check is enclosed
☐ Please charge my credit card (details on reverse)

11AHSDC 000000

Mr. Bill Rehm
#########
##############

The
CENTER for
VICTIMS of
TORTURE

649 DAYTON AVENUE
ST. PAUL, MN 55104
www.cvt.org

Your contribution to the Center for Victims of Torture is tax-deductible. If you wish to use your credit card to make a gift, please fill out the information on the reverse. You may also make a gift via our secure server at www.cvt.org. CVT welcomes gifts of stock as well. To arrange for a transfer, please call Ashley Gotreau at 1-877-265-8775.

❏ **Please charge my credit card:** ❏ VISA   ❏ MasterCard   ❏ American Express   ❏ Discover

Card #_____ Exp. date _____

Signature _____

Phone _____ Email address _____

NOTICE TO CONTRIBUTORS: Many states require charities that solicit funds from the public to register with the state agency regulating charities. Although our financial report is always sent free to anyone requesting a copy, certain states require us to advise you that a copy of our financial report is also available from them. The Center for Victims of Torture, 649 Dayton Avenue, St. Paul, MN 55104

FLORIDA — A COPY OF THE OFFICIAL REGISTRATION AND FINANCIAL INFORMATION MAY BE OBTAINED FROM THE DIVISION OF CONSUMER SERVICES BY CALLING TOLL-FREE, 1-800-435-7352 WITHIN THE STATE. REGISTRATION DOES NOT IMPLY ENDORSEMENT, APPROVAL, OR RECOMMENDATION BY THE STATE. (SC-11363) **MARYLAND —** For the cost of copies and postage, Office of the Secretary of State, State House, Annapolis, MD 21401. **MISSISSIPPI —** The official registration and financial information of the Center for Victims of Torture may be obtained from the Mississippi Secretary of State's office by calling 1-888-236-6167. Registration by the Secretary of State does not imply endorsement. **NEW JERSEY —** INFORMATION FILED WITH THE ATTORNEY GENERAL CONCERNING THIS CHARITABLE SOLICITATION MAY BE OBTAINED FROM THE ATTORNEY GENERAL OF THE STATE OF NEW JERSEY BY CALLING 973-504-6215. REGISTRATION WITH THE ATTORNEY GENERAL DOES NOT IMPLY ENDORSEMENT. **NEW YORK —** Office of the Attorney General, Department of Law, Charities Bureau, 120 Broadway, New York, NY 10271. **NORTH CAROLINA —** Financial information about this organization and a copy of its license are available from the State Solicitation Licensing Branch at (919) 807-2214. The license is not an endorsement by the state. **PENNSYLVANIA —** The official registration and financial information of the Center for Victims of Torture may be obtained from the Pennsylvania Department of State by calling toll-free, within Pennsylvania, 1-800-732-0999. Registration does not imply endorsement. **VIRGINIA —** State Division of Consumer Affairs, Department of Agricultural and Consumer Services, PO Box 1163, Richmond, VA 23218. **WASHINGTON —** Charities Division, Office of the Secretary of State, State of Washington, Olympia, WA 98504-0422, 1-800-332-4483. **WEST VIRGINIA —** Residents may obtain a summary from the Secretary of State, State Capitol, Charleston, WV 25305. Registration with any of these states does not imply endorsement.   12/10

RECYCLED & RECYCLABLE / SOY INK 11-AH2

EXHIBIT 14.2

Year-End Appeal Response Device, Union of Concerned Scientists

I SUPPORT A HEALTHY ENVIRONMENT AND A SAFER WORLD.

Yes, Kevin! I'm proud to have played a key role in UCS's victories this year! But I know we have a great deal of work to do on building a healthy environment and safer world. I'm enclosing my tax-deductible year-end contribution of: [35]

❏ $40   ❏ $35   ❏ $25   ❏ Other $_____

As a member since 1991, your feedback is greatly appreciated.

Mr. John Doe
123 Main Street
Anytown, US 00000
UCS11AJ/12-7-11/SURVEY APPEAL

❏ Please charge my credit card (see back).

My email address is:

_____

Union of Concerned Scientists
Citizens and Scientists for Environmental Solutions

0000402298000011AJ22IC00000UN0000000000040003500254

2011 ANNUAL MEMBERSHIP SURVEY

Membership #:	402298
Member Since:	1991

Please take just a few minutes to answer the following 11 short questions. Your responses will help us strengthen our work for a healthy environment and a safer world. Thank you very much for participating!

Please help us make sure our records are accurate.

1. We want to make sure that our records reflect the correct spelling of your name and address. Please verify your contact information printed above, and note any changes or corrections.

2. Do you receive email updates from UCS?

❏ Yes.

❏ No, but I'd like to. My email address is:

_____

❏ No, thank you.

Please give us feedback on our work.

3. Which areas of UCS' work are of most interest to you? *(Please select your top five.)*

❏ Translating and communicating climate change science

❏ Advocating for fuel-efficient vehicles

❏ Promoting sustainable agriculture

❏ Transforming U.S. nuclear weapons policy

❏ Minimizing the risks of nuclear power

❏ Advancing renewable energy technology

❏ Protecting tropical forests to address climate change

❏ Fighting dirty coal power plants

❏ Restoring scientific integrity in public policy

4. How interesting do you find the following types of information from UCS?

Scale 1-5:
Least interested—Somewhat interested—Very interested

UCS authored scientific research and technical analysis

1 ___   2 ___   3 ___   4 ___   5 ___

Information on advocacy opportunities

1 ___   2 ___   3 ___   4 ___   5 ___

Government policy and legislative updates

1 ___   2 ___   3 ___   4 ___   5 ___

Consumer information

1 ___   2 ___   3 ___   4 ___   5 ___

Other: _____

1 ___   2 ___   3 ___   4 ___   5 ___

Are there other ways you'd like to engage with UCS?

5. Would you like to receive information about the UCS monthly giving program, Partners for the Earth?

❏ Yes.

❏ I'm already a member.

❏ No, thank you.

❏ I'd like to join now! (Please provide your credit card information on the back of the reply form.)

6. Would you be interested in meeting with UCS staff members if they are in your area?

❏ Yes.

❏ No.

7. Have you considered including UCS in your will?

❏ Yes, I've already included UCS in my will.

❏ I've considered it and would like to receive additional information about:

❏ Wills and charitable bequests

❏ Gifts that provide income for life

❏ Making UCS a beneficiary of retirement plans

❏ No, I'm not interested right now.

Please continue on reverse

☐ **Please charge my one-time gift as noted on front.**

☐ **Please enroll me in the Partners for the Earth monthly giving program!**
I authorize UCS to charge my credit card monthly in the amount of:
☐ **$12**   ☐ **$15**   ☐ **$20**   ☐ **$_____**   ($10/month minimum)

☐ VISA   ☐ MasterCard   ☐ American Express   ☐ Discover

Card # _____   Expiration date _____

Signature _____

☐ Please send me information about including UCS in my estate plans.

Our careful and effective use of your donations has earned UCS the highest honors a charity can receive: a four-star rating from Charity Navigator, an accreditation seal from the Better Business Bureau, and an 'A' rating from the American Institute of Philanthropy.

8. How well do you think each of the following UCS publications, our magazine *Catalyst*, our newsletter *Earthwise*, and our e-newsletter *Pulse*, fulfill the following roles? (Please fill in your rating, with 1 being fully agrees with the statement, and 5 being fully disagrees with the statement.)

Provides information that is important to me

___ *Catalyst*   ___ *Earthwise*   ___ *Pulse*

Tells me how my UCS contributions is used

___ *Catalyst*   ___ *Earthwise*   ___ *Pulse*

Gives me information about how to become more involved

___ *Catalyst*   ___ *Earthwise*   ___ *Pulse*

I'd prefer to receive it via email.

☐ *Catalyst*   ☐ *Earthwise*   ☐ *Pulse*

My email address is:

_____

Can we learn a little more about you?

9. What are the primary reasons you support UCS? (*Please check your top three.*)

☐ UCS combines scientific analysis, public policy, and citizen activism to protect human health and the environment.

☐ UCS has a long history of success working with both Republican and Democratic policy makers and administrations.

☐ UCS provides sound scientific expertise for use in national policy debates.

☐ UCS works in collaboration with other environmental, security and health organizations.

☐ UCS develops initiatives on the state level that can be replicated nationally.

☐ Other: _____

10. Please tell us a little about your background. (*If retired, please answer regarding your former career.*)

My occupation is:

_____

Highest degree obtained:

_____

If you are a medical professional or scientist:

My field or specialty is:

_____

11. Have you visited the UCS website at www.ucsusa.org?

☐ Yes.
☐ No.

If yes, when you visit are you (*check all that apply*):

☐ Looking for information about issues you are concerned about

☐ Looking for information about technologies

☐ Making a donation

☐ Checking on the latest policy news

☐ Reading entries at the new UCS blog, *The Equation* (blog.ucsusa.org)

☐ Searching for a specific UCS report or analysis

☐ Seeking opportunities to take action

☐ Other: _____

Another easy way to get timely updates and information from UCS is by signing up for our Online Action Network.

If you would like to do so please provide your email address:

_____

Please provide any additional suggestions and comments on a separate sheet. Although we may not be able to respond individually to all comments, we appreciate hearing from you. Thank you for your feedback and your support!

Please return this survey in the enclosed self-addressed envelope, or mail to:

Union of Concerned Scientists
Two Brattle Square
Cambridge, MA, 02138-3780

To donate online go to www.ucsusa.org/2011

Source: Union of Concerned Scientists, 2011 Member Survey Appeal. Used by permission.

or more gifts of no more than $25, and UCS hopes he'll upgrade to a slightly higher level.

The CVT package components pictured in exhibits 14.3 through 14.6 offer additional, incontrovertible evidence that this is a year-end appeal.

EXHIBIT 14.3
Year-End Appeal Holiday Card, Center for Victims of Torture

Your generosity provides hope and healing to thousands of torture
survivors as they reclaim their lives and rebuild their communities.

Thank you for being part of our community of healing in 2011.
May the year ahead be a year of good health and renewed
hope for you and your loved ones.

*Warmest wishes from all of us at
the Center for Victims of Torture*

PHOTO © JANE REILLY

The mission of the Center for Victims of Torture is to heal the wounds of torture on
individuals, their families, and their communities and to stop torture worldwide.

The
CENTER for
VICTIMS of
TORTURE

649 Dayton Avenue · St. Paul, MN 55104
www.cvt.org

RECYCLED & RECYCLABLE / SOY INK   11-AH5

EXHIBIT 14.4

Year-End Appeal Letter, Center for Victims of Torture

The
CENTER for
VICTIMS of
TORTURE
Restoring the Dignity of
the Human Spirit

Douglas A. Johnson
EXECUTIVE DIRECTOR

December 7, 2011

Dear Mr. Rehm,

As you know, at the end of January, I will step down as CVT's Executive Director. It's been a remarkable 23-year run for me—and I'm profoundly grateful for all the support you've given to the Center for Victims of Torture and to me personally.

You have been with CVT since your first gift in 2007, and I hope the enclosed holiday card from the entire CVT staff shows the depth of our appreciation.

I'm writing you this short note as a follow up to my letter last month that highlighted our achievements in 2011—and pointed to some ongoing challenges in 2012. I asked you to be among those who step forward to make a special year-end gift that will enable CVT's new Executive Director to hit the ground running.

If you've just sent your gift, please forgive this reminder, and accept my heartfelt thanks. And if you haven't yet found time to make a contribution, I urge you to take a moment now to make your year-end gift to the Center for Victims of Torture.

With new and ongoing CVT initiatives being planned in Kenya, Jordan, the Democratic Republic of Congo, Tunisia, Egypt, and here in the United States, we need your continuing help. A gift of $100 would really help; a gift of $200 would help even more.

Thank you again for your generosity and partnership. May your holiday celebrations be filled with joy and the New Year bring you happiness and health.

With warm wishes for the holidays,

[signature]

Douglas A. Johnson

P.S.   One of my favorite Winston Churchill quotes has always been: *"We make a living by what we get, we make a life by what we give."* Your gift of $100 or $200 would be a gift of hope for torture survivors trying to reclaim their lives. Please give generously.

RESTORING THE DIGNITY OF THE HUMAN SPIRIT

The Center for Victims of Torture works to heal the wounds of torture on individuals, their families and their communities and to stop torture worldwide.

649 DAYTON AVENUE · ST. PAUL, MN 55104 · TELEPHONE 1-877-265-8775 · FAX 612-436-2600 · www.cvt.org

11-AH1

EXHIBIT 14.5
Year-End Appeal Outer Envelope, Center for Victims of Torture

THE CENTER FOR VICTIMS OF TORTURE
649 Dayton Avenue • St. Paul, MN 55104 • www.cvt.org

Mr. Bill Rehm
#########
##############

9461041014

RECYCLED & RECYCLABLE / SOY INK   11-AH3

EXHIBIT 14.6
Year-End Appeal Reply Envelope, Center for Victims of Torture

The
CENTER for
VICTIMS of
TORTURE
649 Dayton Avenue   St. Paul, MN 55104
www.cvt.org

ATTN: My Special Year-end Gift Enclosed

THE CENTER FOR VICTIMS OF TORTURE
GIFT PROCESSING CENTER
PO BOX 6030
ALBERT LEA MN 56007-6630

RECYCLED & RECYCLABLE / SOY INK   11-AH6

EXHIBIT 14.7
Year-End Appeal Letter, Union of Concerned Scientists

 Union of Concerned Scientists
Citizens and Scientists for Environmental Solutions

Two Brattle Square   Cambridge, MA 02138-3780
www.ucsusa.org   member@ucsusa.org   (800) 666-8276

Kevin Knobloch, President

December 7, 2011

Mr. John Doe
123 Main Street
Anytown, US 00000
UCS11AJ/12-7-11/SURVEY APPEAL

Dear Mr. Doe,

Before this year draws to a close, I want to thank you one more time for being such a valued partner in all of the Union of Concerned Scientists' work throughout 2011.

We all recognize that the victories won over the past 12 months would not have been possible without your help. A short list of the more notable accomplishments would include:

- California passing our nation's strongest renewable energy standard, mandating that 33% of the state's power come from renewable resources by 2020, a measure that will work to drive the rapid growth of the renewables industry;

- The U.S Senate ratifying the new START arms limitation treaty, which will help reduce the threat that still exists from nuclear weapons;

- An agreement between the Obama Administration and automakers to cut carbon and other pollution through significantly increased fuel efficiency standards, setting the average for all passenger vehicles to nearly 55 mpg by 2025.

UCS played a significant role in helping to shape and win adoption of each of these policies. And that means you should take pride in helping to have brought about these important achievements. These accomplishments are all the more impressive when you consider the fierce, well-funded opposition from industry lobbyists that needed to be overcome.

But Mr. Doe, we can't afford self-congratulation; the progress we've made toward a healthy environment and safer world could be reversed next year … unless we continue working together to ensure that sound science drives our nation's environmental, public health and security policies.

Here's how you can help right now:

1) **Provide your feedback.** We value your input. In case you have not yet returned the Member Survey we sent you a few weeks ago, I've enclosed another copy for you. Your answers will help shape our strategies for winning tough battles over the coming weeks and months.

2) **Send a year-end gift to UCS.** Whether you can build on your record of support for UCS with a tax-deductible gift of $35, $40, or an even more generous one, it's important for you to act now so we can get 2012 off to the strongest possible start.

(over, please)

The holiday card ("Warmest wishes from all of us"), the personalized letter (not just the salutation but the fifth-paragraph copy as well), and the first-class commemorative stamps both on the carrier envelope and on the reply envelope—all these elements are signs of the care and expense the Center for Victims of Torture has invested in what is obviously a very important appeal.

Similarly, the UCS year-end appeal that appears in exhibits 14.7 through 14.10 could hardly be anything but exactly what it is. The phrase "year-end gift" appears repeatedly and the letter is highly personalized on page one.

You can be sure that coal, oil and gas industry lobbyists, the politicians who do their bidding, and climate change deniers aren't waiting for the New Year to ramp up their assaults on standards that protect our environment and health—and science itself.

We can't afford to wait either! That's why I'm asking you to return your survey and year-end gift now so UCS can immediately get going on …

- Pressing the Nuclear Regulatory Commission to improve the safety and security of U.S. nuclear power plants to protect the 120 million U.S. citizens who live within 50 miles of a reactor, and to make sure a disaster like the one in Japan this year does not happen here;

- Working to fully implement the 2025 average vehicle fuel economy standards for cars and light trucks to nearly 55 mpg, and meet the longer-term goal of cutting by 50% our dependence on oil as a source of energy by 2030;

- Continue our efforts to expose those who mislead the public about the reality of global warming, and defending the ability of scientists to maintain their freedom from political interference;

- Working to reduce heat-trapping emissions by shutting down old and dirty coal plants and increasing investments in wind, solar and other renewable energy sources; and,

- Putting independent science and analysis front and center in Washington and nationwide to combat the increasing misuse of science for purely political or financial gain.

Those are just some of our top priorities for 2012, but hopefully enough to show why your support is so urgently needed.

Once again, thank you for sticking with—and fighting alongside—UCS this year. I look forward to working with you to make next year another year of progress toward a healthy environment and safer world.

Sincerely,

Kevin Knobloch
President

P.S.   If you've already sent in your completed survey, please forgive this reminder and accept my thanks for taking the time to provide your feedback. But if you still haven't sent your survey or your year-end tax-deductible gift, I urge you to do so now. Thank you.

♻ RECYCLED & RECYCLABLE / SOY INK 11-AJ1C

Source: Union of Concerned Scientists, 2011 Member Survey Appeal. Used by permission.

Also, for any of the tens of thousands of very long-term UCS members, "Annual Membership Surveys" of this sort are a long tradition that was begun soon after the organization's founding in 1969.

Both of the foregoing examples are traditional direct mail year-end appeals. For at least a decade now, however, we've been learning about the extraordinary power of online appeals in the closing days of the year. Typically, the year-end e-mail sequence includes at least one message preceding or following (or both) a direct mail letter, another message shortly after

---

EXHIBIT 14.8

Year-End Appeal Buckslip, Union of Concerned Scientists

Give with Confidence

We are committed to being good stewards of your money.

Our careful and effective use of your donations has earned UCS the highest honors a charity can receive: a four-star rating from Charity Navigator, an accreditation seal from the Better Business Bureau, and an 'A' rating from the American Institute of Philanthropy.

Thank you for your support!

Our work is noticed nationwide:

"The Union of Concerned Scientists, one of the leading voices in the push to combat global warming…"
—*The Minneapolis Star-Tribune*

"If the deniers of global warming are so concerned about the science, they should heed the Union of Concerned Scientists."
—*The Philadelphia Inquirer*

 Union of Concerned Scientists   Two Brattle Square
Cambridge, MA 02138-3780
www.ucsusa.org   (800) 666-8276

Our financial report is sent free to anyone requesting a copy and certain states require us to advise you that a copy is also available from them. If you desire a copy of our official registration or financial information, please contact UNION OF CONCERNED SCIENTISTS, Two Brattle Square, Cambridge, MA 02138-3780, or any of the following state agencies:

FLORIDA: A COPY OF THE OFFICIAL REGISTRATION AND FINANCIAL INFORMATION MAY BE OBTAINED FROM THE DIVISION OF CONSUMER SERVICES BY CALLING TOLL-FREE 1-800-435-7352 WITHIN THE STATE. REGISTRATION DOES NOT IMPLY ENDORSEMENT, APPROVAL, OR RECOMMENDATION BY THE STATE. (CH-3090) **ILLINOIS**: Charitable Trust and Solicitations Bureau, 100 West Randolph St., 12th floor, Chicago, IL 60601. **MARYLAND**: For the cost of copies and postage: Office of the Secretary of State, State House, Annapolis, MD 21401. **MICHIGAN**: Registration no: 9641. **MISSISSIPPI**: The official registration and financial information of the Union of Concerned Scientists may be obtained from the Mississippi Secretary of State's office by calling 1-888-236-6167. Registration by the Secretary of State does not imply endorsement. **NEW JERSEY**: INFORMATION FILED WITH THE ATTORNEY GENERAL CONCERNING THIS CHARITABLE SOLICITATION MAY BE OBTAINED FROM THE ATTORNEY GENERAL OF THE STATE OF NEW JERSEY BY CALLING 973-504-6215. REGISTRATION WITH THE ATTORNEY GENERAL DOES NOT IMPLY ENDORSEMENT. **NEW YORK**: Office of the Attorney General, Department of Law, Charities Bureau,120 Broadway, New York, NY 10271. **NORTH CAROLINA**: FINANCIAL INFORMATION ABOUT THIS ORGANIZATION AND A COPY OF ITS LICENSE ARE AVAILABLE FROM THE STATE SOLICITATION LICENSING BRANCH AT 1-888-830-4989. The license is not an endorsement by the state. **PENNSYLVANIA**: The official registration and financial information of the Union of Concerned Scientists may be obtained from the Pennsylvania Department of State by calling toll-free, within Pennsylvania, 1-800-732-0999. Registration does not imply endorsement. **VIRGINIA**: State Division of Consumer Affairs, Department of Agricultural and Consumer Services, PO Box 1163, Richmond, VA 23218. 1-800-552-9963. **WASHINGTON**: Charities Division, Office of the Secretary of State, State of Washington, Olympia, WA 98504-0422, 1-800-332-4483. **WEST VIRGINIA**: Residents may obtain a summary from: Secretary of State, State Capitol, Charleston, WV 25305.

REGISTRATION WITH ANY OF THESE STATES DOES NOT IMPLY ENDORSEMENT, APPROVAL, OR RECOMMENDATION BY THE STATE.

RECYCLED & RECYCLABLE / SOY INK 11-AI5A

Source: Union of Concerned Scientists, 2011 Member Survey Appeal. Used by permission.

EXHIBIT 14.9

Year-End Appeal Outer Envelope, Union of Concerned Scientists

 Kevin Knobloch, President

Union of Concerned Scientists   Two Brattle Square
Cambridge, MA 02138-3780

FIRST CLASS MAIL

Mr. John Doe
123 Main Street
Anytown, US 00000
UCS11AJ/12-7-11/SURVEY APPEAL

RECYCLED & RECYCLABLE / SOY INK   11-AJ3C

Source: Union of Concerned Scientists, 2011 Member Survey Appeal. Used by permission.

EXHIBIT 14.10
Year-End Appeal Reply Envelope, Union of Concerned Scientists

⊛ RECYCLED & RECYCLABLE / PRINTED WITH SOY INK   11-A#6   ⊷⊞⊶

32nd Annual UCS Membership Survey

‖ ‖ ‖

PLACE
YOUR
STAMP
HERE

UNION OF CONCERNED SCIENTISTS
PO BOX 4123
WOBURN MA 01888-4123

լսիկլիլ․սիկիկիլիկ․ կիդիկիսիկիկիսիկ․ կիկ․ լ․սիկ

Source: Union of Concerned Scientists, 2011 Member Survey Appeal. Used by permission.

Christmas, and a final e-mail message on the thirtieth of December. The last two e-mails emphasize the tax advantages of giving before New Year's Day. (Even though that advantage is trivial or nonexistent for most donors, mention of it is still a useful trigger for giving.) Exhibits 14.11 through 14.16 offer an example of a year-end e-mail series for AmeriCares.

The date in exhibit 14.11, which shows the first e-mail in this year-end series, is December 9. The "From" line in this message, as in the rest of the series, features AmeriCares' chief executive. The bright, bold "Donate Now" buttons in the graphic sidebar and at the bottom are regular features of the series too.

In exhibit 14.12, AmeriCares employs a harder-hitting subject line ("Help us save lives this holiday season") in a message that contains the same mission-central thrust. The date this message was sent is December 15, ten days before Christmas.

The third e-mail in the AmeriCares year-end e-mail series (exhibit 14.13) is dated December 20, as the holiday shopping season picks up—and many people's thoughts begin turning to year-end giving.

Just two days later, on December 22, the fourth AmeriCares e-mail (exhibit 14.14) arrives, dressed up as a holiday greeting card.

Now, three days after Christmas, AmeriCares delivers the message "Three days left: Save lives now" (exhibit 14.15).

"Donate by midnight tonight—save lives" reads the subject line in the sixth and final message in the AmeriCares year-end e-mail series (exhibit 14.16). Believe it or not, this is the one that brings in a huge share of the money generated by the series as a whole.

EXHIBIT 14.11
Year-End Online Appeal E-mail #1, AmeriCares

Subject: ADV: Counting on you this holiday season
Date: Friday, December 9, 2011 10:53:32 AM ET
From: Curt Welling, AmeriCares
To: Eric Overman

AmeriCares
A Passion to Help. The Ability to Deliver.

Dear Eric,

Around the world and here at home, when disaster strikes, when people are in urgent and desperate need of humanitarian aid — AmeriCares will be there.

With your renewed support today, AmeriCares will be able to continue to provide emergency medical relief and humanitarian assistance to men, women and children plunged into crisis because of natural or man-made disasters.

Donate now to help AmeriCares continue to deliver lifesaving aid to millions in need through our current and ongoing disaster relief programs:

Donate now to provide emergency relief to people in need.

Donate Now

- AmeriCares responded to crisis-level flooding in El Salvador and throughout Central America with shipments of medicines, relief supplies and nutritional supplements along with other emergency aid.
- When a massive tornado left Joplin, Missouri in ruins, an AmeriCares disaster relief expert was on the ground the next day working with partner clinics to assess and then help meet emergency medical aid and relief needs.
- We continue our work in Somalia, Kenya and surrounding countries to help survivors of drought, famine and civil conflict with nutritional supplements, medicines and medical supplies.
- More than 5 million people are struggling to survive in the wake of severe flooding in southern Pakistan, including many families still recovering from the catastrophic 2010 floods, and AmeriCares has supported free medical camps in the flood affected areas.
- **This year, AmeriCares has provided millions of dollars in aid in response to natural and man-made disasters around the globe.**

For almost 30 years, we have partnered with leaders in the pharmaceutical and medical equipment industries who donate tons of free medicines, medical supplies and emergency relief supplies. Then AmeriCares delivers those lifesaving cargos via air, sea or land to trusted and effective partners on the ground who use it where it is needed most.

But we need your support today to ensure that when disaster strikes, when people are in crisis they will get the help they need, wherever they are, whenever they need it.

We wish you a happy holiday season and thank you for your ongoing commitment.

Sincerely,

Curt Welling
President and CEO, AmeriCares

Donate Now

Share this email on **Facebook** and **Twitter**

A PASSION TO HELP. THE ABILITY TO DELIVER. ®
Privacy Policy © 2011 AmeriCares | 88 Hamilton Avenue | Stamford, CT 06902

CHARITY NAVIGATOR

Unsubscribe

Tell A Friend

View this message on the web

EXHIBIT 14.12
Year-End Online Appeal E-mail #2, AmeriCares

Subject: ADV: Help us save lives this holiday season

Date: Thursday, December 15, 2011 8:00:00 AM ET

From: Curt Welling, AmeriCares

To: Eric Overman

Dear Eric,

Every day, men, women and children die from illnesses that are preventable or easily treatable if the appropriate medications were available. AmeriCares Global Medical Assistance program is delivering lifesaving medicines and medical supplies worldwide.

This holiday season, will you help us save more lives?

We need your renewed support today more than ever so AmeriCares Global Medical Assistance and aid programs will be able to continue to reduce suffering and restore health around the world.

Nearly 2 billion people — one-third of the world's population — have inadequate access to medicines. These families are not just victims of news-making catastrophes; they also suffer from almost unnoticed natural disasters and ongoing "silent disasters" caused by grinding poverty and civil conflict.

Help us save lives

Make a tax-deductible donation

AmeriCares partners with leaders in the pharmaceutical and medical equipment industries who donate tons of free medicines, medical supplies and emergency relief supplies. Then we deliver those lifesaving cargos via air, sea or land to trusted and effective partners on the ground who use it where it is needed most. But we can't deliver these vital supplies without your support!

And because AmeriCares delivers donated medicines and medical supplies to an established network of locally based clinics, hospitals and health care providers around the world and here in the United States, the impact of the contributions supporters like you provide is multiplied many, many times over.

Your tax-deductible contribution will help AmeriCares provide health and hope through our Global Medical Assistance and other lifesaving programs.

Thank you for your ongoing commitment.

Sincerely,

Curt Welling
President and CEO, AmeriCares

Donate Now

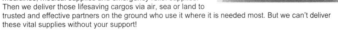

Share this email on **Facebook** and **Twitter**

A PASSION TO HELP. THE ABILITY TO DELIVER. ®
Privacy Policy © 2011 AmeriCares | 88 Hamilton Avenue | Stamford, CT 06902

Unsubscribe

Tell A Friend

View this message on the web

EXHIBIT 14.13

Year-End Online Appeal E-mail #3, AmeriCares

Subject: ADV: Help those who need it most this holiday season.

Date: Tuesday, December 20, 2011 8:00:23 AM ET

From: Curt Welling, AmeriCares

To: Eric Overman

Dear Eric,

<u>With your help this holiday season, AmeriCares will continue to do whatever it takes to save families' lives.</u>

Your earlier support for our work helped us save lives and was very much appreciated. But so much more help is needed and your renewed support now would enable us to continue delivering help and hope to people in crisis around the globe.

<u>Please make a special year-end tax-deductible gift today to ensure that AmeriCares can continue to provide vital aid to those who need it most.</u>

This holiday season, help those who need it most.

Photo courtesy REUTERS/Akhtar Soomro

Donate Now

Wherever a child is vulnerable to disease…

A pregnant mother needs prenatal vitamins…

A village clinic needs antibiotics to save lives…

A family is driven from their home in a country plunged into turmoil…

Where surgeons need medical supplies…

A community has been destroyed in a natural disaster…

Or children are suffering…

…You and AmeriCares are there to help!

<u>Please give from your heart during this very special season — so many families need AmeriCares and we need you.</u>

Happy holidays, and thank you for your ongoing commitment.

Sincerely,

Curt Welling
President and CEO, AmeriCares

Donate Now

Share this email on **Facebook** and **Twitter**

A PASSION TO HELP. THE ABILITY TO DELIVER. ®
Privacy Policy © 2011 AmeriCares | 88 Hamilton Avenue | Stamford, CT 06902

Unsubscribe

Tell A Friend

View this message on the web

EXHIBIT 14.14
Year-End Online Appeal E-mail #4, AmeriCares

Subject: ADV: Best wishes for the holidays
Date: Thursday, December 22, 2011 8:00:24 AM ET
From: Curt Welling, AmeriCares
To: Eric Overman

Dear Eric,

In this special season, we send you our best wishes for the holidays.

Your generous spirit and commitment inspire us all.

Your support for our work is very much appreciated. Thank you for giving the gifts of hope and health to people who need it most around the world and right here in the United States.

Sincerely,

Curt Welling
President and CEO, AmeriCares

Donate Now

Share this email on **Facebook** and **Twitter**

A PASSION TO HELP. THE ABILITY TO DELIVER. ®
Privacy Policy © 2011 AmeriCares | 88 Hamilton Avenue | Stamford, CT 06902

Unsubscribe

Tell A Friend

View this message on the web

EXHIBIT 14.15
Year-End Online Appeal E-mail #5, AmeriCares

Subject: ADV: 3 days left: Save lives now.

Date: Wednesday, December 28, 2011 8:00:55 AM ET

From: Curt Welling, AmeriCares

To: Eric Overman

Donate Now

Dear Eric,

Time is running out- you have only 3 days to make your year-end lifesaving gift to AmeriCares.

Your earlier support for our work was very important to us, and much appreciated. This past year, AmeriCares saved lives in more than 90 countries — and in all 50 states here at home. Your renewed support today will help us deliver health and hope — in the form of lifesaving medicines, medical supplies and humanitarian aid.

Help us carry our critical work into 2012 by renewing your support now with a year-end tax-deductible contribution to AmeriCares.

Your donation today will help us continue to save lives around the world in 2012.

For almost 30 years, we have partnered with leaders in the pharmaceutical and medical equipment industries who donate tons of free medicines, medical supplies and emergency relief supplies. Then AmeriCares delivers those lifesaving cargos via air, sea or land to trusted and effective partners on the ground who use it where it is needed most.

Please don't wait - make your year-end gift today to ensure that AmeriCares can continue to provide vital aid to those who need it most.

Thank you again and best wishes for a healthy and happy new year.

Sincerely,

Curt Welling
President and CEO, AmeriCares

LAST CHANCE
Make a tax-deductible gift to AmeriCares

URGENT

Donate Now

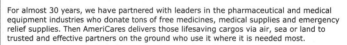

Donate Now

Share this email on **Facebook** and **Twitter**

A PASSION TO HELP. THE ABILITY TO DELIVER. ®
Privacy Policy © 2011 AmeriCares | 88 Hamilton Avenue | Stamford, CT 06902

CHARITY NAVIGATOR

Unsubscribe

Tell A Friend

View this message on the web

EXHIBIT 14.16
Year-End Online Appeal E-mail #6, AmeriCares

Subject: ADV: Donate by midnight tonight - save lives
Date: Saturday, December 31, 2011 8:00:28 AM ET
From: Curt Welling, AmeriCares
To: Eric Overman

Donate Now

Dear Eric,

Last chance — midnight tonight is the deadline to make your year-end lifesaving gift to AmeriCares!

Your earlier support for our work was very important to us, and much appreciated. This past year, AmeriCares saved lives in more than 90 countries — and in all 50 states here at home. Your renewed support today will help us deliver health and hope — in the form of lifesaving medicines, medical supplies and humanitarian aid.

Your renewed support now will help us continue to save lives worldwide in 2012.

Millions of families depend on AmeriCares for crucial medical aid — for emergency relief when threatened by natural disasters, armed conflict and for basic medical care due to chronic poverty. **They depend on AmeriCares and we depend on you.**

But time is running out — make your year-end tax-deductible gift to AmeriCares by midnight tonight.

Thank you again and best wishes for a healthy and happy New Year.

Sincerely,

Curt Welling
President and CEO, AmeriCares

Make your **tax-deductible** gift by midnight!

URGENT!

Donate Now

Donate Now

Share this email on **Facebook** and **Twitter**

A PASSION TO HELP. THE ABILITY TO DELIVER. ®
Privacy Policy © 2011 AmeriCares | 88 Hamilton Avenue | Stamford, CT 06902

Unsubscribe

Tell A Friend

View this message on the web

How Year-End Appeals Are Different from Other Fundraising Appeals

The end of the year is a special time for most US nonprofit organizations. A spirit of generosity holds sway, and donors turn to thoughts of tax deductions, including charitable giving. In fact, many of the donor motivations described in chapter 1—loneliness, to cite just one example—are felt most strongly during the year-end holidays.

Year-end appeals are a major source of support for the nation's nonprofit organizations, because an estimated 40 percent of all charitable giving takes place during the final three months of the year. These appeals can be either annual (or membership) renewal mailings or special appeals (seeking gifts for earmarked purposes). But the fundraising letters that charities mail during this time tend to exhibit most of the following six characteristics:

1. There are usually references to the season (particularly in letters from religious organizations). The benefits of year-end tax deductions are commonly mentioned too. Often the two are connected.

2. Ask amounts are usually variable. The generosity of year-end giving makes it possible for most groups to invest a little more in personalizing their appeals.

3. For the same reasons, many charities spend more on producing their year-end appeals than they do on fundraising letters mailed at other times of the year—not just on personalization but also on paper stock, ink colors, and premiums, such as holiday greeting cards.

4. A favored theme is "looking back, looking forward." The widespread tendency in the United States to think about New Year's resolutions lends itself to this Janus-like approach.

5. More often than at other times of the year, charities may launch multipart appeals, consisting of a series of two or three letters, perhaps even combined with a telephone call.

6. Year-end appeals are often mailed to large proportions of the donor file.

In addition to year-end fundraising letters, most savvy fundraisers now send a series of e-mail appeals along the lines of the AmeriCares example shown above. While e-mail typically brings in few gifts at other times of the year, online year-end appeals can be very lucrative. My colleagues and I conclude from several years of experience that at least one-third of all gifts sent in response to e-mail appeals are received in the month of December—and up to half of all that money is received on December 31!

So much for that one type of specialized appeal to donors. In chapter 15, "Recruiting Monthly Sustainers," we'll examine another type.

Chapter Fifteen:
Recruiting Monthly Sustainers

Offering Small Donors a Chance for Greater Impact

For a great many donors, the option of making modest monthly contributions to a favored nonprofit organization is an attractive proposition. Some US charities persuade 5 percent, 10 percent, or more of their donors to *convert* to this lucrative arrangement—lucrative because a monthly gift of $10 amounts to much more in the course of a year than infrequent gifts of $25. In much of the rest of the world, monthly (or *regular* or *committed* giving) is the rule rather than the exception. Even though there is much greater resistance to monthly giving here in the United States—due probably to our more complex banking system and to deeper distrust of nonprofit organizations than is found in Europe, for example—monthly gifts may still constitute one-third or more of a charity's small-donor income.

Monthly contributors in the United States are typically called *sustainers* or *pledge donors*. They are often converted by a telephone call or mailing of the sort typified by the Bread for the World letter and response device reproduced in exhibits 15.1 through 15.3.

This is unquestionably a sustainer conversion mailing because

- The words "each month," "monthly gift," or "monthly giving" appear six times on the front side of this appeal. It could hardly be more obvious.

- The copy dwells on the convenience and impact of monthly gifts rather than on the specific programs that constitute Bread for the World's work.

- The sustainer program has its own name, "Baker's Dozen"—itself clearly a sign of the ongoing character of the program.

- The suggested gift amounts on the reply device are modest, even though joining this program will, in effect, make members into significant donors because of the cumulative impact of their gifts.

EXHIBIT 15.1
Sustainer Invitation Reply Device and Letter, Bread for the World

Yes, I'd like to join the Baker's Dozen giving program and start making monthly

gifts of : [ ] $10   [ ] $15   [ ] $20   [ ] $_____

[ ]   I'd like to make my monthly gifts by electronic funds
transfers from my bank account. I've enclosed a check for my
first month's gift, and my signature below authorizes my future gifts.

Signature _____ Date _____

Baker's Dozen
Monthly Giving to End Hunger

Jane A Doe
1234 Any Street
Any Town, AS 00000
BFW10MB / July 2010 / Package D

10MB

9999999

Bread for the World
50 F Street NW, Suite 500
Washington, DC 20001
1-800-822-7323 www.bread.org

breadfor**theworld**
HAVE FAITH. END HUNGER.
50 F STREET NW, SUITE 500
WASHINGTON, DC 20001
1-800-822-7323 www.bread.org

July 2, 2010

Dear Ms. Doe,

Your active membership in Bread for the World is very encouraging. Your faithful financial support has enabled us to move forward at a time when many other groups have been forced to cut back.

I'm writing to invite you to take one more step — a small step that will have a very big impact. I'd like you to join the growing number of Bread for the World members who participate in our Baker's Dozen monthly giving program.

A gift of just $10 a month adds up to significant annual support. And because we have lower costs — and more stable income — with Baker's Dozen gifts, your contributions have an even greater impact.

And please continue to write or call your members of Congress. Urge them to make ending hunger at home and abroad a national priority.

Your involvement is especially critical right now. This is a time of constraint and controversy here in Washington. Yet the administration and Congress are moving forward to make our nation's foreign assistance more effective in reducing hunger. As a result, critical aid will reach more hungry people more quickly. Nutrition for mothers and children will be a higher priority. And small farmers in Africa will have the chance to grow more food for their families and others.

By joining the Baker's Dozen giving program today, you will make it possible for Bread for the World and Bread for the World Institute to continue to play a leadership role in these encouraging developments. Thank you!

Sincerely,

David Beckmann

David Beckmann
President

P.S.   Please take a moment right now to write your first check and send it along with the enclosed authorization form.   Your monthly gifts will be transformed into a Baker's Dozen.   Thank you!

RECYCLED & RECYCLABLE / PRINTED WITH SOY INK   10-MB2

REMEMBER

In order to sign up for the Baker's Dozen, please enclose a check that will serve as your first monthly gift.

My authorization to transfer my gift from my checking account on the 20th of each month shall be the same as if I had personally signed my check to Bread for the World or Bread for the World Institute. This authorization shall remain in effect until I notify Bread for the World that I wish to end this agreement. I understand that a record of each monthly gift will appear on my bank statement and serve as my receipt.

Contributions to Bread for the World are not tax-deductible since its members lobby Congress on behalf of hungry people. Tax-deductible gifts may be made to Bread for the World Institute to support research and education, including the annual Hunger Report. Please make out your check accordingly. You may discontinue your monthly bank transfers at any time. Just call 1-800-822-7323 ext. 132, or send an e-mail to memberservices@bread.org.

Please visit www.bread.org and learn how you can help persuade Congress
to protect and strengthen tax credits that enable low-income families to feed their children.

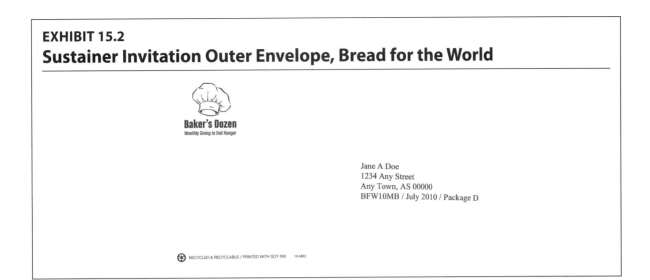

EXHIBIT 15.2
Sustainer Invitation Outer Envelope, Bread for the World

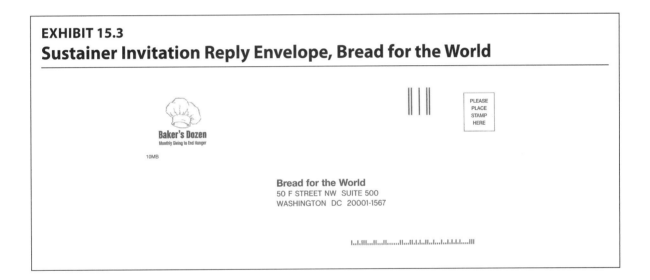

EXHIBIT 15.3
Sustainer Invitation Reply Envelope, Bread for the World

- The means of payment is unorthodox, requiring that members authorize their banks to transfer funds directly from their accounts into Bread for the World's account. (The organization has settled on bank transfers alone as the mechanism of payment, because the number of donors making this type of payment who drop out of the Baker's Dozen program is significantly less than it would be among donors making credit card payments—and checks are only very rarely accepted in sustainer programs operated by any nonprofit today, as the dropout rate is extremely high.)

Bread for the World may be in a minority in its continuing use of direct mail to recruit monthly sustainers. Telephone conversion is more common. However, e-mail has also become a favored channel in recruiting sustainers. Exhibits 15.4 and 15.5 are examples from an e-mail and

EXHIBIT 15.4
Sustainer Conversion E-mail, AmeriCares "Partners in Caring" Program

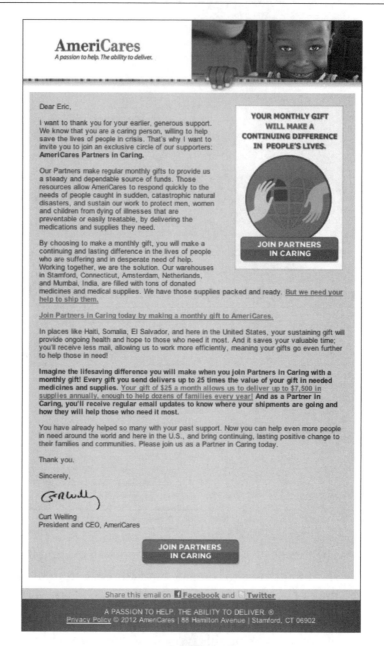

EXHIBIT 15.5

Landing Page Lightbox Invitation, AmeriCares "Partners in Caring" Program

webpage sustainer conversion appeal from one of the largest charities in the United States, AmeriCares.

How Sustainer Invitations Are Different from Other Fundraising Appeals

Joining the monthly sustainer program of a nonprofit organization requires a special commitment that relatively few donors demonstrate, and it's often difficult for a charity to convert its donors to this highly advantageous arrangement. Many organizations find that the response to direct mail conversion letters is not high enough to justify the cost. Telephone conversion is more typical—probably because prospects for monthly giving programs have many questions that can't necessarily be answered satisfactorily by mail. Online appeals, too, are widely used to recruit monthly donors. Still, some nonprofits continue to find conversion mailings cost effective. These letters typically share some or all of the following six attributes:

1. Sustainer conversion mailings are rarely sent to all small donors. Normally, a nonprofit will select only those donors it believes show the greatest promise of accepting the invitation to join a sustainer program. They tend to be donors who (a) are of long-standing and can thus be presumed to be committed to continuing their support and (b) consistently give small and frequent contributions. In some larger organizations, for example, only those donors who've shown a pattern of giving three or more gifts per year will be deemed strong prospects for monthly giving.

2. The emphasis tends to be on the prospect's relationship with the organization rather than on the issues or programs in which the organization is involved.

3. A principal argument for joining a monthly giving program is that it will allow a donor to achieve greater impact—partly because of the reliability and predictability of her gifts but also because the cumulative amount will allow her to become, in effect, a "major donor," despite the modest size of each contribution.

4. The letter (or the phone script) devotes as much attention as necessary to explaining the program's logistics, which often raise questions in donors' minds.

5. Unlike the example in exhibit 15.1, most sustainer conversions emphasize that a monthly sustainer may opt out of the program at any time. This gives donors a sense that they remain in control even though payments will be made automatically.

6. There is frequently some incentive offered to donors to join a sustainer program. Sometimes the incentive is tangible—a coffee mug, T-shirt, or lapel pin, for example—and sometimes it consists largely of convenience. In any event, a sustainer invitation will emphasize the personal benefits of joining the program.

A monthly sustainer (or pledge) program is one way to raise the level of giving of donors who habitually make modest contributions. Another way to increase the giving level is covered in the next chapter, "Soliciting High-Dollar Gifts."

Chapter Sixteen:
Soliciting High-Dollar Gifts

Framing the Case for Major Contributions

Direct mail fundraising typically attracts modest gifts, usually of less than $100. Online gifts tend to be larger but rarely average much more than $100. Within the last couple of decades, however, direct response fundraisers have come to understand that similar techniques, carefully honed for greater impact on upscale donors, can generate gifts of $500, $1,000, or more. The so-called high-dollar appeals that seek (and increasingly yield) such gifts are fast becoming a fixture in the pantheon of nonprofit fundraising. Exhibits 16.1 through 16.5 show one such high-dollar upgrade package.

The National Organization for Women mailed this appeal package, which is typical of the genre in many ways:

- Clearly, this is a leadership appeal—a request that's far out of the ordinary, if only because it leaves the gift amount up to the donor. In nearly all other circumstances, this is unwise. Most direct response donors reflexively give small amounts that are far below their means. But any donor who has given $250 or more has clearly demonstrated a higher level of commitment and might be relied on to give serious thought to how much she might contribute.

- This appeal suggests giving an unusually large sum of money—as much as $50,000. I wouldn't dream of suggesting anything even remotely that high in a run-of-the-mill direct response appeal.

- The contents of the package are held together with a paper clip, which betrays the hands-on treatment this appeal required.

EXHIBIT 16.1

High-Dollar Appeal Reply Device, National Organization for Women

2012 ACTION PLAN

REPLY MEMORANDUM

FROM: Mr. John Doe
           123 Main Street
           Anytown, AS

A
JQS999
12345

TO: Terry O'Neill, President
           National Organization for Women

Thank you, Terry, for sending me NOW's 2012 Action Plan to address the very real threats to our hard-won victories for women's rights in the year ahead. I agree we must take immediate action and I want to help NOW implement the urgent strategies outlined in the proposal you enclosed.

❑ I have reviewed the giving chart below, and I have decided to help
with a generous gift of $_____.

GIVING CHART

To raise the funds needed for the initiatives outlined in the attached proposal, I will need help from a lot of extraordinary people. The chart below shows some suggested donation levels. Thank you for your generosity. — Terry

Number of Gifts Needed	Amount of Gift	Total
2	$50,000	$100,000
5	$25,000	$125,000
10	$10,000	$100,000
20	$5,000	$100,000
50	$2,500	$125,000
100	$1,000	$100,000
250	$500	$125,000
500	$250	$125,000
Campaign Total		**$900,000**

Please make your check payable to NOW, and return it with this form in the enclosed envelope. See reverse to make your gift by credit card. Thank you.

You can also donate securely online at www.now.org

Contributions to the National Organization for Women are not tax-deductible. NOW is a non-profit, tax-exempt organization working politically and legislatively to advance women's rights.

1100 H Street, NW ■ Suite 300 ■ Washington, DC 20005 ■ www.now.org

EXHIBIT 16.2
High-Dollar Appeal Letter, National Organization for Women

National Organization for Women

February 24, 2012

Ms. Jane Doe
123 Any Street
Anytown, AS 00000

Dear Ms. Doe,

As we gear up for perhaps the most critical election year ever for women's rights and lives, your commitment as one of NOW's strongest supporters is absolutely crucial.

You have been a vital partner in our work beating back attacks on hard-won gains for women's rights and dignity. And we recognize that the support and inspiration provided by thoughtful, committed members like you is truly our strength. This year, we need your dedication more than ever.

That's why I have prepared the enclosed copy of NOW's **2012 Action Plan**, explaining how we need to ramp up our efforts in the coming months to help ensure a victory for women in November.

We must fight back to avoid devastating losses like 2010 that would guarantee the end to safe, legal abortion in this country. With so much at stake, I urge you to review the proposal carefully and decide what Leadership Gift you're able to make to help put our winning strategy into action.

Our top priorities in 2012 are to urgently mobilize grassroots activists and educate voters on: "personhood amendments" in as many as a dozen states that would define life as beginning at conception; marriage equality measures; and electing more feminist candidates to Congress and state legislatures — to counter the right-wing lawmakers bent on enacting radical anti-choice legislation and gutting essential programs that women and families depend on. At the same time, we're working on legislative and policy initiatives to strengthen women's rights, reproductive health and financial security.

The goal of NOW's 2012 Action Plan is to replicate our important past successes like our historic 2008 voter mobilization campaign and last summer's stunning victory over a personhood ballot measure in Mississippi. With the far right pouring huge sums of cash into candidate and ballot initiative campaigns, NOW urgently needs $900,000 to fully implement our organized, proven grassroots strategy. I know that sounds like a big sum, but the challenges are real and the stakes are high!

To make our plan a reality, we must have our most loyal members standing with us. I know we have you to thank for many of our past successes, and I hope I can count on you once again. Please take a few moments right now to review our plan and return your Leadership Gift to help make it a reality. Thank you for doing your part!

Sincerely,

Terry O'Neill

Terry O'Neill
President

1100 H Street, NW ■ Suite 300 ■ Washington, DC 20005 ■ 202.628.8669 ■ www.now.org

EXHIBIT 16.3

High-Dollar Appeal Proposal, National Organization for Women

2012 Action Plan

A proposal prepared for

Ms. Jane Doe

by

The National Organization for Women

February 24, 2012

1100 H Street, NW ■ Suite 300 ■ Washington, DC 20005 ■ www.now.org

A Challenging Time for Women's Rights

With the right wing's assault on women's freedom, health and financial security intensifying, the 2012 election is shaping up as one of the most critical votes for women in modern U.S. history. That's why the participation of NOW and the support of our most dedicated members is so vital.

At the federal level, conservatives are pulling out the stops to seize control of the White House and Congress. If they succeed, they will be able to move forward with major restrictions on reproductive freedom like the draconian **No Taxpayer Funding for Abortion Act** — which would not only codify the Hyde Amendment's ban on public funds to pay for abortion services for low-income women, but would also eliminate abortion coverage in most private employer insurance plans and allow many hospitals to refuse to provide even life-saving abortions.

Complete conservative control of Congress would open the floodgates to the far right's plans to slash Social Security, Medicare, Medicaid and other federal programs that women disproportionately depend on. And a right-wing victory in November would also deal a major blow to efforts to secure equal marriage rights, workplace protections and other civil rights for lesbian, gay, bisexual and transgender (LGBT) people.

Anti-choice forces are also hoping to strengthen their grip on state legislatures, in order to add to the hundreds of state restrictions on reproductive freedom that have been enacted in recent years — over a hundred in 2011 alone.

Meanwhile, radical right groups are pushing to put "personhood" initiatives on the ballot in as many as a dozen states, which would outlaw not only abortions, but also common birth control methods and even some fertility treatments. Extremists have also succeeded in putting constitutional bans on same-sex marriage on the ballot in North Carolina and Minnesota, and are gearing up for a major push to defeat a ballot measure that would extend marriage equality to LGBT couples in Maine.

To counter the right wing's vast financial advantages, NOW has created the 2012 Action Plan described in this document. The plan includes the following goals:

- Defeating rabidly anti-choice ballot measures, like the so-called "personhood" initiatives that threaten all aspects of women's reproductive choice;
- Supporting marriage equality measures;
- Electing more feminists to office; and
- Laying the groundwork for legislative and policy initiatives.

To reach these objectives, NOW is working to register voters, educate them about the issues at stake and make sure that they get out to vote. NOW is also mobilizing our 170,000-strong online activist network, providing grassroots campaign training to our chapters, forging strong partnerships with groups who share our goals, and preparing to send NOW staff and officers into the field in key states.

To fully implement this ambitious action plan, NOW must raise $900,000 in the next 90 days. We're counting on our strongest supporters to step up and help us turn this blueprint for victory into reality.

NOW's 2012 Goals

Electing More Feminists to Office

Women across the country are suffering the consequences of the 2010 elections, when right-wing forces won control of the U.S. House of Representatives and tightened their stranglehold on dozens of state governments. These extremists have launched an all-out assault on women's reproductive health and financial security, and are bent on rolling back recent advances toward full equality for LGBT people. The key to heading off threats is to change the make-up of our representation.

To fight back, NOW has made electing more champions of women's rights to office at the federal, state and local levels our top 2012 election priority. To accomplish this, we're planning to register a critical mass of pro-women voters, educate them about what is at stake, and make sure that they get to the polls to support feminist candidates. NOW is also playing a leadership role in a powerful coalition that is working to double the number of women in Congress and state governorships by 2022. And we are publicly challenging candidates to support legislation critical to women's rights and lives.

Winning Ballot Measures on Reproductive Freedom

In 2011, anti-choice forces attempted to ram through a so-called "personhood" provision in Mississippi which would have amended the state constitution to define a fertilized egg as a "person." If passed, this amendment would have criminalized not only all abortions, but also some forms of contraception and even in vitro fertilization and stem-cell research. Thanks to a concerted, all-out grassroots effort by NOW and our allies, the measure was defeated. But undaunted by their failure, radical-right extremists are ramping up their assault, pushing to get personhood amendments on the ballot in up to 12 states this year, including Georgia, Colorado, South Carolina and Arkansas. And that means we need to launch the same kind of defense on a much wider scale.

NOW is working with allied organizations to keep these personhood initiatives off state ballots, and we will mobilize powerful grassroots campaigns to defeat any that survive our challenges.

Threats to Marriage Equality

Meanwhile, conservatives are pushing back hard against recent LGBT civil rights victories by attempting to add same-sex marriage bans to the state constitutions of Minnesota and North Carolina. And they are using every weapon at their disposal to defeat a ballot measure in Maine that would give LGBT couples equal marriage rights.

We'll be working closely with LGBT rights advocates to defeat proposed state constitutional bans on same-sex marriage, help win the marriage equality vote in Maine and achieve equal marriage rights through legislation in states like New Jersey and Maryland.

Laying the Groundwork for Legislative and Policy Initiatives

Winning in November is a critical step towards protecting women's rights and lives and defending our past advances. But our work isn't done there. With a favorable change in the makeup of Congress and our state legislatures, NOW must be ready to fight for legislation that protects reproductive rights, strengthens women's financial security, advances LGBT civil rights, and sets fair taxation and spending priorities.

In addition to preparing to push for stronger reproductive rights at the federal and state levels, NOW is also working with partners to craft proposals that would strengthen Social Security to improve benefits for chronically low-wage/low-employment workers and people with disabilities, and extend them to same-sex couples and caregivers who are overwhelmingly women. And NOW is gearing up for an ambitious post-election campaign to repeal the discriminatory Defense of Marriage Act and enact other vital equality measures.

The 2012 Action Plan

Voter Registration, Education and Mobilization

NOW is currently working with more than 20 pro-women groups to register women to vote and educate them about the stakes in the 2012 elections. This partnership is designed to maximize resources, prevent duplication of effort and avoid gaps that our opponents can capitalize on. NOW is also working with the HERvotes campaign (www.hervotes.us), using social networking and other cutting-edge tools to mobilize women voters in 2012 around preserving women's health and economic rights that are now at serious risk.

NOW is already coordinating our local chapters to take part in these efforts, providing online webinar trainings to chapter leaders, and connecting them with our allies in their local areas. And with your help, NOW will provide educational materials and online resources for voters and grassroots activists, to help spread the word about how much is on the line in 2012. The momentum of issues important to women could rest on feminist candidates like U.S. Senate hopefuls Tammy Baldwin and Elizabeth Warren who are standing up for women's rights, health and financial security.

The scale of our efforts – and our success – lies very much in the hands of dedicated supporters like you.

Budgeted Cost: $350,000

Training and Deploying Grassroots Field Activists

An essential part of reaching NOW's 2012 election goals is to train campaign field activists, then use sophisticated resource and needs assessments to connect them with areas or campaigns where their work will have maximum impact.

NOW has already begun online trainings for our chapters and e-activists that will cover the fundamentals of grassroots campaigning, including registering and educating voters, conducting phone banks and door-to-door canvasses, creating effective messaging strategies, and utilizing social media. With your help, we will present two of these webinars each month through November. And NOW is creating special online action kits for activists involved in state personhood amendment and marriage equality ballot measure campaigns, so they have the critical tools they need to succeed.

In addition to this online training activity, NOW will take a hands-on approach, matching up experienced campaign activists with NOW leaders and other volunteers, to prepare them to operate effectively in the field. And if possible, NOW officers and staff will be assisting efforts in election battleground states where their organizing skills will have the greatest effect for candidate and ballot measure campaigns.

After November, these trained activists will serve as NOW's post-election vanguard, as we work to make the most of our election successes to protect reproductive freedom, strengthen women's financial security and equality, and achieve full civil rights for LGBT people with new state and federal level allies.

Budgeted Cost: $550,000

Conclusion

NOW faces formidable obstacles in the 2012 elections, including the far right's huge funding advantages. But with a coordinated plan to register and educate voters on issues important to women, train grassroots activists, impact candidate and ballot measure campaigns, and prepare for post-election legislative and policy initiatives, we can elect a critical mass of feminists and win important victories for women's rights and lives. We can protect what generations of feminists fought so hard for and make new advances for the generations ahead. The key is to get the strong, early support of NOW's most committed members and raise the $900,000 needed to fully implement our comprehensive 2012 Action Plan.

The National Organization for Women needs the strength and dedication of our most committed donors for the pivotal year ahead, more than ever before. Please join us by making a generous Leadership Gift to NOW's 2012 Action Plan today.

- The stapled, five-page "2012 Action Plan" was obviously expensive to prepare and would not be cost effective as an insert in an appeal to low-dollar donors. There's no off-the-shelf brochure or flyer in this package!

- The carrier envelope measures 9 by 12 inches and is printed in purple ink on hefty, textured stock. It has an expensive look and

EXHIBIT 16.4
High-Dollar Appeal Carrier Envelope, National Organization for Women

EXHIBIT 16.5
High-Dollar Appeal Reply Envelope, National Organization for Women

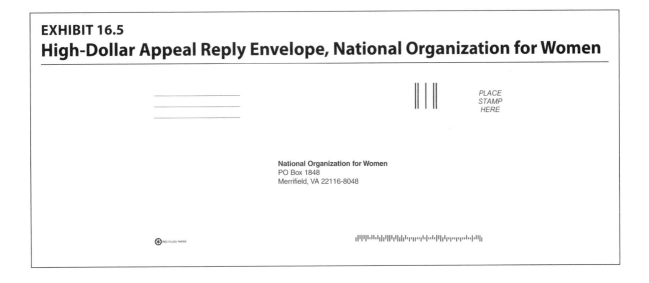

feel, obviously upscale from the typical direct mail solicitation. And, though you can't see it on this example, the envelope bore first-class stamps.

What is *atypical* of this high-dollar package is the range of possible gift levels. Frequently, a high-dollar package will focus on one giving level—most often, the minimum contribution required to join an annual giving club or society. In this case, the levels correspond with the gifts enumerated in the *giving pyramid* on the reply device. (A giving pyramid, typically found in major donor fundraising campaigns, is a useful device in high-dollar fundraising too.) And the package makes no mention of the annual giving commitment that normally is associated with a high-dollar club.

How High-Dollar Appeals Are Different from Other Fundraising Letters

A high-dollar package may be used in the service of a great many fundraising purposes, even recruiting new donors. More typically, however, these high-cost efforts are directed at a nonprofit's most generous and responsive supporters—as special appeals or upgrade efforts, for example. But whether used in mailings to the *house file* (the list of previous donors) or in mailings directed at promising online supporters, high-dollar fundraising letters usually share at least five characteristics:

1. The ask amount is high. And that amount isn't just the highest in a string where the lowest suggested amounts let a donor off easy. If there's a choice of gift levels, every choice is a big number.

2. The packaging is often very expensive. These are upscale appeals, designed to communicate a feeling of exclusivity. High-dollar packages accomplish this aim by looking and feeling different from most other direct mail fundraising letters. Sometimes they're different in size, shape, texture, and color as well as in their elegant design. High-dollar appeals embody what Hollywood calls *high production values*.

3. Almost always, high-dollar appeals are personalized, and often extensively so. Your chances of obtaining a $1,000 gift are slim with a letter beginning "Dear Friend."

4. The copy is often upscale in tone and approach. Many high-dollar fundraising letters are built around snob appeal or exclusivity (for example, offering invitations to "exclusive" or "intimate" events or societies).

5. Most important, a strong high-dollar appeal features a uniquely appropriate marketing concept: an offer to match the high-level ask. A genuine high-dollar letter usually doesn't just ask for a larger sum of money than other fundraising letters do; it supplies the donor with a special and credible reason to send the amount of money asked for. In other words, a high-dollar letter has a marketing concept all its own. In the NOW example in this chapter, that concept is embodied in the "2012 Action Plan." (See chapter 6 for a detailed discussion of this concept.) And to reinforce the marketing concept, there may be only a

single specified gift level. Often the offer involves a *gift club* or *giving society* that entails unique benefits or privileges.

High-dollar packages are a type of special appeal used to upgrade existing donors who have given enough in the past to be considered high-dollar prospects. In chapter 17, "Going for Bigger Gifts," we'll explore another type of special appeal—the sort used to upgrade low-dollar donors.

Chapter Seventeen:
Going for Bigger Gifts

Persuading Donors to Make an Extra Commitment

Most nonprofit organizations slyly imply in their appeals to donors or members that a gift that's larger than the donor's previous gifts would be . . . well, better. They do this by suggesting gift amounts that are more generous than those earlier gifts by some prescribed amount—say, 25 percent or 50 percent or just $10 more.

However, there is a special class of fundraising appeal specifically designed to solicit increased gifts. These *donor upgrade* letters—sometimes special appeals or year-end appeals, sometimes membership or annual giving *renewal* letters—go out of their way to supply reasons why a donor's increased level of support will bring additional benefits.

The response device and the first page of a letter reproduced in exhibits 17.1 and 17.2—from a high-dollar package for Save The Bay that's reproduced in its entirety at www.josseybass.com/go/fundraisingappeals—illustrate three of the elements commonly encountered in donor upgrade efforts:

- You can tell at a glance that the purpose of this appeal is to upgrade Jane Doe's support. The reply device requests a gift of $250 or more, clearly a larger amount than Doe has ever contributed in the past. Jane Doe is a member of the Save The Bay high-dollar club, the Protector's Circle, and a gift of $250 or more will renew her membership in this leadership group.

- Two gift amounts are suggested, with a third, open alternative, allowing Doe the opportunity to select the level most comfortable for her.

- The letter ingeniously introduces the argument for increased donations by telling the story of a conversation between the executive director who signed the letter and the group's regionally famous founder.

EXHIBIT 17.1
Donor Upgrade Response Device, Save The Bay

PROTECTOR'S CIRCLE
MEMORANDUM *of* ACCEPTANCE

To: David Lewis
        Executive Director, Save The Bay

From: Ms. Jane Doe
        123 Any Street
        Any Town, AS 00000-0000
        STB12XA/2-17-12/Pkg 1: Major Donors
                                            000000   12XADOEA

David, I am proud to renew my membership in the Protector's Circle to help Save The Bay
continue to restore and protect San Francisco Bay. I agree with the key conservation strategies
in your Proposal and am eager to help you reach your financial goals for 2012 and beyond.
Enclosed is my Protector's Circle gift of:

[ ] $250   [ ] $500   [ ] $_____

1-A-0

Funding Opportunities to Restore and Protect San Francisco Bay

To reach our 2012 Protector's
Circle goal of $125,000, gifts of
all sizes are needed and deeply
appreciated. Please review the
chart at right and make the most
generous gift you can today.
Thank you for your leadership,
your commitment and your
participation.

Thank you for
your commitment
and your generosity.

Number of Gifts Needed	Amount of Each Gift	Total Amount	Cumulative Amount
1	$15,000	$15,000	$15,000
2	$10,000	$20,000	$35,000
5	$5,000	$25,000	$60,000
10	$2,500	$25,000	$85,000
15	$1,000	$15,000	$100,000
25	$500	$12,500	$112,500
50	$250	$12,500	$125,000

1330 Broadway, Suite 1800
Oakland, CA 94612-2519
www.saveSFbay.org

To charge your gift, please complete the following:

Amount of gift: $_____

☐ Visa   ☐ MasterCard   ☐ American Express   ☐ Discover

Card # _____ Expiration date _____

Signature *(required)* _____

☐ **Please keep me posted. My email address is:** _____

It's easy to sign up for fun and rewarding volunteer adventures on our website.
Please visit our online events calendar at www.saveSFbay.org/volunteer.
If you prefer to register by phone, just call us at (510) 463-6850.

Protector's Circle Benefits of Membership

CREEK LEVEL — $250 to $499 Annual Contribution

- Recognition in the Protector's Circle Book of the Bay on display at Save The Bay's office
- Five Native Seedlings from our nursery planted in your honor at one of our marsh restoration sites
- Recognition in our Annual Report
- Invitations to our special events

COVE LEVEL — $500 to $999 Annual Contribution

All of the above benefits plus:
- Invitations to Behind the Scenes Nursery Field Trips

ESTUARY LEVEL — $1,000 to $2,499 Annual Contribution

All of the above benefits plus:
- Periodic Program Updates from Senior Staff and the Executive Director

DELTA LEVEL — $2,500 to $4,999 Annual Contribution

All of the above benefits plus:
- Saving the Bay DVD for your own personal library

MARSH LEVEL — $5,000 to $9,999 Annual Contribution

All of the above benefits plus:
- Special Seminar on San Francisco Bay Ecosystems

BAY LEVEL — $10,000 or more Annual Contribution

All of the above benefits plus:
- Bay Cruise aboard Potomac, President Franklin D. Roosevelt's personal yacht anchored at Jack London Square in Oakland

1330 Broadway, Suite 1800
Oakland, CA 94612-2519
www.saveSFbay.org

RECYCLED & RECYCLABLE / SOY INK   12-XA2

EXHIBIT 17.2
First Page of Donor Upgrade Letter, Save The Bay

1330 Broadway, Suite 1800
Oakland, CA 94612-2519
www.saveSFbay.org

David Lewis
Executive Director

February 17, 2012

Ms. Jane Doe
123 Any Street
Any Town, AS 00000-0000
STB12XA/2-17-12/Pkg 1: Major Donors

Dear Ms. Doe,

I want to tell you about an important conversation I had with Save The Bay co-founder Sylvia McLaughlin at our 50th Anniversary Gala last fall.

As we spoke of our five decades of progress, she said, "David, how do you plan to keep Save The Bay strong?" After a moment of thought, I answered, "One of our achievements with huge potential is the creation of a select group of leaders committed to a healthy Bay—**the Protector's Circle**."

Sylvia knows about the Protector's Circle, and the generous individuals like you, Ms. Doe, who are part of this special group. She is behind this critical initiative 100 percent and said, "David, it seems to me that we need to increase the size and the financial power of the Protector's Circle. There is so much to do to achieve our goals. But with everyone's help, it can be done."

I am writing you today to thank you again for stepping forward and becoming a member of the Protector's Circle. Your leadership and your commitment are making a critical difference in our work to restore and protect our beloved San Francisco Bay.

But as Sylvia said, with everyone's help it can be done. So I am also enclosing a personalized Proposal prepared exclusively for you which presents you and your fellow members of the Protector's Circle with opportunities to help make a lasting difference in the health of our Bay.

When you review your Proposal, you'll see that our 2012 goal for the Protector's Circle is $125,000. To help us achieve that goal, I'm hoping you will make a gift of $250 or $500 as soon as possible.

The reasons for the urgency are no secret. Our Bay is being threatened by Cargill's destructive—and totally misguided—plan to fill in up to 1,435 acres of salt ponds that should be protected and restored to wetlands to benefit wildlife, water quality and the region's quality of life.

(over, please)

RECYCLED & RECYCLABLE / SOY INK   12-XA1   1-A-0

How Donor Upgrade Appeals Are Different from Other Fundraising Appeals

Fundraising appeals of many types—including special appeals, renewals, and high-dollar appeals—frequently feature donor upgrade options, but those options are rarely emphasized. A true upgrade letter lays out a set of reasons why the donor should give more—and the argument to give more is a central theme in the copy, not an afterthought. This is the primary characteristic of an upgrade letter.

For example, a special appeal might seek gifts equal to or greater than the donor's highest previous contribution (HPC) to the charity. The reply device might even offer three alternative giving levels: the HPC, the HPC plus 25 percent, and the HPC plus 50 percent. But that alone won't make the letter an upgrade appeal. To qualify for that characterization, the letter needs to build a case for the increase in support. In inflationary times, that case might be to help the organization cope with steadily rising costs, and the letter might illustrate just how quickly costs are rising by giving concrete examples. Or the letter might spell out how much more the charity can accomplish if the donor sends a gift that's 25 percent or 50 percent larger than in the past. More commonly, however, an upgrade appeal is distinguished from a special appeal because it invites the donor to join a special group or giving category that requires significantly higher gifts. (That's the case with all the examples in this chapter.)

Three additional traits are shared by most upgrading efforts:

1. Upgrade letters customarily spotlight opportunities to join giving clubs or otherwise feature special benefits, premiums, or incentives for making the larger gifts requested. (Keep in mind that some or all of those benefits or incentives may be intangible.) In other words, there's a marketing concept appropriate to the request for a larger gift.

2. Upgrade efforts frequently offer two, three, or more alternative levels of support. Although this approach isn't universally used in upgrading efforts, it's common because the purpose of such efforts is usually to secure the largest possible gift—and the letter writer rarely knows how much that's likely to be.

3. Personalization and high-quality paper stock are often used in upgrade appeals—to match the ambitious request.

Case Study: AIDS Project Los Angeles Upgrade Appeal

The package illustrated in exhibits 17.3 through 17.5 is a simple straightforward upgrade appeal—in this case, an invitation to join the AIDS Project Los Angeles "Leadership Council" with a gift of $1,000 or more.

Often, high-dollar upgrade appeals of this sort focus exclusively on one giving level, most often the lowest. In this example, however, donors are offered a choice of giving levels from $1,000 to $25,000 and

EXHIBIT 17.3
Leadership Council Appeal Upgrade Letter, AIDS Project Los Angeles

LEADERSHIP COUNCIL

APLA
AIDS Project Los Angeles

The David Geffen Center
611 S. Kingsley Drive
Los Angeles CA 90005
www.apla.org

Thursday, February 8, 2007

APL07XA/01-2007/PKG 1: ALL
Ms. Jane Doe
123 Any Street
Any Town, AS 00000

Dear Ms. Doe,

Thank you for your generous support of AIDS Project Los Angeles.

As a donor of APLA since 2003, your support for our programs and services has been extraordinary. I am grateful for your partnership in helping people who are struggling with HIV/AIDS—and I hope you know the enormous difference you are making in our community.

Like you, perhaps, my initial involvement in APLA's work was deeply personal. I lost my twin brother, Greg, to AIDS in the summer of 1995.

Greg was just 34 years old when he died, and even though I was living in Chicago and couldn't be with him as much as I wanted to be, I know he wasn't alone. Thanks to AIDS Project Los Angeles, and the wonderful services they provide to people with AIDS, Greg received the care and attention he needed right 'til the very end.

APLA's Home Health program helped my brother live his final days in comfort. Even more than that, APLA staff and volunteers helped him die with dignity. I'll never forget that. It was then and there that I decided to become involved with APLA, and do everything I could to help them fulfill their mission on behalf of other people living with HIV/AIDS.

Ms. Doe, I'm writing to invite you to join me in becoming a member of APLA's Leadership Council with your gift of $1,000 or more. I've just renewed my support for 2007, and I hope you won't think me presumptuous in asking you to do the same.

AIDS Project Los Angeles depends on the generosity of its *Leadership Council* to help underwrite their programs and services—so I urge you to take a moment now to consider supporting APLA at a higher level than you've ever given before.

Your gifts totaling $1,000 in 2006 were extremely helpful.

(Over, please)

Ms. Jane Doe
Page Two

Time and again, throughout the 12 years I've been involved with APLA, I've seen the people of Los Angeles step forward to help people living with HIV/AIDS.

Your support for APLA has been extraordinary, and it gives me the courage to make an extraordinary request of you. Will you consider making a gift of $1,000 or more—and joining APLA's *Leadership Council* today?

The *Leadership Council* provides the financial foundation for APLA's life-sustaining services and HIV prevention programs. By renewing your commitment at this time, you will help improve the lives of people struggling with AIDS, you will help protect a new generation from the scourge of HIV infection, and you will help advocate for fairer and more effective HIV-related public policy.

In short, you will help advance APLA's core mission on every level.

As a member of the *Leadership Council*, you will continue to receive special recognition and exclusive benefits. You'll be invited, for example, to attend gatherings reserved for Council members only, where you will have an opportunity to meet with APLA Executive Director Craig Thompson. You will also receive special briefings and be given VIP treatment at APLA events.

You will receive enduring recognition on the Donor Wall of Honor in The David Geffen Center, on the APLA website, and in the Annual Report published each spring.

Even more important, you'll be joining with other generous, caring, and compassionate friends whose annual gifts help to underwrite APLA's programs and services.

On behalf of the *Leadership Council*, I'm extremely grateful for your steadfast support, and I look forward to seeing you at one of our events in 2007.

With heartfelt thanks,

Jeff York
Member, APLA *Leadership Council*

P.S.   I'm increasingly mindful that it's the commitment of people like you and me—not the commitment of our government—that enables APLA to provide its life-saving programs. Please renew your leadership support today.

MEMORANDUM *of* ACCEPTANCE

TO: Jeff York, Member
        APLA Leadership Council

FROM: APL07XA/01-2007/PKG 1: ALL
        Ms. Jane Doe
        123 Any Street
        Any Town, AS 00000   07XADOEB 5254   0

YES, I accept your invitation to become a Member of APLA's *Leadership Council.* I am honored to join with you in ensuring that AIDS Project Los Angeles has the resources to advance its life-saving mission. Please enroll me as a Member at the following level:

☐ I wish to become a *Member* with my gift of $1,000.
☐ I wish to become a *Friend* with my gift of $2,500.
☐ I wish to become a *Sponsor* with my gift of $5,000.
☐ I wish to become a *Patron* with my gift of $10,000.
☐ I wish to become a *Benefactor* with my gift of $25,000.

☐ I don't wish to become a Member of the *Leadership Council* at this time, but I'd like to make a special gift of $ _____.

☐ Please list my/our name(s) on the Donor Wall of Honor, the APLA website, and in APLA's 2007 Annual Report as:
_____.

☐ I prefer my/our gift remain anonymous.

LEADERSHIP COUNCIL

APLA
AIDS Project Los Angeles

The David Geffen Center
611 S. Kingsley Drive
Los Angeles CA 90005
www.apla.org

Your gift to AIDS Project Los Angeles is fully tax-deductible.

* Please see reverse if you'd like to charge your *Leadership Council* gift to your credit card.

7-XA2

☐ **I prefer to make my Leadership Council gift by:**

   ☐ VISA   ☐ MasterCard
   ☐ American Express

Amount: $ _____

Card Number: _____

Exp. date: _____

Signature: _____

☐ **I'd like to receive occassional email updates from APLA. My email address is:**
_____

Will your employer match your generous gift?

☐ **I have enclosed my employer's matching gift form.**

MEMBERSHIP LEVELS

MEMBERS who make gifts of $1,000 to $2,499 are recognized in APLA's Annual Report, on APLA's website, and on the Wall of Honor in the main reception area of The David Geffen Center. They are invited to two major donor events each year and receive a subscription to *The Optimist*.

FRIENDS who make gifts of $2,500 to $4,999 receive all of the benefits listed above and also receive advance invitations to all APLA functions and events, including a personal tour of APLA's offices.

SPONSORS who make gifts of $5,000 to $9,999 receive all of the benefits listed above and also receive two invitations to the VIP breakfast preceding AIDS Walk Los Angeles, two invitations to APLA's Annual VIP Oscar Party, an opportunity to have dinner with a senior APLA staff member, and personal handling of requests and other VIP services.

PATRONS who make gifts of $10,000 to $24,999 receive all of the benefits listed above and also receive four invitations to the VIP breakfast preceding AIDS Walk Los Angeles, four invitations to attend APLA's Annual VIP Oscar Party, and an opportunity to have dinner with APLA's Executive Director and Board Chair.

BENEFACTORS who make gifts of $25,000 and above receive all of the benefits listed above and also receive eight invitations to the VIP breakfast preceding AIDS Walk Los Angeles, six invitations to attend APLA's Annual VIP Oscar Party, VIP access to all APLA events, and special recognition opportunities for selected programs.

LEADERSHIP COUNCIL

AIDS Project Los Angeles

BENEFITS OF MEMBERSHIP

The *APLA Leadership Council* is comprised of a group of leaders in our community who make a significant financial contribution on an annual basis to AIDS Project Los Angeles. Council members express their deep commitment to helping people affected by HIV disease, reducing the incidence of HIV infection, and advocating for effective HIV-related public policy through their generous annual gifts of $1,000 or more.

Council members receive exclusive benefits and enduring recognition. All members are invited to events reserved only for *APLA Leadership Council* members, for discussions with APLA Executive Director Craig E. Thompson and other prominent leaders involved in HIV/AIDS prevention. Council members also receive a complimentary subscription to APLA's quarterly newsletter, *The Optimist*, and other expressions of appreciation.

AIDS Project Los Angeles
The David Geffen Center • 611 S. Kingsley Drive • Los Angeles CA 90005
www.apla.org • 213-201-1564

EXHIBIT 17.5
Leadership Council Appeal Outer Envelope, AIDS Project Los Angeles

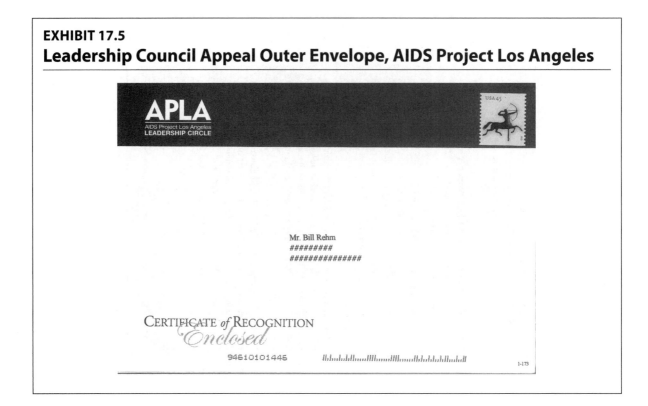

above. Note the benefits offered at each of these levels: you'll see an abundance of special events (probably more typical of Los Angeles than of this particular organization!). Note also the multiple instances of personalization. Just imagine your chances of securing a gift of $1,000 or more with a "Dear Friend" letter!

Now that you have what I hope is a clear picture of how upgrade efforts work, I'd like you by my side in chapter 18 as we examine the topic of "Seeking Annual Gifts."

Chapter Eighteen:
Seeking Annual Gifts

Building Long-Term Loyalty, One Year at a Time

The backbone of most direct response fundraising programs—indeed, of most fundraising programs generally—is an annual membership or "Annual Fund" program. Most such programs use a technique borrowed from the magazine subscription business (remember magazines? those slick, colorfully printed periodicals?) to maximize donor participation: they mail a series of letters (or *notices*), stopping only when a member's gift is finally received. Smaller nonprofits may limit their *renewal series* to three or four such notices. Larger organizations with huge donor databases may send out ten notices or more (just as do major national magazines).

The Be The Match membership renewal device reproduced in Exhibit 18.1 contains three elements that are both important and typical of the renewal notices used by nonprofits. (The full package can be seen online at www .josseybass.com/go/fundraisingappeals.)

- This is clearly about renewing annual membership—since the headline says so!

- The form offers several different membership levels, so that the recipient may upgrade voluntarily.

- The message is extremely brief and focused almost exclusively on the relationship between the individual member and the organization.

EXHIBIT 18.1

Annual Fund Renewal Response Device, Be The Match

2012 ANNUAL FUND RENEWAL

SUPPORTER SINCE:	2004
YEAR OF LAST GIFT:	2011
THIS RENEWAL FOR:	2012

Yes, I want to provide hope and healing to marrow transplant patients and their families. Enclosed is my special gift to support Be The Match®'s 2012 Annual Fund campaign:

❑ $25 ❑ $38 ❑ $50 ❑ $_____

❑ My check is enclosed.

❑ Please charge my credit card. *(See reverse.)*

Mr. John Doe
123 Main Street
Anytown, AS 00000
BTM12AA/4-13-12/PKG1: Annual Fund Appeal High Value

12AA23IB 30599

BE ✿ THE MATCH®

3001 Broadway Street NE | Suite 601
Minneapolis, MN 55413-1753

Please see reverse to charge your gift. Return this form with your renewal of support. Be The Match is a 501(c)(3) organization and your contribution is fully tax-deductible. Thank you!

BE ✿ THE MATCH®

3001 Broadway Street NE | Suite 601
Minneapolis, MN 55413-1753
BeTheMatch.org

April 13, 2012

Dear Mr. Doe,

I'm writing to thank you for your generous support of Be The Match®—and to urge you to take a moment today to renew your support for our 2012 Annual Fund campaign.

As a long time supporter of Be The Match®, you may remember that this is the time of year when we ask you—and <u>all</u> our supporters—to renew your annual support. Your gift at this time of year will enable us to plan our resources more effectively and will also save you from receiving repeated renewal notices throughout the year.

**So I ask you to take a moment—today if possible—to renew your
2012 Annual Fund support with a gift of $25 or $38.**

Since your first gift to Be The Match® in 2004, you have helped to provide hope and healing to thousands of patients needing marrow transplants.

In 2011 alone, with your support, we were able to help 5,500 patients receive a marrow transplant from an unrelated donor—and grow the Be The Match Registry® by more than 650,000 potential new transplant donors! Since our founding in 1987, more than 50,000 patients have benefitted from life-saving transplants!

Mr. Doe, please always remember, no matter how you have taken part in Be The Match® previously, <u>our good work depends on you and you are making a tremendous difference</u>.

I am profoundly grateful for all your support over the years. Please know that whatever additional contribution you are able to make to Be The Match® during our 2012 Annual Fund campaign, you will always be appreciated for your continuing support, your strength and compassion, and your confidence in our work. I extend to you my most sincere gratitude.

With thanks,

Christine Fleming

Christine Fleming
President

P.S. Your last gift of $25 in 2011 made such a difference. If you are able to match that gift—or even make a gift of $38—I will be enormously grateful.

Please charge my:

☐ VISA   ☐ MasterCard   ☐ American Express   ☐ Discover

Name: _____

Amount: $_____   Expiraton date: _____

Card #: _____

Signature: _____

☐ Yes, I want to receive occasional updates from Be The Match®.

My email address is: _____

How Renewal Letters Are Different from Other Fundraising Appeals

Annual renewal efforts are of two general types: annual fund appeals (most commonly coming from schools and colleges) and membership renewal series (which aren't limited to organizations with formal membership structures but are most frequently used by them). Both types usually share the following five characteristics:

1. There are clear and explicit references to membership dues or the annual gift. In other words, it's unmistakably clear that the organization expects the donor's support, this year and every year.

2. The letter focuses on the process of renewal, repeating an action taken last year (and maybe for many years past).

3. The case is usually made in general and institutional terms rather than focusing on a particular program or special need. An annual gift, after all, represents support for the institution, not for some limited aspect of its work.

4. Renewal letters are typically short. The most important point to make in such letters is "please renew"—and that may be all you really need to say.

5. The element of time and its limits is always at least implicit: "this year's dues," "your expiration date," "the deadline for renewing."

Case Study: Corporate Accountability International's Annual Membership Renewal Series

Exhibits 18.2 through 18.5 show the outer envelopes of the four efforts in Corporate Accountability International's membership renewal series, just to give you a sense of the changing character of these reminder notices as time goes by. (The full packages are shown in color at www.josseybass.com /go/fundraisingappeals.)

Here's how a renewal series typically works:

- All of last year's active members, plus many of those whose membership has lapsed, are mailed the first effort in the series. Those who respond with gifts are then immediately thanked and cycled into a sequence of special appeals. They will not receive any subsequent renewal notices.

- Nonresponders to the first effort will receive the second some four to six weeks later. They too will be acknowledged for their renewed support, removed from the renewal process, and included in any special appeals the organization may subsequently send.

- The later efforts, numbers three and four in this case, will function in an identical manner, mailed at intervals of approximately one month. Through this process, by the time the entire series has been mailed, a substantial proportion of the organization's members will have renewed.

- However, some members ignore renewals and respond only to special appeals. Those mailings, which take place only once the renewal series is well under way, serve to reactivate an additional number of members. (In many organizations, there is no meaningful distinction made between *members* and *donors*.)

For a great many nonprofit organizations, the renewal series is the backbone of the small-donor fundraising program. Renewals often account for a huge proportion of the revenue from direct mail, telephone, and online fundraising programs.

EXHIBIT 18.2

First Membership Renewal Effort Outer Envelope, Corporate Accountability International

CORPORATE
ACCOUNTABILITY
INTERNATIONAL
CHALLENGING ABUSE, PROTECTING PEOPLE
10 Milk Street, Suite 610 | Boston, MA 02108

Your 2012 Membership Renewal is Enclosed

Mr. John Doe
123 Main Street
Anytown, US 00000
CAI12RA /March 14, 2012/ Renewal 1/A

RECYCLED & RECYCLABLE / PRINTED WITH SOY INK   12-RA3   318

EXHIBIT 18.3

Second Membership Renewal Effort Outer Envelope, Corporate Accountability International

Ms. Jane Doe
123 Any Street
Any Town, AS 00000

Over the years, my colleagues and I have succeeded in dramatically boosting revenue for new clients in the very first year of our work with them. Usually, the number one reason we accomplish this is that we introduce an annual renewal series. So, if your organization isn't taking advantage of this unusually lucrative technique, I suggest you hasten to do so ASAP!

Now let's look at an activity that is tragically undervalued in the nonprofit sector: thanking your donors.

EXHIBIT 18.4

Third Membership Renewal Effort Outer Envelope, Corporate Accountability International

MEMBERSHIP SERVICES
Corporate Accountability International
10 Milk Street, Suite 610
Boston, MA 02108

RECYCLED & RECYCLABLE / SOY INK   9-RC3

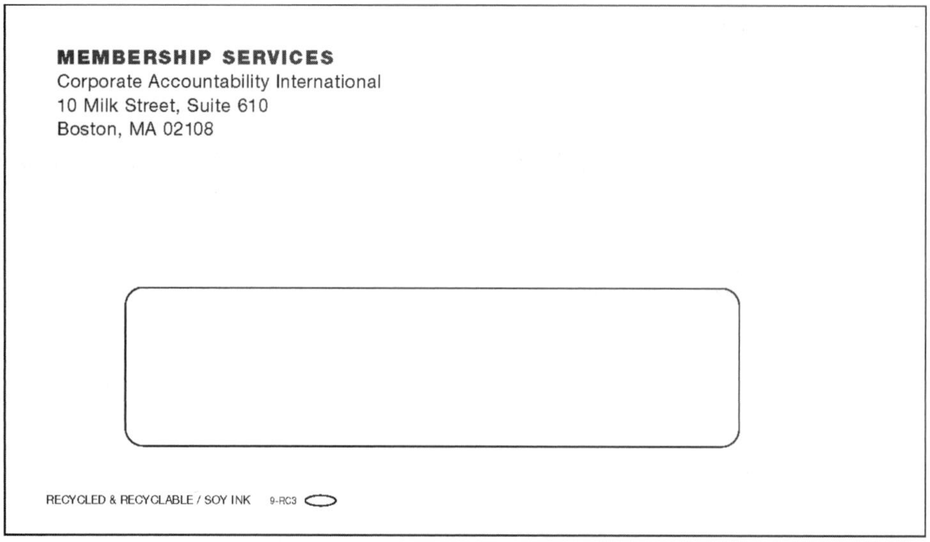

EXHIBIT 18.5

Fourth Membership Renewal Effort Outer Envelope, Corporate Accountability International

CORPORATE ACCOUNTABILITY INTERNATIONAL
CHALLENGING ABUSE, PROTECTING PEOPLE
10 Milk Street, Suite 610 | Boston, MA 02108

FINAL Membership Renewal **Notice Enclosed**

Mr. John Doe
123 Main Street
Anytown, US 00000
CAI12RD /June 7, 2012/ pkg 1:Renewal Donors

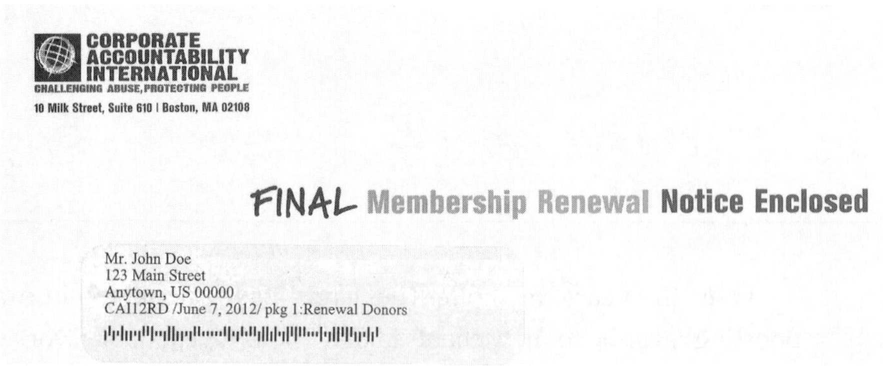

Chapter Nineteen:
Thanking Your Donors

Friend-Raising before Fundraising

You probably figured this out a long time ago: writing fundraising letters is no way for your organization to make a quick buck. Raising money by mail, online, or by telephone, like fundraising conducted by any other means, is a long-term process. The fundraising appeals you send as that process unfolds may differ dramatically from one another because your relationships with donors change over time. You know much more about your donors in the later stages of the process than you do at the earlier, and your appeals will reflect that knowledge in ways that are both obvious and profound. But there's one element all effective fundraising letters share: they show appreciation.

Even when you're writing a prospective donor who's known to you only as a name on a list, it's sound practice to find a way to compliment her while you make your case for a gift—and then to thank her in advance for agreeing to help. It's the *polite* thing to do.

When you write to a proven donor to solicit additional support, it's important to reinforce her goodwill (and her memory) by thanking her for her past generosity. It's not only polite to do that; it's sure to make your appeal work better.

And when you're asking a donor to make an extra special effort to upgrade her support—by joining a high-dollar club or a monthly sustainer program, for example—you'll get the best results when you include repeated, heartfelt thanks in your letter. After all, the donors you select to include in most upgrade campaigns are very special people who've already given you more money or given more frequently or for a longer period of time than all the rest of your supporters. It's polite, effective, and natural to thank them in an upgrade appeal.

In other words, every fundraising appeal is a thank-you.

Even so, that's not enough. The savviest fundraisers learn early on that they need to send special letters or e-mails and sometimes even make special phone calls dedicated exclusively to thanking their donors.

How Thank-You Letters Are Different from Other Fundraising Letters

The Center for the Victims of Torture donor acknowledgment letter reproduced in exhibits 19.1 through 19.4 is an excellent example. From the outer envelope teaser through all the remaining elements of this package (except

EXHIBIT 19.1
Thank-You Outer Envelope, The Center for the Victims of Torture

EXHIBIT 19.2
Thank-You Letter, The Center for the Victims of Torture

Thank you!

December 2, 2011

Mr. Bill Rehm
Ms. Joanne Ruby
########
###############

Dear Mr. Rehm and Ms. Ruby,

Thank you for your gift of $100.00 to the Center for Victims of Torture, which we received on November 29, 2011. Your support is especially helpful now as we come to the end of 2011 and begin to implement our new plans for 2012.

This past year—in countries all around the world—CVT helped thousands of clients to rebuild lives devastated by torture. Your partnership made this possible.

As you may know, in 2011 CVT significantly expanded our work in the Dadaab refugee camps in Kenya, where conditions are especially dire for refugees fleeing Somalia. These camps were originally built to house 90,000 refugees, but are now home to more than 450,000 men, women, and children—including thousands of the torture survivors now receiving care from CVT.

And, for more than 26 years we've extended care to torture survivors living in Minnesota. This year we've helped over 250 clients and more than 500 family members from 42 countries rebuild their lives. We've also developed a new initiative, Healing in Partnership, to help hundreds of arriving refugees who endure mental health symptoms as a result of torture and war-related traumas. By using culturally adapted mental health screening tools, refugees needing mental health care are identified and directed to the best resources within the community.

Thank you again for your continuing and generous support, which makes this work possible.

With warm regards,

Douglas A. Johnson
Executive Director

Contributions to the Center for Victims of Torture are tax-deductible. No goods or services were provided in return for this gift. Please keep this letter for your tax records.

649 DAYTON AVENUE ST. PAUL, MN 55104 • TELEPHONE 1.877.265.8775 • FAX 612.436.2600 • www.cvt.org

Does your employer match your contributions to the Center for Victims of Torture?

Your contribution to CVT may accomplish even more if your company or organization matches contributions by you and other employees. Some of the many corporations that match gifts to CVT are listed below.

AIG
Alliant Techsystems, Inc.
Altria Group, Inc.
American Express Foundation
Amgen Foundation
Aspect
BP Foundation, Inc.
Briggs and Morgan, LLP
Burlington Northern Santa Fe
   Foundation
Cardinal Health Foundation
The Clorox Company Foundation
Community Solutions Fund
The Di Salvo Ericson Group
Dorsey and Whitney Foundation
Equifax Foundation
Fair Isaac

Follett
GMAC—RFC
Halleland Lewis Nilan &
   Johnson LLP
Insurance Services Office, Inc.
JP Morgan Chase Foundation
Thrivent Financial
Mal Warwick Associates
MasterCard International
The May Department Stores
   Company
McKnight Foundation
McMaster—Carr
The Meredith Corporation
   Foundation
Metris Foundation
Microsoft

Moody's Foundation
Nokia
Nuveen Investments, LLC
Oswald Family Foundation
The Pew Charitable Trusts
Pfizer Foundation
Sam's Club Foundation
Schatz Group GMAC Real
   Estate
Star Tribune Foundation
Thompson West
Tyco
U.S. Bancorp
W. K. Kellogg Foundation
Xcel Energy Foundation

**Check with your personnel department or human resources manager
to find out if your company will match your gifts to CVT.**

We use your contributions wisely! We are proud that **91 cents of every dollar** contributed goes directly to programs and projects that benefit torture survivors. The Center for Victims of Torture meets all the requirements of The American Institute of Philanthropy and Charities Review Council.

You may visit our web site, www.cvt.org, to view our annual report and financial statements. You may also request a free copy of our audited financial reports by writing us at 649 Dayton Avenue, St. Paul, MN 55104.

The Center for Victims of Torture can be found under Human/Civil Rights Organizations in the Combined Federal Campaign, Number 11943.

EXHIBIT 19.3
Thank-You Reply Device, The Center for the Victims of Torture

Other Ways You Can Help

☐ I'd like to join CVT's online advocacy network and receive e-mail updates:

E-mail address: _____

☐ Please don't exchange my mailing address.

    Mr. Bill Rehm
    Ms. Joanne Ruby
    #########
    ##############

THE CENTER FOR VICTIMS OF TORTURE
649 DAYTON AVENUE ST. PAUL, MN 55104 · 1.877.265.8775 · www.cvt.org

☐ I'd like to make an additional
gift to support CVT's work:

☐ $100   ☐ $50
☐ $25   ☐ $_____

☐ I've enclosed a check.
☐ Please charge this gift to my credit card:

Card # _____

Expiration Date _____

Signature _____
20601 REN-LO

11-YA2A

Please see reverse side for ▶
important information.

EXHIBIT 19.4

Thank-You Insert, The Center for the Victims of Torture

You're making a difference!

Thank you for joining with thousands of other compassionate and generous friends of the Center for Victims of Torture. Your financial support enables us to fulfill our mission to heal the wounds of torture on individuals, their families, and their communities and to stop torture worldwide. Torture is a crime against humanity that is perpetrated in more than 100 countries around the world. It is used to control populations by destroying leaders and frightening communities.

There are an estimated 500,000 torture survivors now living in the United States. Many are refugees or persons who have been granted or are seeking political asylum. Torturers leave behind talented and highly trained individuals who once were productive, but now are disabled. Left un-addressed, these disabilities can trap survivors in a cycle of hopelessness and despair. Yet it is possible for them to break free with our help and hard work—and to heal from the deep wounds of torture.

Founded in 1985, the Center for Victims of Torture was the first organization of its kind in the United States. CVT has pioneered a unique, multi-disciplinary treatment program that enables torture survivors to reclaim their lives. Together, we're making a difference!

CLIENT CARE

More than 30,000 torture survivors live in Minnesota, where CVT provides care and rehabilitative services at our healing center in St. Paul. Our clients have come from more than 70 nations—in Africa, Asia, the Middle East, Eastern Europe, and Latin America. They come to CVT wanting desperately to regain productive lives of dignity—for themselves, for their families, and for their communities. But first they must overcome the legacy of torture: physical pain, nightmares, anxiety, depression, and a combination of reactions that are grouped together as post-traumatic stress disorder.

To help torture survivors heal from these deep wounds, our physicians, psychiatrists, psychologists, nurses, and social workers employ

With your support, the Center for Victims of Torture reaches out to thousands of people who have suffered torture during civil conflicts in Africa and the Middle East.

a multi-disciplinary program designed to meet our clients' extraordinary needs. Healing torture survivors is a complex and difficult task, and our professional staff are widely regarded as international experts in this emerging field of work.

IN AFRICA AND THE MIDDLE EAST

The Center for Victims of Torture also operates programs in Kenya, Jordan, and the Democratic Republic of Congo. Last year, over 2,100 survivors received services in refugee camps and in communities where refugees have returned. Since beginning our work, CVT international staff has trained more than 300 local staff, many of whom are refugees themselves, to serve as mental health specialists.

CAPACITY BUILDING INITIATIVES

No one organization can provide services for the hundreds of thousands of torture survivors now living in the United States. However, many survivors can be greatly helped if they receive care from others in the community who—through training on the effects and symptoms of torture— ▶

understand how to respond appropriately. CVT's training programs serve as models for other organizations in the United States and abroad.

- CVT has trained more than 25,000 health and human service providers in Minnesota to identify symptoms related to torture and provide appropriate care for survivors. The project also helps torture survivors receive sensitive and appropriate care wherever they receive health and human services.

- CVT organized the National Consortium of Torture Treatment Programs and provides assistance to an emerging network of over 30 groups throughout the United States. We help these centers build their clinical skills; create strong, local organizations; and strengthen their public education and advocacy programs.

- When we were founded, CVT was the third center of its kind in the world. Now, more than 200 programs worldwide care for torture survivors. We are assisting centers in 17 different countries that have the potential to become regional leaders in the torture treatment movement.

- Through the New Tactics in Human Rights Project, CVT works with leading international organizations and activists. The project has researched and catalogued more than 120 tactics—the actions people take to create solutions—in the field of human rights.

Our 12 years of work in Africa have resulted in rebuilding the lives of 18,000 men, women and children in Guinea, Sierra Leone, Liberia and the Democratic Republic of Congo.

EDUCATION AND PUBLIC POLICY

The Center for Victims of Torture is able to speak with a very unique voice against torture. We understand torture's real purpose and its consequences. CVT was the leading force behind the passage of the Torture Victims Relief Act, which authorized millions of dollars in U.S. government support for programs to assist torture victims in the U.S. and abroad. With our staff in Washington, D.C., and in collaboration with other torture treatment centers, we continue to advocate for increased funding for torture rehabilitation programs, and the need for additional public and private funding remains extraordinary.

If you have questions, please contact us:

The
CENTER for
VICTIMS of
TORTURE

We're always happy to hear from friends of the Center for Victims of Torture. Our annual report—including financial statements—is available by visiting our web site: www.cvt.org. You'll find a wealth of other current information there as well.

Please call or write if you wish to receive printed materials.

649 DAYTON AVENUE ST. PAUL, MN 55104 • TELEPHONE 1.877.265.8775 • FAX 612.436.2600 • www.cvt.org

11-YA5A

for the reply envelope, which isn't shown), the message is consistently "thank you!" This package displays seven elements that clearly set it apart as a thank-you and nothing more:

- The outer envelope sets the tone with a bold "THANK YOU" teaser.

- The letter specifically refers to the date and amount of the gift.

- The back of the letter promotes corporate matching gifts, which can be a significant source of revenue.

- The text of the letter reinforces the case for giving and counters what commercial marketers call "buyers' remorse."

- The message is brief and to the point, so as not to muddy the thank-you theme.

- The response device offers "Other Ways You Can Help," giving donors the opportunity to join CVT's online advocacy network.

- The insert provides further reinforcement for the donor with a headline reading "You're making a difference!"

Why You Need to Write Thank-Yous

Focus group research consistently turns up comments like the following:

"I sent them some money over a year ago, but I never got a thank-you. Well, never again!"

"I've been giving to them for years, twenty, twenty-five bucks at a time. They got a hundred bucks from me recently—and all they sent back was the same preprinted postcard they always send. How much do you think they're going to get the next time around?"

"The thing that burns me up is getting a thank-you about two months after I send a check—after they've already asked me for more money! I won't give to a group that's that disorganized . . . or rude."

Why do remarks like these so commonly emerge from focus group research? Because so many charities defy what I call the Golden Rule of Donor Acknowledgments: thank your donors promptly!

Consider my alter ego—whom I call the Phantom Donor. This generous soul sends $15, $20, or $25 gifts once or twice a year to some of the nation's top nonprofit organizations—and studies the mail that comes in return.

Several years ago, the Phantom paid special attention to the donor acknowledgment practices of some favorite charities. The experience was sobering. The Phantom mailed a round of $15 checks to twenty organizations, all on the same day and accompanying the most recent reply device and reply envelope received from each of the mailers. Eight weeks later, the Phantom Donor had been thanked by only fifteen of the twenty groups. One of them, the American Red Cross, got out a thank-you (admittedly only a postcard) within less than one week. But few others arrived within the first month. The typical response time was five to seven weeks.

That performance was pathetic. And we're not talking about the mom-and-pop charity down on the corner. These were some of the most successful nonprofit mailers in America—groups such as the Humane Society of the United States, Common Cause, and the Christian Appalachian Project. In fact, most direct mail fundraisers do a downright poor job of thanking their donors. The donor acknowledgment practices of those big charities simply mirror what goes on throughout the independent sector.

Charities that cut costs by refraining from mailing thank-yous or by sending such cut-rate items as preprinted postcards are all missing the boat, because they can do so much better. But even worse is to defy the Golden Rule of Donor Acknowledgments.

The most heartwarming and informative thank-you copy will be wasted on a donor who may already have forgotten that he sent you a check. (If you doubt donors react this way, run a couple of focus groups, and ask donors what they think.) In fact, I'm so concerned about the widespread failure to heed the Golden Rule of Donor Acknowledgments that I'll offer a corollary: Send even a "bad" (that is, impersonal) thank-you if you can get it into the mail much faster than a "good" (that is, personal and specific) one!

Here, now, are a few other pointers for effective donor acknowledgments:

Writing an Effective Thank-You

- Reassure your donors that it was a good idea to send a gift. Don't let them suffer from buyer's remorse. Reinforce their original belief that your group is effective, caring, and worthy of their support.

- Be warm and friendly. If they're new donors, welcome them to the "family."

- Praise their generosity. Tell them how, by joining with other supporters, they're having a significant impact on your work.

- Reaffirm your gratitude at the end of the letter or in a P.S.

- Give examples of recent organizational successes donors can feel proud of.

Most fundraisers believe it's advisable to suggest another gift in a thank-you package—and I agree with them when it's a "soft" ask that no one could possibly interpret as arm-twisting. There are circumstances in which I don't think such an approach is advisable, but it's often worth considering. For example, in emergencies and with important deadlines approaching, it might be unnatural not to ask for additional support. In any case, it's almost always a good idea to enclose a reply envelope, even if you're not soliciting an additional gift.

To explore some of the numerous possibilities opened up by thank-you packages, let's take a look at the diverse styles and approaches followed by those fifteen mailers who (eventually) thanked the Phantom Donor—a contributor to the newsletter I edited for twenty-five years who had mailed $15 unsolicited contributions to those mailers several months previously. The story that follows is based on a study conducted several years ago, but I can find no evidence that practice in the nonprofit sector has changed in material ways in the years since then.

How Some of the Country's Top Fundraising Mailers Thank Their Donors

A Number 10 window envelope was far and away the preferred choice of the fifteen mailers who responded to the Phantom's unsolicited contributions. Not a single one used a closed-face (nonwindow) envelope, although CARE opted for a self-contained *fast-tab* envelope. There were also two postcards (from the Red Cross and from the National Organization for Women).

Of the envelope packages received, nearly half featured teasers. Nothing flashy, just a simple "thank you" in five out of the six cases. The sixth got fancier: "A special note of thanks."

As I mentioned earlier, some direct mail pros argue that a thank-you is the best time to solicit another contribution—a "get 'em while they're hot" mentality. All the thank-you packages sent to the Phantom (except the two postcards) included a return envelope to be used for subsequent gifts. However, only seven of these thirteen mailers directly pitched for funds by including reply devices. The most aggressive approach was the attempt to seek an immediate upgrade through membership in a monthly giving club. Two environmental groups opted for this stratagem: Greenpeace USA and the National Audubon Society. Significantly, in both cases letter copy emphasized the long-term commitment needed in the day-to-day battle to save our environment.

Most of the packages consisted of copy that was short and to the point. Aside from the two postcards, the Phantom received six short-form receipts, one of which also incorporated a membership card. Of the seven actual letters, five were of the one-page variety. The exceptions were the two monthly sustainer packages: Greenpeace used a two-page letter, Audubon a three-pager.

One intriguing point about the two longer pieces was that these were the only letters that were not personalized. Both instead used a variation on the "Dear Supporter" salutation—ironically, a rather impersonal way to elicit a substantial upgrade.

Almost all the acknowledgments straightforwardly and profusely thanked the Phantom—from a simple "your gift makes a difference" to the gushy "you are special to us and we hold you in our hearts and minds." Religiously oriented groups were likely to add a "God bless you."

Generally, the message was upbeat and gracious, reminding the Phantom Donor of the good work being accomplished by the group (to make her—or him—feel better about parting with fifteen bucks). Occasionally, though, the tone was more downbeat, and the Phantom was treated to a lecture on the ills faced by the organization. The Republican National Committee, for example, was up in arms about the "Clinton/Democrat tax and spend frenzy," while the World Wildlife Fund informed the Phantom that many species "are on the brink of extinction."

Four of the thirteen letter packages contained inserts. What was particularly striking was that all four were on the subject of planned giving. Each of these inserts incorporated a return coupon for requesting additional information. In two other instances—where a planned giving brochure was not enclosed—a checkoff box was included on the reply device for requesting further material.

Most of the Phantom's charities avoided sending premiums. The Billy Graham Evangelistic Association was a notable exception. As in previous acknowledgment packages, the Graham organization included a 300-page paperback book and a reprint from its monthly magazine. Only two other groups mailed premiums, apart from the Nature Conservancy's membership card. St. Joseph's Indian School sent a prayer card, and Father Flanagan's Boys' Home included an excerpt from a book by its executive director. The latter also enclosed a "handy" wallet calendar that was "made in our own print shop."

Father Flanagan's Boys' Home also alerted the Phantom to be on the lookout for a future premium. The personalized copy declared, "In my next letter, because you are one of our family, I'm sending you an honorary certificate of citizenship." Two weeks later the certificate arrived—with another appeal for funds.

Despite bells and whistles and occasional high-pressure requests for additional donations, few donor acknowledgments generate even enough revenue to cover their costs. Nevertheless, savvy (if far from speedy) fundraising mailers go to all this trouble and expense not just because it's thoughtful and polite to send thank-yous but also for the following three reasons. The first two are obvious and easily confirmed by testing; the third presents a more fundamental reason to invest in timely and appropriate donor acknowledgments.

1. Thank-yous increase response to subsequent appeals.
2. Thank-yous increase donor loyalty.
3. Thank-yous help build long-term relationships with donors.

To give you a better sense of what I mean, I'm going to guide you through a thank-you package from another major fundraising mailer—one not on the Phantom's charity list.

Case Study: An Example of a Great Thank-You Letter

The Southern Poverty Law Center, in Montgomery, Alabama, sent out a masterful donor acknowledgment package that consisted of an outer envelope and two notebook-sized pages, printed on one side only (see exhibits 19.5 and 19.6). Many fundraisers insist you should include a self-addressed reply envelope in every communication with your donors, but there was none in this package (much less a personalized reply device that might generate a bounce-back gift). I'll bet, though, that this warm, informative acknowledgment generated gifts at least an order of magnitude greater than the few, paltry bounce-back contributions that might have resulted if the package had included a reply envelope.

This package was mailed first class. Had it been mailed bulk rate instead (to save on postage), the Southern Poverty Law Center couldn't have used

---

EXHIBIT 19.5
Thank-You Outer Envelope, Southern Poverty Law Center

Bobby Person
Route 1, Box 407
West End, North Carolina 27376

EXHIBIT 19.6

Thank-You Letter, Southern Poverty Law Center

Bobby Person
Route 1, Box 190
West End, North Carolina 27376

October 15, 1993

Ms. ⸻
⸻
⸻, CA 947⸻

Dear Ms. ⸻,

I understand from my friends at the Southern Poverty Law Center and its Klanwatch Project in Montgomery that you recently sent a gift to help in their work.

I wanted to show some appreciation for the work the Center did for me and I wrote them a letter of thanks. They asked if I would share my feelings with you so that you might better understand that their work touches the lives of real people in a meaningful way. I was more than glad to help by writing you directly.

When I needed their help to protect me from harassment from members of the Ku Klux Klan, they spent hundreds of hours and several thousand dollars to protect my family and me.

Let me tell you about my case.

I am a black person living in a small rural North Carolina community and work as a guard at a state prison. I wanted to advance myself and asked my supervisor for permission to take the sergeant's examination. No black man had ever been sergeant of the prison guard.

I did not know at the time that one of the white guards was a Klansman. That night, a Klan cross was burned in the dirt road in front of my house. My wife and children were terrified. A few nights later, several Klansmen wearing sheets and paramilitary uniforms, and carrying guns, drove up in front of my home and threatened to kill me. My children were so frightened that they did not sleep well for months. Later, shots were fired at the guard tower at night from cars passing on the road.

The lawyers from the Southern Poverty Law Center filed suit against three Klansmen suspected of this harassment. They also filed suit to stop the Carolina Knights of the KKK from operating their paramilitary army. After a few months, they received a court order stopping the Klan paramilitary training. The three Klansmen who harassed me and my family also stood trial and were ordered to stop.

Since the Center came to my aid, I am proud to tell you that I won the promotion to sergeant.

You may have heard of some of the big cases the Center has handled. Many of these cases receive national publicity and many have made significant advances in human rights. My case is not very important in the long run and you may not ever have heard about it, but it was important to my family and me to be able to call on a group of lawyers who had the money to go after the Klan and who are experts in how to stop Klan terrorism. Funds were available to help me only with help from people like yourself.

Now the Center has expanded its work with a new educational project to encourage the teaching of tolerance in our schools.

For the first time in history, an organization exists that is not only fighting the Klan in the courtroom, but also in the classroom by helping teach children the value of tolerance.

Please continue your financial support of the Center. This is a long, hard fight that needs people like yourself committed to working for a future when all people live in peace and harmony.

My family and I want to thank you personally for the generous gift that you gave the Center.

Sincerely,

Bobby Person

Bobby Person's name and address as the return address on the outer envelope. (Under postal regulations still in force in the United States at this writing, a nonprofit organization must correctly identify itself on the outer envelope to qualify for the nonprofit postal discount.) Why mail first class? With a first-class letter from a person unknown to the recipient, the package had an air of mystery about it and unquestionably received high readership—far higher, in all likelihood, than a letter identified as coming from the center would have garnered.

Clearly, the Southern Poverty Law Center chose to invest in its future relationships with donors by spending a modest sum on thank-yous like these. You'd be well advised to consider whether this technique makes sense for your own organization. It probably does, because the revenue generated from future appeals to new donors is likely to dwarf the investment you've made in acquiring and converting first-time donors to loyal donors through such techniques as this. And far more of your new donors are likely to respond to those future appeals (and more generously so) if they feel you've treated them like part of the family.

It's really that simple. Treat every one of your donors like Grandma or Uncle Paul, and your organization will reap the rewards for many years to come. If you do all that, you may just find that your organization is eventually enriched by the ultimate gift, a legacy. We'll take up that subject in chapter 20.

Chapter Twenty:
Promoting Legacy Gifts

Seeking the Ultimate Commitment

Direct mail fundraising—indeed, all direct response fundraising, including telemarketing and e-philanthropy—works because lots of people contribute small gifts, and many of them continue to do so, year after year. Most people who specialize in other aspects of fundraising deal in gifts that are substantially larger than the typical direct response gift, sometimes running into hundreds of thousands or millions of dollars. Viewed from one perspective, legacy fundraising is a bridge between the direct marketers who typically traffic in small contributions and the traditional fundraisers who are often discontent if the gifts they secure don't run into six or seven figures, or more. That's because legacy gifts in the United States tend to be comparable in size to the major gifts, foundation grants, and corporate contributions that constitute the bread and butter of traditional fundraisers.

In most organizations, legacy fundraising is confined to a special office or department, typically called by the inelegant and unfortunate name *planned giving*. Such offices are usually staffed by specialized, often highly paid major gift officers who are knowledgeable about the legal ins and outs of complex wills and trusts—the stuff that wealthy people usually come to grips with in middle age or later. All too often, planned giving officers scorn the modest legacies that might come from retired schoolteachers, postal employees, or service personnel. In other words, they rarely lift a finger to solicit those gifts. Direct response fundraising techniques, principally direct mail, are the most effective way to reach these people. It's important that those nonprofit organizations likely to benefit from legacy fundraising turn to direct response, for three reasons.

Reasons to Use Direct Mail for Legacy Fundraising

- The overwhelming majority of legacy gifts are in the form of bequests, which typically consist of a sentence or two in an individual's will, living trust, or estate plan. Research shows that direct mail is the most effective way to market legacy giving through bequests.

- So-called planned giving officers, for reasons of their own, tend to concentrate on wealthy individual prospects who may be candidates for multimillion-dollar legacy gifts (often in the form of complex tax-avoidance trusts that require lawyers, accountants, and other high-priced help to establish). But the vast majority of legacy gifts come from individuals who are not rich—the very same people who normally relate to and support charities primarily through the mail.

- The tools used by sophisticated direct mail fundraisers—statistical analysis and segmentation—are by far the most cost-effective way to identify prospective legacy donors.

EXHIBIT 20.1
Legacy Response Device, Bread for the World

A Legacy of Hope

☐ Please send more information, without obligation, about:
   ☐ How IRAs can be used for charitable gifts
   ☐ Charitable gift annuities
   ☐ Charitable lead and remainder trusts

☐ I would like more information on remembering Bread for the World in my will.

☐ I've established a charitable bequest to Bread for the World or Bread for the World Institute. Please add my (our) name(s) to the Legacy of Hope display:

_____
PLEASE PRINT YOUR NAME(S) AS YOU WISH IT (THEM) TO APPEAR.

Mr. John Doe
123 Anv Street
Any Town AS 00000
BFW07LA/2-13-07/Others

Phone _____ / _____

0
07LA

All information about charitable bequests and other planned gifts is held in the strictest confidence.

1   07LA B

Bread for the World Institute welcomes gifts of stocks and securities. To arrange transfers, please contact Molly Pearce at 1-800-822-7323, ext. 137.

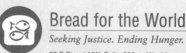

Bread for the World
Seeking Justice. Ending Hunger.
50 F Street NW, Suite 500   Washington, DC 20001-1567
1-800-822-7323   www.bread.org

The Bread for the World renewal device shown in Exhibit 20.1 illustrates several of the characteristics that are commonly found in direct mail promotions for legacy giving:

- There's no mistaking the fact that this mailing is about legacy giving, since the headline makes it clear at the outset.

- The options offered to donors include opportunities both to declare a bequest previously arranged and to inquire about legacy giving possibilities. This reflects the reality that a large proportion of legacy gifts are never disclosed to the charity they benefit until after the will is probated.

- The form emphasizes in bold print (on the right-hand side) that any response will be "held in the strictest confidence." This is a matter of considerable importance to most legacy givers.

How Legacy Promotion Letters Are Different from Other Fundraising Appeals

Nonprofit organizations may promote legacy giving through a variety of forms and techniques. Among these are special newsletters mailed periodically both to declared legacy donors and to prospects, occasional letters specifically promoting bequests sent to the most likely legacy donors, legacy clubs or societies that celebrate donors who commit to leaving legacies, information about legacy giving (sometimes including special software to calculate tax benefits) on the charity's website, and recognition at special events and in annual reports. However, the most effective promotional efforts, regardless of the medium employed, display the following four features:

1. They emphasize bequests rather than planned gifts of the sort that are usually of interest only to wealthy donors.

2. They dwell on the organization's vision and mission, not on the mechanics involved in leaving a legacy. Legal and accounting information is, at best, only marginally interesting to most donors. Many regard it as a turnoff.

3. The request to declare a legacy gift typically notes that going public shows leadership by providing an example to other donors.

4. The primary purpose of most legacy giving promotions is not to secure a legacy commitment by return mail (or on the phone or by e-mail): it is to engage the donor in a dialogue that, at length, may

result in such a commitment. Leaving a legacy requires a major commitment—psychologically as well as financially. Many donors take a long time to think about the prospect.

Case Study: Project Bread Bequest Promotion

Exhibits 20.2 through 20.6 show the full contents of a straightforward legacy promotion mailing to selected donors of Project Bread, a Boston-based antihunger organization. There are several noteworthy aspects of this mailing:

- The letter was mailed in a closed-face envelope (rather than a window). Since this mailing was generic (nonpersonalized), the donor will have to supply her name and address on the reply form. Obviously, Project Bread could have afforded to use personalization in this mailing. Instead, though, the organization opted to underline the confidentiality of the appeal by including no personalized elements inside the package.

- The letter is short and very much to the point: "establishing a charitable bequest." And there's no doubt how the money will be used: "to provide life's most basic necessity—food—to all our neighbors in need."

EXHIBIT 20.2
Legacy Promotion Outer Envelope, Project Bread

Project Bread™
Feeding people,
nourishing hope

145 Border Street
East Boston, Massachusetts 02128

Mr. John Doe
123 Any Street
Any Town AS 00000

RECYCLED & RECYCLABLE / PRINTED WITH SOY INK   6-LA3

EXHIBIT 20.3
Legacy Promotion Letter, Project Bread

Dear Friend,

Your generous and faithful support of Project Bread has made a profound difference in the lives of hungry people in Massachusetts. Thank you.

Despite our accomplishments, over 400,000 people in Massachusetts are struggling to feed themselves and their families. Right now, thousands of hard-working families are being forced to choose between paying ever higher heating bills, providing medical care for their children—or putting food on the table.

Emergency services are a vital part of Project Bread's goal to alleviate hunger in the Commonwealth. However—if we are to finally end hunger in our state—emergency services must be complemented by preventative efforts. Our work to prevent hunger is based on the premise that hunger has become a <u>public health crisis in Massachusetts</u>—one that involves both physical and emotional trauma. For children especially, hunger threatens their ability to grow and learn.

That's why I hope you will consider continuing your support of our work by making a planned gift to Project Bread—The Walk for Hunger, Inc.

Specifically, by establishing a charitable bequest that benefits Project Bread, you will reaffirm your commitment to ensuring that families have enough to eat. Legacy gifts provide financial support for hundreds of food pantries and soup kitchens. These planned gifts also enable Project Bread to develop and implement hunger prevention programs that protect the state's most vulnerable citizens—children and the elderly—from hunger.

I hope you will decide to include Project Bread in your estate plans. Taking this small step now will have a big impact for years to come. Your bequest will also <u>inspire others to join you</u> in supporting our efforts to end hunger in Massachusetts.

Thank you for all you do to provide life's most basic necessity—food—to all our neighbors in need.

Sincerely,

Lori Miller
Director of Individual Giving

145 Border Street • East Boston, MA 02128 • Tel 617-723-5000 • Fax 617-248-8877
www.projectbread.org • info@projectbread.org

6-LA1

EXHIBIT 20.4
Legacy Promotion Brochure (Outside), Project Bread

A Commonwealth
...where everyone
is free from hunger

Other Creative Ways to Help

You can also designate Project Bread as the beneficiary of insurance policies or retirement plans. In some cases, you or your heirs may also realize significant tax savings. Project Bread also accepts gifts of securities (stocks and bonds). To discuss these and other possibilities, please contact Lori Miller at 617-239-2560 or via e-mail at lori_miller@projectbread.org.

When you remember Project Bread in your will or living trust, you create a legacy of hope and opportunity for hungry families in Massachusetts. For more information on making a bequest or other legacy gifts to Project Bread, please contact Lori Miller at 617-239-2560 or via e-mail at lori_miller@projectbread.org.

Project Bread's tax identification number is 04-2931195.

Project Bread™
Feeding people,
nourishing hope

145 Border Street
East Boston, MA 02128
617-723-5000
FoodSource Hotline at 1-800-645-8333
www.projectbread.org

RECYCLED & RECYCLABLE / SOY INK   6-L45

Continue your legacy of feeding the hungry in Massachusetts.

For nearly 40 years, Project Bread – The Walk for Hunger has worked to create solutions to the problem of hunger in our midst. The progress we've made has been possible because of thousands of compassionate volunteers, walkers, and donors. Together, we have raised more than $59 million to help hungry families. In 2005, Project Bread supported over 400 soup kitchens and food pantries that served 40 million meals. In addition, through collaboration with civic leaders and community groups, Project Bread has played a leadership role in developing public policies that address hunger and nutrition, especially among children.

Now, you have the opportunity to assist hungry families for years to come. By including Project Bread in your estate plan, you can leave an enduring legacy of support for efforts that feed people and nourish hope.

The Legacy of Compassion and Good Health

You don't need to be wealthy to make a gift that will have an impact on future generations. A charitable bequest to Project Bread in your will or living trust will serve as a powerful testimony to your conviction that no one should have to struggle to provide food for themselves or their families in Massachusetts.

No matter how modest your assets, establishing a will or living trust can ensure your estate is settled quickly—and with fewer complications for your family and loved ones.

You Can Make a Bequest

You may find the following wordings to be helpful. These brief descriptions are not intended as legal or financial advice. Please consult your attorney or financial planner.

- **TO MAKE A SIMPLE BEQUEST**

"I give and bequeath to Project Bread – The Walk for Hunger, Inc., of 145 Border Street, East Boston, Massachusetts, 02128, the sum of $ _____ (or a specific item of property, such as real estate, stocks or bonds, automobile, etc.) to be used as the organization determines."

- **TO MAKE A RESIDUAL BEQUEST**

You may choose to leave the residue of your estate after you have provided for family members and other beneficiaries. "I give and bequeath to Project Bread – The Walk for Hunger, Inc., of 145 Border Street, East Boston, Massachusetts, 02128, the residue of my estate, to be used as the organization determines."

- **TO MAKE A PERCENTAGE BEQUEST**

"I give and bequeath to Project Bread – The Walk for Hunger, Inc., of 145 Border Street, East Boston, Massachusetts, 02128, _____ % (name a specific percentage) of the total value of my estate to be used as the organization determines."

EXHIBIT 20.5
Legacy Promotion Reply Device, Project Bread

CONFIDENTIAL REPLY

☐ I'm considering including Project Bread in my estate plan. Please send me additional information about leaving a charitable bequest or other planned gift.

☐ I have already included Project Bread in my estate plans.

☐ I prefer that my charitable plans remain anonymous.

Project Bread™
Feeding people,
nourishing hope

145 Border Street
East Boston, MA 02128
Tel 617-723-5000
www.projectbread.org

PLEASE PRINT:

Name _____

Address _____

City _____ Zip _____

Email address (optional) _____

Phone: _____ - _____

☐ Please call me. The best time to reach me is:
☐ morning   ☐ afternoon   ☐ evening

Please be assured that there is no obligation, and that all information about charitable gifts and bequests will be held in the strictest confidence.

6-LA2

EXHIBIT 20.6
Legacy Promotion Reply Envelope, Project Bread

Project Bread™
Feeding people,
nourishing hope

PLEASE
PLACE
STAMP
HERE

Confidential:
Please Route to Lori Miller

Project Bread
145 Border Street
East Boston, MA 02128-1903

RECYCLED & RECYCLABLE / SOY INK   6-LA6

- The brochure was developed exclusively for this mailing. It's no off-the-shelf general promotional brochure. Rather, it dwells on the topic at hand: creating "a legacy of hope and opportunity for hungry families in Massachusetts."

- The reply form is headlined "Confidential Reply." Its purpose is not to secure a commitment but rather to initiate a conversation with the donor, probably by telephone.

- The reply envelope, also marked "Confidential," is directed to a single, dedicated individual. This presumably will increase donors' confidence in the confidentiality of the process.

With this chapter, we come to the end of part 3. In part 4, we'll venture into the brave new world of integrated, multichannel fundraising, with an emphasis on the growing importance of cyberspace.

What you've read so far is largely about writing direct mail fund-raising letters. Of course, you can't help but to have noticed that I've been referring frequently to fundraising through other channels, using the phrase *integrated, multichannel fundraising*. Now at last it's time for me to put all these comments in context. In this part of the book, we'll examine the ins and outs of integrated, multichannel fundraising, with an emphasis on electronic communications, or online media, if you prefer. Here you'll come face-to-face with the nitty-gritty of the business, reviewing

- How a multichannel fundraising campaign is like a turkey sandwich with all the trimmings
- What you can (and can't) expect from online fundraising
- The anatomy of an e-mail appeal
- The eight cardinal rules for writing e-mail appeals
- How writing e-mail is different from putting words on paper
- The paramount importance of engaging and cultivating online supporters
- How to prepare your website for success in multichannel fundraising
- Driving dialogue with social media
- Making use of mobile communications

Chapter Twenty-One:
Rounding Out Your Appeal with Online Media and More

If you're like most people who raise money by mail for nonprofit causes and institutions, chances are the only fundraising *channel* you use is direct mail. You probably have a website, and perhaps you also manage an e-mail program, which may or may not involve fundraising. If your organization is well established and boasts tens or hundreds of thousands of supporters, you may even be trying to coordinate your direct mail and online communications with one another (though probably with mixed success, at best). If your organization is small, you might not even have had the resources to attempt to integrate direct mail and online communications. In this chapter, you'll learn why it's important to integrate those channels—and others as well—and how you can accomplish that to optimize your fundraising results.

How a Multichannel Fundraising Program Is Like a Turkey Sandwich with All the Trimmings

Think of that upcoming direct mail fundraising letter as a slice of turkey. Smoked turkey, if you prefer. Free-range, even! But, no matter how tasty the turkey, it won't make for a satisfying meal all by itself. You need to add a few things if you're going to make an enjoyable turkey sandwich.

The situation is much the same in direct response fundraising today. To achieve your twin goals of raising more money and building stronger relationships with your donors, you've got to do more than just send them stand-alone direct mail letters from time to time. Just "getting by" has gotten a lot more complicated these days:

- Just as you'll need a roll or two slices of bread to start turning that slice of turkey into a sandwich, you'll want to update your website so that recipients of your letter who go there to check you out will be urged to respond with gifts—and so they can respond online with a credit card instead of having to write a check and mail it back to you.

- You'll probably want a slice of cheese to add heft to that sandwich and make the flavor more complex. So, too, you'll no doubt elect to send an e-mail message to the same donors who will receive your letter, either before you mail it or afterward, or both. E-mail will boost response to your letter as well as bring in a number of gifts online.

- But that sandwich won't be very inviting if all it consists of is turkey, cheese, and bread. Surely, you'll choose to ignore that diet and slather on mustard and mayonnaise. The extra zing will help ensure that you devour the whole thing, not stop after just a few bites. Similarly, in a fundraising campaign, calling some or all of the donors by phone will elicit many more gifts—and give your donors opportunities to ask questions and send feedback.

- As an experienced sandwich maker, you know you're not yet done. You'll want to add lettuce, of course, and pickles too, if you like that sort of thing. A similar impulse will lead you to make sure that your website and e-mail are easily readable on smartphones, iPads, and other mobile devices. If you have in hand some of your donors' mobile telephone numbers, you might even want to send them a text message to reinforce your fundraising campaign.

Now that (I hope) you can see the logic of multichannel fundraising, it's time to dive into the topic in earnest, beginning with an examination of what you might expect from online communications in particular.

What You Can (and Can't) Expect from Online Fundraising

Get out your pencil and notebook now. It's time for a pop quiz.
Question: Which one of the following statements is true?

a. The most important thing about raising money online is the capacity to accept donations on your website.

b. E-mail costs so much less than direct mail that it's rapidly replacing mail as the fundraising medium of choice.

c. Nonprofit organizations in the United States are raising more than 40 percent of their revenue online.

d. Most organizations now acquire more new donors online than off-line.

e. Social media and mobile communications are dominating online fundraising.

Careful now—this is a trick question.

Have you got it? You figured out that *not one* of these answers is true? Go to the head of the class! But hold on, because that's only part of a story that seems to be rapidly changing every twelve months. Fundraising online continues to show strong growth every year, but it's a world in itself, with its own rules, quirks, and culture. If you plunge in blindly, heedless of the idiosyncrasies and challenges of communication online, you may find that fundraising in the digital arena is anything but simple and cheap.

For starters, here are a few of the inescapable facts about online fundraising:

- Strong e-mail cultivation, not the web, is still the key to raising money online today. A high-impact website is absolutely necessary, but it's far from sufficient. If you build it and just let it sit there, they *won't* come.

- Online fundraising revenue is growing at an astounding rate—an estimated 35 to 40 percent annually. In 2010, according to one widely cited study, online fundraising yielded $22 billion, representing approximately 7.5 percent of the $290 billion contributed by American donors that year. Numerous reports speak of annual increases of 25 percent or more during the last several years.

- Those donors who give across multiple channels, though few in number, have higher donor value. But while small, the numbers continue to grow from year to year, and both online and multichannel donors will continue to grow in importance to your program's success.

- One of the Internet's competitive advantages over other media is speed. In your direct mail fundraising program, you may allow months to elapse between conception and the mailbox. That would lead to utter failure online. It's no accident that most of the first successful online fundraisers were disaster relief agencies, advocacy organizations, and political campaigns—because all of them rise or fall with breaking news. To make the Internet work for you as a fundraising tool, you'll need to find some way to introduce a strong sense of urgency into your appeals.

- Social and mobile media are growing rapidly but are still a very small portion of fundraising, apart from appeals after disasters. However, as you'll see below, they're both still important channels for empowering supporters and building an audience to activate at key times. So, while only a handful of organizations ever raised more than $100,000 on Facebook, I believe we'll see supporters engaged with your organization through these channels beginning to become your most loyal ones.

- In online fundraising, you'll encounter a bonus: it's quick and easy to test variations in copy and design. Decades of research into the habits and expectations of direct mail donors have given us considerable insight into what's likely to work in the mail, and what isn't. (Even so, our best guesses are wrong far too often!) With most online, e-mail, social, and mobile platforms, easy testing options are available, with immediate results. From a subject line to the placement of a graphic in an e-mail or on your website, you can test it, and quickly.

Demographic considerations are important in the online fundraising arena.

Web users are typically younger than direct mail respondents, although not as much younger as you might expect. After all, the median direct mail donor for most nonprofits tends to be fifty-five or older, and for some organizations the median age can reach into the seventies. But the fact that teenagers and twenty-somethings have grown up with the Internet and can often be found in cyberspace at any hour of the day or night doesn't mean that they're now rushing into philanthropy. Yes, online donors tend to be younger than direct mail donors, typically in their forties and fifties rather than their sixties or seventies. But online communications reach older folks as well as youngsters—and it's the older ones who disproportionately respond to appeals for money. After all, the fastest growing group of participants in Facebook the last few years has been women ages forty-five to sixty-five.

One more thing about demographics: don't automatically discount those target audiences outside the typical direct mail marketplace as having little fundraising potential. Generation Xers and Yers who are engaged by nonprofits often support up to five organizations with annual gifts exceeding $100. In the years ahead, it will be important to engage these populous demographic cohorts before others do.

Oh, one last, important point: The technical demands of raising money online can be daunting. Chances are, unless you or a member of your staff is a dyed-in-the-wool geek with a broad knowledge of what works online, you'll find your organization's performance on the Internet to be limited if you try going it alone. For starters, you'll need to sign up with an online service provider that specializes in working with nonprofits to manage the technical aspects of maintaining your list, sending out e-mail messages and e-newsletters, and hosting your website. You're also likely to find it advisable to hire an online fundraising consultant. Let the consultant keep up with the proliferation of online opportunities on your behalf—and stick to raising money yourself.

To explore this high-potential medium and determine how to make the most of it, let's first take a look at some of the most frequently used media in an integrated, multichannel campaign.

Channel by Channel, the Nuts and Bolts of Multichannel Fundraising

No doubt about it: the prophets of "convergence"—the pundits who envision all our communications channels merging into one—have been proven wrong. Instead, new electronic channels continue to appear, year after year, each one disrupting all those that appeared before it.

Recent Google research indicates that we Americans now divide our viewing time primarily among four media devices: smartphone, tablet, PC or laptop, and TV, with the smartphone now the most commonly used to initiate action. Depend on it. No matter your intention, your online fundraising message will be seen on a variety of devices, and each device will determine the way your message comes across. That's why a multichannel fundraising campaign can't be limited to direct mail and e-mail if it's to achieve optimal results.

For the most broadly based fundraising campaigns, you'll employ at least three or four of the following channels:

- Direct mail

- E-mail

- Your website

- Outbound telemarketing

- Social media

- Mobile messaging

- Online advertising

Now let's examine each of those channels in turn, reviewing their special characteristics and exploring how they may be used in combination with the other media you select.

Direct Mail

Whatever other channels you might employ in a fundraising campaign, you'll almost certainly use direct mail. But today's direct mail no longer stands alone. Even if you only send your donors a mailing and take advantage of no other medium, at a minimum you'll want to include in the letter and on the reply device the URL for the donation page on your website (exhibit 21.1). One instance might be in the body of the letter, a second on the reply device, and a third in the return address on your outer envelope (exhibit 21.2).

EXHIBIT 21.1
Promotion of Online Giving in a Direct Mail Letter, Save The Bay

2011 ANNUAL MEMBERSHIP RENEWAL

<u>YES</u>, I want to renew my annual support of Save The Bay—and help restore, protect and advance the health of San Francisco Bay. Enclosed is my 2011 membership renewal gift of:

❑ $50 ❑ $75 ❑ $100 ❑ $_____

❑ **I'm increasing my support for Save The Bay by making an online gift at www.saveSFbay.org/renew2011. Please send me a commemorative 50th Anniversary bookmark as a thank you gift.**

John Doe
Anytown, AS 00000
123 Main Street
STB11RB/ 02/18/11 /PKG1:1ST RENEWAL: DRIVE 2 WEB TEST

179697 11RB51CC

350 Frank H. Ogawa Plaza
Suite 900 • Oakland, CA 94612
510.452.9261 • www.saveSFbay.org

Save The Bay is a 501(c)(3) non-profit organization. Your gift is fully tax-deductible. To charge your membership renewal to your credit card, please see the reverse side. If you'd like to renew your support online, please visit www.saveSFbay.org/renew

350 Frank H. Ogawa Plaza
Suite 900 • Oakland, CA 94612
510.452.9261 • www.saveSFbay.org

February 18, 2011

Dear John,

I'm writing to ask you to take a moment today to renew your membership support for Save The Bay in 2011—our 50th Anniversary Year.

As I noted in my letter to you last month, we have our work cut out for us this year—particularly as we learn the details of the budget cuts that face the State of California in the year ahead and as we continue to see urban sprawl and runoff pollution threatening our shoreline.

Environmental stewards like you know and understand the importance of our work, and I'm encouraged by the progress we have made together for the past 50 years.

In 2011, with your help, we will redouble our efforts to:

- <u>Reduce plastic waste</u>—especially single-use plastic bags like those outlawed recently in Marin County and San Jose—bags that endanger wildlife, smother wetlands and pollute our waters.

- <u>Re-establish 100,000 acres</u> of healthy wetlands around the Bay that provide habitat protection for hundreds of fish and wildlife like harbor seals and shorebirds and protect communities from sea-level rise.

- <u>Block Cargill</u> from paving over 1,436 acres of restorable wetland habitat to create a new city of 30,000 people in Redwood City.

John, you've already been generous. Your gift of $50 in 2010 was tremendously helpful—and I hope you'll consider renewing your membership support in 2011 with a gift of that amount or more.

I assure you that your gift will be used carefully and efficiently to protect and restore San Francisco Bay for you and for future generations to enjoy.

Please renew your 2011 membership support today—and then go out and experience the Bay. These late winter months are an extraordinary time to celebrate San Francisco Bay!

With many thanks,

David Lewis,
Executive Director

P.S.   If you wish to take a moment now to make your gift online, please visit our secure server at www.saveSFbay.org/renew2011. It's convenient for you and efficient for us—and as a gesture of thanks, we'll send you a commemorative 50th Anniversary bookmark.

EXHIBIT 21.2

Promotion of Online Giving on the Front and Back of a Direct Mail Outer Envelope, Save The Bay

350 Frank H. Ogawa Plaza
Suite 900 · Oakland, CA 94612
510.452.9261 · www.saveSFbay.org

YOUR CHOICE OF TWO RENEWAL OPTIONS:

John Doe
Anytown, AS 00000
123 Main Street
STB11RB/ 02/18/11 /PKG1:1ST RENEWAL: DRIVE 2 WEB TEST

a) the regular old-fashioned good feeling option

b) the expedited good feeling option with
   a special "thank you" gift thrown in for
   renewing your membership online at
   saveSFbay.org/renew2011

RECYCLED & RECYCLABLE / PRINTED WITH SOY INK   11-RB3B

Renew your membership online instantly!
It's easy, fast, safe, and secure. saveSFbay.org/renew2011

E-mail

There's no question about it: despite a flood of predictions that "e-mail is dead" (very similar to the continuing cries that "direct mail is dead"), e-mail remains the workhorse online, producing the most tangible and predictable results (just as direct mail continues to be the most reliable source of gifts from direct response fundraising overall).

An e-mail campaign can be undertaken either as a stand-alone fundraising tool or integrated with direct mail and other media in a multichannel campaign. Either way, there may be a single e-mail message or a series of them.

To put the value of e-mail as a fundraising tool in perspective in the online world, it's worth remembering the findings revealed in the *2012 eNonprofit Benchmarks Study*: between 18 percent and 47 percent of online revenue is driven by e-mail.

Even so, don't expect the e-mail components of your campaign to produce a large share of your revenue (except, perhaps, in a year-end campaign, a topic I'll address later). Nor is e-mail especially effective in prospecting for new donors. E-mail works better at cultivating prospective donors than it does recruiting them. A large proportion of the people who respond to e-mail messages, even fundraising messages, will take almost any action you ask of them—except send money.

EXHIBIT 21.3
Online Fundraising by Channel: E-mail versus Other Online Channels

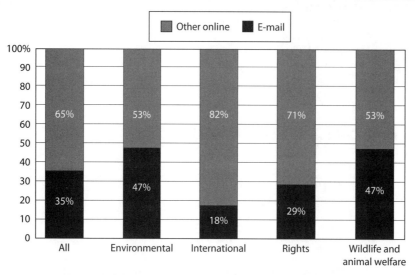

On average, 35% of online revenue was sourced to direct e-mail appeals. The remaining 65% came from other sources, such as unsolicited web giving and peer referrals.

At 18%, the international sector had the lowest average share of money raised via e-mail, which may be due to an increase in unsolicited web giving received during emergencies.

Source: M+R Strategic Services, *2012 eNonprofit Benchmarks Study*, available at www.e-benchmarksstudy.com.

As you can see in exhibit 21.3, e-mail appeals account for only about one-third of online fundraising revenue. Another third—35 percent—was driven by direct mail.

Much of the time, e-mail's *fundraising* function in a multichannel campaign is to boost response to your direct mail letter. The e-mail message you send—or messages plural, in many campaigns—must parallel and reflect the copy in the letter, citing the same key facts about the campaign and using much of the same language and imagery.

Make sure you've considered the following options when designing a multichannel fundraising campaign:

- *Integrated e-mail appeal.* E-mail should play a part in most fundraising campaigns, if only to precede and/or follow an expensive mailing (with e-mail calling attention to the mailing, or prompting response after the fact, or both). In such cases, it's usually best to schedule the e-mail to arrive in sync with the date the mail is expected to arrive in homes or within a few days afterward. The most notable exceptions to integrating e-mail are direct mail new-donor acquisition efforts—and even those efforts should be followed up with an e-mail welcome series for those new donors who provide e-mail addresses.

- *E-mail welcome series.* A series of three or four e-mails spread over a one-to three-week period will give you the opportunity to explain more about your organization and its work, offer additional opportunities to become engaged, invite new donors to join a monthly sustainer program, and even to solicit second gifts. Such a series for new donors or members is one of the most valuable ways to use the e-mail medium.

- *Multipart e-mail appeal series.* At critical times, such as year-end or when you're launching an especially important campaign, it's important to integrate a multipart e-mail series into the overall program design. (For an example, see the matching grant appeal for Be The Match in chapter 13.) Keep in mind that online revenue is far more seasonal than off-line revenue, with as much as 60 percent of online revenue received during the month of December alone, and one-third of that on December 31. In other words, it's absolutely essential to deploy e-mail aggressively at year-end.

- *Online donation bounce-back.* In addition to any donor acknowledgment program you may already have in place, it's important to prepare a *bounce-back* e-mail message to be sent instantly to any donor who contributes a gift online. Your e-mail system should be programmed to do this. A bounce-back message serves both as a thank-you for each gift and, by citing the gift amount, as a receipt for tax reporting or record keeping.

- *E-mail cultivation messages.* Don't ever forget to make use of the low-cost option of e-mail to cultivate your donors. Is there a great impact story to tell? Has your recent campaign met its goals? Has the organization won an award for its work or received a high-profile endorsement? Has there been a breakthrough in your organization's work in the field? Whatever the circumstance, send your donors a brief message to share the good news and thank them again for their support.

Your Website

The home page and donation pages on your website are crucial to the success of any multichannel campaign, because every other channel is designed to drive traffic there. Here's how you can make the most of this high-value real estate.

The natural starting point when getting your toes wet in multichannel fundraising is your website. Even if your appeal will be delivered exclusively through direct mail, there are two important steps for you to take:

1. *Make use of your home page.* Even if you include a custom URL in your direct mail appeal to offer donors or prospects the option of giving online, fewer than half of them will go directly to any custom

EXHIBIT 21.4
Home Page Fundraising Promotion, AmeriCares

donation page you may have (see item 2 in this list). The majority
of those who go online will either Google your organization or go
directly to your home page. The numbers of those who go online after
reading a letter from you are growing fast, so this step has become
essential in fundraising. Its importance grows whenever you add
e-mail or social media messaging to your campaign. If you don't have
a callout to the campaign on your home page, such as I described
above (also see exhibit 21.4), the proportion of donors and of prospects who *convert* (by donating) will start to fall. (This *conversion rate*
is one of the key metrics in online fundraising and marketing.)

2. *Build a dedicated donation page (landing page).* Most online fundraising
   platforms (Convio, Blackbaud, and Salsa, for example) allow you to
   customize a section of your campaign donation page with messaging
   and images specific to your appeal. It's especially important to take
   advantage of this capability if your campaign includes other online
   components that drive traffic to the donation page (as it should!). In
   some systems, there's an added advantage to doing so: setting up a

landing page for each campaign makes your backend tracking and reporting easier. And that can be advantageous even if you're not appealing for money: the landing page might help you track those who sign up for a sustainer program or who take action in support of your advocacy efforts.

Outbound Telemarketing

Forget the squeamishness of your board or your own distaste for calling donors. Of all the media at our disposal today, the telephone usually offers the highest response rates by far. One big problem is that telemarketing is, next to direct response TV, the most expensive medium a nonprofit might consider to deliver a fundraising message. The art of telephone fundraising rests on your skill, or that of your consultant, in weighing the trade-off between cost and the anticipated return. Another problem is that most folks under thirty or thirty-five these days don't have landlines anymore . . . and cell numbers are not *appendable* at this point.

Because of cost concerns, telemarketing is used today primarily for high-value-added campaigns such as recruiting monthly donors, soliciting gifts of $1,000 or more, or upgrading donors who have demonstrated both loyalty and generosity. If one or more of these goals is part of your campaign, it's definitely worth considering a telemarketing drive as part of the mix. (In addition to *outbound* telemarketing—where your organization or an agency working on your behalf directly calls your donors or prospects—you may also want to consider *inbound* telemarketing. By offering donors a toll-free number they can call at any time of the day or night, you might see your response rise. However, inbound telemarketing is generally available only to nonprofits with very large direct response programs.)

Limitations on space and time prevent me from covering the topic of telephone fundraising in this book. I suggest you contact a consultant or agency that specializes in raising money by phone to learn more about this very important channel—and if you decide to hire one to assist your fundraising campaign, be sure to ask for competitive bids and check references carefully.

Social Media

As anyone who is awake in the twenty-first century is aware, social media are growing fast. Facebook reportedly has more than one billion users, and Twitter well over half that number. Pinterest, a relative newcomer to the industry, attracts more than one hundred million visitors monthly, behind only Facebook and Twitter, even though the number of its active users is tiny by comparison.

High traffic numbers notwithstanding, social media sites have not yet proven to be fruitful fundraising venues. However, in a multichannel campaign, it makes perfect sense to take advantage of as many of these channels as you can, writing campaign updates on your Facebook page, tweeting frequently, and drafting short copy to accompany an image you post on Pinterest. These efforts will provide additional points of contact between your campaign and your donors or prospects, and they'll help build a broader base of supporters who may be activated later to participate in future campaigns.

One of my favorite articles about social media appeared in *Fast Company* magazine under the title "Social Networking Affects Brain Like Falling in Love" (July 1, 2010). Yes, believe it or not: immersing yourself in Facebook, Twitter, or Pinterest releases oxytocin, a long-familiar human hormone, sometimes called the *cuddle chemical*, that generates empathy, generosity, and trust. So, while social media still lag far behind other forms of digital fundraising as revenue generators, their importance for your organization's future can't be understated. Simply put, communication through social media engenders trust. For example, nearly twice as many people trust anonymous bloggers (30 percent) as trust mainstream advertising (17 percent). And a whopping 83 percent trust peer reviews.

But, as they say in direct mail, *there's more!*

Donors *prefer* fundraising through social media (or at least they say they do). When Convio asked donors what channel they thought was the most appropriate for solicitations, more than half said they favored being asked for money by a friend on behalf of an organization. A peer-to-peer module available on most online fundraising platforms, enhanced with social media tool sets, makes this easy. You see this all the time with charity runs, walks, and bicycle races. You've probably been invited to participate in such events. If so, have you noticed how you get the same request to support the same charity from the same friend year after year?

Be careful now. I'm certainly not suggesting you eliminate your direct mail program and start raising all your money on Facebook! If you do, you'll probably be out of a job within weeks, as your organization's revenue diminishes to a trickle. However, as an investment in donor engagement, donor cultivation, and an uncertain future, you'd be well advised to invest a few hours a week in social media—or enlist an intern or a volunteer in posting on behalf of your organization. You'll be surprised how steadily your online presence will grow, attracting supporters you could never reach through any other means (especially those treasured younger prospects who will mature into donors if they stick with you through the years).

Don't get me wrong: I'm not saying that any specific platform—even Facebook or Twitter—will prove to be the key over the long term. They may not even be in business ten years from now. What's important for you and your organization is to begin engaging your constituents through this nearly ubiquitous new medium. Once you engage your supporters on social networks and through peer-to-peer fundraising, they'll seek you out as new networks develop.

Be on the lookout for some of these opportunities to integrate social media, if you haven't already started to do so:

- Enhance your "Get Involved" section on Facebook with relevant messages simultaneously with each appeal. Post updates on actions taken, videos produced, and photos of beneficiaries, participants, or donors.

- Update your Facebook background image and message to match your appeal. Image requirements change frequently, but specs can be found on Facebook's website.

- Post messaging on your social media platforms to support every advocacy campaign.

- Build your online list.

- Support your direct mail donor acquisition campaigns with posts that reflect the copy in your control letter and link to the campaign landing page on your website.

- Drive peer-to-peer fundraising with occasional incentives offered online for supporters who bring in the greatest number of donors or the most money.

- Share impact stories, photos, and videos related to the call to action in your appeal.

Online Advertising

For some campaigns, advertising on Facebook makes good sense. The ads are small, and words are few, but Facebook's one billion "active" users make it easy to microtarget by demographic and lifestyle characteristics—and exceedingly easy to test. However, you'll find that selecting the segments to expose to your ad is the hard part. Finding the right images and the right few words to test is straightforward by comparison.

Another widely employed advertising opportunity is Google AdWords. These are tiny ads that appear in the upper right-hand corner of the results pages when you search for a term on Google. Exhibit 21.5 shows what I found there when googling the term *environmental protection*.

EXHIBIT 21.5

Google AdWords Promotions, "Environmental Protection" Search Result

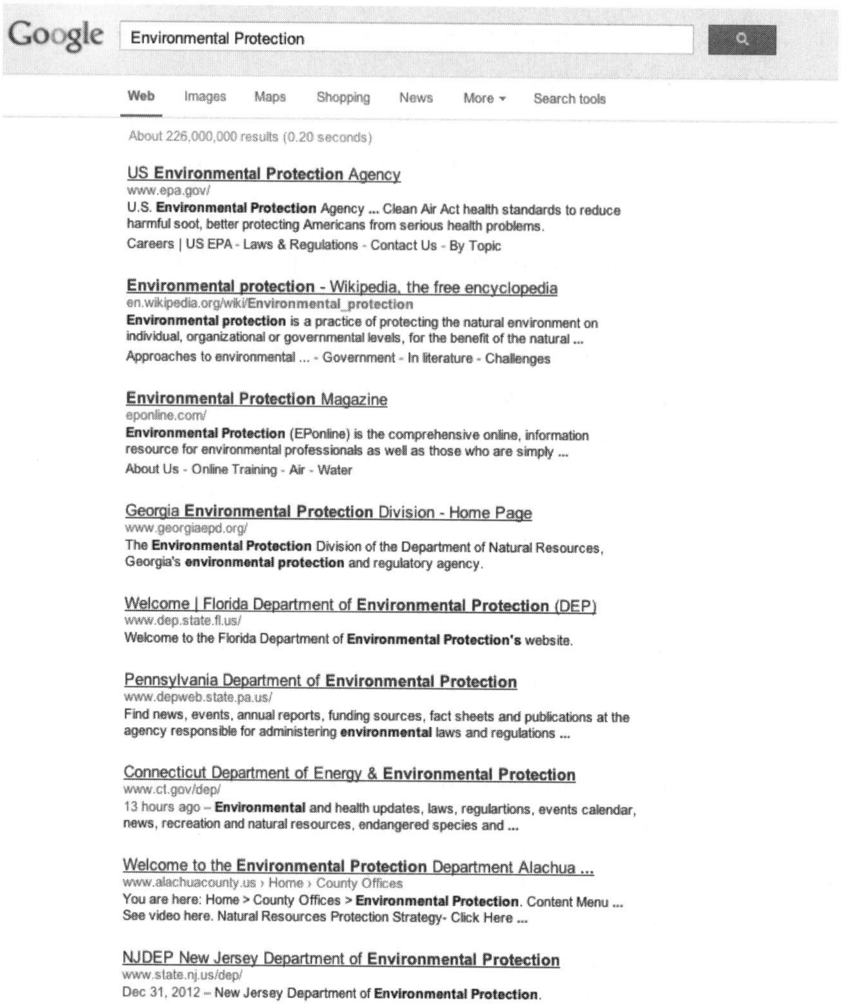

Each of the organizations whose ads appeared alongside my search results—all of them nonprofits, as it turns out—had chosen the AdWord (or *keyword*) *environmental protection* and related words. No doubt, each had also listed many other keywords, so that its ads would appear on lots of other pages as well. Businesses (and nonprofits too, for that matter) can "buy" AdWords in an auction system somewhat similar to the pricing mechanism on eBay. But many nonprofits receive large numbers of free *impressions* in the form of a Google Grant. For example, the company might grant to Greenpeace, say, one million *hits* or impressions for any AdWord advertising that organization chooses to do on Google. (You can learn more about the offer and how to apply for a Google Grant at www.google.com/grants.) A word of warning, though: managing and analyzing the results of advertising on Google can be daunting for a novice. It's best to get help from someone who has had experience wrestling with Google's complex management process.

Mobile Messaging

Online activity is quickly moving from big screens to small ones, and no wonder! Already there are more than six *billion* cell phones in the world. With world population at seven billion, that means there is one cell phone for almost every person on the planet—and don't forget that a lot of people are far too young (or far too poor) to own phones! Of course, it's true that the number of smartphones, capable of accessing the Internet, is smaller, but that may not be the case for long, since an estimated 700 million smartphones were estimated to have been sold globally in 2012 alone.

The first step in approaching this massive market is to optimize your website and your e-mail appeals for mobile platforms. (If you don't understand what optimization is all about, check in with your programmer or your online fundraising consultant.) It's also advisable to begin building a list of mobile phone numbers and to begin sending text messages to supporters (at first, at least, not to raise money but to strengthen your relationships with them). Most such lists are very small—just 1.2 percent of the size of e-mail lists, according to the *2012 eNonprofit Benchmarks Study*—but they're very responsive. A series of short messages sent via SMS (text messaging) can drive a lot of phone calls or similar actions in support of your campaign. However, according to PayPal, e-mail is the largest single driver of mobile activity . . . so don't overlook e-mail when you're going for gifts from mobile devices.

"Whoa, My Head Is Starting to Hurt!"

You may well be wondering why it makes sense to go to all this trouble of engaging your supporters through so many channels. After all, direct mail still yields the bulk of donor revenue. However, donor attitudes and habits are changing, and the way donors interact with the causes and institutions they support is starting to change as well.

The fundamental reality is this: *fundraising today is all about donor choice.* You simply have to make it as easy as possible for your supporters to engage with you when and where they're ready. If you don't, the competition will.

I know, I know, you don't have "competition"—you're a just a friendly nonprofit. But, like it or not, that viewpoint is wrong. In the United States alone, there are more than one million tax-exempt charitable and educational organizations (the exact number varies depending on how you count them).

Globally, I estimate the total at more than ten million. No matter how you look at it, there's only so much money to go around, and if your organization isn't inside your donors' circle of awareness, the chances you'll continue to receive their support will surely diminish.

If losing donors to the competition doesn't get you started designing multichannel campaigns, then consider the following:

- Online philanthropic revenue consistently rises by more than 25 percent annually, and frequently by 35 percent to 40 percent, while direct mail revenue growth has slowed considerably.

- According to a recent Convio study, donors who gave via mail and online had a twelve-month donor value almost 150 percent higher than single-channel donors.

- Upward of 35 percent of web *white mail* donations (funds not tagged to specific campaigns) are driven by direct mail.

- Fifty percent of donors surveyed in 2012 said they prefer to give online when they receive a letter in the mail from a charity, according to a study by the communications firm Big Duck.

- Studies have reported that over 70 percent of new donors check your website before they respond to your direct mail package. And over 60 percent of major donors tend to research your organization online before writing a check!

Investing in multichannel fundraising starts to sound better and better in light of all this, doesn't it?

However, once you do, you'll need to know how to adapt your appeal to the requirements of all those channels. So, please join me now in chapter 22, "Writing Online Appeals."

Chapter Twenty-Two:
Writing Online Appeals

Even assuming you've already written and designed a direct mail fundraising appeal, writing the additional components of a multichannel campaign may seem daunting. It's true that the style and format of online copy are different and that much of what works in the mail most assuredly does *not* work online. However, the message is the same, the motivators are the same, and the need to convey impact is the same too, so it's easier than you might think. To give you a sense of the process, let's take a look now at the basic electronic component of any multichannel campaign: e-mail.

Anatomy of an E-mail Appeal

The appeal displayed in exhibit 22.1 won the Package of the Year Award from the Direct Marketing Fundraisers Association for 2006 because of the unusually strong results it yielded. Even after many years, it's worth reviewing because it so clearly illustrates the strengths of the e-mail channel and because it uses no graphic images or video, making it more accessible for smaller organizations that lack the capacity to handle imagery. From top to bottom the e-mail message in exhibit 22.1 is a whole different species from any direct mail fundraising letter. Consider each of these elements:

1. *From.* Direct mail testing often shows that the identity of a letter signer may have little or no impact on the results of a mailing. Not so in e-mail. If the "from" line at the top of your e-mail doesn't reflect someone or something recognizable to your supporters—your organization's name, the personal name most familiar to your supporters (probably that of your executive director), a celebrity name, or some combination of those elements—the odds are great that your message will go straight into the trash.

2. *Subject.* The "subject" line, equivalent to a headline in a space ad, is probably the single most important textual element of an e-mail

---

EXHIBIT 22.1
Award-Winning E-Mail Appeal, MoveOn.org

From: Nita Chaudhary, MoveOn.org Political Action [mailto:moveon-help@list.moveon.org]

Sent: Thursday, April 26, 2007 1:52 PM

To: Madeline

Subject: This is a brave man

George Bush keeps saying that he's the one who supports the troops and those of us who want to end the war don't. Someone has to take him on for that. And John Bruhns—who served in Iraq as a sergeant—is the man to do it.

MoveOn members chose John to be the subject of a TV ad by Oliver Stone as part of our VideoVets project. After coming home, John decided he could no longer remain silent. He says keeping our troops in Iraq without end is "wrong, immoral, and irresponsible." He's brave and patriotic, and his first-hand truth is an essential antidote to the administration's lies.

Can you chip in $25 so we can get John's story on TV and spread it across the internet? Click below to watch the video and contribute:

https://pol.moveon.org/donate/videovets2.html?id=10248-8035350-IQPyZs&t=4

We talked to John this morning, and he's really moved by this whole experience. Here's a note he asked us to pass on to MoveOn members:

> *I'm overwhelmed by the statements of those who saw my video. I can't put into words how honored I am that people were so moved by it. For so long I felt so helpless—in a sense that there was nothing I could do to make a difference in regards to ending the war and educating the American people on the reality of the situation. I made a promise to myself in Iraq that if I was lucky enough to make it home I would do everything in my power to help transition us out of the war. Thank you all so very much for giving me this tremendous opportunity. I am very grateful.*

Oliver Stone and his team are working on the ad as we speak. And John is getting ready to get on a plane and go work with them. We want to make sure as many people as possible hear John's message about the real cost of war.

Can you chip in $25 to help get John's message out there through a big online and TV ad campaign?

https://pol.moveon.org/donate/videovets2.html?id=10248-8035350-IQPyZs&t=5

The president is accusing Congress of playing politics with our troops because they want a plan that starts a responsible redeployment this year. John's video—along with the interviews of all the VideoVets participants—prove that supporting our troops does NOT mean supporting the president's reckless policy in Iraq.

The truth is that it's President Bush and his Republican allies who have not supported the troops. Our brave men and women are stranded in the middle of a civil war, with inadequate protection and resources—and the president wants to send more still.

Supporting our troops is more than a catch phrase. The way to support our troops is to listen to them and their families. Folks like John have stepped up to get the truth out there.

Please help us get John's story out to counter the administration's spin on Iraq.

https://pol.moveon.org/donate/videovets2.html?id=10248-8035350-lQPyZs&t=6

Oliver Stone did a special interview with us about why he chose to get involved. Click below to watch it:

http://pol.moveon.org/videovets?id=10248-8035350-lQPyZs&t=7

Thanks for all you do,

-Nita, Laura, Karin, Patrick and the MoveOn.org Political Action Team

Thursday, April 26th, 2007

P.S. One thing John makes clear is the need to safely redeploy our troops. The fight to end the war is heating up in Congress right now. We thought you might enjoy this note from Senator Feingold. Click below to read it:

http://www.moveon.org/r?r=2538&id=10248-8035350-lQPyZs&t=8

Support our member-driven organization: MoveOn.org Political Action is entirely funded by our 3.2 million members. We have no corporate contributors, no foundation grants, no money from unions. Our tiny staff ensures that small contributions go a long way. If you'd like to support our work, you can give now at: http://political.moveon.org/donate/emailhtml?id=10248-8035350-lQPyZs&t=9

PAID FOR BY MOVEON.ORG POLITICAL ACTION, http://pol.moveon.org/
Not authorized by any candidate or candidate's committee.

Subscription Management:

This is a message from MoveOn.org Political Action. To change your email address, update your contact info, or remove yourself (Madeline) from this list, please visit our subscription management page at: http://moveon.org/s?i=10248-8035350-lQPyZs

appeal. The subject line, similar to the outer envelope copy, must tease the recipient (but not so much that she chuckles and trashes the message) and offer a benefit (but without triggering spam filters). However, teasing can backfire when you're seeking an annual renewal or a year-end gift. Remember, *test the subject line!* And if you resend your message after a day or so to those who haven't opened your message, write a new subject line.

3. *Lead.* In a direct mail fundraising appeal, you might well lead with a story about how some hapless individual's life has been turned around by the miraculous service your organization has provided. Not in e-mail—unless that story is highly emotional and very short. The first few lines of your message may be all that the recipient ever sees—because he's probably viewing your e-mail through a *preview pane.* A wordy or unclear lead will guarantee that the message goes straight into the trash. The direct mail device known as the *Johnson Box*—a sentence or two of copy that appears above the salutation—can be put to work in e-mail too. Sometimes response will rise significantly if you place your

most dramatic and compelling sentence at the very top of the message, because it's certain to be read, even through a preview pane.

4. *Graphic.* Most online fundraising appeals today incorporate graphics, video, or both. In most cases, the upper right-hand corner contains a *sidebar* that consists of a small amount of text below a photo or a video link. However, graphic elements do tend to reduce the deliverability of e-mail. Many e-mail delivery services work hard to ensure their messages, including graphics, avoid the spam filters at Gmail, Hotmail, Yahoo!, AOL, Comcast, and the other big e-mail providers. To work effectively with your e-mail delivery service you'll probably need to contract for help from a qualified provider of online assistance for nonprofits, such as Blackbaud, which has the clout to get the attention of anyone in the industry.

5. *Links.* The rule of thumb in raising money by e-mail is to include at least three click-through links to a donation page on your website— one near the beginning, one in the middle, and one toward the end of the message. These links should lead to a donation landing page separate from your home page like the one shown in exhibit 22.2. (Rather than construct an individual landing page for each link, I recommend that you embed a unique source code within each link. That way, you can track which link draws the most traffic.)

6. *Unsubscribe.* Include instructions on how to get off your e-mail list (*unsubscribe*) in every message. In fact, most e-mail delivery services hardwire this into their systems. If people don't want your messages, make it easy for them to stop, and for you to avoid accusations of spamming.

With the possible exception of a graphic image, every e-mail appeal you send should absolutely, positively include every one of the foregoing elements. And each of them is worth every bit of attention you can pay to ensure that you've got them all just right.

One more important point about e-mail appeals: in direct mail fundraising, we sometimes lamely urge our donors to "pass along to a friend, colleague, or family member" any duplicate appeal they receive. Naturally, you can probably count on the fingers of one hand the number of times this has actually happened. But online, it's a different story. The capacity for *viral* messaging, in which one donor forwards an appeal from you to twenty friends, or two hundred, is one of the advantages of the Internet. You're unlikely to raise a lot of money that way or recruit a large number of new donors, but there may be some—and it's practically free anyway. So it's a mistake not to offer your donors an opportunity to "pass along" your appeal to others. However, the proper place to make that request is not in the solicitation itself but on the landing page or in the thank-you message you send upon receipt of the gift.

EXHIBIT 22.2
Landing Page for Award-Winning Online Appeal, MoveOn.org

MoveOn.ORG
POLITICAL ACTION®   CAMPAIGNS | SUCCESS STORIES | DONATE | SIGN UP | ABOUT

Help get John Bruhns' story out there

George Bush keeps saying that he's the one who supports the troops and those of us who want to end the war don't. Someone has to take him on for that. And former Sergeant John Bruhns—who served in Iraq—is the man to do it. He's the subject of a new ad by Oliver Stone. Your contribution will help us spread his story--and those of the other VideoVets participants--far and wide through a big TV and online advertising campaign. **Can you contribute?** Complete the form below to contribute.

replay   embed url

No video? Click here.

1 YOUR INFORMATION

Your Name
E-mail
Billing Address
City
State
Billing Zip
* Occupation
* Employer

2 SELECT AN AMOUNT

○ $25   ○ $100   ○ $500   ○ $2000
○ $50   ○ $250   ○ $1000   Other $

3 CREDIT CARD INFORMATION

Credit Card Number (VISA/MC/AMEX)

Verification #   Expiration Date (mo/year)

4 CONTRIBUTION RULES

By checking the box below I confirm that the following statements are true and accurate: 1) I am a United States citizen or a permanent resident alien. 2) This contribution is not made from the general treasury funds of a corporation, labor organization or national bank. 3) This contribution is not made from the treasury of an entity or person who is a federal contractor. 4) The funds I am donating are not being provided to me by another person or entity for the purpose of making this contribution. 5) If under 18: I am contributing knowingly and voluntarily with my own funds.

* ☐ I have read all of the rules above and I certify that I comply with each of them.

☐ Remember my data (except credit card information) for next time.

Submit Contribution »

* Required by federal law

How Writing E-mails Is Different from Putting Words on Paper

Take, for example, the typical special appeal package illustrated in exhibit 22.3. There's nothing out of the ordinary in this direct mail letter sent by the AIDS Project Los Angeles (APLA)—unless you count the generic approach (rather than a personalized one) to previous supporters. Just try, though, to e-mail an appeal structured like this one to your supporters, and you'll see quickly enough that what works in the mail falls flat online.

To gain a sense of the specific differences between the online and printed approaches, take a look at the same appeal *repurposed* in an online format in exhibit 22.4. (This repurposed appeal was prepared for this book and was not sent. If it had been e-mailed, "unsubscribe" language would have appeared below the image shown.) The appeals shown in exhibits 22.3 and 22.4 convey almost exactly the same message. But the e-mail version isn't just the original letter transposed into e-mail—it's truly repurposed. Note the significant differences between the two versions:

- The e-mail appeal is shorter—much shorter. That reflects the more limited attention span of e-mail recipients. Research estimates that you've got an average of eight seconds to grab the attention of a direct mail recipient and induce her to read the letter. Online, you'd be lucky for a recipient to scan your message for half that time. Many e-mail recipients simply highlight all incoming messages, preparing them for deletion—and then preserve the few they really want to read by removing the highlighting. It's a cruel world out there in cyberspace!

- The e-mail appeal gets right to the point. Note the headline and the caption above the photo on the right-hand side. Then read the first sentence of the e-mail appeal and compare it with the lead of the direct mail letter. There's no mistaking the point of this electronic appeal, even when only its top portion is viewed through a preview pane.

- Clearly, this HTML appeal—the format in which the overwhelming majority of e-mail messages are sent these days—features graphic

---

EXHIBIT 22.3

Direct Mail Fundraising Appeal Package, AIDS Project Los Angeles

The David Geffen Center
611 S. Kingsley Drive
Los Angeles, CA 90005
www.apla.org

Ms. Jane Doe
123 Any Street
Any Town AS 00000
APL07AC/6-12-07/MATCHING GRANT APPEAL

INSIDE:

Special Matching Gift Offer Will Double Your Gift!

RECYCLED & RECYCLABLE / SOY INK   7-AC3   1

AIDS Project Los Angeles

The David Geffen Center
611 S. Kingsley Drive
Los Angeles, CA 90005
www.apla.org

June 5, 2007

Dear Friend and Supporter,

I'm writing to you today with some wonderful news for AIDS Project Los Angeles and for people in our community living with HIV/AIDS.

At a time when many other AIDS service organizations are seeing diminishing support from corporations, APLA continues to receive an annual $100,000 Matching Gift offer from Wells Fargo Bank.

> For the next 100 days, Wells Fargo Bank will match
> all contributions from current APLA members—dollar
> for dollar—up to $100,000. For a limited time, you can
> double the impact of your gift through the Wells Fargo
> Matching Gift offer.

This is tremendous news—and we are appealing to our core donors like you to step forward and participate in this generous offer. Unlike many other challenge grants with specific program guidelines, the Wells Fargo offer will allow APLA to use the $100,000 in matching funds wherever the need is greatest.

That means we'll be able to increase our funding this summer to increase the HIV prevention and outreach efforts taking place in neighborhoods that have been hardest hit by AIDS. We'll be able to expand our Home Health Services to provide bedside care for people who are seriously ill with AIDS. And we'll be able to meet the growing needs of low-income clients who count on APLA each week for groceries and other necessities of life.

These are challenging times for AIDS service organizations across the country. This week marks the 26th anniversary of the first reported case of AIDS and we are reminded that more than 25 million people around the world have already died of AIDS—including 30,000 people living right here in Los Angeles.

I feel privileged to live and work in Los Angeles where we have steadfast supporters like you to help us get through these challenging times. And to continue serving our clients in the year ahead, we need the matching gift support of our core donors this summer.

As you may know, government support for our services is decreasing. Federal funding through the Ryan White CARE Act is again being threatened—and Los Angeles County just can't count on receiving the same amount of HIV prevention education funding this year as we received last year.

There are over one million Americans living with HIV, and more than 59,000 of them live right here in Los Angeles County. Many of these individuals turn to APLA for help each year—and only through our partnership with friends like you and Wells Fargo Bank are we able to meet this growing need for our services.

> **If you are able to send a $25 contribution to APLA today, it will be matched immediately and APLA will have $50 to help someone in our community living with HIV/AIDS. Your gift of $100 will become $200, and will go twice as far in providing groceries to APLA clients at one of our food distribution centers. Your $500 gift will actually enable APLA to provide $1,000 worth of home health care visits to persons who are too ill to leave their homes.**

Please know that I'm personally grateful to you for your compassion, your confidence in APLA, and your continuing support for persons living with HIV/AIDS.

I urge you to help us take advantage of this extraordinarily generous offer by Wells Fargo Bank and help APLA qualify for every dollar of the $100,000 grant. I can assure you that your gift will be matched, but the difference you make in the life of someone struggling with AIDS will be unequaled.

Thank you, once again, for staying with us.

With high hopes,

Craig E. Thompson

Craig E. Thompson
Executive Director

P.S.   As you may know, Wells Fargo Bank has a proud history of supporting APLA and giving back to the community. APLA has been a grateful beneficiary of Wells Fargo gifts for several years, and I hope you'll join us this year by sending in a gift of $25, $50, $100, $500, or more within the next 100 days and help us reach our $100,000 goal. For more information on Wells Fargo and their charitable giving, please visit their website, www.wellsfargo.com. Thank you.

$100,000 Wells Fargo Matching Gift Campaign

TO: Craig E. Thompson, Executive Director
AIDS PROJECT LOS ANGELES

FROM: Ms. Jane Doe
123 Any Street
Any Town AS 00000
APL07AC/6-12-07/MATCHING GRANT APPEAL

07ACDOEA
0
5254

ABOUT: Doubling My Support for APLA's Programs and Services

YES, I wish to take advantage of Wells Fargo's Matching Gift offer and double the amount of my gift to AIDS PROJECT LOS ANGELES. I understand my gift will be matched dollar for dollar. Enclosed is my special contribution of:

[ ] **$100 — turning my gift into a $200 contribution to APLA**
[ ] **$200 — turning my gift into a $400 contribution to APLA**
[ ] $_____

Do you prefer to make your gift by credit card?

☐ VISA   ☐ MasterCard   ☐ American Express

Name on card: _____

Account number: _____

Exp. Date: _____   Gift Amount: _____

Signature: _____

To contribute online via our secure server, please visit: **www.apla.org.** *Your gift to AIDS Project Los Angeles is fully tax-deductible.*

1

APLA
AIDS Project Los Angeles

The David Geffen Center
611 S. Kingsley Drive
Los Angeles CA 90005
www.apla.org

RECYCLED & RECYCLABLE / SOY INK   7-AC2

APLA
AIDS Project Los Angeles

ATTN: Special Wells Fargo Matching Gift

7-AC6

AIDS PROJECT LOS ANGELES
GIFT PROCESSING CENTER
2550 NINTH STREET SUITE 1059
BERKELEY CA 94710-2551

EXHIBIT 22.4

Repurposed Online Version of Direct Mail Appeal, AIDS Project Los Angeles

Double Your Impact
for people living with HIV/AIDS

Wells Fargo is matching all donations to APLA up to $100,000 through DATE

Dear Friend,

At a time when many other AIDS service organizations are seeing diminishing funding from the government and corporations, AIDS Project Los Angeles has a critical opportunity to increase support for the 59,000 people in our community living with HIV/AIDS.

For the next 100 days, Wells Fargo Bank will match all contributions to APLA – dollar for dollar – up to $100,000.

Please, have your gift matched today!

This opportunity is especially exciting because, unlike many other challenge grants with specific program guidelines, Wells Fargo is allowing APLA to use the matching funds wherever the need is greatest.

▶ **Have your gift matched today!**

This means that – if we meet our goal of $100,000 – we'll be able to:

Bring our HIV prevention and outreach efforts to neighborhoods that have been hardest hit by AIDS.

Expand our Home Health Services to provide bedside care for people who are seriously ill with AIDS.

Meet the growing needs of low-income people who count on APLA each week for groceries and other necessities of life.

With government support decreasing and federal funding through the Ryan White CARE Act being threatened — Los Angeles County just can't count on receiving the same amount of HIV prevention education funding this year as we received last year.

If we want to continue bringing our services to the people who need them in the year ahead, we need the matching gift support of our donors this summer. Please have your gift matched today!

While the dollars you donate will be doubled, the difference you make in the life of someone struggling with AIDS will be unequaled.

I hope you'll take this opportunity to make that difference. Thank you in advance for your generous contribution, and thank you, once again, for staying with us.

With high hopes,

Craig E. Thompson

Craig E. Thompson
Executive Director

leadership in prevention, advocacy & service

611 South Kingsley Drive
Los Angeles, CA 90005
213.201.1600 Main line
213.201.1500 Clientline

elements that would appear intrusive in a direct mail format. Sure, some mailers use headlines and photos in their letters. However, such graphic elements are likely to look out of place in most direct mail appeals. As you've probably deduced from the earlier chapters in this book, I use graphics very sparingly in direct mail letters. My tendency is to do so online as well—and there is a growing body of evidence that's calling into question the wisdom of loading up e-mail messages with graphics.

- There are three asks in the letter. Even in the much shorter e-mail message, there are three asks, too. Each of the three underlined passages links to a giving page on the organization's website.

Those are specific differences. As you can see, though, the difference in the look and feel of the two versions is greater than the sum of these parts. E-mail is an entirely different medium from print—and if that contrast doesn't show in your e-mail appeals, you'll find your online campaigns falling far short of their goals.

The Cardinal Rules of Writing E-mail Appeals

Fundraisers and commercial marketers alike are constantly evaluating their efforts and gaining new insight when it comes to writing e-mails. However, there are certain basic guidelines that are worth observing and are unlikely to be overturned by later experience.

- The from line should be consistent in all your e-mail appeals. Use your organization's name on that line rather than the name of an individual person or a department.

- Avoid using the recipient's name in the subject line, since that will make your message appear to be spam.

- Make sure that the top two to four inches of your appeal—the portion that will show through a preview pane—is compelling enough to induce readers to open the message and read it all.

- Limit the length of your lines to fifty to sixty characters.

- Just as in direct mail, make sure there's plenty of white space on all sides and between paragraphs.

- Limit paragraphs to no more than five lines.

- Don't overload your message with web links. Include only those you must: your landing page (perhaps three times) and your home page, plus a contact link and an opt-out link at the bottom.

- Minimize your use of asterisks, stars, and other typographical devices (they may trigger spam filters).

- Test each message before sending it.

- Test each message before sending it. (No, this is not a typo, it just merits repeating!) This essential part of a good e-mail program can give you much insight into what copy works for the from line and subject line and in the body of an e-mail. Sadly, it is often overlooked. (Don't make me add it a third time!)

Keep in mind that timeliness is one of the keys to success online. This doesn't just mean you must respond to headline-grabbing events within hours, if possible—it also means you need to send appeals to newly acquired online supporters within thirty days. Click-through rates drop after that point, and much more dramatically after sixty days.

Eight Ways Writing E-mail Appeals Is the Same as Writing Direct Mail Letters

1. Donors respond to the same lofty goals and aspirations online as they do in direct mail. Your organization's vision and mission are the most important motivators. While techniques such as challenge grants, premiums, thermometers (or other symbols of a campaign's promise), or clever campaign concepts may work a little better online than they do in the mail—so long as they are absolutely clear at a glance—contributions online come from the same space in our hearts, minds, and spirits as they do in direct mail. (If you need a refresher course in the fundamentals of donor motivation, check out the motivational hierarchy developed by Abraham Maslow.)

2. A direct mail appeal will fall flat if its marketing, or creative, concept isn't absolutely clear without a second look. The same is true of an e-mail appeal. From the subject line to the lead to the language on the landing page, the marketing concept must ring true. At no point in the process should you muddy the waters by introducing ideas that are inconsistent with the marketing concept.

3. Successful fundraising online is no less dependent than fundraising by mail on making it easy for the donor to give. You go to great lengths to prepare a response device that is tightly connected, thematically and visually, to the main letter. You should devote no less attention to the landing page where people actually use their credit cards to donate.

4. Just as your direct mail letters must come across as personal, one-to-one communications, so too must your e-mail appeals. Use "I" and "you" as liberally as possible.

5. Direct mail offers abundant opportunities to boost response and increase cost effectiveness through segmentation. The same is true online (and at lower cost). At first, you may want to limit yourself to appeals that are identical for all your donors. However, as you build a database of response data—far more detailed and intricate than you could ever build through the mail—you'll find that the possibilities for segmentation online appear endless. It's worth learning how to

fine-tune your e-mail fundraising program with variable copy and ask amounts. But don't get carried away: as in direct mail, the most broadly useful segmentation is based on a donor's highest previous contribution (HPC).

6. In direct mail, the major factors influencing the success of an appeal are the list, the offer, and the format. That's no less the case with e-mail. One major difference is that although renting or exchanging donor, member, subscriber, or activist lists or demographically defined lists is normal in direct mail marketing, list buying is more complicated online and usually involves exchanges with other organizations. The lists generally available for rental don't work for online fundraising and will also subject you to complaints that you're spamming, even if the names are allegedly on an *opt-in* list, meaning people have given permission for their use.

7. Urgency is a critical element in direct mail. Unless your appeal conveys a sense that it really makes a difference for the donor to respond right away, chances are high that he'll simply put your letter aside intending to "get to it later"—which of course happens infrequently. (Siegfried Vögele, whose work I wrote about in chapter 2, estimated that approximately half these responses will be lost.) In e-mail, urgency is even more the name of the game. If your organization can e-mail a relevant message about a headline event within a couple of hours of the event, or a day at most, you may generate many times more revenue than you would have had you waited an extra day or two. One of the prime virtues of online communication is its speed. You need to make the most of it.

8. True fundraising—not those one-off gifts that come from donor acquisition campaigns but the renewal and special appeal gifts that stiffen the backbone of the development process—depends on involving donors. In direct mail, a form of involvement can come from a device as simple as a survey or petition or as substantial as a phone conversation with a legacy giving officer in a follow-up to a letter. In electronic communications, the possibilities of involvement are much more numerous. The most common of the involvement techniques is the e-newsletter.

In exhibit 22.5, "How to Assess an E-mail Fundraising Appeal," you'll see the cheat sheet I've prepared to keep you focused on the most important factors in writing solicitations for funds through e-mail. It is the e-mail version of the evaluation form for direct mail that appeared in exhibit 8.7.

Creating an Effective E-Newsletter

Building relationships in the ephemeral world of online communication is a challenge. If your donors find it easy to discard your direct mail appeals unopened, they can delete your e-mail appeals even more easily. Paradoxically, though, relationships grow strong over time only if the frequency of contact is high—once monthly at a minimum. Today's most successful online fundraisers e-mail their supporters much more frequently—weekly, two or three times weekly, or even daily. But if your organization is small, thinly budgeted, or able to craft a credible appeal only infrequently, then an e-newsletter may be a useful tool for building interest among your online supporters and advancing the process of involving them in your organization. One such product is pictured in exhibit 22.6.

Most e-newsletters are published in HTML format, like the sample in exhibit 22.6. That way, you can include graphics and photos as well as web links shrunk to manageable size ("Click here," for example). A few organizations—a diminishing number—still use plain text. (A handful of organizations send their newsletters as Adobe PDF attachments, but these are likely to be treated as spam.) However, most organizations that send e-newsletters offer their supporters a plain text version as an option.

Then there are the formatting questions that arise about the newsletter's layout. Some publishers insist that a long form is best—one that includes the full text of each article in sequence. Others maintain that readership increases when the e-newsletter itself contains only a one- or two-paragraph summary of each article, followed by a link to the full text on another website. Still others say that such long summaries are distracting and a single sentence plus a link to the website will suffice. There is no conclusive evidence yet available that one of these approaches consistently works better than the others. However, my own experience suggests that because brevity works better online than wordiness, a newsletter that appears shorter is more likely to gain and keep readers than one that goes on for page after page of text.

Keep in mind that an electronic communication—like any message sent to supporters—needs to be interesting, substantive, and written in a lively style. Most e-newsletters are boring. Ideally, a newsletter should include news. Short of that, it ought to include enough human interest and colorful information that your supporters will want to read it.

What structural elements should you include in an e-newsletter? The possibilities are endless of course. However, I strongly recommend that you publish shorter newsletters relatively often rather than longer ones infrequently, and that you consider incorporating at least the following elements into each issue.

EXHIBIT 22.5

How to Assess an E-mail Fundraising Appeal

First, rate e-mail on each criterion by circling your rating: 5 = best, 0 = worst.

#	Criterion	Rating	Weight	Total
1	Speaks *to* the reader, *from* the signer. Uses the singular personal pronouns, "you" and "I."	0 1 2 3 4 5	× 2 =	
2	Talks about benefits, not needs.	0 1 2 3 4 5	× 3 =	
3	The *offer* is unmistakably clear. Benefits to donor are compelling. Asks for a specific amount of money or other explicit act.	0 1 2 3 4 5	× 3 =	
4	Subject line is compelling, relevant, or personal without seeming cheesy.	0 1 2 3 4 5	× 2 =	
5	Establishes urgency—that is, makes the case to take action *now*.	0 1 2 3 4 5	× 2 =	
6	Sender is recognizable.	0 1 2 3 4 5	× 2 =	
7	Powerful writing style: short words, emotion, short sentences, short paragraphs; no ten-dollar words, foreign expressions, abbreviations, acronyms. Uses Anglo-Saxon, not Latin.	0 1 2 3 4 5	× 2 =	
8	Formatted and designed for easy reading. Uses white space, bullets, underlining, a P.S.	0 1 2 3 4 5	× 1 =	
9	Appeal is as long (or as short) as necessary to make the case. Must address all the unspoken questions a reader's likely to have.	0 1 2 3 4 5	× 1 =	
10	Graphics used are eye-catching, compelling.	0 1 2 3 4 5	× 3 =	
11	Landing page follows naturally from the message and makes it easy to take action.	0 1 2 3 4 5	× 2 =	
12	Effectively uses color, graphics, white space to emphasize essentials: benefits, deadline, call to action.	0 1 2 3 4 5	× 1 =	
	TOTAL			
	Total the 11 ratings. (Remember: 0 × 5 = 0!)			

Second, evaluate your score. With as many as 5 points available for each of the eleven criteria, and weighting factors that total 24, a perfect score is 120 points. You may translate a numerical score into a letter grade as follows.

Rating	Letter Grade	Meaning
110–120	A+	No more need be said.
100–109	A	Give that writer a pat on the back!
80–99	B	Shows lots of promise.
60–79	C	Needs some improvement.
30–59	D	Requires a lot of work. Maybe better to start from scratch!
0–29	F	Uh oh!

Source:

EXHIBIT 22.6

Sample E-newsletter, Sierra Club

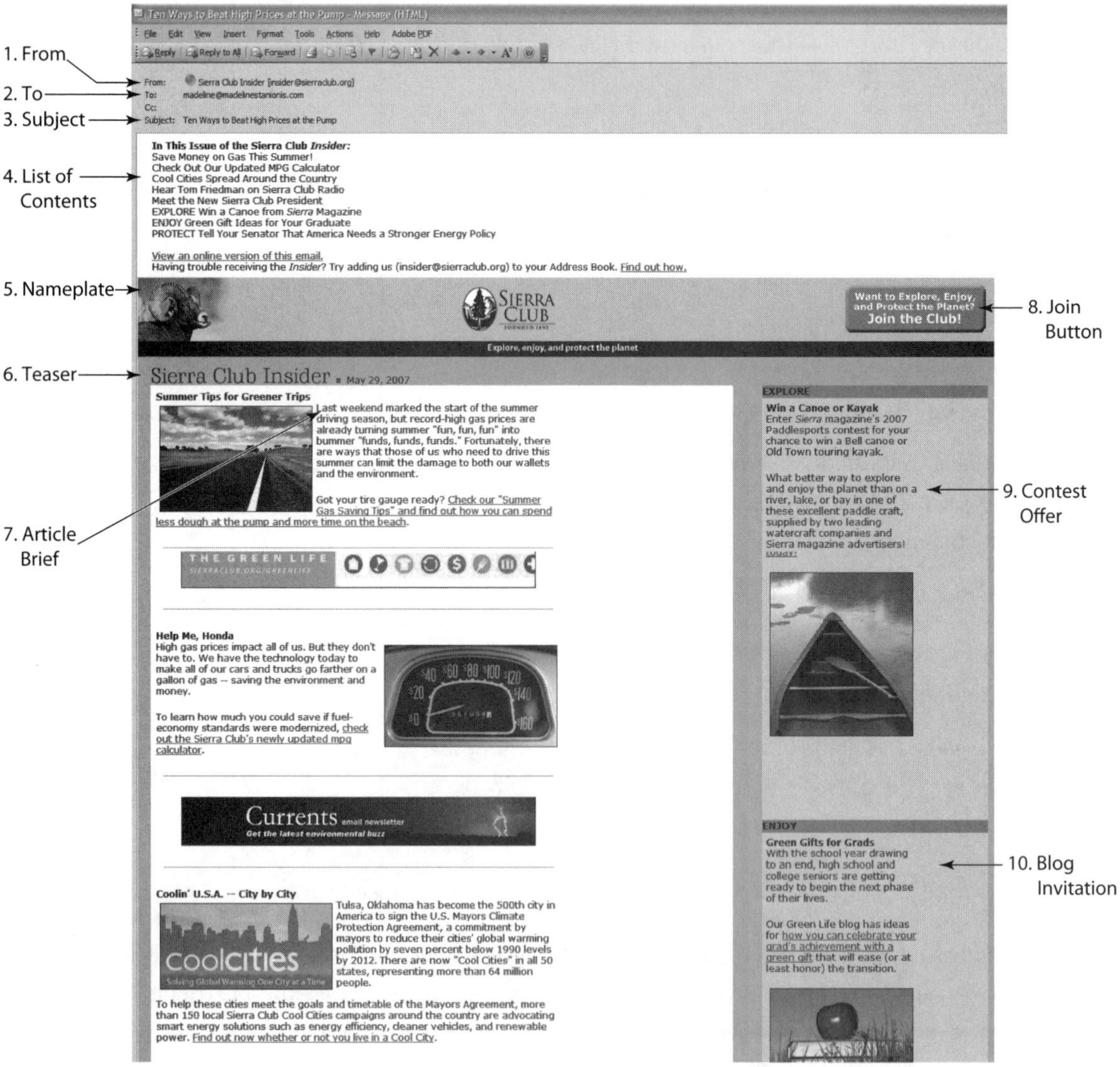

1. From
2. To
3. Subject
4. List of Contents
5. Nameplate
6. Teaser
7. Article Brief
8. Join Button
9. Contest Offer
10. Blog Invitation

Ten Ways to Beat High Prices at the Pump - Message (HTML)

File Edit View Insert Format Tools Actions Help Adobe PDF

Reply | Reply to All | Forward

From: Sierra Club Insider [insider@sierraclub.org]
To: madeline@madelinestanionis.com
Cc:
Subject: Ten Ways to Beat High Prices at the Pump

In This Issue of the Sierra Club *Insider:*
Save Money on Gas This Summer!
Check Out Our Updated MPG Calculator
Cool Cities Spread Around the Country
Hear Tom Friedman on Sierra Club Radio
Meet the New Sierra Club President
EXPLORE Win a Canoe from *Sierra* Magazine
ENJOY Green Gift Ideas for Your Graduate
PROTECT Tell Your Senator That America Needs a Stronger Energy Policy

View an online version of this email.
Having trouble receiving the *Insider*? Try adding us (insider@sierraclub.org) to your Address Book. Find out how.

SIERRA CLUB

Want to Explore, Enjoy, and Protect the Planet? Join the Club!

Explore, enjoy, and protect the planet

Sierra Club Insider ▪ May 29, 2007

Summer Tips for Greener Trips
Last weekend marked the start of the summer driving season, but record-high gas prices are already turning summer "fun, fun, fun" into bummer "funds, funds, funds." Fortunately, there are ways that those of us who need to drive this summer can limit the damage to both our wallets and the environment.

Got your tire gauge ready? Check our "Summer Gas Saving Tips" and find out how you can spend less dough at the pump and more time on the beach.

THE GREEN LIFE
SIERRACLUB.ORG/GREENLIFE

Help Me, Honda
High gas prices impact all of us. But they don't have to. We have the technology today to make all of our cars and trucks go farther on a gallon of gas -- saving the environment and money.

To learn how much you could save if fuel-economy standards were modernized, check out the Sierra Club's newly updated mpg calculator.

Currents email newsletter
Get the latest environmental buzz

Coolin' U.S.A. -- City by City
Tulsa, Oklahoma has become the 500th city in America to sign the U.S. Mayors Climate Protection Agreement, a commitment by mayors to reduce their cities' global warming pollution by seven percent below 1990 levels by 2012. There are now "Cool Cities" in all 50 states, representing more than 64 million people.

coolcities
Solving Global Warming One City at a Time

To help these cities meet the goals and timetable of the Mayors Agreement, more than 150 local Sierra Club Cool Cities campaigns around the country are advocating smart energy solutions such as energy efficiency, cleaner vehicles, and renewable power. Find out now whether or not you live in a Cool City.

EXPLORE

Win a Canoe or Kayak
Enter *Sierra* magazine's 2007 Paddlesports contest for your chance to win a Bell canoe or Old Town touring kayak.

What better way to explore and enjoy the planet than on a river, lake, or bay in one of these excellent paddle craft, supplied by two leading watercraft companies and Sierra magazine advertisers!

ENJOY

Green Gifts for Grads
With the school year drawing to an end, high school and college seniors are getting ready to begin the next phase of their lives.

Our Green Life blog has ideas for how you can celebrate your grad's achievement with a green gift that will ease (or at least honor) the transition.

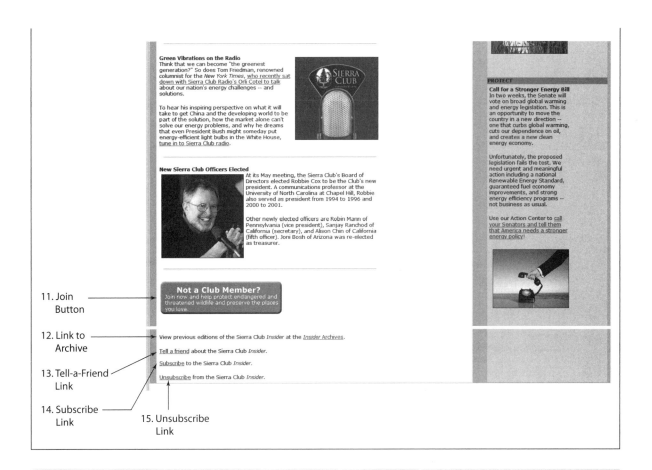

Green Vibrations on the Radio
Think that we can become "the greenest generation?" So does Tom Friedman, renowned columnist for the *New York Times*, who recently sat down with Sierra Club Radio's Orli Cotel to talk about our nation's energy challenges -- and solutions.

To hear his inspiring perspective on what it will take to get China and the developing world to be part of the solution, how the market alone can't solve our energy problems, and why he dreams that even President Bush might someday put energy-efficient light bulbs in the White House, tune in to Sierra Club radio.

New Sierra Club Officers Elected
At its May meeting, the Sierra Club's Board of Directors elected Robbie Cox to be the Club's new president. A communications professor at the University of North Carolina at Chapel Hill, Robbie also served as president from 1994 to 1996 and 2000 to 2001.

Other newly elected officers are Robin Mann of Pennsylvania (vice president), Sanjay Ranchod of California (secretary), and Alison Chin of California (fifth officer). Joni Bosh of Arizona was re-elected as treasurer.

Not a Club Member?
Join now and help protect endangered and threatened wildlife and preserve the places you love.

View previous editions of the Sierra Club *Insider* at the *Insider* Archives.

Tell a friend about the Sierra Club *Insider*.

Subscribe to the Sierra Club *Insider*.

Unsubscribe from the Sierra Club *Insider*.

PROTECT
Call for a Stronger Energy Bill
In two weeks, the Senate will vote on broad global warming and energy legislation. This is an opportunity to move the country in a new direction -- one that curbs global warming, cuts our dependence on oil, and creates a new clean energy economy.

Unfortunately, the proposed legislation fails the test. We need urgent and meaningful action including a national Renewable Energy Standard, guaranteed fuel economy improvements, and strong energy efficiency programs -- not business as usual.

Use our Action Center to call your Senators and tell them that America needs a stronger energy policy!

11. Join Button

12. Link to Archive

13. Tell-a-Friend Link

14. Subscribe Link

15. Unsubscribe Link

• *List of contents*. Not all e-newsletters lead with this abbreviated listing of articles, but experience online seems to suggest that this approach increases readership—so long as the entries are brief and the language is clear. Perhaps that's because at least some of the list of contents will show through on a preview screen—and one of the several articles listed may be a greater incentive to open and read the newsletter than the opening lines of a single article.

• *Limited number of articles*. Some e-newsletters are jam-packed with contents—ten, twelve, or even fifteen articles—but I don't recommend that. I believe that the more digestible your newsletter, the more it will be read. I would opt more readily for a daily newsletter that includes a single article than a weekly newsletter containing seven. And I most assuredly would not wait until I'd accumulated a critical mass of articles—fifteen, twenty, or more—and then publish a monthly issue. A hefty print newsletter might—I say *might*—be more attractive than a flimsy one. Online, though, it will discourage readership.

• *Appeal for funds—sometimes, not in every issue*. Some direct marketers advocate asking for money at every opportunity. I don't. Your readers are expecting content from you—interesting, useful information—not an appeal for funds at every turn. I believe fundraising efforts are more effective when they're interspersed with substantive material, not a predictable and inevitable part of every communication. In any case, newsletter appeals don't usually generate a lot of donations unless your supporter list is very large.

- *Pass-along option*. The most effective location for an invitation to pass along your newsletter is at the very top of each issue. It's intrusive of course, and may be esthetically undesirable. Many fundraising organizations relegate this link to the bottom of the newsletter.

- *Call to action or other involvement opportunity*. Though I believe requests for money ought to be sent sparingly, I feel very different about requests for action. The biggest and most responsive e-mail lists are those built through such devices as grassroots lobbying and consumer-generated content (material written by supporters rather than by you or your staff). The more involving you can make your newsletter, the more likely it

is your subscribers will open it regularly. And make no mistake—the frontline challenge in e-mail is similar to that in direct mail: getting the recipient merely to open your message. Typical open rates nowadays are in the range of 10 to 20 percent, with rates between 20 and 30 percent qualifying as above average, and rates north of 30 percent being exceptionally good.

- *Unsubscribe option*. I regard it as a cardinal sin to e-mail an electronic newsletter without including a link to a site where the recipient may opt out of her subscription. It's not just bad practice to omit an unsubscribe option—it's a CAN-Spam Act must. (That means it's illegal!)

- *Copyright and publisher information*. It's wise to include both a current copyright notice and the name and contact information of your organization. These elements signal an element of professionalism and thus heighten the credibility of an e-newsletter.

One more word of advice: just as I've urged you to write your fundraising letters in an informal, conversational style, I implore you to do so in your e-newsletters. Not only do online readers trend younger, they're also accustomed to the greater informality of the web.

Prepare Your Website for Multichannel Engagement

As I suggested earlier, the first two places to focus your website efforts are the home page and campaign landing page. Each is worth a closer look.

Home Page

If you've got a knack for writing teasers, you'll probably have an easy time crafting the copy for a headline and blurb to place on or near the top of your website's home page. The objective in doing so is to capture the attention of visitors to your site and persuade them to go directly to the campaign landing page by clicking on the link in your blurb. For example, if you're working for an animal protection organization, you might write something along the following lines:

Kiss this baby goodbye?

[Small photo of bloodied young seal on an ice floe]

Only with your help can we can stop this atrocity.

[Bold, bright button here, labeled **TAKE ACTION!**]

[Note: clicking anywhere on this blurb will link to the landing page.]

However, once you've written and designed that blurb, you may find that securing home page real estate, especially at the top, can be daunting. With every department and program fighting for limited space on the site, you may find yourself embroiled in organizational politics. It's best to anticipate this problem and make every effort to head it off by obtaining blanket permission from senior management in advance.

Why is a position near the top of the home page so important? Consider this: someone who has just received your appeal might only spend three seconds on your home page before leaving if he doesn't find messaging relevant to the campaign that brought him there in the first place. And that's critical because 70 percent of the people who receive your direct mail appeals will visit your website before deciding whether to give again. (You won't forget that, will you?)

Here's an interesting experiment. Take an informal poll of your organization's staff. Ask what percentage of your home page should be dedicated to helping raise funds. Answers might range from as low as 15 percent to 60 percent or higher. Now, examine your home page and measure the proportions. If you're above 30 percent, congratulations—you're doing well! Some organizations have only 5 percent dedicated to helping them achieve one of their most important goals. Fight for your key appeals to have prominent placement. You'll be glad you did.

Now here are five things to remember when trying to get your message across on the home page:

1. *Location, location, location.* According to recent studies as well as our old friend Siegfried Vögele, website visitors look at information in the pattern of a reversed F, starting at the top left, working their way over, down the side, and into the middle. For key campaigns, and certainly at year-end, make sure your appeal message is at the top and center-left of the home page.

2. *Make it fast and easy.* Messaging and usability (ease of reading and taking action) trump design for website success. So make sure you use high-impact language. With only three seconds or so of a visitor's

attention, you must quickly ask her to take an action, explain (or illustrate) why that action is important, and provide the next step.

3. *Pay attention to keywords.* If your organization hasn't configured its website to ensure a higher volume of traffic through the process known as *search engine optimization* (SEO), talk to your programmer or consultant. You're overdue for SEO. Once that work has been done, the organization will have created a list of keywords that reflect the nature of its work and priorities. And whenever you write copy for the site—or for e-mail too, for that matter—you'll need to include in your message as many of those keywords as you can and also avoid keywords that violate organization policy. For example, an old folks' home may favor the use of *dignity*, *aging*, and *geriatric* but want to avoid *old*, *senior citizen*, *death*, and *dying*. Since most people who go online find your site though a search, make sure your copy supports SEO goals instead of hindering them. Ask the powers that be for the relevant word lists.

4. *Empower your donors!* Don't ever forget that fundraising isn't about you and your organization. It's about helping your donors realize how much they accomplish as part of your team. Your organization simply serves as the link between donors and beneficiaries. Focus your messaging on "you" and "your" not "we" and "us."

5. *Highlight the link to action.* It's not enough to ask people to "click here." You'll need to include a prominent "DONATE" or "ACTION" button in the blurb you write.

Landing Page

When a donor clicks on one of the links you've embedded in your e-mail appeal, or the home page message supporting your appeal, she'll be transported to a specified landing page on your website. Smaller organizations tend to link donors to a generic donation page, but I don't recommend that. In direct mail, it's almost always important to enclose a separate reply device that matches the letter in theme, tone, and appearance. The landing page should do that too. See exhibit 22.7 for an example.

The landing page is the business end of an online appeal, equivalent to the reply device in direct mail. How you design and write this form can be critical to the success of your e-mail appeal. The landing page must look and feel like the appeal itself. It's wise to limit, or even eliminate, links to other pages on your site. Be certain the ask is clear and that you've restated the creative, or marketing, concept of the appeal, repeating the language in the appeal, just as you would in direct mail. Offer several giving options.

EXHIBIT 22.7
Landing Page for Online Appeal, AmeriCares

Use a one-column format (rather than two) where you ask for personal information. (Testing has shown that one-part forms usually outperform multiple-part forms and that the one-column approach outpulls the two-column format.) And above all, keep this form simple.

Driving Dialogue with Social Media

While explicit fundraising campaigns are occasionally appropriate in social media, such channels as Facebook, Twitter, and Pinterest are more frequently (and more successfully) used as engagement opportunities for both current and new supporters. Empowering these supporters to make positive and social change is key to driving success in this channel.

Most of the time, your posts on social media should relate to current circumstances, such as headline news or especially notable news about your organization, and not rely on scheduled organizational updates. A social media page or post is not the place to repurpose your organizational brochure! From time to time, though, you'll need to spur on the conversation with hard-driving, often urgent, messaging to induce your supporters to become engaged. This might include a few sentences for a Facebook post, a tweet, or the few words you write to accompany an image "pinned" on Pinterest.

Keep the copy brief. (Twitter will do that for you, with its 140-character limit on messages!) When supporting a multichannel campaign with a post on Facebook, for instance, you'll need to craft a strong headline and a two-sentence description of the main message in your appeal, followed by a one-sentence call to action. Include a video about the campaign or the issue, or a high-impact photo. Then follow all that with a one-paragraph summary of the story in your appeal, including a description of how a supporter can help. Conclude by repeating the call to action. And don't forget to use the words "you" and "your," be timely, create urgency, and talk *with*, not *to*, your supporters.

You can see many of these elements, and how your abbreviated copy might be deployed, in the "Aware in Care" campaign from the National Parkinson Foundation (exhibit 22.8), which illustrates several different Facebook ads.

These Facebook ads drove visitors to the National Parkinson Foundation's Facebook page, where they could learn how to help simply with a click or two online (exhibit 22.9). The first 10,000 of those who "liked" the Foundation's page made it possible for the organization to distribute valuable diagnostic kits to people in need.

The Foundation posted Facebook updates continuously throughout the campaign, even after the first 10,000 kits had been handed out. Note the update in exhibit 22.10 asking for feedback from those who actually received the kits—a post that also helped supporters see what impact they achieved.

EXHIBIT 22.8
Facebook Ads, National Parkinson Foundation "Aware in Care" Campaign

National Parkinson Foundation

"Like" NPF to help us give away 10,000 free Aware in Care kits that contain vital tools and information for people with Parkinson's.

👍 Like · Raise Moremoney likes this.

National Parkinson Foundation

75% of people with Parkinson's have medication complications in the hospital. Click "Like" to help us change the odds.

👍 Like · Raise Moremoney likes this.

National Parkinson Foundation

"Like" NPF today to help give 10,000 people with Parkinson's the power to take charge of their care.

👍 Like · Raise Moremoney likes this.

National Parkinson Foundation

Parkinson's patients spend twice the time hospitalized as other people. Click "Like" to help change the odds.

👍 Like · Raise Moremoney likes this.

National Parkinson Foundation

Click "Like" now to give a person with Parkinson's an Aware in Care kit that will ensure they get the treatment they need.

👍 Like · Raise Moremoney likes this.

National Parkinson Foundation

You can help beat Parkinson's – click "Like" to give a person with Parkinson's an Aware in Care kit to get the treatment they need.

👍 Like · Raise Moremoney likes this.

EXHIBIT 22.9
Facebook Post, National Parkinson Foundation "Aware in Care" Campaign

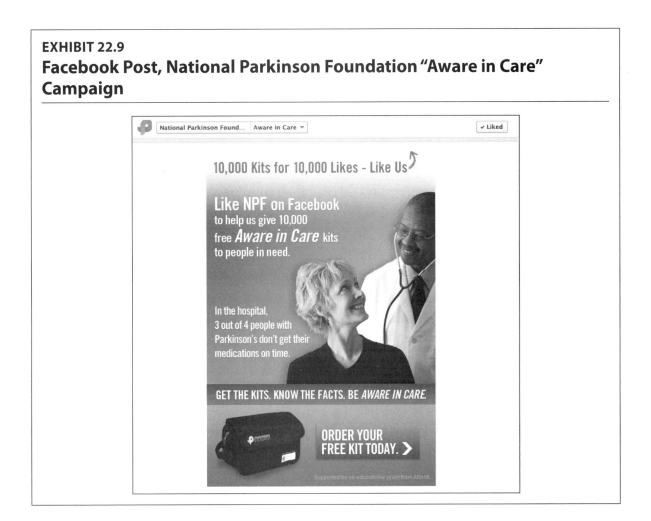

EXHIBIT 22.10
Facebook Update, National Parkinson Foundation "Aware in Care" Campaign

The New Frontier of Mobile Marketing

Did it register in your mind when I wrote some pages back that most online action today is initiated through mobile devices such as smartphones and tablets?

That fact is one of the most significant markers in today's digital landscape that point toward the future. Unfortunately, the implications for your work as a fundraiser aren't nearly so clear. No doubt, mobile communications will loom large in your fundraising program in years to come. However, to date there are few large-scale success stories. For the time being, if only as a hint of what's to come, it's worth looking at two applications of mobile marketing: text to give and outbound mobile cultivation.

Text to Give

If you have any thoughts at all about mobile fundraising, they probably relate to the Red Cross text-to-give program launched in the wake of Hurricane Katrina in 2005. Although it contributed only a small fraction of the relief funds raised for New Orleans and the Gulf Coast, that program was a qualified success. If you're involved in raising money to respond to humanitarian emergencies, you should have a plan in place to accept text donations and deploy mobile fundraising messages within hours of the first news report (minutes would be even better). In the aftermath of any disaster, the lion's share of the contributions is received within the first seventy-two hours. Beyond that point, receipts rapidly dwindle as the news media steadily shift from around-the-clock coverage to an occasional follow-up story. Here are the basic guidelines to follow for text-to-give fundraising:

- Swing into action immediately—absolutely no later than twenty-four hours after the first headlines appear—and continue messaging with increased frequency during the first seventy-two hours as more information becomes available.

- Prominently feature your text-to-give phone number and keyword (for example, "Text 'donate' to 55555 to make a $10 donation now") in all outbound messages and media during those seventy-two hours. That includes e-mail, press releases, and public statements by representatives of your organization.

- Make sure your messages are brief and that the urgency of the situation grabs the reader's attention.

- In advance, have in place a plan for postdisaster mobile cultivation. Currently, you can identify the donations you receive via text only by the mobile telephone numbers from which they were sent. They're not accompanied by either a physical or an e-mail address. To increase the chances of repeat giving from text donors, then, it's important to initiate outbound cultivation messaging immediately after new text donors are acquired.

Mobile Cultivation

Many organizations are gathering mobile numbers from their supporters, developing mobile communication streams, and keeping in touch through messages sent directly to supporter by phone. (You can acquire mobile phone numbers either through an emergency fundraising campaign or by inviting your donors themselves to opt in to a mobile messaging program.) First, however, you'll need to optimize both your website and your e-mail messaging program to be read on mobile devices. If your message won't display correctly, they can't read it. If they can't read it, they can't donate.

Exhibits 22.11 and 22.12 show first an e-mail and then the mobile-optimized version of that e-mail for an appeal from AmeriCares. The mobile version is easy to read right from a smartphone—and without a complete redesign or overhaul. The optimization process is simple and straightforward—it involves adding a snippet of HTML code to the e-mail's header—but you'll probably need to consult your programmer or online fundraising or marketing consultant for help.

Mobile optimization is a must if you want to raise money through mobile phones. Navigating traditional online forms via mobile phone is extremely difficult at best.

Exhibit 22.13 is the mobile-optimized donation form for the AmeriCares appeal illustrated immediately above. As you can see, it resembles a direct mail response device, with motivational language and imagery at the top and an easy-to-navigate form below. Constructing a form like this requires more than simply adding a snippet of code, but you'll need to invest in a mobile donation page before you launch a mobile cultivation program.

Keep in mind that all mobile messaging needs to be both timely and succinct.

Even More Techniques to Involve Your Donors Online

Cyberspace is a direct marketer's dream. The possibilities for dialogue and involvement are unlimited, and new technologies that increase the available options appear to be coming on the market almost monthly. Here are just some of the possibilities that come to mind at this writing, over and above the use of social networks such as Facebook, Twitter, and Pinterest. Some are well tested, others just now coming into view. They're all worth your consideration as donor involvement devices as well as list-building efforts if you want to develop an innovative online fundraising program.

1. *Activism.* If your organization engages in lobbying of any sort . . . if your mission includes public education . . . if you are seeking to

EXHIBIT 22.11
E-mail Appeal, AmeriCares

AmeriCares
A passion to help. The ability to deliver.

Dear FirstName,

Your monthly support as a member of Partners in Caring gives health and hope to families in crisis around the world and here at home.

This video is a token of our appreciation for you, and a reminder of the vital impact you have as a monthly donor to AmeriCares.

These last few months have been a time of almost unprecedented disaster and difficulty for millions of families around the world. We've been in action around the clock, helping people in desperate need. But our resources are almost stretched to their limits.

Please consider making an additional end of year, tax-deductible donation, and together we will continue AmeriCares lifesaving mission, as outlined in this powerful new video.

Thank you for your support during this special time of year.

Sincerely,

Curt Welling
President and CEO, AmeriCares

Donate Now!

Share this email on Facebook and Twitter

A PASSION TO HELP. THE ABILITY TO DELIVER. ®
Privacy Policy © 2011 AmeriCares | 88 Hamilton Avenue | Stamford, CT 06902

EXHIBIT 22.12
Mobile-Optimized Appeal, AmeriCares

AmeriCares
A passion to help. The ability to deliver.

Dear FirstName,

Your monthly support as a member of Partners in Caring gives health and hope to families in crisis around the world and here at home.

This video **is a token of our appreciation for you, and a reminder of the vital impact you have as a monthly donor to AmeriCares.**

These last few months have been a time of almost unprecedented disaster and difficulty for millions of families around the world. We've been in action around the clock, helping people in desperate need. But our resources are almost stretched to their limits.

Please consider making an additional end of year, tax-deductible donation**, and together we will continue AmeriCares lifesaving mission, as outlined in this** powerful new video**.**

Thank you for your support during this special time of year.

Sincerely,

Curt Welling
President and CEO, AmeriCares

Donate Now!

Share this email on ☰Facebook and Twitter

A PASSION TO HELP. THE ABILITY TO DELIVER.®
Privacy Policy © 2011 AmeriCares
88 Hamilton Avenue | Stamford, CT 06902

EXHIBIT 22.13
Mobile-Optimized Donation Form, AmeriCares

change public opinion about a high-profile issue (or one whose profile you want to raise) . . . then online activism may provide you with an opportunity to advance your mission while involving supporters online. Just as direct mail letters sometimes include action devices such as petitions or postcards, you can incorporate action devices into your online appeals and e-newsletters. Activism is the single most effective way to build a large database of online supporters.

2. *Quiz*. A quick-and-dirty quiz that consists of no more than half a dozen questions relevant to your organization's work can do double duty as a clever way to attract traffic to your website and as a way to educate the public about the issues you address.

3. *Survey*. There are many types of surveys—everything from an informal questionnaire included in your electronic newsletter to an online survey directed at a statistically valid sample of your e-mail list. If your primary goal is to promote involvement, an informal survey may be a winner. If you are seeking actionable data about your online prospects, then you probably need to hire a third-party supplier with a large screening panel that will permit statistically valid results. Short of that, surveymonkey.com and other sources of inexpensive software make it easy for you to manage the survey process.

4. *Poll*. Like surveys, polls can be conducted either informally or formally. For instance, you can structure an informal poll that serves to attract new visitors to your site and to give your existing supporters an opportunity to become involved. You might ask visitors to "vote" on a yes or no question (or several questions), and report the results in real time on your site. Polls of this type are popular and appear to remain effective as involvement devices—especially if you offer voters a chance to add comments that will be posted online.

5. *Game*. Some well-heeled and venturesome nonprofits have invested large sums of money in developing professional-quality games that have helped them gain a foothold on the World Wide Web. See, for example, the United Nations World Food Programme's website for its game Food Force, at www.food-force.com. Exhibit 22.14 reproduces the home page.

6. *Video*. Video can bring life to an e-mail appeal or a web page. A testimonial from a celebrity, an up-to-the-minute report from a program officer in the field, an update from the executive director—any of these, and many more, can deepen a supporter's experience of your organization. It might also increase response, although some organizations have found it doesn't. What's more, you can post the video on

EXHIBIT 22.14
Food Force Home Page, United Nations World Food Programme

YouTube and reach more people at no cost. (In fact, you can construct your own unique, branded channel on YouTube.) There's a catch, however. Experience shows that only short videos generally work well online. That eight-to-ten-minute video your organization has produced to introduce your organization's work at house parties will likely fall flat online. Think two-minute productions, or three at most. Even forty-five- or sixty-second videos can be helpful. Many viewers tune out after no more than one minute.

7. *Animation.* Animation is often cute, sometimes funny, and—every once in a while—genuinely effective. At its best, a truly clever animated short can induce your donors to send it along to all their friends, triggering a viral-marketing success story. But animation can also come across as amateurish and silly. It is exceedingly difficult to produce an animated video that will work online (no matter how clever or hilarious you may think it is). Use animation sparingly, and only if you know what you're doing (or have hired someone who does).

8. *Podcast.* Many people like downloading audio podcasts to their iPods or other devices. They're much easier to make than videos, but you'll still need to find an interesting subject and a good speaker and do a

professional job on the recording. Then you can include a link to your podcast in an appeal or an e-newsletter for your activists, donors, or prospects.

9. *Contest.* Some of direct mail's biggest successes have been built on the back of a sweepstakes offer or other contest. In e-mail it's easier. "The first 50 donors to this campaign will receive a free [something-or-other]." Or: "As a supporter of this cause, your e-mail address will be entered into a drawing. You could be one of the 100 lucky donors who will win a free [something-or-other]." Or: "Your winning 50-word essay may be selected for posting right here on our website along with nine other lucky winners." However, if you launch a campaign of this sort with any significant scope, you may run afoul of state laws that require registration and limit your options in a variety of ways.

10. *Q&A.* One way to ensure a growing body of content on your website while involving your supporters as well is to offer quick answers to people's questions about the field or issue your organization addresses. In each issue of your e-newsletter, you can highlight this service by offering a link to the Q&A page of your site and featuring an especially interesting, recent question and answer. Your growing archive of these Q&As will become an attraction in its own right, drawing more attention to your organization.

11. *Testimonials.* Studies in word-of-mouth marketing show that testimonials—whether from rank-and-file donors or buyers or from experts or celebrities—are regarded as highly credible by the public. A well-crafted testimonial from one of your donors might be substantially more persuasive to an ambivalent donor than a message from you. And donors (like most people!) are often pleased to endorse a service or an organization that pleases them. All you have to do is ask—in your e-newsletter, for example. Then, if you wish, you can feature these testimonials both in your e-newsletter and on your website. The prominence given donor testimonials is likely to attract others to offer their own.

12. *Friend-get-a-friend.* Asking donors to recruit friends, neighbors, coworkers, or relatives is a technique that surely predates direct mail. Properly framed, it works, sometimes very well. It's ordinarily one of the cheapest ways to prospect for new donors. Online the possibilities for friend-get-a-friend campaigns are numerous. The simplest approach is simply a request in every e-newsletter for the reader to pass along a copy—ideally, by entering the names and e-mail addresses of one or more prospects on a landing page on

your website, thus triggering e-mail messages to these prospects that incorporate the text of the newsletter. You might also attempt a purer form of viral marketing by sending a video or animated short to your supporters and suggesting they share it with all their friends. Or you could take the process a step further and offer some form of prize or other incentive to those donors who recruit the largest number of new donors, activists, or e-newsletter subscribers. However, the most successful friend-to-friend efforts in online fundraising revolve around special events such as walkathons, bike-athons, and the like.

13. *User-generated show-and-tell.* Animal welfare organizations have involved and energized thousands of supporters by encouraging them to post photos of their pets online. You may not be able to make such a beguiling offer, but some variation on this show-and-tell technique could work for you. For example, you might ask supporters to post their own personal stories, with or without photos. You could ask them to post their photos and explain why they feel the issue you're addressing is important, then post their entries on a Google map to show your supporter base across the nation or the world.

14. *Personalized landing pages.* If your online vendor is up to the task, you can embed personal data in the landing page for a link included in a supporter's e-mail appeal or e-newsletter. This way you can build an individualized ask, just as you might do in a direct mail appeal.

These fourteen online involvement devices are relatively straightforward and technically undemanding. New technologies—what geeks call collectively Web 2.0—offer abundant new possibilities for involvement. Many of these are much less straightforward. Here are just a few examples:

15. *Blogs.* According to the Neilson people (the folks who also estimate how many people watch TV shows), there were more than 181 million blogs online in 2012. So you might feel left out if your organization doesn't offer your supporters at least one blog. But make sure you know what you're getting into. It's easy and cheap to create a blog, but it's quite another thing to maintain it on a daily, or even a weekly, basis. It's also easy (at least for some people) to write thousands of words. It's harder to write in a colorful, uniquely personal, and hard-hitting style that will engage readers and keep them coming back for more. Before you take the plunge, think hard about what you're taking on.

16. *Do it yourself (DIY).* One of the newest trends—and it may eventually become the most important—is giving your supporters online tools that enable them to become fundraisers for you. This is friend-to-friend

fundraising at its best. The method has been used for decades for events like the American Cancer Society's Relay for Life, where runners create *personal pages* online and send their friends and colleagues there to donate. Now organizations are creating *charity badges* and other widgets that supporters can place on their Facebook pages, their websites, or their blogs, inviting visitors to donate. Donation totals are updated in real time, and the organization can also update news content on the badges.

Which Comes First—the Chicken or the Egg?

If you're confused by all these references to a seemingly endless list of channels, tools, and links, join the club. Even old-timers in this area, now typically called a *space*, can be overwhelmed at times by all the options. Nobody, but nobody, can keep track of them all, since new software and services seem to come online on almost a daily basis. However, there is a growing body of experience in raising money and selling goods and services online, so it's now possible to set some priorities. For example, we know now that the first step in venturing online to raise money must be a website, since those who respond to e-mail or web advertising need somewhere to go. (You can hardly ask them to mail you a letter!) The second step is to collect e-mail addresses from your supporters, and that's followed by the development of some regular means of communicating with those supporters through an e-newsletter, action alerts, or e-mail appeals (or, more likely, some combination of those mechanisms).

As you can see in Exhibit 22.15, surveys conducted by MarketingSherpa, a leading online source of data about online commerce, landing pages emerge as the top choice for testing a value proposition online. This means, in effect, that when you test variables on a landing page, you're most likely to observe a great enough response to determine which of one or more variations will yield the best results. I believe it follows that the landing page is thus the single most important element in "closing the sale"—that is, in fundraising terms, securing a gift. Important as it is to craft a powerful e-mail appeal that will motivate prospects to click through to the landing page, it's even more important to optimize the design of the landing page, so that the largest possible number of prospects will actually follow through by contributing gifts.

The Immediate Future of Online Appeals

Online fundraising has brought millions of new donors into the world of philanthropy thanks to fundraising campaigns for humanitarian relief following the South Asian tsunami and Hurricanes Katrina and Rita. Leading

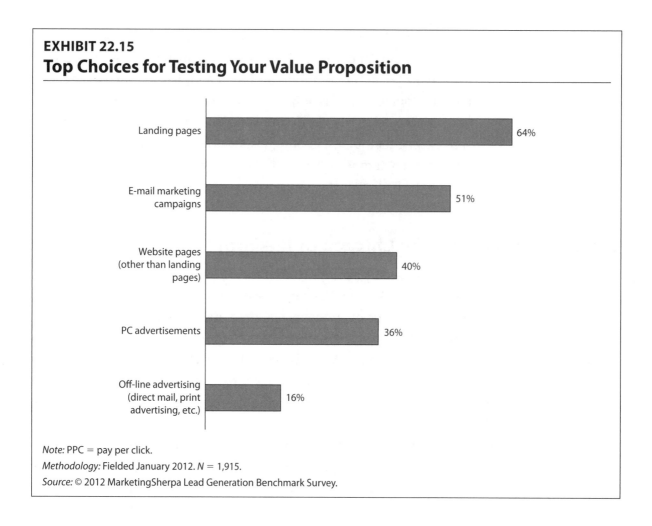

EXHIBIT 22.15
Top Choices for Testing Your Value Proposition

Landing pages — 64%
E-mail marketing campaigns — 51%
Website pages (other than landing pages) — 40%
PC advertisements — 36%
Off-line advertising (direct mail, print advertising, etc.) — 16%

Note: PPC = pay per click.
Methodology: Fielded January 2012. *N* = 1,915.
Source: © 2012 MarketingSherpa Lead Generation Benchmark Survey.

advocacy organizations have enlisted hundreds of thousands, even millions of supporters online. In political fundraising too, the impact of the Internet has been substantial, especially in US presidential campaigns starting in 2004. President Obama's 2008 election campaign famously recruited 750,000 online donors, and his effective use of online fundraising continues to play an important role in building his support on the ground. Other nonprofits have gained footholds online through significant investments in marketing. For all these organizations, online techniques are locating new donors who are not responsive to other communications media. The most successful US nonprofits have 10 percent or even 15 percent of their small donors giving online—and typically giving much higher average gifts than direct mail donors—and those numbers are growing while direct mail returns for these nonprofits may be flat or declining. Clearly, for some nonprofit organizations, the advent of the Internet has been a major boost.

I remain optimistic that electronic communications will continue to gain prominence in our work as fundraisers. I'm convinced that an investment of time, effort, and money in learning the techniques of online fundraising will eventually pay off handsomely. And I *know* that online communications already contributes in a major way to raising money through integrated, multichannel campaigns.

Additionally, we're finding that donors engaged in social fundraising have higher retention rates than those who don't. Think about it: once I've asked my friends and family to support or donate to a charity on my behalf, I'm going to be pretty vested in that charity's success, aren't I?

For the immediate future, though, the more traditional direct marketing channels of mail and the telephone will continue to dominate the quest for individual contributions in the nonprofit sector. Direct mail is, and will remain for some time to come, the workhorse in your annual fund, annual campaign, or membership program—and the likely source of the overwhelming majority of later major and legacy gifts.

However, online will continue to grow as a recipient of funds driven by direct mail as well as continue to grow as its own force as a generator, not just a recipient, of donor contributions. Donor choice will drive this change. Digital's benefits, impact, and results simply continue growing from year to year.

Now that I've run you through the wringer, covering just about every communication medium except tin cans on a string, it's time to shift gears again and elevate this fast-moving vehicle to about 30,000 feet, where we can view the entire fundraising landscape in perspective. That's my topic in chapter 23, "The New Keys to Success in Fundraising Today."

Chapter Twenty-Three:
The New Keys to Success in Fundraising Today

What I'm about to tell you is certainly not news to you—that the world of nonprofit fundraising has changed in fundamental ways in the past two decades, and even in the five years since the second edition of this book was published. You know that. But if you're like most people engaged in the business of raising money, you may not have a handle on what those changes mean from a practical perspective—what the implications are for how we go about our business on a day-to-day basis.

When I began raising money professionally more than thirty years ago, the fundraising field consisted primarily of people who worked on major gifts, foundation grants, corporate giving, special events, and, increasingly, direct mail. And those people really didn't talk to one another. Fundraising today is vastly more complex—and we can't afford not to understand at least a little about what everyone else is doing.

So in these few pages, I'm going to take you on a tour of this strange new world of fundraising in the twenty-first century. This will be a quickie tour, a Big Picture tour. I'm not going to write about click-through rates or fundraising ratios or data mining. Instead, I'll attempt to give you an overview of the new guiding principles that I believe have to be followed if we're to be successful in fundraising today and tomorrow.

Integrated, multichannel fundraising is a given in this complex new fundraising environment. As new channels of communication—and expression— have opened up in recent years, our personal habits have evolved. Are you dependent on e-mail today in your work? In your personal life? Do you have a Facebook page and perhaps a Twitter account? Do you use a mobile telephone? Is it an Internet-enabled smartphone? Whether or not you would answer yes to any of these questions, you're well aware that fast-growing numbers of people around the world do answer yes to *all* these questions.

In this greatly changed communication environment, in which the personal habits and preferences of hundreds of millions of people have changed so dramatically, I don't believe the roadmaps of the past will help us anymore. In fact, following the old directions can quickly take us way off course. We can't think about fundraising simplistically as a matter of hiring a collection of specialists in different fundraising techniques. We have to think about fundraising in a *holistic* fashion. We can't even cleanly separate donors into institutional and individual donors anymore, because they're often the very same people!

What we're facing is a truly new fundraising environment. Not just a bewildering profusion of new technologies, but new generations of donors . . . with new and unfamiliar attitudes . . . and new levels of acceptance and rejection of the techniques we use to raise money for the causes we care about.

Maybe things will become simple someday, when all our communication technologies truly converge and we all plug into one big network in the sky. Pundits have been telling us to expect that for the past two decades and more. But convergence in that sense is a long, long way off. And as the economist John Maynard Keynes famously told us, "In the long run we're all dead."

Today's Route to Riches?

So what are the routes to fundraising success in this new, unfamiliar world? Can you get there by doing something simple? "Telling your story," maybe? Or being "creative"? There are people in the field who seem to think easy answers like that will do the trick.

You know, of course, that life is never that simple. And you probably have a healthy degree of skepticism about the assumptions of the past—the conventional wisdom. But before we start exploring the central principles of fundraising today, let's take a look at three of the most common bits of conventional wisdom of the past few years.

Myth #1: "Online fundraising will make direct mail obsolete."

First, let's consider the widely accepted belief that online fundraising will make direct mail obsolete.

Ever since the World Wide Web went public in 1992, pundits and some online practitioners alike have been telling us that direct mail is doomed. By tomorrow—or the day after tomorrow, at the latest—donors will move online to give, and direct mail will go the way of the buggy whip.

Guess again! In the United States, direct mail still accounts for at least twenty and perhaps as much as forty times the revenue brought in by online fundraising in all its varieties (and that includes e-mail, the web, and social networks).

Now, some experts will tell you that online revenue already accounts for 10 percent or even 15 percent of all philanthropic gifts in the United States. Unfortunately, that's just not true. Their methodology is flawed. It's true that online revenue is rising rapidly—probably 35 to 40 percent per year in most years—but today online activities really account for less than 5 percent of revenue. It will take a *very* long time for that 5 percent to grow to 15 percent—and that would still be only about one-third as much as comes in by mail.

Myth #2: "Younger people will all go online to give."

Now here's another widely shared misconception: that younger people will only give *online*. For starters, people under forty really don't give at anything even approaching the rates of people over forty. They may not have any money to give. They're active consumers and use their money to buy stuff. And it may take many years and a lot of life experience for them to accept the importance of sharing through philanthropy.

But that's only half the story. A Convio study of 1,500 donors turned up some very interesting data. For example, take people like me who are too old to be Baby Boomers. Seventy-seven percent of us gave via checks by mail compared to 24 percent via the web. No surprise there. But contrast that with the Millennials or Generation Y. Those are the people who were born from the mid-1970s to the early 2000s. Twenty-six percent gave via mail and just 29 percent via the Web. In other words, the youngest people studied responded just about as well to direct mail appeals as they did to online appeals!

Myth #3: "Social networking is the key to success in fundraising."

Maybe you've already discovered for yourself that social networking isn't the route to fundraising riches. Yes, there have been success stories about raising money via social networks. Recently some nonprofit organization reportedly raised a couple of million dollars that way. But stories like that are few and far between. They're what social scientists call outliers. Social networks aren't even on the radar screen as a route to success in fundraising.

Could this change? As Facebook becomes ever more strongly embedded in the flow of people's day-to-day lives, as now seems to be the case—well, maybe. Eventually. Not today or tomorrow.

Where's the Yellow Brick Road?

What's the road to success in fundraising today? How do you get onto the yellow brick road and follow it to the riches we all know are out there?

Now, keep my warning in mind: I'm not going to give you any simple answer. I won't reveal a step-by-step, five-point plan to meet all your fundraising challenges. I take you—and myself—more seriously than that.

OK, then. There's no map, and you certainly won't get there in a straight line. But there is a way to get there. *And it's all about how well you treat the people who care about the work your organization is doing.*

Today, you can't approach fundraising through a collection of specialized silos, such as major gifts and e-mail fundraising, and expect to bring in buckets of money. Nor can you play the old numbers game so popular in direct marketing. For most people involved in this game, the objective of it was to build the largest possible donor list, no matter what the value of the donors or how many of them gave just once and then never again.

Today, best practice in fundraising follows four guidelines, or principles, of donor care (exhibit 23.1), and I'm going to examine each of them in detail.

Principle #1: Choice

The first of these overriding principles is *choice*—meaning *donor choice*. Now, you've probably heard about donor choice in the past. For many years now, we've been hearing that community-wide fundraising campaigns like those of United Way were encountering more and more resistance from donors. And many individual nonprofit organizations have been reporting lately that they're having trouble attracting enough support with generalized or institutional campaigns. What we're hearing is that we've got to offer donor choice. But rarely does anyone really explain what donors want to

EXHIBIT 23.1
The Four Principles of Donor Care

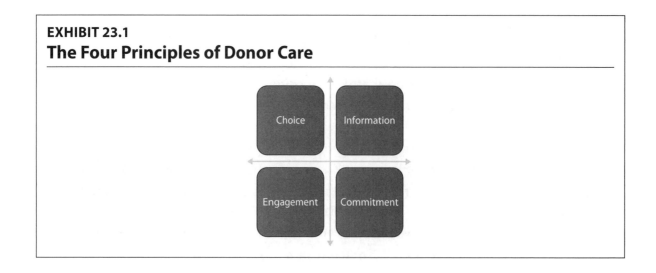

choose—or what's likely to happen when you give them the opportunity to do so. I'll take a look at all that, so you can determine what sorts of choices to offer your donors when you're writing that next appeal.

Principle #2: Information

The second of the principles is *information*. No doubt you've heard people urging you to give more information to your donors. But what kind of information? And how do you give it to them? I'll look into those questions.

Now, keep in mind the difference between *data* and *information*. One way to describe the distinction is to say that *data* consist of all that stuff people are throwing at us all day, every day—online, by mail and phone, on TV, and now even on our mobile phones. Practically none of that is interesting to us. We regard it as *spam* or *junk mail* or worse. It's all data. By contrast, *information* is data put together in a way that makes it understandable . . . delivered in a way and in a time and place that makes us notice it . . . and, most important of all, that makes it *relevant* to us. You need to know what information will make your appeals more readable—and your donors more responsive.

Principle #3: Engagement

The third of the principles I'll address in this chapter is *engagement*. You've probably heard it referred to as *donor involvement*, which seems like it's more or less the same thing. However, I use the term engagement to mean something at least a little deeper and more meaningful than involvement. After all, in direct mail we speak about *involvement devices*. Usually, all an involvement device requires you to do is sign your name or move a sticker from one sheet to another or fill out a short and simple survey. Engagement in the sense I talk about requires a lot more than that. I'll take a look at what engagement means—and at different ways you can bring it about. Understanding engagement in this sense will enable you to write more powerful—and more engaging—appeals.

Principle #4: Commitment

Fourth is *commitment*. Now, some of us have been measuring commitment for a long time. We call that measurement *long-term donor value* (or, sometimes, *lifetime value*). There's no question that's an important concept. In a way, all of us in fundraising are supposed to be working to increase our donors' long-term value. But how often do we think about how to go about that? What can we actually do, day-to-day, to build long-term value?

That's what I'll try to do as I examine donor commitment in its many forms and stages. I'll make an effort to understand what commitment is all about—and how to deepen it.

So, if you remember nothing else from the time you spend reading this chapter, please commit these four words to memory: *choice, information, engagement, commitment*. These are the new signposts on the road to fundraising success.

Please join me first in taking a look at the principle of *choice*.

The Four Dimensions of Donor Choice

Now, why is choice important? If you think about it for a minute, you'll understand. Yesterday's donors—my generation, and the generations before me—placed an enormous amount of trust in established institutions, including nonprofit organizations. We simply sent them our gifts and trusted them to use the money as they saw fit. But in the 1960s, '70s, and beyond, people encountered what was originally called the *credibility gap*, starting with the federal government but gradually extending to all of society's major institutions. People growing up against that backdrop learned to *distrust* established institutions.

Now, add to that the tendency we've all seen in increasing numbers of donors to demand a say in how we use their money. That's true of people today in practically every age group up to age sixty or so. And that's why donor choice is so important today.

Now, in thinking about choice, it's convenient to consider the four main dimensions that may enter into your donors' or prospects' decision making: program, location, channel, and intermediary. I'll explain each in turn.

• Program. When people talk about donor choice, they often mean choice of *program*. Most nonprofits resist offering choices of this sort because of the inefficiencies and possible accounting and reporting problems caused by earmarking funds for specific programs. However, my colleagues and I have consistently found over the years that about 70 percent of donors will elect to leave the choice to you if you offer that general option. Perhaps that will make program choice a little easier for your CFO to swallow!

• Location. But donors are at least equally concerned, and probably more concerned, about *where* their funds are used. In fact, many donors will *only* support local charities. Their concept of philanthropy is to give back to their communities. If your organization is regional or national and has both a central office and satellite offices or chapters, you'll probably receive at least a little bit better response if you solicit gifts that will go to the donor's nearest local office. And that response may be much better if the money will stay in-country rather than going outside the borders. However, at the same time, there are donors who are concerned above all with the Big Picture. They're looking for nationwide or global impact, so they tend to seek out causes that address the biggest issues in the broadest ways.

• Channel. More and more these days, donors are developing new communication patterns as technology continues to evolve. A donor you recruited by mail ten years ago might now insist on communicating—and giving—only online. Another one who has been a supporter only through your website might only become a responsive donor when you start to send her old-fashioned mail or call her on the phone. The bottom line is that most of your donors today have incorporated many channels into their day-to-day lives—e-mail, telephone landlines, and mobile phones, at a minimum. And collectively they use more than one channel to connect with your organization—or want to do so. Some may prefer one channel, others another. You've got to start learning what those preferences are, and offer donors choices that will maximize the likelihood of getting the gifts you need.

• Intermediary. Now, I hope you know that practically none of your donors think they're supporting your *organization*. The gifts they send you are intended to support the *people you're helping*. You're just a conduit to those individuals, as far as your donors are concerned. Your job is connect donors with beneficiaries—and don't ever forget it!

And do I have to tell you again that your organization isn't the only charity on the block? In the United States, there are, by various counts, between one and one-and-a-half million nonprofits. If your mission is truly unique, your organization is truly exceptional. But that's unlikely. Chances are, lots of others are doing more or less the same work. And if they're doing a better job of meeting donors' needs and respecting their preferences than you are, your donor file is going to shrink. Guaranteed.

Now let's turn to the second of my four guidelines, or principles: *information*.

The Four Varieties of Information

Don't forget the distinction I drew between data and information. It may have been a little unorthodox, as definitions go, but it works for fundraising. When you're informing your donors, you've got to make sure what you're telling them is interesting *to them*. That means you don't send newsletters about staff comings and goings . . . about the executive director's recent big honor . . . or statistics about how many people you've served. Far too often, articles like that appear in nonprofit newsletters—and they're *boring* to donors. You've got to answer *their* questions, not yours.

OK, so let's take a look now at each of the four broad varieties of information that may be interesting to your donors: information about results and also institutional, financial, and personal information.

• Results come first. For the great majority of your donors, results are at the very top of their wish list for information from you. Think about it: you've just sent $50 to your favorite charity to support a big new campaign because you really care about the issue it addresses. Won't you want to know what happens with that campaign? Now think a little more: if the campaign doesn't go well, if unanticipated problems arise, wouldn't you want to know that too? Wouldn't you resent it if you never heard a thing? And, not so incidentally, wouldn't you also resent it if the charity told you the campaign was a huge success—and later you learned some other way that it was really a big failure?

What I'm trying to tell you is that your donors don't want propaganda. They get enough of that every day from commercial marketers. (It's called advertising.) They want to know what's really going on. And if you level with them—really level with them—your relationships with them will get stronger and stronger.

• Institutional information. But some prospects and donors, especially your most loyal and committed donors, want to know who's minding the store. This is particularly important when your organization serves a local community. This means knowing who's on the board of directors. Who the staff members are, and what skills they have. How long the organization's been in business. How decisions are made. How big the budget is.

• Financial information. Now, I don't mean you should be including all your financial information in your donor appeals. For most donors, most of the time, this is data, not information. But it all needs to be posted on your website, at a minimum. And it must be included in an annual report. By the way, you *should* publish an annual report every year. It doesn't have to be beautifully designed and lavishly printed. It doesn't even have to be on paper! For many organizations, an annual report on the website may be enough. But an annual report is a basic requirement of a nonprofit's contract with society.

If you listen to the self-appointed charity watchdogs, you'd probably think that all donors really want from you in the way of information are financial reports. These are the people whose obsession with "fundraising costs" has poisoned the well for all US nonprofits by persuading the public that the only thing that matters about an organization's operations is what percentage it spends on raising money. In fact, if I had the time, I could easily show you how this percentage is almost always both irrelevant and misleading.

Of course, some donors clearly do care about this stuff (even if they didn't know that before they were told they should). And some care about other financial matters, such as your chief executive's salary. So the easier you make it for them to access that information, the better. This means not just filling out government forms but publishing clear, easily understandable financial reports and making them available to anyone who asks.

- Personal information. But financial information about your organization is only part of the picture. As far as many donors are concerned, *their own* financial information is at least as important—as you'll know if you've ever fielded incoming calls from donors. Partly because of all the attention given to privacy concerns in recent years, your donors really care what your records show about their past giving. And it's hard to blame them, because so many nonprofit organizations do an incredibly sloppy job of data entry, misspelling names, adding or dropping digits, and entirely missing some gifts.

To do a really good job of fundraising, you've got to have this information at your fingertips—or at least be prepared to provide it within a day or so. You'll do an even better job if you make it easier for the donors themselves to review the same information, ideally by giving them direct access online or sending them an annual summary like the hypothetical example in exhibit 23.2.

Now let's turn to the concept of engagement. To understand this idea as I conceive of it, you need to get your head around a new way of looking at donors.

EXHIBIT 23.2
Hypothetical Personal Financial Report

Mr. Warwick, your contributions in 2012 totaled $265.

Date	Amount	Program or Event Supported	Received via
January 10	$50	Membership Renewal	Mail
April 23	$100	Media Campaign	E-mail
September 9	$50	Lobby Day	Event
December 12	$65	Year-End Appeal	Mail

Thank you for your continuing support as a member of the Director's Circle!

The Four Routes to Donor Engagement

Most of the time, we think of donors as just that: people who send us money. But donors may have multifaceted relationships with us—for example, as volunteers, as former staff members, as providers of in-kind products or services, or as direct beneficiaries of our work. For them, and possibly even for us, those other aspects of their relationships may be even more important than their financial support. And even donors who are currently *only* donors may be able to contribute more meaningfully to our work in nonfinancial ways than they do as donors. So, don't think of engagement in a narrow way as a means to get more money from them. Take a holistic view. Think of the possible benefits for both parties in a broader relationship.

- *Volunteering*. First, if your organization offers volunteer opportunities, you have one of the easiest and sometimes the fastest routes to donor engagement. People who volunteer for a charity are three times as likely to contribute funds as those who don't. But that's only one aspect of the picture. Most analysts in the United States value volunteer service at $15 per hour, so a person who volunteers, say, three hours a week throughout the year is giving an extra contribution worth more than $2,000 that year. Moreover, some volunteer programs require highly trained and specialized skills that may be worth many times that much. Volunteers' contributions of time and skill are probably worth a lot more than the value of all their financial contributions.

   As you know, running a volunteer program isn't easy. And it's absolutely essential that your volunteer program provide a rich and rewarding experience. That takes skill and entails management and training costs. So take care: a badly run volunteer effort can turn people *off* just as quickly as a good one can turn them on.

- *Advocacy*. The second route to donor engagement is *advocacy*. Increasingly, with the continuing growth of e-mail and the Internet as inexpensive ways to involve supporters, grassroots advocacy efforts (or campaigning) are becoming an ever more familiar way for nonprofits to recruit new supporters. Such efforts have become equally important as means to broaden nonprofits' relationships with people who already support them. But it's a mistake to think of advocacy as consisting exclusively of sending out e-mail action alerts asking supporters to send an e-mail to the president or a member of Congress. There are far more meaningful ways for these donors and other supporters to engage in advocacy on your behalf. For example, they might print out, sign, and mail actual letters—on real paper! Or make telephone calls. Or attend meetings or rallies or demonstrations . . . or walk picket lines . . . or join delegations of citizens to visit legislators . . . or even climb up the side of a high-rise to hang a banner! All this is advocacy—and those few people who choose one of these more active ways to support you are worth their weight in gold. They're certainly worth paying a *lot* of attention to!

- *Consultation*. Yet another route to engagement is to consult your supporters. Keep in mind the old axiom about major donors: "If you want advice, ask for money. If you want money, ask for advice." Donors always feel appreciated—and more involved in your work—when you solicit their views. And of course you can do that not just by phone but by e-mail, direct mail, face-to-face at events, or in informal focus groups.

But don't limit yourself to asking for your donors' *opinions*. Use the most appropriate channel to acquire *meaningful personal information*: what motivates their giving . . . which of your programs is most important for them . . . whether your organization is a top philanthropic priority. In other words, seek out the sort of information that will help you tailor your fundraising appeals more closely to donors' individual interests and giving habits.

- *Access*. For some donors, however, there's simply no substitute for face-to-face contact. Giving them access to staff members, or in some cases the members of the board, can be a huge incentive for some people to give, or give more. And supplying a donor with the e-mail address and direct phone number of her own personal contact on the staff will enhance her feeling that her support is truly valued.

Direct access like this won't pay off just in increased giving. Perhaps equally important, it will lead to positive word of mouth for your organization. Favorable *buzz* like this can be invaluable—a thousand times as valuable as any advertising you might pay for. That's what we're learning from studies in the emerging field of word-of-mouth marketing. Buzz leads to wider public awareness of your work and even to new donors. Remember: people will listen with less skepticism to friends and acquaintances than they will to your organization making the same claims!

The Four Levels of Donor Commitment

Last among the four principles I've developed is *commitment*. Remember, as I wrote earlier, the level of commitment roughly corresponds to a donor's long-term value. So it's our job as fundraisers to find ways to deepen our supporters' commitment.

Naturally, a person's commitment to your organization can be located anywhere on the continuum from nonexistent to total. The old way of looking at this was to divide people into suspects, prospects, one-time donors, multi-donors (or regular donors), major donors, and legacy donors. But the world doesn't really work that way anymore. Today's landscape is broader, a lot more complicated, more multifaceted. To take all the new circumstances into account, and to keep things as simple as I can, I like to identify donors in terms of four levels of commitment: the Tourist, the Visitor, the Resident, and the Lifer.

• *The Tourist.* First, there's the casual contact you might experience from what I call a *Tourist.* You know people like this—far too many, in fact. A Tourist is someone who lands on your website from a search engine and stays for a minute or two . . . or drops by your office out of sheer curiosity to bother the receptionist with naive questions . . . or mails back the survey you sent in your donor-acquisition campaign—without a check. Chances are, Tourists are simply looking for freebies. They're not likely to give you any money. Unless you can find some way to grab them with an irresistible story or an offer that's impossible to turn down, you're probably never going to see them again. But it's a mistake to isolate yourself entirely from Tourists. Just enough of them eventually do something meaningful to make their contact worthwhile for you—perhaps sending an action e-mail or signing up for your online newsletter, so that you obtain at least their e-mail addresses and can approach them again. My friend Marcelo Iniarra calls these people *trysumers*: they'll try something if it's free.

• *The Visitor.* At a higher level of commitment is the *Visitor.* A Visitor might arrive in the same fashion as a Tourist—through a search engine or Facebook, perhaps. But the Visitor's intent may be a tad more serious than the Tourist's, and she becomes a little more involved—maybe subscribing to your free newsletter, attending an inexpensive or free event, or even giving a small donation.

We used to say that the most critical phase in the fundraising process was to persuade one-time donors to give a second gift, precisely because fewer than half of them do. Now, though, as so many nonprofits are acquiring far more names online than off, the game has changed. Our biggest challenge now is to get Visitors more involved—in other words, we need to increase their level of commitment—and not just concentrate on the much smaller number of people who actually donate money. Because, as Visitors become more committed, more and more of them will become donors.

• *The Resident.* Chances are, your organization has lots of *Residents*— and I'll bet you didn't even know it! These are folks who have apparently come to stay. Some have contributed to you on several occasions and maybe are even monthly donors. Others may be former or retired staff or board members who left on the best of terms. Some are the volunteers who come back again and again. To the extent that you get to know them well, you have a good chance to deepen their commitment. As a practical matter, that means you gather pertinent personal information and integrate it into your communications with them.

Long-term volunteers can turn into annual or monthly donors, or even join your board of directors. Former board or staff members may become major donors. And any of these people can leave legacies. Regardless of whether they're donors now, their future value is potentially enormous.

- *The Lifer*. At the highest level of commitment is the *Lifer*. This is a person who has stuck with you over the years, through your organization's ups and downs, contributing steadily to the best of her ability. But, as with Residents, those contributions may not be financial. A Lifer might be a volunteer who has been around since the organization was founded. Or a director who's never left the board because you don't have a rotation policy. Or a regular donor whose monthly gifts have steadily increased over the years, putting her into the ranks of major donors. Or even a loyal small donor whose modest gifts have come in every year for decades, despite the fact that nobody in the organization has ever met her!

In all these cases, Lifers may well be candidates for legacy gifts. In fact, it's from this group that the overwhelming majority of legacies are likely to come. Longevity is the single best indicator of the likelihood of a bequest.

Perhaps it occurs to you that this typology that arranges the stages of donor commitment suggests a new configuration of the donor pyramid. That old cliché in fundraising, when applied to direct response, was typically rendered along the lines illustrated in exhibit 23.3. The new configuration appears in exhibit 23.4.

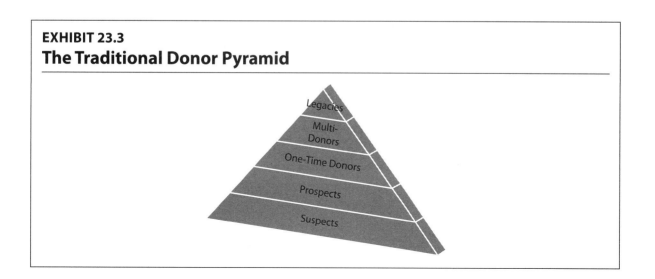

EXHIBIT 23.3
The Traditional Donor Pyramid

EXHIBIT 23.4
The New Supporter Pyramid

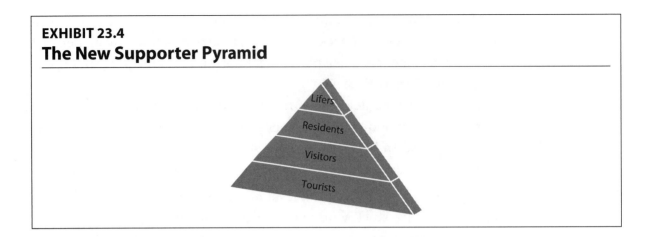

As you compare these two pyramids, you'll see that their titles differ in an important way. In the old days, we spoke of the *donor* pyramid. Nowadays, taking a broader view of our work as fundraisers, we need to focus on the universe of *supporters*. It matters what our constituents do, whether or not they ever become donors. A Resident who has never given us a dime of her own money might well have played a key role as a volunteer in helping us secure a multimillion-dollar gift from a friend of hers—and perhaps even leave a rich legacy when she passes away herself. Even a casual comment by a Visitor at a fundraising event might provide the critical information needed to connect your fundraising staff with the right person at a local corporation that will later become a reliable source of volunteer help and in-kind donations.

So, as we wrap up the main body of this book, make a mental note to remember my four guidelines. They're the keys to success in today's new and fast-changing fundraising environment: choice, information, engagement, and commitment.

I suggest you take a moment now to review the contents of part 5, a set of resources I've designed to help you in your day-to-day work of raising money for your organization.

This is the part where I invite you to steal my ideas as you might see fit. The resources that follow lay out for your unregulated use a bag full of treatments for the dread disease of writer's block:

- Sample multichannel campaign calendar
- Twenty great e-mail subject lines
- Sixty successful outer-envelope teasers
- Fifty-four strong leads for fundraising appeals
- Ninety ways to use the word "You" in a fundraising appeal
- Sixty-three ways to handle awkward copywriting transitions
- Forty-one powerful ways to end a fundraising appeal
- Fifty-eight ways to start a P.S. in a fundraising appeal
- Fifteen ways how *not* to get results

There are two ways to use these resources: (1) as an amusing assortment of copywriting ideas that will reassure you because there are so many of them and so varied a collection or (2) as a crutch you can lean on as you start writing an especially troublesome appeal.

Appendix A:
Sample Multichannel Campaign Calendar

	Week 1	Week 2	Week 3	Week 4	Week 5
Mail:					
Segment 1		Challenge Appeal			Challenge Follow-Up Appeal
Segment 2		Challenge Appeal			VS Pin
Segment 3		Challenge Appeal	Statement Extra Gift Ask		
Segment 4					
Phone:					
Phone				Challenge Campaign	
Phone E-mails			Pre-Call E-mail	Post-Call E-mails	
Online:					
E-mail	List Acquisition Buy	Newsletter		Message 1	Message 2
Action		Advocacy #1		Message 1	
Web				Medium Feature Donation Button	
Social				Launch w/Tweet FB/ Blog/ Tumblr Image	Periodic Campaign Updates
Mobile					

	Week 6	Week 7	Week 8	Week 9	Week 10	Week 11	Week 12
		Animal Times		Campaign 2		Deadline 10/31	Newsletter
		Animal Times			Campaign 2		Newsletter
		Animal Times	Statement Extra Gift Ask	Campaign 2 w/Upgrade			Newsletter
	Mailing TBD						
	→→→					In-house 2nd Ack	
	→→→						
	Message 3	Message 4 (Action E-mail)	Message 5	Message 6	Message 7	Message 8	
		Advocacy #2				Message 2	
	→→					Countdown on Button & Intercept	
	→→					Deadline Tweet FB/Blog/ Tumblr Image	
				Outbound Text #1	Outbound Text 2 & 3	24 Hour SMS	

Appendix B:
Twenty Great E-mail Subject Lines

Words of caution: every e-mail is unique, and every story you tell is unlike every other. Also, the success of subject lines varies wildly. But every one of these subject lines got great response, and subject lines can easily be tested.

1. Thank You
2. 125,396 reasons you are amazing (*Note: the e-mail goes on to describe the 125,396 kids who have been helped thanks to the organization's services.*)
3. [Insert Name] is matching all gifts
4. Testing Fixes (*Note: This was an e-mail about sample testing.*)
5. Thank you for saving my life
6. Your $1 is worth more than $1
7. 17 children die every minute
8. She doesn't want to lose another child
9. Today only: An Oxfam membership for less
10. Multiply the power of your gift 12 times
11. Ignore us and we'll go away
12. $1 = $2
13. Did you get a check?
14. The ant and the grasshopper
15. Your boss is not your doctor (duh)

16. The end?
17. Rachel Maddow
18. Triple the Impact
19. Final Hours
20. You did it

Appendix C:
Sixty Successful Outer-Envelope Teasers

It's hard to make general statements about outer-envelope teasers, much less lay down rules and regulations about how to write them. Instead, I'll do three things in this appendix: (1) list some of the many different kinds of teasers and show an example of each, (2) tell you about thirty of the teasers that have impressed me the most, and (3) list thirty all-time favorite teasers from five of my peers in the practice of raising money by mail. My hope in approaching the subject this way is to tickle your imagination. Perhaps I'll help lead you to write a few all-time favorite teasers for your own fundraising letters!

What You Can Accomplish with a Strong Teaser

To increase the likelihood the reader will open your appeal, you might write a teaser to fill any one of a number of needs—for example:

Function	Example
Describe the contents	*Membership Card Enclosed*
Establish urgency	*Your response needed within 10 days.*
Hint at advantages	*R.S.V.P.*
Flag the importance of the contents	*Membership Survey*
Start a story	*She was only 11 years old. She was as old as the hills.*
Offer a benefit	*Your Free Gift Enclosed*

Function	Example
Ask a question	*Would you spend $1 a day to save the life of a child?*
Pique curiosity	*What do these people have in common?*
Challenge the reader	*Take this simple quiz to learn your Health I.Q.*

There are both advantages and pitfalls in every one of these approaches. For example, the reader might answer a loud NO! to the question you pose, be totally unconvinced by your effort to establish urgency, or be miffed by the offer of a free gift. In other words, none of these approaches is guaranteed to work.

Nevertheless, teasers can deliver. Let's take a close look now at thirty of them that really do—at least as far as I'm concerned.

Thirty of My Own Favorite Teasers

My own all-time favorite outer-envelope teaser from the fundraising field was one I didn't write. It's pictured at the top of exhibit C.1. Judge for yourself whether it inspires you. It certainly intrigued a lot of other people. That teaser has been remailed for many years and has helped recruit hundreds of thousands of members for Handgun Control, Inc. (now called the Brady Center to Prevent Gun Violence).

The best teaser I've ever written myself was the one that appears on the second envelope in exhibit C.1. It worked well, I believe, because the letter (which I didn't write) asked readers to do precisely what the envelope copy implied: to "give Nellie Red Owl a piece of their minds"—by jotting down a greeting or comment that could be read on the air of the Native American–run radio station that was the beneficiary of this appeal. In other words—and this is key, I believe—the teaser didn't just sucker readers into opening the envelope. It delivered.

Here are a few of my other recent favorites:

- PRE-PAID FEDERAL EXPRESS ENVELOPE ENCLOSED

    From the National Republican Senatorial Committee (Washington, DC), rubber-stamped in red ink on an 11½-by-14½-inch brown kraft envelope bearing six postage stamps.

- Open Carefully . . . You may unleash a powerful spirit

    From the Smithsonian Institution (Washington, DC)—typeset in red ink on a white 6-by-9-inch window carrier next to a full-color illustration of a Native American ceremonial mask.

EXHIBIT C.1
Exemplary Outer-Envelope Teasers

ENCLOSED:
Your first real chance
to tell the National
Rifle Association to
go to hell! . . .

Source: Copyright © Handgun Control, Inc. Used by permission of Handgun Control, Inc.

Nellie
Red Owl
wants a
piece of
your
mind . . .

- "I read your <u>State of the World</u> every year."—Bill Clinton

  Maybe you should too . . .

  From Worldwatch Institute (Washington, DC)—in large blue type dominating a white Number 10 window envelope.

- NOTICE OF ENROLLMENT:

  Membership card enclosed.
  Confirmation requested.

  From KQED (San Francisco)—printed in blue and black ink on a 3⅞-by-7½-inch white window envelope.

- Because many people who sell alcohol think pennies are more important than human lives . . .

  From MADD (Mothers Against Drunk Driving, Irving, Texas)—typeset in red ink on a white Number 10 window envelope next to a second window through which a real penny shows.

- Bill Moyers

    From the Southern Poverty Law Center (Montgomery, Alabama)—typeset in bold black type in the corner card of a brown kraft Number 11 window carrier.

- "We believe every American has the right to be different and not be punished for it." <u>Don't open this envelope unless you agree!</u>

    From the American Civil Liberties Union (New York)—typeset in black ink on a tan Number 10 window envelope, with the word "Don't" underlined in bold red.

- Critical that you read this today. W.B.W.

    URGENT: SOMALIA UPDATE

    From Project HOPE (Millwood, Virginia)—a note handwritten in black ink above a headline in a broad yellow band stretching across the bottom of a 4-by-8-inch white window envelope.

- DO NOT FORWARD

    CRITICAL INFORMATION PREPARED FOR:

    [My name and address]

    PETITIONS ENCLOSED FOR:

    PRESIDENT GEORGE BUSH

    SENATE MAJORITY LEADER GEORGE MITCHELL

    HOUSE SPEAKER TOM FOLEY

    IMMEDIATE RETURN REQUESTED BY:

    [Date]

    From Common Cause (Washington, DC)—alternately typeset and laser-printed in blue, black, and red ink on a white personalized packet 9¼ by 13½ inches.

- OK, THE ELECTION WENT OUR WAY. <u>NOW WHAT?</u>

    AN IMMODEST PROPOSAL ENCLOSED FOR:

    [My name and address]

    From the Victory Fund (Washington, DC)—printed in blue and red on a white Number 10 window envelope.

- Your Sierra Club membership EXPIRES THIS MONTH!

    From the Sierra Club (San Francisco)—typeset in bold black and blue on a white Number 10 carrier.

- Would <u>you</u> go to jail to keep a puppy from being tortured?

    WE ARE!

    From Last Chance for Animals (Tarzana, California)—typeset in black and red ink above and below a photograph of a pathetic puppy showing through a large second window on a white Number 10 envelope.

- The Favor of a Reply is Requested . . .

  From the American Association of University Women (Washington, DC)—the latest example of an old chestnut that seems to work so often, typeset in an elegant face across the top of a window on a cream-colored Number 10 carrier.

- FREE SEEDS ENCLOSED

  This miracle tree could mean a new life for the world's poor . . .
  NOTE: If no seeds are visible, tip the envelope.

  From the New Forests Project (Washington, DC)—typeset in white and red type within and below a broad band of dark green across the front of a two-window Number 10 outer envelope (with seeds showing through the second window).

- CHANGE THE FACE OF TELEVISION!

  THIS AIN'T NO MICKEY MOUSE CLUB

  From In the Life/Media Network (New York)—printed in purple and gold across the front of a white Number 10 window envelope, alongside playful drawings and a shieldlike circular emblem featuring a Mickey Mouse hat.

- Would you give $10 . . . just $10 . . . to help save a child's life?

  From St. Jude Children's Research Hospital (Memphis, Tennessee)—handwritten in dark blue ink on the back of a white 3⅞-by-7½-inch window carrier.

- PULL HERE FOR YOUR FREE BACKPACK

  (details inside)

  From the National Audubon Society (New York)—set inside a band of red and blue on a perforated strip outlined in dashes above a personalized membership card that appears in an odd-sized window at the center of a 6-by-9-inch white outer envelope.

- A personal reminder

  From the Sierra Club Legal Defense Fund (San Francisco)—handwritten and underlined with a scrawl in dark blue ink across the face of a gray 4-by-7½-inch window envelope.

- Have you heard about Bill Clinton's NEW TAX? Details Inside . . .

  From Americans for a Balanced Budget (Falls Church, Virginia)—handwritten above the window on a white Number 10 envelope.

- What would you do with 500,000 pounds of BEANS?

  From Feed the Children (Oklahoma City)—handwritten in red ink in the upper-left-hand corner of a white Number 10 window outer envelope.

- RELAX!

  Both of you.

  (A $10 nest egg will do it.)

  (Do not fold. Bumper sticker enclosed.)

  From the Nature Conservancy (Arlington, Virginia)—on one of the most unusual and celebrated membership acquisition packages of recent years: printed in black ink in several different typefaces and at different angles, alongside fingers pointing to a full-color portrait of a startled-looking ostrich and my name and address showing through the window of a white 6-by-9-inch outer envelope.

- Bill Clinton

  430 South Capitol Street, SE

  Washington, DC 20003

  VIA AIR MAIL

  From the Democratic National Committee (Washington, DC)—"typed" upper left in black and printed in dark blue on the right on what appears to be a standard bluish Number 10 airmail envelope (with red and blue stripes around the perimeter).

- IMPORTANT SURVEY ON GUN CONTROL ENCLOSED

- *From the Coalition to Stop Gun Violence (Washington, DC)—typeset in huge red letters on a self-contained, 11-by-15-inch "doormat" package beneath an official-looking address section that includes a personalized "Registered Survey Number."*

- Christmas Card Enclosed . . .

  From Habitat for Humanity International (Americus, Georgia)—typeset above the window on a bright red 6-by-9-inch outer envelope beneath a corner card reading only, "Rosalynn Carter."

- Here's <u>your</u> chance to help stop filth on television.

  From the American Family Association (Tupelo, Mississippi)—printed in large blue letters across the face of a Number 11 white window envelope.

- Enclosed: Important Information Regarding U.S. Government Grants

  From World Vision (Monrovia, California)—typeset in black in the upper-left-hand corner of a closed-face white 5¾-by-8⅜-inch envelope.

- STEP INSIDE FOR A TASTE OF

  The Good Life

  YOUR FREE TICKETS FOR A PRIVATE TOUR ARE ENCLOSED

  From the Oakland Museum/Museum of California Foundation (Oakland, California)—set in contrasting typefaces in red and green inks on the front of a Number 10 white window outer envelope embellished with nondescript but elegant-looking designs in pale pink and continued on the back in simple red block letters.

- Do you want to lose the Property Tax Exemption for your home?

    From the People's Advocate, Inc. (Sacramento, California)—printed in black above the window on a white Number 10 outer envelope.

Another Thirty All-Time Favorite Teasers

Taste in teasers is a function of style as well as the character and circumstances of the charities that use them. To give you a broader range of examples than my own files and taste will permit, I turned for help to my colleagues in the Association of Direct Response Fundraising Counsel (ADRFCO), the trade association for companies that provide direct mail fundraising services to nonprofit organizations. Several firms responded to my call for nominees for the All-Time Favorite Fundraising Envelope Teasers.

I received eighteen nominees from Charlene Divoky (Divoky & Associates). The following are the ones that teased me the most:

- P.S. We named the duck Harold.

    Community Service Society of New York

- Why don't woodpeckers get headaches?

    Boston Public Library Foundation

- The committee's decision is official . . . your Kind Human Award is enclosed.

    Northeast Animal Shelter

- Me? Sleep in a subway station?

    Community Service Society of New York

- Enclosed: The Life or Death Seed Catalog

    U.S. Committee for UNICEF

- She finally allowed herself to be rescued.

    Northeast Animal Shelter

Michael P. Scholl (Direct Mail Decision Makers, Inc.) sent me twenty-five teaser candidates. Here are the ones I liked the most:

- How Sister Alice became GRANDMA

    Missionary Sisters of the Immaculate Conception

- Father Carl . . . brutally murdered

    Passionist Missions

- One of the hardest letters I've ever had to write

  Missionary Servant of the Most Blessed Trinity

- Fr. Bob is an Alcoholic and he's going through a private hell!

  Guest House

- Rejoice with me . . .

  Old Saint Mary's Church, San Francisco

- She arrived at the Grotto with tears in her eyes

  Missionary Sisters of the Immaculate Conception

Here are a few of the best teasers I received from the late Wendy Fisher (Mailworks):

- <u>FACT:</u> At 91, Emily Smithtown doesn't have a friend in the world. Not even one.

  Little Brothers/Friends of the Elderly

- Think kids are safer at home than on the street? <u>Think again.</u>

  Night Ministry/Youth Shelter Network

- FACT: Last year we distributed over 22 million pounds of food to hungry people.

  FACT: It wasn't enough.

  Greater Chicago Food Depository

- Will you be killed by a handgun in the next 23 minutes?

  [*On back flap*]: Someone will be.

  Illinois Citizens for Handgun Control

- Come. Step with me for a minute into Emily's apartment.

  Little Brothers/Friends of the Elderly

- She dared to have a dream—that one day her beloved mountain gorillas would be safe.

  Safe to roam their Viruna mountains in search of food . . . safe to give birth . . . rear their young . . . safe—so that their species can survive.

  Dian Fossey nurtured her dream . . . she died with that dream . . .

  But her beloved gorillas are still not safe.

  Dian Fossey Gorilla Fund

Here are some verbal letter-openers from Robert E. Hoagland (then at L. W. Robbins Associates):

- They Were the Last Words Lisa's Parents Expected to Hear . . . And They Changed Her World Forever!

  Joslin Diabetes Center

- What Has No Wings, Flies, and Is Called an Angel?

  Arkansas Children's Hospital Foundation

- "When it Comes to Courage, This Kid Is an All-Star!"

  Dana-Farber Cancer Institute/The Jimmy Fund

- Your Personal Emergency Relief Kit

  Open to Activate

  American Red Cross of Massachusetts Bay

- The Cat Licked Her Face. And for a Moment, the Woman and the World Were Young Again.

  Bide-a-Wee Home Association

Here are some of the teasers suggested by my colleague Bill Rehm (Mal Warwick & Associates):

- They're at it again!

  California telephone customer alert

  Toward Utility Rate Normalization

- My son was 29 years old when he died.

  Hyacinth Foundation

- [*In handwriting*] I need to know what <u>YOU</u> think.

  Wellstone Alliance

- Can you remember where you were on June 5, 1981?

  Shanti Project

- IMPORTANT NOTICE about your telephone bill

  Please read before paying

  Toward Utility Rate Normalization

- ARE YOU PREPARED FOR FIRE?

  Checklist enclosed

  American Red Cross/Bay Area

- WELCOME BACK!

  Toward Utility Rate Normalization

Appendix D:
Fifty-Four Strong Leads for Fundraising Appeals

1. Thank you . . . !
2. I'm writing you today . . .
3. You are among the first . . .
4. You may be surprised to learn . . .
5. Did you know that . . . ?
6. Don't you wish . . . ?
7. It's no secret that . . .
8. You've probably said to yourself . . .
9. Think about it for a moment.
10. Let's face it.
11. If you sincerely want to . . .
12. I wish you could have been with me when . . .
13. I was sure you'd want to know that . . .
14. I can't get the image out of my mind . . .
15. I still wake up in the middle of the night . . .
16. I've just returned from . . .
17. I need to hear from you this week about . . .
18. I don't want to waste words or paper . . .
19. I don't usually write such long letters . . .
20. We tried to reach you by phone . . .
21. According to our records, your membership has lapsed.
22. Will you please take a moment right now to renew your membership?

23. I want to tell you a story about . . .

24. You won't believe it.

25. As I was passing through _____ recently, I . . .

26. I've just returned from . . .

27. I want to tell you about a remarkable . . .

28. I'm writing to invite you . . .

29. I'd like to take just a few moments of your time to . . .

30. I hope you'll take a moment right now to . . .

31. Because you've been so generous . . .

32. I'm writing you this urgent letter today because . . .

33. It's been awhile since I heard from you . . .

34. I have exciting news for you!

35. I'm writing you today because _____ is [are] in grave danger.

36. Have you ever wondered . . . ?

37. Do you ever feel . . . ?

38. I want to share a recent experience with you.

39. I want to give you the latest information on . . .

40. I hope you'll be as excited as I am to learn . . .

41. Have you ever wanted to be part of . . . ?

42. Have you ever said to yourself . . . ?

43. If you've always wanted to . . .

44. Haven't you wondered how you could help . . . ?

45. It's no surprise that . . .

46. It's hard to believe, but . . .

47. I know you'll be interested to know that . . .

48. I know you'll want to be a part of this . . .

49. Let's be frank.

50. I have a secret.

51. You've been chosen . . .

52. If you've seen the recent headlines, you're well aware . . .

53. Someone you know . . .

54. I'd like to say it isn't so.

Appendix E:
Ninety Ways to Use the Word "You" in a Fundraising Appeal

1. Thank you for . . .

2. Thank you very much for . . .

3. Thank you again for . . .

4. As you know . . .

5. I'm writing you today . . .

6. I'm sure you'll agree that . . .

7. With your generous support, . . .

8. Because you helped, . . .

9. You are among the first . . .

10. You're the kind of person who . . .

11. I know that you . . .

12. Would you believe that . . . ?

13. As I wrote to you recently, . . .

14. Did you know that . . . ?

15. I don't know about you, but I . . .

16. Will you spend just pennies a day to . . . ?

17. How many times have you said to yourself . . . ?

18. You're among the few I can count on to . . .

19. I was delighted to hear from you.

20. You're among our most generous supporters.

21. Now, at last, you can . . .

22. You're in for a pleasant surprise.

23. Have you ever wondered . . . ?

24. . . . may astonish you.

25. You may never forgive yourself if . . .

26. The benefits to you are substantial.

27. You can rely on . . .

28. You'll be joining the ranks of . . .

29. None of this would be possible without your generous help.

30. You owe it to yourself to explore this opportunity.

31. You've helped in the past, and your generosity . . .

32. Your membership gift . . .

33. You're one of our most generous supporters . . .

34. You've been with us for a long time, and . . .

35. As one of our newest members, you . . .

36. I want to tell you about . . .

37. It's people like you who . . .

38. I know, like me, you must feel . . .

39. You're such an important friend . . .

40. Through the years, you've been . . .

41. You've shown just how much you are . . .

42. You may be shocked . . .

43. You may be surprised . . .

44. I've noticed you haven't . . .

45. Working together, you and I . . .

46. You're one of the few people who truly understand . . .

47. You should be proud of what we've accomplished together.

48. With your special gift, _____ can . . .

49. Your gift can make the difference between . . .

50. You can help them [grow strong, live a better life] . . .

51. You helped prevent . . .

52. When _____ happened, you were there.

53. Have you ever felt as if . . . ?

54. Have you ever wished you . . . ?

55. Please believe me—you can . . .

56. Like me, you may . . .

57. I can tell you from my own experience . . .

58. I've seen firsthand how you . . .

59. When you join . . .

60. I'll be pleased to send you . . .

61. I need to hear from you by _____ . . .

62. I'll keep you informed . . .

63. I'll want to keep you involved . . .

64. It may seem to you . . .

65. You've helped so many people with . . . !

66. Now you can play a leadership role . . .

67. Can you believe . . . ?

68. Have you seen . . . ?

69. What would you think if . . . ?

70. Because of people like you . . .

71. You're just the kind of person who . . .

72. How can you, as a _____, . . . ?

73. You and others like you are _____ 's only hope!

74. Have you ever noticed . . . ?

75. Can I rely on you to . . . ?

76. I hope you'll consider . . .

77. You're someone who . . .

78. You can rest assured that . . .

79. You may never again have an opportunity to . . .

80. You're not someone to stand by while . . .

81. Your gift really will make a difference.

82. What can you do? These _____ [*supply a number*] things:

83. You too can be part of this project.

84. I want you by my side (again) at this critical time.

85. This is all possible because of you.

86. You probably had no idea . . .

87. Find out for yourself.

88. Here's a new opportunity for you.

89. For you, free of charge.

90. Reserved for you:

Appendix F:
Sixty-Three Ways to Handle Awkward Copywriting Transitions

1. As I'm sure you'll understand, . . .
2. But that's not all.
3. [*Use subheads.*]
4. But now, for the first time, . . .
5. Today, more than ever, . . .
6. Best of all, . . .
7. Here's why:
8. Think of it:
9. One thing's for sure:
10. The truth is, . . .
11. To show you what I mean, . . .
12. I'm hoping you'll agree.
13. And there's more:
14. It's that simple!
15. It's now or never.
16. There's never been a better time.
17. Am I claiming too much? I don't think so.
18. That's why I'm writing you today.
19. In addition, . . .
20. Not only that, but . . .

21. And . . .

22. Now, . . .

23. Next, . . .

24. [*Indent paragraph*]

25. Before I tell you . . .

26. As you can see, . . .

27. Because it's people like you who . . .

28. Because there's no time to lose.

29. But wait, that's not all.

30. Why am I so concerned? Because . . .

31. Let me explain . . .

32. In a moment I'll tell you more about _____. But first, . . .

33. And, most important of all, . . .

34. That's what _____ is all about.

35. It may seem hard to believe, but . . .

36. There's so much at stake!

37. Let me tell you more.

38. That's why I'm asking you to do three things right now.

39. The recent news from _____ is shocking, but I'm sure you know . . .

40. To clarify what I mean . . .

41. Now is the time to . . .

42. But wait: there's more.

43. Just imagine:

44. Consider the consequences:

45. In other words, . . .

46. Put yourself in their place:

47. Time is of the essence.

48. Can you think of a better way to . . . ?

49. It's sad but true:

50. I know how you feel about _____ because you . . .

51. Will you help?

52. Are you willing to take the next step to . . . ?

53. Why wait?

54. It's clear that . . .

55. Despite the lack of media attention . . .

56. I think you'll agree that . . .

57. The truth hurts.

58. I know this isn't pleasant . . .

59. As you know very well . . .

60. Act now, and we'll . . .

61. If you really think about it . . .

62. Ask yourself:

63. Now that you know . . .

Appendix G:
Forty-One Powerful Ways to End a Fundraising Appeal

1. Thank you for caring so very much!

2. You may not know their names, but they'll carry thanks in their hearts for your kindness and generosity.

3. From the bottom of my heart, thank you!

4. Your investment will bear dividends for years to come.

5. I'm sure you'll be glad you did.

6. Isn't that what life is really all about?

7. So you can't lose!

8. Don't miss this unique opportunity!

9. It's up to you.

10. May I hear from you soon?

11. The future is in your hands.

12. And that can make all the difference in the world!

13. I'm counting on you!

14. In return, you'll have the satisfaction of knowing that . . .

15. Together, we will . . .

16. With your help, we'll . . .

17. The satisfaction you'll receive is indescribable.

18. Thank you for joining me in this . . .

19. I'm looking forward to hearing from you very soon.

20. Together, I know we can . . .

21. When you look back at this moment in history . . .

22. Please, if you feel the way I do, . . .

23. I can't think of a better gift to give our children and grandchildren than . . .

24. Thank you for your compassion.

25. I know you won't be disappointed.

26. Please, send your gift today.

27. And I promise to send you _____ just as soon as . . .

28. Thank you for taking the time to help.

29. I know I can count on you!

30. My warmest wishes to you.

31. You'll be so glad you decided to help!

32. You'll be proud to be part of . . . !

33. The _____ are depending on you!

34. _____ won't forget you!

35. I can't thank you enough.

36. I believe you'll make the right choice.

37. Please act today!

38. This is your chance to . . .

39. With your help, _____ will have a chance to . . .

40. Please show them they're not alone!

41. The future of your children and your children's children hangs in the balance.

Appendix H:
Fifty-Eight Ways to Start a P.S. in a Fundraising Appeal

1. Thank you again for . . .

2. If you respond within the next _____ days, you'll receive . . .

3. If you send $_____ or more, you'll receive . . .

4. There's not much time.

5. The enclosed _____ are yours to keep—our gift to you.

6. Please use the enclosed _____ to . . .

7. If $_____ is too much for you to give at this time, will you consider a gift of $_____ or $_____ ?

8. We need to _____ by _____, so please send your gift today.

9. Your gift of $_____ makes it possible for . . .

10. Please don't set this letter aside.

11. Remember, if you respond by . . .

12. Please take a look at the _____ I've enclosed for you.

13. As a special benefit for the first _____ people who respond, I'll . . .

14. And remember, your gift is tax deductible.

15. I've always regarded you as one of our strongest supporters, so . . .

16. Please don't wait.

17. Every day that goes by . . .

18. I hope I can count on receiving your gift in the next _____ days.

19. Please, as always, feel free to contact me at [telephone number] if you have any questions about . . .

20. If you decide not to join us in this crucial effort, I hope you'll take a moment to write and tell me why.

21. Just as soon as I return from _____, I'll let you know how . . .

22. I need to send that shipment of _____ in the next _____ days, so . . .

23. Don't forget:

24. You've come through so many times in the past, and I hope I can count on you again now.

25. _____ need[s] your help today.

26. Did you know that . . . ?

27. If you act by . . .

28. Your gift of $ _____ will make it possible for _____ to get _____.

29. $ _____ is just _____ per day!

30. For less than a cup of coffee a day, . . .

31. I promised _____ that . . .

32. When I look into the eyes of . . .

33. Unless you and I act immediately, . . .

34. Please know that your gift is _____ 's only hope for _____.

35. Without your help, _____ doesn't stand a chance.

36. Won't you please take out your checkbook now and . . .

37. I hope I can count on you to respond by . . .

38. Take a moment right now to look at the enclosed _____. I'm sure you'll feel the same as I do:

39. I hope you'll enjoy—and use—the enclosed _____.

40. Remember, to reach our goal by _____, we need . . .

41. I can't stress enough how much your support will mean to us!

42. Without your support, I can't . . .

43. It's members like you who . . .

44. There's no better time to . . .

45. Don't miss this chance to . . .

46. I'd like to hear your thoughts about . . .

47. Don't delay.

48. If your check and this letter have crossed in the mail, . . .

49. What may seem a small gift to you can . . .

50. I know it's hard to imagine _____, but . . .

51. Put yourself in _____ 's place for a moment.

52. All it takes to _____ is $ _____ !

53. If you and I don't do something right now, . . .

54. If you won't help, who will?

55. Remember, every day that goes by without our help, . . .

56. Please find it in your heart to give. Even just a little gift will help!

57. _____ need[s] to know that someone cares.

58. Thanks to friends like you, . . .

Appendix I:
Fifteen Ways How *Not* to Get Results

I can best approach the rules of copywriting through the back door, by advising you on how to avoid the most common errors I see. There are at least fifteen. They're described below, beginning with the five I believe cause the most trouble.

1. Chaotic Thinking

Effective writing begins (and ends) with clear, disciplined thought. As William Strunk Jr. and E. B. White put it so elegantly in *The Elements of Style:* "Design informs even the simplest structure, whether of brick and steel or of prose. You raise a pup tent from one sort of vision, a cathedral from another. This does not mean that you must sit with a blueprint always in front of you, merely that you had best anticipate what you are getting into." So before you lay a finger on the keyboard or position your pen on paper, *make up your mind what it is you want to communicate.* Decide where you want to go and how you'll get there. If necessary, outline the steps you'll take along the way. If you don't decide in advance what the point is, it's unlikely you'll get it across.

2. Hemming and Hawing

There may still be a place for slow and easy writing that meanders from point to point, but I think that approach went out of style with William Faulkner—and there is no room for such laziness when you're writing to achieve results. Get to the point—the quicker the better! Unless you can devise a clearly superior lead sentence, I suggest you start a letter with the words, "I'm writing to you today because . . ." That approach won't win a prize in a creative writing contest, but it does force you to communicate quickly and directly the result you're hoping to achieve with your letter. Creativity doesn't raise money, but directness does. If your writing doesn't get to the point, your readers' eyes and minds will wander off to more satisfying pursuits. Bluntness is usually a wiser and more productive course than subtlety.

3. Boring Leads

If you're faced with the task of writing a six-page letter or a ten-page memo, you'd better be sure your opening paragraph—and especially the opening sentence—is intriguing enough to pique your readers' interest. And that goes double for a letter intended to secure a gift or sell a product.

Writing that engages the reader often begins with a question, a challenge, a human-interest story, a bold assertion, a familiar phrase turned on its head—or straightforward, unalloyed directness. The special circumstances and conditions of your writing assignment (or simple inspiration) may suggest that one of these approaches is ideal. But it may be enough simply to sum up the points you're going to make—if you state them dramatically enough and set the proper tone for the audience you're addressing—for example:

> *I'm writing today to invite you to join me in launching a historic initiative with vast potential to improve the quality of life in our community.*

For a general audience, that pompous lead might guarantee your letter will quickly make its way into the proverbial circular file. But for a high-brow group with a demonstrated commitment to your community and a connection to the person who signs the memo or the letter, the boldness of your claim may be captivating.

4. Run-On Sentences

Writing of any type suffers from overlong sentences; a letter to raise money or sell software can die a horrible death from this malady. If a sentence is longer than three typewritten lines, analyze it, looking for a way to break it down into two or three simpler and shorter sentences. Almost always, you'll get your point across more effectively if you do so.

Keep this in mind: a reader dedicated enough to tackle Proust or Joyce may be willing to concentrate hard enough to follow a tortured thought all the way to a long-overdue period. (Understandably, the period is sometimes known as a *full stop*.) But *your* readers aren't likely to pay that much attention. Long sentences will test readers' limited attention span, and you'll come up the loser.

5. Failure to Use Visual Devices to Guide the Reader

A novelist who is highly skilled in moving the reader from one page to the next may be able to do so with the power of words alone. Most of us aren't so lucky, and our readers, who often have far more meager incentives to read on for page after page, are typically far less tolerant. To write effectively for impact, you'll probably need to make liberal use of subheads, bulleted or numbered series, boldfaced section headings, and other devices to break the monotony of gray, unbroken text. Only by providing your readers with clues that are visible at a glance can you make your writing actually *look* easy to read—and you'll substantially reinforce that impression by using short sentences and short paragraphs. Signals such as these send an important message to the reader: that you're writing for *her* benefit, not for your own.

6. Inconclusive (and Uninteresting) Endings

A strong appeal requires a forceful ending as well as a thought-provoking lead. It's not enough to sum up and repeat the strongest points made along the way. A letter should end on a high note: affirming the relationship between the signer and the recipient and relating the appeal to the organization's mission and the values that inspire it. End with something readers will remember.

7. Vague Language

Bad writing is full of excuses, qualifications, exceptions, and caveats. For example, a sales letter might begin:

> *Most people agree, this product is one of the best things since the hula hoop.*

Well, is it the best—or isn't it? If "most people" agree, then why not write instead:

> *This incredible product will knock your socks off! Take it from me—it's the best thing since the hula hoop!*

When a writer constantly relies on evasions, they signify fuzzy thinking. If you can't make your case in clear, unequivocal language, it's time to reexamine the reasoning that led you to conclude the case that you're presenting was defensible. Your readers won't become excited about helping you if your writing doesn't clearly convey what you want, and why, and when.

8. Overwriting

Inexperienced and insecure writers frequently overuse adjectives and adverbs, robbing their writing of clarity and impact. As Strunk and White wrote in *The Elements of Style*, "The adjective hasn't been built that can pull a weak or inaccurate noun out of a tight place." If you want to write for results, try doing so without using any adjectives at all. You can go back later and insert an adjective or two for the sake of precision or honesty. To the extent you exercise restraint, your readers will thank you—and they'll reward you with the ultimate gift to a writer: they'll go on reading.

9. Ten-Dollar Words

Like overwriting, the use of long, obscure, and highly technical language is a form of showing off. It's not necessary to write *cessation* when *end* will do, or use *communicate* when you can get the point across with *say* or *write*. Unfortunately, this sort of thing is all too common in writing today, and communication suffers as a result. Board chairs and chief executive officers are especially susceptible to this malady. Avoid it like any deadly (shall I say *communicable*?) disease.

10. "Business English"

The tendency to use widely accepted but grammatically incorrect—and often abysmally wordy—constructions is one of the afflictions of contemporary writing, and it infects a great deal of advertising and fundraising copy. Stay clear of abominations such as the following; choose their equivalents in acceptable English—or shun them altogether:

Avoid Using	What to Use Instead
accordingly	so
along the lines of	like
and/or	[*Leave this one to the lawyers!*]
as to whether	whether
at this point in time	now [*or*] today
dialogue	talk

enclosed herewith	I'm sending you
etc.	[*Use very sparingly*]
finalize	finish
for the purpose of	for
implementation	[*Just do it!*]
in order to	[*"To" will suffice*]
inasmuch as	because
in the event that	if
interface	work with [*or*] meet
make use of	use
owing to the fact that	because
per your request	as you asked
prioritize	set priorities
prior to	before
pursuant to	according to
quite [*or*] very	[*Lilies sell better without gilt!*]
results-wise	result is that
revert back	revert
the foreseeable future	[*How far away is that?*]
with a view to	to

Then there are all those words wasted because writers insist on doubling up, presumably out of some deep, hidden fear that they'll otherwise fail to get the point across. For example:

Avoid Using	**Why?**
exact opposites	[*"Opposites" will suffice*]
the reason is because	[*Which is it: "the reason is" or "because"? Choose one!*]
final conclusion	[*If it's the conclusion, isn't it final?*]
actual experience	[*As opposed to an unauthentic experience?*]
continue on	[*Is the alternative "continue off"?*]
end result	[*Give me a break!*]

You get the point. From now on, I trust you'll be on guard against these boring and objectionable word wasters. While you're at it, please put the following words on your list of what to avoid:

Avoid Using	Why?
hopefully	[*Do you really hope so? Given the way this word is so frequently misused, I think that's unlikely. But if you really hope so, then say it!*]
frankly	[*This word is commonly used when its opposite is intended. It puts the reader on guard. So does, "To be honest with you."*]
irregardless	[*The correct word is "regardless."*]
very unique	[*If something's unique, it's one of a kind. Drop the "very."*]

Every one of these words and phrases is a violation of common sense. (Strunk and White comment, sometimes at greater length, about some of these examples in their *Elements of Style*.)

11. Stilted Language

Just because a word is grammatically correct, properly spelled, and precisely expresses the thought you want to convey, you shouldn't assume it's the *right* word. When you're seeking to achieve results, it's important to write as you speak, using familiar, everyday words. The best way to guard against problems of this sort is to give your writing a road test: read your letter aloud before you let anyone else see it. If you have trouble pronouncing a word or phrase, chances are it will trip up your reader too. Find another way to say what you've written.

12. Lack of Agreement

One of the most common violations of the rules of grammar typically happens because the writer fails to decide in advance what point a sentence is to make. This confusion is often reflected in a mismatch between subject and verb or between a pronoun and its antecedent—for example:

If members choose not to attend, you may obtain a discount instead.

There's nothing wrong with this sentence that a little forethought wouldn't have cured. Here is one possible approach:

Members who choose not to attend are eligible for discounts.

This alternative wording is less likely to trip up the reader, who could easily do a double take on the original. The second version is also two words shorter, making it that much easier to read.

13. Dangling Modifiers

Closely related to the preceding problem, this common error typically arises from the same source: foggy thinking. I know of no way to describe it other than to use the grating language of the grammarian or to give examples:

An example of the very best the community had to offer, the mayor awarded her the prize last year.
Loaded with valuable benefits, I thought the product was the best I could buy.

To avoid the confusion caused by mismatches like these, try revising them. Usually, there are numerous acceptable alternatives. Here's one alternative for each example:

The mayor awarded her the prize last year because she exemplified the very best the community has to offer.
It was simply loaded with valuable benefits—the best product I could buy, I thought.

You don't need to know what a modifier is: all you have to do is remember when you near the end of the sentence what you were writing about when you started it.

14. Overuse of the Passive Voice

There are times when the passive voice is unavoidable, or at least convenient—in the following, for instance:

The snowfall was unprecedented, but the streets were plowed clean in record time.

In this example, which is about streets and snow, not people, it's not important *who* plowed the streets (although the members of the street-plowing crew might have a different opinion). The point of the sentence is clear. Nothing is lost by the use of the passive voice. The corresponding active-voice statement is no clearer or more elegant than the passive one:

Snow accumulated to an unprecedented depth, but the crews plowed it clean in record time.

Usually, however, the passive voice detracts from the impact of a statement. The passive voice is frequently used to evade straightforward assertions of fact. Thus it rarely helps you sell products or obtain charitable gifts. Consider the following example:

> *Voting members of the museum are required to attend one meeting per year to preserve their status and receive all these discounts.*

That sentence reads like a passage from a rulebook, not a promise of benefits that might entice someone to join the museum. Try this instead:

> *As a voting member of the museum, you'll receive all these discounts if you attend just one meeting per year.*

Writing for results requires communicating conviction. The active voice helps the writer to be direct and permits the reader to grasp the point more quickly.

15. Atrocious Spelling

My mother always said that respect for spelling died in the 1950s when educators decided there was a better way to teach reading than by using phonetics. I think she was right. I know few Americans younger than I who can spell worth a damn (and I'm really *old*). Fortunately, most of us who live by the word are likely to use Word (from, heaven help us, Microsoft!), which features a spell-checking utility. I heartily recommend spell-checking as a partial answer for the spelling-impaired (only partial, because it won't pick up words that are correctly spelled but wrong in context). Using such a program requires only a few seconds, yet it may rescue you from years of mortification. Perhaps you don't care whether there are spelling errors in your copy, *but I do!*

For example, I will cast a dark eye on you if I catch you committing all-too-common spelling errors, such as any of the following egregious examples:

- *except* (meaning "exclude") instead of *accept* (meaning "receive" or "acknowledge")

- *it's* instead of *its* (when used as the possessive form of it)

- *affect* (meaning "act on" or change something) instead of *effect* (meaning "do" or "bring about as a result")

- *loose* (as in "loose screw" or "loose clothing") instead of *lose* (as in "lose your keys")

If you heed the fifteen points just outlined and if you're faithful to Strunk and White's rules of grammar and vocabulary in *The Elements of Style* and Rudolf Flesch's "25 Rules of Effective Writing," from *How to Write, Speak and Think More Effectively*, you'll avoid most of the common mistakes that can prevent you from communicating effectively. You'll also be more likely to achieve the results you intend from your fundraising appeals.

Index

A

Acquisition (prospect) campaigns, 127–139; caution on e-mail appeals, 133, 139; coregistration campaign, 134–137, 139; cultivation of donors as key to, 133; defined, 43; direct mail, 127–131; Facebook campaign, 134, 135, 137, 139; online, 133–139; petition campaign, 134, 136; unique characteristics of, 130–131; welcome series e-mails, 138, 139

Address labels, 49, 60, 61

Advocacy, 306–307

AIDS Project Los Angeles (APLA): direct mail special appeal repurposed for online appeal, 265–271; upgrade appeal, 207–212

AmeriCares: home page fundraising promotion, 254; landing page for online appeal, 281; mobile-optimized e-mail appeal, 285, 286–288; online sustainer conversion appeal, 188–189; online year-end appeal, 177–183; reply device, 83

Amplifiers, 28

Annual fund renewal appeals: characteristics of, 215–216; defined, 215; example of, 213–215

Archiving wave of rejection, 31–32

Asking for action: as attribute of effective fundraising appeal, 41–42; in e-newsletters, 278; pre-writing thinking about, 73; on website home page, 280

Asking for money: as cardinal rule, 105; in donor acquisition appeals, 130, 131; in e-newsletters, 277–278; high-dollar appeals, 191, 192, 199–200; importance of, 9; pre-writing thinking about, 73; special appeals, 161, 164; sustainer conversion appeals, 185, 186, 187; in thank-you packages, 225–226; upgrade appeals, 203, 204, 206, 208, 209; in welcome packages, 144, 152; year-end appeals, 167–170, 184

Assessment: of direct mail fundraising package, 110–113; of e-mail appeal, 273, 275–276

Association of Direct Response Fundraising Counsel (ADRFCO), 325

B

Basic questions, 29

Be the Match Foundation: annual fund renewal appeal, 213–215; special appeal, 155–163

Beliefs of donors, and charitable giving, 15, 18

Benefits: basing appeal on, 104–105; named in successful fundraising appeals, 56–57, 61; in postscripts, 92; pre-writing thinking about, 75; of sustainer conversion, 190; tax, 17; in upgrade appeals, 205, 207, 211, 212; in welcome packages, 141, 145

Billy Graham Evangelistic Association, 227

Blogs, 292

Bread for the World: direct mail sustainer conversion appeal, 185–187; legacy promotion reply device, 234–235

Buckslips, 107, 176

Buyer's remorse, 141, 224

C

Camp Fire USA, fundraising letters reviewed by focus group, 35–39

Campaign to Abolish Poverty appeal, 63–68; fundraising letter, 64, 65–66; outer envelope, 63–64; reply device, 64, 67; reply envelope, 64, 68

Cardinal rules of e-mail appeals, 271–273

Cardinal rules of fundraising letters, 95–110; ask for money, 105; base appeal on benefits, 104–105; create sense of urgency, 108–109; example illustrating, 96–97, 104, 105, 107–108, 109, 110; format your letter, 107–108; length of letter, 109–110; psychological considerations, 110; use easy-to-understand English, 107; use "I" and "you," 95, 104; write package, not letter, 106–107

CARE, 226

Case, 45

Celebrities: lift letters from, 58–60; as motivators for charitable giving, 13; and online appeals, 261, 289–290, 291

Center for Victims of Torture (CVT), The: thank-you letter, 220–224; year-end appeal, 167–168, 170–174

Channels: donor choice of, 303; new, for charitable giving, 11; selecting, for fundraising appeals, 43–44. *See also* Multichannel fundraising

Charitable giving: average size of donation, 10, 191; demographics of, 248, 299; donors' motivations for, 9–19

Charity badges, 293

Cheshire labels, 49, 60, 61

Children's Health Fund (CHF), online acquisition campaign, 133–139

Choice: as donor care principle, 300–301, 302–303; as motivating charitable giving, 18–19; as reality of current fundraising, 259; in special appeals, 161

Clichés, 119–120

Closed-face envelopes, 86

Colloquialisms, 119

Community building, as motivation for charitable giving, 15–16

Comprehensive second dialogue, 27–28

Contractions, 122

Conversion rate, 254

Copy platform, 76

Corner cards, 47

Corporate Accountability International, 216–218

Corruption, charitable giving to get back at, 13

Credibility gap, 302

D

Dashes, 60, 121–122

Dates: on appeals mailed bulk rate, 49, 50, 58, 108–109; deadline, in postscripts, 53, 57–58; on donor acquisition letters, 131; in renewal appeals, 216; sample multichannel campaign calendar, 313–315; in special appeals, 164. *See also* Time

Demographics: of charitable giving, 248, 299; of Facebook users, 248, 255

Design: for easy reading, 107–108, 347; importance of, 40

Dialogue: fundraising letters as like face-to-face, 26–28; in personal fundraising visit, 22–24; transition from short to comprehensive second, 27–28

Dialogue Method, 21, 24

Direct mail: as channel in integrated multichannel fundraising, 249–250, 251; Vögele's research on, 21–33

Direct mail appeals: assessment of, 110–113; first twenty seconds of reader's reception of, 32–33, 79; myths about, 298–299; as packages, 4; postscript of, 27, 92; repurposing, for e-mail appeals, 265–271; waves of rejection of, 30–32

Divorky, Charlene, 325

Doctors Without Borders, 78–79

Donative intent, 17

Donor acquisition appeals. *See* Acquisition (prospect) campaigns

Donor care principles, 300–310; choice as, 300–301, 302–303; commitment as, 301, 307–310; engagement as, 301, 306–307; information as, 301, 303–305

Donor upgrade appeals. *See* Upgrade appeals

Donors: demographics of, 248, 299; do-it-yourself (DIY) fundraising by, 292–293; house file of, 200; reasons for responding to fundraising appeals, 9–19; revised categories of, 308–310; techniques for online involvement with, 285, 289–293. *See also* Readers

Duty, charitable giving motivated by, 17–18

E

Earthjustice, 127–130

Elements of Style, The (Strunk and White), 116, 345, 348, 352

Ellipses, 122

E-mail appeals: cardinal rules for writing, 271–273; elements of, 261, 263–264; example of award-winning, 262–263; form for assessing, 273, 275–276; mobile-optimized, 259, 283–285, 286–288; repurposing direct mail appeals for, 265–271

E-mails: in acquisition (prospect) campaigns, 133, 138, 139; bounce-back, 253; as channel in integrated multichannel fundraising, 250, 252–253; as fundraising appeal component, 87, 252–253; as integrated special appeal component, 162–163; underlining in, 92; to welcome new donors, 41, 141, 142–144, 253; as year-end appeal component, 175, 177–183, 184, 253. *See also* Subject lines

Emotions: appealing to, when writing fundraising letters, 75, 107, 110; as motivating charitable giving, 16

Enclosures. *See* Inserts

E-newsletters: example of, 276–277; recommended elements of, 277–278; tips on creating, 274, 278

Engagement: as donor care principle, 301, 306–307; using social media for, 281–283

Envelopes, outer: closed-face, 86; direct mail promotion of online giving, 251; as essential component of direct mail appeals, 4; example of, in poorly constructed appeal, 63–64; examples of well-written, 47–49, 90, 101; focus-group review of design for, 36; high-dollar appeals, 199; legacy promotions, 236; mailing labels on,

49, 60, 61; membership renewal series, 217, 218; methods of applying postage to, 48; "recycled paper" notation on, 49; signatures on, 47–48; special appeals, 155, 160; sustainer conversion appeals, 187; teasers on, 86, 89–90, 319–327; thank-you packages, 220, 224, 226, 228; upgrade appeal, 212; writing, 89–90; year-end appeals, 173, 176

Envelopes, reply: as essential component of direct mail appeals, 4; example of, in poorly constructed appeal, 64, 68; examples of well-written, 62–63, 101; high-dollar appeals, 199; legacy promotions, 240, 241; special appeals, 161; sustainer conversion appeals, 187; thank-you packages, 226; year-end appeals, 173, 177

Examples, learning from, 4–5

F

Facebook: in acquisition (prospect) campaigns, 134, 135, 137, 139; advertising on, 137, 257, 282; as channel in integrated multichannel fundraising, 247; demographics of users, 248, 255; engaging supporters using, 281–283; fundraising using, 256, 257

Facts: about online fundraising, 247–248; added during revision, 77; distinguishing people you're writing to, 72; overcoming donor skepticism with, 39; in postscripts, 92; in successful fundraising appeals, 15, 54, 55. *See also* Information

Father Flanagan's Boys' Home, 227

Fear, as motivating charitable giving, 16

Feelings. *See* Emotions

Figures of speech, 120

Filing-away wave of rejection, 31–32

Filters, 28

First run-through, 31

Fisher, Wendy, 326

Flesch, Rudolf, 117–119, 352

Focus groups: Camp Fire fundraising letters reviewed by, 35–39; cost-effective alternative to, 40

Format: for easy reading, 107–108, 347; importance of, 40

Freemiums, 12

Fundraising: common myths about, 298–299; holistic approach to, 297–298; personal visits for, 22–24. *See also* Multichannel fundraising; Online fundraising

Fundraising appeals: attributes of effective, 41–42; components of, 4, 45; detailed look at successful example of, 47–63; example of poorly constructed, 63–68; qualities of successful, 44–45; reasons donors respond to, 9–19; selecting channels for, 43–44; types of, 43, 125. *See also* Direct mail appeals; Online appeals; Packages; Writing fundraising appeals; *specific types of appeals*

Fundraising letters: common elements of, 45; deciding whether to open, 24–26; detailed look at successful example of, 49–58; editing, 2; as essential component of direct mail appeals, 4; example of poorly constructed, 64, 65–66; focus-group findings on length of, 39; for high-dollar appeals, 193; legacy promotions, 236, 237; as like face-to-face dialogue, 26–28; readers' unspoken questions about, 29–30; review of, 35–39, 40; for special appeals, 158–159, 160; for sustainer conversion appeals, 185, 186; as top source of new gifts, 11; for upgrade appeals, 203, 206, 208–209; urgency as component of, 11–12; for year-end appeals, 172, 174–175. *See also* Cardinal rules of fundraising letters

G

Gifts, charitable. *See* Charitable giving

Giving pyramids, 192, 199–200

Giving something back, as motivating charitable giving, 18

Global Fund for Women, welcome package, 145–151

Golden Rule of Donor Acknowledgments, 224, 225

Google AdWords, 257–259

Greenpeace USA, 226

Guilt, as motivating charitable giving, 16–17

H

Handbook of Direct Mail (Vögele), 21

Handgun Control, Inc., 320, 321

Hero images, 87, 163

High-dollar appeals, 191–201; defined, 43, 191; example of, 191–200; telemarketing for, 255; unique characteristics of, 200–201. *See also* Upgrade appeals

Hitchcock, Stephen, 85

Hoagland, Robert E., 326

Home pages, 253–254, 278–280

Hope Is Alive!, procedure for writing fundraising appeal for, 86–94

House file, 200

How to Write, Speak and Think More Effectively (Flesch), 117, 352

Human interest stories, 39

Humor, 120

I

"I": cardinal rule on using, 95, 104; in e-mail appeals, 272; in successful fundraising letter, 50, 54

Indicia, 48, 62, 130

Information: data vs., 301, 303; as donor care principle, 301, 303–305; length of letter determined by, 39; as motivating charitable giving, 14–15; types desired by donors, 304–305. *See also* Facts

Inserts: direct mail package example, 100–103; legacy promotions, 238–239, 241; planning giving brochures, 102–103, 154, 227; thank-you packages, 222–223, 224, 227; welcome packages, 154

Integrated multichannel fundraising. *See* Multichannel fundraising

Interfaith Alliance, 81–82

Involvement. *See* Engagement

Involvement devices, 301

Irony, 120

Italics, 122–123

L

Landing pages: building, 254–255, 280–281; examples of, 137, 189, 265, 281; importance of,

293, 294; links to, 264; "pass along" notation on, 264, 291; personalized, 292

Language: to be avoided, 347–350; easy-to-under-stand, 107, 348–350; for readability, 117–119

Leads: avoiding boring, 346; examples of strong, 329–330; recommended direct, 345–346; writing, 91

Legacy promotions, 233–241; defined, 43; direct mail as channel for, 233–234; examples of, 234–235, 236–241; unique characteristics of, 235–236

Length: cardinal rule on, 109–110; of donor acquisition letters, 130; information as determining, 39; of online appeals, 39, 109; of paragraphs, 107; of sentences, 118; of special appeal letters, 164; and success of appeal, 15; of thank-you letters, 226

Letters. *See* Fundraising letters; Lift letters/notes

Lift letters/notes, 58–60, 160

Logos, 36, 48, 49, 50, 60

Loneliness, charitable giving as way to fight, 13–14

M

Ma, Yo-Yo, 58–60

Mail, time spent reading unsolicited, 25

Mail responsiveness, 10–11

Mailing labels, 49, 60, 61

Marketing concepts: defined, 42, 71; developing, 85, 86; examples of, 77, 86; high-dollar appeals, 200–201; how to write, 76–77; role in reply device, 77–83

Membership renewal series: characteristics of, 215–216; defined, 215; example of, 216, 217–218

Metaphors, 120

Mills-Peninsula Hospital Foundation, 90

Mobile messaging: as channel in integrated mul-tichannel fundraising, 259, 283–285, 286–288; growth of fundraising by, 247

Modifiers, dangling, 351

Monthly giving programs. *See* Sustainer conver-sion appeals

MoveOn.org, 262–263

Multichannel fundraising, 245–260; direct mail channel, 249–250, 251; e-mail channel, 250,

252–253; mobile messaging channel, 247, 259, 283–285, 286–288; as necessary in new fundraising environment, 297–298; online advertising channel, 257–259; online fund-raising as element of, 246–248, 249–250, 251, 298–299; reasons for engaging in, 259–260; sample calendar, 313–315; social media chan-nel, 255–257, 281–283; telemarketing channel, 255; turkey sandwich analogy for, 245–246; value of, 123–124; website channel, 253–255, 278–281

Murdoch, Colin, 47, 48, 53, 54, 56, 57, 63

N

Nagel, David, 97, 100, 104, 105, 107, 108, 110

National Audubon Society, 226

National Organization for Women: high-dollar appeal, 191–200; thank-you postcard, 226

National Parkinson Foundation, 282–283

Nature Conservancy, 227

New donor enrollment forms. *See* Reply devices

No Kid Hungry, 142–144

O

Ocean Conservancy, 80

Offers, 45

Online advertising: as channel in integrated multichannel fundraising, 257–259; on Face-book, 282

Online appeals, 261–295; celebrities and, 261, 289–290, 291; in e-newsletters, 274, 276–278; length of, 39, 109; for mobile media, 259, 283–285, 286–288; setting priorities in, 293, 294; in social media, 255–257, 281–283; for sustainer conversion, 187–189; techniques for promoting donor involvement, 285, 289–293; using "you" in, 95, 272; on websites, 278–281, 293, 294. *See also* E-mail appeals

Online fundraising: direct mail promotion of, 249–250, 251; facts about, 246–248; future of, 293–295; myths about, 298–299. *See also* Multi-channel fundraising

Opinions, charitable giving to express, 14

Outer envelopes. *See* Envelopes, outer

P

Packages: acquisition (prospect) campaigns, 127–130; assessment of, 110–113; determining contents of, 86–88; direct mail appeals as, 4; illustrating cardinal rules, 96–103; to thank donors, 219–231; to welcome new donors, 141, 145–154; writing, as cardinal rule, 106–107

Pass-along option, 264, 278, 291

Passive voice, 351–352

Personalization: of appeal mailed bulk rate, 54; high-dollar appeals, 200; landing pages, 292; legacy promotions, 236; special appeals, 164; of successful fundraising appeal, 86, 87, 88; of thank-you letters, 224, 226; upgrade appeals, 207, 212; welcome packages, 145; year-end appeals, 174, 184

Phantom Donor, 224–225, 226–227

Pinterest, 255

Planned giving: brochures on, 102–103, 154, 227; office of, 233. *See also* Legacy promotions

Pledges, 43, 185. *See also* Sustainer conversion appeals

Podcasts, 290–291

Postage: bulk rate, 49, 50, 108–109, 130; methods of applying to outer envelope, 48; on reply envelope, 62; special appeals, 164; thank-you package, 228, 231

Postscripts (P.S.): deadline dates in, 53, 57–58; importance of, 27, 92; ways to start, 341–343; writing, 92

Premiums: on buckslips, 107; examples of, 60, 61, 100; as motivating charitable giving, 12, 105; in thank-you packages, 227

Product questions, 29, 30

Project Bread, legacy promotion mailing, 236–241

Propositions, 45

Prospect campaigns. *See* Acquisition (prospect) campaigns

Punctuation, 121–122

Putting to one side wave of rejection, 32

Q

Questions: to answer before writing fundraising appeal, 71–76; Vögele on readers' unspoken, 25, 27, 28–30

R

Readability, 117–119

Readers: deciding whether to open fundraising letters, 24–26; first twenty seconds of direct mail letter with, 32–33, 79; unspoken questions of, 25, 27, 28–30; waves of rejection by, 30–32. *See also* Donors

Recruiting new donors/supporters. *See* Acquisition (prospect) campaigns

"Recycled paper" notation, 49, 55, 62

Red Cross, 225, 226, 284

Regular giving programs, 43. *See also* Sustainer conversion appeals

Rehm, Bill, 47, 127, 160, 161, 327

Rejection, waves of, 30–32

Religious beliefs, as motivating charitable giving, 18

Renewal appeals, 213–218; defined, 43, 213; example of annual fund renewal notice, 213–215; example of membership renewal series, 216, 217–218; outer envelopes, 217, 218; reply device, 214–215; unique characteristics of, 215–216

Repetition, 122

Reply devices: acquisition packages, 127–130; asking for money on, 98, 105; direct mail promotion of online giving, 250; drafting, 88–89; as essential component of direct mail appeals, 4; example of, in poorly constructed appeal, 64, 67; example of, in successful fundraising appeal, 60–61; high-dollar appeals, 192; legacy promotions, 234–235, 240, 241; renewal appeal, 214–215; role of marketing concept in, 77–83; special appeals, 155, 156–157, 161; sustainer conversion appeals, 185, 186; thank-you letters, 221, 224, 226; upgrade appeals, 204–205, 210–211; welcome packages, 144, 146; when to write, 77; year-end appeals, 167–170

Reply envelopes. *See* Envelopes, reply

Republican National Committee, 227

Response devices. *See* Reply devices

S

San Francisco Conservatory of Music appeal, 47–63; fundraising letter, 49–58; lessons from, 63; lift letter, 58–60; outer envelope, 47–49; reply device, 60–61; reply envelope, 62–63

Save The Bay: direct mail promotion of online giving, 250, 251; upgrade appeal, 203–206

Scholl, Michael P., 325

Semicolons, 121

Sentence structure, 120–121, 346

Sierra Club, 276–277

Signatures/signers: avoiding multiple, 104; e-mail appeals, 261; noticed by readers, 27, 54; on outer envelope, 47–48; pre-writing thinking about, 74–75

Similes, 120

Social media: as channel in integrated multichannel fundraising, 255–257, 281–283; growth of fundraising using, 247. *See also* Facebook

Social networking, myth about fundraising role of, 299

Southern Poverty Law Center, 228–231

Special appeals, 155–165; defined, 43, 155; direct mail package, 155–161; online materials, 162–163; repurposing direct mail, for online version, 265–271; unique characteristics of, 164–165

Spelling errors, 305, 352

St. Joseph's Indian School direct mail package, 96–109; fundraising letter, 96–97, 104, 105, 107–108, 109, 110; as illustrating cardinal rules, 95; inserts, 100–103; interrelated contents, 106; outer envelope, 101; reply device, 98–99, 105; reply envelope, 101

Strunk, William Jr., 116, 345, 348, 352

Subheads, 92–93

Subject lines: in e-mail series, 177; examples of great, 317–318; importance of, 32, 45, 261, 263; testing, 263, 271; writing, 89

Sustainer conversion appeals, 185–190; asking for money, 185, 186, 187; defined, 43; direct mail, 185–187; envelopes, 187; letters, 185, 186; online, 187–189; reply devices, 185, 186; unique characteristics of, 189–190; value of monthly giving to nonprofits, 185; via telephone calls, 185, 187, 189

T

Target audience, 43

Tax benefits, as motivating charitable giving, 17

Teasers: defined, 86; examples of strong, 320–327; possible functions of, 319–320; on special appeals, 155; on thank-you outer envelopes, 220, 224, 226; writing, 89–90

Telemarketing, 255

Telephone: mobile, 259, 283–285, 286–288; for sustainer conversion appeals, 185, 187, 189

Thanking donors: with bounce-back e-mails, 253; in every fundraising appeal, 219; Golden Rule of Donor Acknowledgments, 224, 225; with welcome packages/series, 153, 154

Thank-you packages, 219–231; asking for money in, 225–226; defined, 43; examples of, 220–224, 228–231; features of, from top fundraising mailers, 226–227; inserts, 222–223, 224, 227; outer envelopes, 220, 224, 226, 228; reasons for sending, 224–226, 228; reply devices, 221, 224, 226; reply envelope, 226; thank-you letters, 220–221, 225, 229–230; unique characteristics of, 220, 224

Thinking, pre-writing, 72–76, 116, 345

Time: first twenty seconds of direct mail letter with reader, 32–33, 79; needed to write fundraising letters, 85; spent deciding whether to open fundraising letter, 24–26; spent reading unsolicited mail, 25. *See also* Dates

Typefaces, 48

U

Underlining: in e-mail copy, 92; in fundraising letters, 92, 93; tips on using, 122–123

Union of Concerned Scientists (UCS), year-end appeal, 167, 169–170, 174–175, 176–177

United Nations World Food Programme, game on website, 289, 290

Unspoken readers' questions: answering, 27, 28–29; defined, 25; types of, 29–30

Upgrade appeals, 203–212; asking for money, 203, 204, 206, 208, 209; benefits listed in, 205, 207, 211, 212; defined, 43, 203; examples of, 203–206, 207–212; reply devices, 204–205, 210–211; unique characteristics of, 206–207; upgrade letters, 203, 206, 208–209

Urgency: creating sense of, 108–109; in e-mail appeals, 273; as necessary component of fundraising letters, 11–12; pre-writing thinking about reasons for, 75–76

V

Values, as motivating charitable giving, 15, 55, 56

Videos, 289–290

Vögele, Siegfried: on amplifiers vs. filters, 28; on behavior of website visitors, 279; Dialogue Method of, 21, 24; on first twenty seconds of direct mail letter with reader, 32–33, 79; on fundraising letter as like dialogue, 26–28; on postscripts, 27, 92; on readers' unspoken questions, 25, 27, 28–30; on time spent reading unsolicited mail, 25; on transition from short to comprehensive second dialogue, 27–28; waves of rejection identified by, 30–32

Volunteers, 306, 308–309, 310

W

Websites: address on fundraising appeal letters, 49; as channel in integrated multichannel fundraising, 253–255; hero images on, 87, 163; home pages, 253–254, 278–280; techniques for involving donors, 285, 289–293. *See also* Landing pages

Welcome packages/series, 141–154; defined, 43, 141; examples of, 142–144, 145–151; possible enclosures, 154; reasons for sending, 152–154; unique characteristics of, 143–144, 152

White, E. B., 116, 345, 348, 352

White mail donations, 260

Words: easy-to-understand, 107, 348–350; "I," 50, 54, 95, 104, 272; importance of, 40; readability and, 118–119; underlining or italicizing, 92, 93, 122–123; "you," 50, 54, 95, 104, 272, 331–334

World Wildlife Fund, 227

Writing, 115–124; common errors to avoid in, 345–352; Flesch's rules of effective, 117, 352; lessons from teaching brother about, 115–116; necessity of revising, 2, 123; recommended book on basics of, 116; for results vs. to describe or report, 119–123; ways to handle awkward transitions in, 335–337

Writing fundraising appeals: always including thank-you, 219; caution on formulas for, 45; considering subheads and underlining before, 92–93; eight-step procedure for, 85–94; for e-mail campaigns, 271–273; fundamental law of, 42; psychological considerations, 110; questions to answer before, 71–76; sample strong leads, 329–330; ways to end, 339–340, 347. *See also* Cardinal rules of fundraising letters

Y

Year-end appeals, 167–184; appeal letters, 172, 174–175; asking for money, 167–170, 184; defined, 43; direct mail, 167–175, 176–177; envelopes, 173, 176; online, 175, 177–183, 184, 253; reply devices, 167–170; unique characteristics of, 184

"You": cardinal rule on using, 95, 104; in e-mail appeals, 272; in successful fundraising letter, 50, 54; ways to use, 331–334